HUSSERL

The Arguments of the Philosophers

EDITOR: TED HONDERICH

Grote Professor of the Philosophy of Mind and Logic,
University College London

The purpose of this series is to provide a contemporary assessment and history of the entire course of philosophical thought. Each book constitutes a detailed, critical introduction to the work of a philosopher of major influence and significance.

Already published in the series

HUSSERL

David Bell

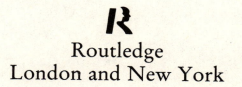

Routledge
London and New York

First published in 1990
by Routledge
11 New Fetter Lane, London, EC4P 4EE

Simultaneously published in the USA and Canada
by Routledge
a division of Routledge, Chapman and Hall, Inc.
29 West 35th Street, New York, NY 10001

Printed in Great Britain by
TJ Press (Padstow) Ltd,
Padstow, Cornwall

British Library Cataloguing in Publication Data
Bell, David, 1947. apr. 24–
Husserl. – (The Arguments of the philosophers)
1. German philosophy. Husserl, Edmund
I. Title II. Series
193
ISBN 0–415–03300–4

Library of Congress Cataloging in Publication Data
Bell, David Andrew.
Husserl/David Bell
p. cm. – – (The Arguments of the philosophers)
Bibliography: p.
Includes index.
1. Husserl, Edmund. 1859–1938. I. Title. II. Series.
B3279.H94B39 1989

193 – – dc 20   89–6293

For Diane, Alex, and Madeleine

Contents

CONTENTS

Preface

My original intention was to write a short, introductory, critical conspectus of Husserl's philosophical thought as a whole. I still indeed hope that something of this aim has been realized in what follows; but there have been many readjustments and compromises on the way. The desire to be brief, for example, was impossible to reconcile fully with the desire to be comprehensive; and likewise I found it difficult to be simultaneously both introductory and critical, without, that is, becoming unacceptably dogmatic in the process.

This book is introductory in the specific sense that it presupposes no acquaintance whatsoever with Husserl's philosophy on the part of the reader, but instead aims to provide an account of the content, the context, and the development of his thought – an account which, it is hoped, may then itself form the basis for such an acquaintance. The book is not, however, 'introductory' in any sense which implies that it is elementary, or which presupposes no acquaintance with *non*-Husserlian philosophical problems, doctrines, concepts, methods, and terminology. And in this connection I am particularly aware that I have on a number of occasions invoked or alluded to the ideas of other philosophers – Kant, Frege, Merleau-Ponty, and Wittgenstein, for example – in ways that will not, perhaps, be perspicuous to those not already familiar with them, and, moreover, in ways that are often regrettably dogmatic, in that they assume without defence a possibly problematic or idiosyncratic interpretation of those ideas. In extenuation I can only plead the desirability of keeping the final size – and, indeed, price – of the book within reasonable bounds.

The need for brevity has not, however, prevented me from including a prolegomenon whose subject matter is the early philosophy of Franz Brentano – and a word needs to be said here in justification of this apparent digression. Brentano stands to Husserl in very much the same relation in which, say, Frege stands to Wittgenstein: one can no more

hope to gain a sympathetic understanding of Wittgenstein's presuppositions, preoccupations, and procedures in ignorance of his inheritance from Frege than one can hope to gain an understanding of Husserl's
in ignorance of his inheritance from Brentano. And in both cases the
reason is the same: neither Wittgenstein nor Husserl enjoyed a widely-
based, formal education or training in philosophy; on the contrary, their
respective philosophical outlooks were initially formulated in the context
of, and in response to, an extremely narrow set of philosophical concerns
– the concerns, predominantly, of a single philosopher. Husserl's early
philosophy is Brentanian through and through (though this is not of
course to deny the influence of others on him – Bolzano, Lotze, Stumpf,
Kant, and Frege, amongst others). Nevertheless, the mere fact of Husserl's
indebtedness to Brentano, however great, would of itself be insufficient
to warrant the inclusion of a lengthy section devoted exclusively to a
consideration of the latter's philosophy. Rather, that section is there
because without it a large number of Husserlian doctrines, methods, and
assumptions would remain at best arbitrary and unjustified, and at worst
inaccessible. For Husserl himself writes, especially in his early works, as
if for a reader already familiar with what is meant by such Brentanian terms
as, say, 'psychology', 'mental', 'physical', 'presentation', 'intuition',
'evidence', 'aggregate', 'moment', 'thing', 'intention', 'inexistence', 'real',
and 'phenomenon'. What these terms of art mean is, however, very far
from obvious, and familiarity with them, and with the doctrines that they
are used to articulate, can hardly be presupposed on the part of present-day
readers of Husserl's works. The prolegomenon, it is hoped, will go some
way towards filling this lacuna.

There is a great deal in Husserl's thought which I find objectionable. I
have not always made this disagreement explicit, however, and at a
number of points I have consciously refrained from all critical comment,
no matter how inadequate the ideas under discussion might seem to be.
One reason for this omission is that Husserl himself is in many ways his
own best critic: his philosophical development is characterized by a
number of phases, each of which, with the exception of the first, is
motivated by the need to overcome the perceived shortcomings and
weaknesses of the one preceding it. It is often unnecessary, therefore, to
indicate the ways in which a given doctrine or method is objectionable, or
how it might be strengthened; for in his subsequent work Husserl very
often does just this himself. I should stress, however, that in what follows
absence of explicit critical comment on a particular point only rarely
signifies acceptance of, or agreement with it.

My original intention to write a short work covering Husserl's
philosophical thought as a whole was an early casualty. It simply proved
impossible to deal adequately with every strand – even every major strand
– of that thought. Two omissions are massive enough to demand mention

here: there is nothing in what follows concerning Husserl's complex and changing phenomenological theories of time; and neither is there anything about his views on ethics and value theory. Less importantly, but still regrettably, there is little or no discussion of Husserl's treatment of problems concerning geometry, token-reflexive expressions, the history of philosophy, apophantics, the nature of European civilization, and much else besides. To have incorporated discussions of these topics would not, I think, have substantially altered the philosophical portrait of Husserl that emerges in this book – but it would have required a book of at least twice the length.

The amount of material presently available to the Husserlian scholar is genuinely daunting. Amongst other items, the Husserl Archives in Louvain contain over 40,000 pages of Husserl's shorthand manuscripts; something in excess of 7,000 pages of Husserl's writings have now been published in German – in addition, that is, to those works which Husserl himself published; and the secondary literature on Husserlian phenomenology is so vast as to be all but unsurveyable. In the sequel I have been sparing in my references both to the available secondary literature, and to the unpublished and posthumously published works of Husserl. My policy has been to provide an interpretation of Husserlian phenomenology that is grounded, first and foremost, in the writings which Husserl himself published, or at least prepared for publication, during his lifetime.

Some of Husserl's works are not yet available in English, and some others are not available in reliable translation. In quoting from the former works I have translated Husserl's German myself; but even in those cases where there is already an English version I have often found it necessary to provide my own translation, either by modifying an existing one or, at times, by retranslating a passage in its entirety. And so, although quotations from Husserl's writings are always followed by a reference to a published English translation, if there is one, this should not be taken as indicating that the passage in question has been taken *verbatim* from that translation.

Although I have not usually included references to the secondary literature on Husserl, even where it bears directly on problems that I discuss, I would like to acknowledge at the outset the help and stimulation I have received from works by, amongst others, Bachelard, Chisholm, De Boer, Dreyfus, Føllesdal, Gurwitsch, Simons, and Smith and McIntyre.

While writing this book I received assistance from a number of institutions to which I would like to express my gratitude. Sheffield University and The British Academy both provided grants enabling me to visit the Husserl Archives in Louvain; and the time I could spend in Louvain was usefully extended by the tenure there of a Visiting Professorship, in the

Hoger Instituut voor Wijsbegeerte of the Catholic University. I owe a considerable debt to the Radcliffe Trust, and another to the Alexander von Humboldt-Stiftung, for the two research fellowships without which this book could never have been completed, could never, indeed, have been contemplated. My thanks go also to the respective staffs of the Husserl Archives, Louvain, and the Universitätsbibliothek der Freie Universität Berlin, for their friendly co-operation and practical assistance. Sheffield University and its Department of Philosophy were generous in freeing me from my normal duties and allowing me to pursue my research in Louvain and Berlin.

It gives me pleasure to record here my gratitude to Roderick Chisholm, Michael Dummett, Hidé Ishiguro, Kevin Mulligan, Günther Patzig, Peter Simons, Barry Smith, and Ernst Tugendhat, who read parts of earlier versions of the present work. Their encouragement was invaluable; and their comments not only saved me from innumerable errors but also suggested many valuable improvements.

To Frank Bock in Louvain, and to Helmut and Anna Nitschke in Berlin go my warm thanks for all the help which they so generously, and so effectively, provided.

My final and by far my greatest debt is to my family, who had to suffer not only my absence, but also at times my presence, during the writing of this book. Their tolerance, generosity, and support during this period was, as always, unfaltering and unstinted. This book is dedicated to them.

Abbreviations
and References

References to the works of Husserl, and to their English translations, have been incorporated into the text using the following system of abbreviations.

CM §*n*/p.*m* *Cartesianische Meditationen* (in *Hus* I), section *n*; *Cartesian Meditations*, translated by D. Cairns, page *m*.

Crisis §*n*/p.*m* *Die Krisis der europäischen Wissenschaften und die transzendentale Phänomenologie* (in *Hus* VI), section *n*; *The Crisis of European Sciences and Transcendental Phenomenology*, translated by D. Carr, page *m*.

EU §*n*/p.*m* *Erfahrung und Urteil: Untersuchungen zur Genealogie der Logik*, section *n*; *Experience and Judgement*, translated by J.S. Churchill and K. Ameriks, page *m*.

FTL §*n*/p.*m* *Formale und transzendentale Logik* (in *Hus* XVII), section *n*; *Formal and Transcendental Logic*, translated by D. Cairns, page *m*.

HSW *Husserl: Shorter Works*, ed. by P. McCormick and F.A. Elliston.

Hus N *Husserliana – Edmund Husserl: Gesammelte Werk*, vol. number *N*.

Ideas §*n*/p.*m* *Ideen zu einer reinen Phänomenologie und phänomenologischen Philosophie. Erstes Buch: Allgemeine Einführung in die reine Phänomenologie* (in *Hus* III), section *n*; *Ideas: General Introduction to Pure Phenomenology*, translated by W.R. Boyce Gibson, page *m*.

Ideas II *Ideen zu einer reinen Phänomenologie und phänomenologischen Philosophie. Zweites Buch: Phänomenologische Untersuchungen zur Konstitution*, (in *Hus* IV).

Ideas III	*Ideen zu einer reinen Phänomenologie und phänomenologischen Philosophie. Drittes Buch: Die Phänomenologie und die Fundamente der Wissenschaften* (in *Hus* V).
LU N, §*n*/p.*m*	*Logische Untersuchungen,* Investigation number N, section *n*; *Logical Investigations,* translated by J.N. Findlay, page *m*.
PdA	*Philosophie der Arithmetik* (in *Hus* XII).
PP §*n*/p.*m*	*Phänomenologische Psychologie* (in *Hus* IX), section *n*; *Phenomenological Psychology,* translated by J. Scanlon, page *m*.
PRS	*Philosophy as Rigorous Science,* translated by Q. Lauer, in *HSW*.
PV p.*n*/p.*m*	*Pariser Vorträge* (in *Hus* I), page *n*; *The Paris Lectures,* translated by P. Koestenbaum, page *m*.

* * *

PES	Franz Brentano, *Psychology from an Empirical Standpoint,* ed. by L.L. McAlister, translated by A.C. Rancurello *et al.*

Full details of all these works can be found in the Bibliography.

Acknowledgements

Parts of Chapter I are taken, with substantial modifications, from a paper which appeared in *Brentano Studien*,vol. 2, 1989; parts of Chapter III are likewise taken from a paper which appeared in the *Proceedings of the Aristotelian Society*, supplementary volume no.62, 1988; I thank the editors and publishers for permission to use this material again. The example of Husserl's handwriting which forms part of the cover design of this book is taken from the *Nachlass*, Manuscript No. K I 20, p.124a, and is reproduced here with the kind permission of Prof. S. IJsseling, Director of the Husserl Archive, Louvain.

Prolegomenon: Brentano's Legacy

One should not seek anything behind the phenomena; they are the lesson themselves.

GOETHE

Prolegomenon:
Brentano's Legacy

Introduction

Like his contemporaries Gottlob Frege and Bertrand Russell, Husserl began his academic life as a mathematician. He studied mathematics at the universities of Leipzig, Berlin (where he was taught by both Kronecker and Weierstrass), and Vienna, where in 1882 he received his PhD for a dissertation entitled 'Contributions to the Theory of the Calculus of Variations'. Although he had in fact studied philosophy as a subsidiary subject – in Leipzig, for example, with Wilhelm Wundt – there is little evidence that his interest in the subject was, during this period, more than cursory.[1] And in 1883 he left Vienna for Berlin to take up a post as assistant to Weierstrass. At this time he felt himself to be, according to his wife, 'totally a mathematician'.[2]

Within a year this feeling changed, and Husserl again left Berlin for Vienna; this time, however, to study philosophy with Franz Brentano. Husserl himself later recalled that during this period 'my philosophical interests were increasing and I was uncertain whether to make my career in mathematics, or to devote myself totally to philosophy. It was Brentano's lectures that finally settled the matter' (*HSW* p.342). Between 1884 and 1886 Husserl attended Brentano's lectures, seminars, and discussion groups, visited him often at home, and even accompanied him on his summer holidays.[3] Brentano's teaching, Husserl reports, 'gave me for the first time the conviction that encouraged me to choose philosophy as my life's work.' (*HSW* p.342).

When Husserl began studying with him, Brentano held the position of a mere *Privatdozent* in Vienna University, having recently resigned the chair of philosophy there, and as such he was not permitted to supervise advanced research or to examine *Habilitationsschriften*. It seems likely that this is why, at Brentano's suggestion, Husserl went in 1886 to study with Carl Stumpf in the University of Halle, where, a year later,

3

he submitted his *Habilitationsschrift* entitled 'On the Concept of Number. Psychological Analyses'. This, Husserl's first philosophical essay, along with the *Philosophy of Arithmetic* of which it came to form a part, are works conceived and executed within an almost entirely Brentanian framework. Unfortunately Husserl's reliance on this framework – his use, that is, of methods, doctrines, concepts and terminology inherited from Brentano – is left very largely unexplained in his early works; and as a result those works are all but inaccessible to readers unfamiliar with that inheritance.

The present chapter comprises an introduction to Brentano's early philosophy, and, in particular, to those aspects of it that exercised a profound and pervasive influence on Husserl's philosophical thought – not merely in his first works on the foundations of arithmetic and logic, but indeed throughout his entire intellectual life as a philosopher. At the most general level Husserl inherited from Brentano a vision of the nature, the goals, and the methods of philosophical enquiry; and more specifically he inherited from him doctrines concerning, for example, phenomena, intuitions, presentations, judgements, consciousness, intentionality, meaning, language, logic, science, truth, certainty, evidence, and analysis. By examining the nature of this Brentanian legacy, with respect to both its content and its rationale, we can begin to understand elements in Husserl's thought that would otherwise remain either impenetrably obscure, or puzzlingly arbitrary and idiosyncratic.

Philosophy and psychology

During the second half of the nineteenth century the discipline of psychology, in spite of pioneering work by, amongst others, Herbart, Lotze, Wundt, and Stumpf, had not yet clearly distinguished itself from philosophy, and had by no means yet declared its independence of it. Symptomatically, for example, all of the psychologists just mentioned occupied chairs of philosophy, and virtually all of them wrote about ethics, logic, and metaphysics, as well as about topics belonging unproblematically within empirical or experimental psychology. But if psychology had yet to acquire a subject matter and a methodology distinctively its own, it was nevertheless, even in an inchoate form, a discipline capable of generating a great deal of intellectual excitement. And part of this excitement was doubtless a result of the realization, in the wake of the liberation from traditional intellectual and religious constraints brought about for example by Darwin, that there could indeed be a 'science of the mind', just as empirical – perhaps even just as experimental – as the more familiar sciences of nature.[4]

The challenge and the excitement of a potentially new way of investigating the human mind resulted, in 1874, in the appearance of two epoch-making works. One was *The Principles of Physiological Psychology* by Wilhelm Wundt,[5] a man widely recognized to be 'the first who without reservation is properly called a psychologist'.[6] In the Preface to this book, Wundt self-consciously announces his intention to 'mark out a new domain of science' which would essentially involve 'the experimental treatment of problems in psychology'.[7] The other work was Brentano's *Psychology from an Empirical Standpoint*.[8]

As originally conceived, this work was to have been a massive affair consisting of six books, organized, according to Brentano's original plan, as follows:

> The first book discusses psychology as a science, the second considers mental phenomena in general. A third . . . will investigate the characteristics of, and the laws governing [mental] presentations; the fourth will concern itself with the characteristics and laws of judgements; and the fifth with those of emotions. . . . The final book will deal with the relationship between mind and body.(p.xv)

It is clear that Brentano intended the first two books, entitled respectively *Psychology as a Science* and *Mental Phenomena in General*, to comprise an investigation of, and introduction to, the most fundamental methods and concepts characteristic of psychology. So they were not intended to make a contribution *within* empirical psychology; their function was to be essentially second-order: to examine the methods, and analyse the most basic concepts to be employed, subsequently, in the empirical investigation of mental phenomena. The first two books are, in other words, largely *philosophical* in character: their contributions lie within areas such as epistemology, the philosophy of science, and, especially, the philosophy of mind. The remaining four books, on the other hand, were supposed to establish the most important empirical laws governing mental phenomena, and so would constitute a straightforward contribution to empirical psychology rather than philosophy. The first two books appeared in 1874, and together make up the work we now know as *Psychology from an Empirical Standpoint*; the other four books never appeared at all. As a result, and in spite of its title, Brentano's book as we have it contains in fact very little by way of psychology from an empirical standpoint; it does, however, contain a great deal of philosophy.

Further: during the period in which his influence on Husserl was at its height, it seems that Brentano's interests were again inclined more to philosophy than to empirical psychology; he wrote to Stumpf in 1886: 'I am now completely a metaphysician and I must confess that after having been a psychologist for a couple of years I'm glad of the change'.[9] Indeed Stumpf himself is in no doubt that throughout his career 'in his innermost soul Brentano's metaphysical interests predominated over all others', and that consequently it would be 'quite wrong . . '. to view psychology as the starting point of his systematic philosophizing'.[10]

The point I wish to stress, then, is this: although Husserl was undoubtedly influenced, and formatively, by Brentano's so-called 'psychology', and although, more generally, Husserl was clearly excited by the revolutionary new ways of studying the human mind that were beginning to emerge at precisely the time he became interested in philosophy, it was not at all 'empirical psychology' which captured his imagination; rather he was fired by a distinctively philosophical discipline which Brentano liked to call 'descriptive psychology', or 'psychognosy', or, sometimes, 'descriptive phenomenology'.[11] As used by Brentano, the term 'descriptive psychology' is immensely unfortunate; for, in the first place, it suggests that we are dealing with an empirical science, even though Brentano's investigations belong within philosophy of mind; secondly, the discipline is in practice more analytic than merely 'descriptive'; and thirdly, its results are not contingent generalizations, but necessary, *a priori* truths. Because it is, especially to modern ears, so very misleading, I shall henceforth largely drop the term 'descriptive psychology' and talk instead about Brentano's contributions to descriptive *phenomenology*. In other words I shall distinguish between, on the one hand, his views concerning an empirical science called *genetic psychology*, and on the other hand, his views concerning the philosophical discipline of *descriptive phenomenology*.[12]

So-called genetic psychology, according to Brentano, aims at a causal explanation of the origin and succession of mental phenomena: 'it is concerned with the laws according to which these phenomena come into being and pass away' (p.369); and its findings, like those of physiology, will comprise inductively based generalizations which are contingent, *a posteriori*, and merely probabilistic. And partly because they are generalizations from contingent facts, the laws established by genetic psychology will, Brentano says, remain ineluctably 'inexact' – they will comprise at best a mere approximation to the truth:

> There are . . . two factors which prevent us from acquiring
> an exact conception of the highest laws of mental succession: first, they
> are only empirical laws dependent upon the variable influences of
> unexplored physiological processes; secondly, the intensity of mental
> phenomena . . . cannot be subjected to measurement. (p.70)

On the other hand, and in sharpest contrast to genetic psychology, Brentanian *phenomenology* is *a priori*; its results are 'exact', 'apodictic', and 'self-evident'; and it arrives at general truths and laws immediately: 'at one stroke, without induction'.[13] From this point on our concern will be exclusively with Brentano's doctrines concerning the philosophical discipline of descriptive phenomenology; I will henceforth ignore, that is, matters internal to the empirical science of genetic psychology. Brentano's contributions to the latter were few (*Psychology from an Empirical Standpoint*, as we have it, is almost entirely a work of descriptive phenomenology); and Husserl contributed to it nothing at all.

Phenomena, mental and physical

What, then, is the nature of Brentano's early philosophy?[14] One of his most basic and distinctive intuitions concerns the nature of mental phenomena in general. Mental phenomena, he believed, are essentially dynamic, comprising acts, activities, events, and processes – rather, that is, than such comparatively inert and static 'contents' of consciousness as ideas, impressions, images, concepts and the like.

Two ways of modelling the human mind predominated in the second half of the nineteenth century. On the one side stood the classical empiricist model of the mind as a largely passive, static, transparent medium of awareness on which experiences impress themselves. According to this model, perception, memory, imagination, judgement, association of ideas and the rest are just so many vicissitudes of mental life, so many things which, so to speak, befall us. Now a natural consequence of such a doctrine is the emphasizing of 'contents' of consciousness at the expense of the mental acts and activities of which they *are* the contents: clearly if one takes the mind to be largely passive, and if one takes consciousness itself to be simply a transparent awareness accompanying mental phenomena, then all interest must focus on those contents, if only because on this model there remains little or nothing else that can be talked about. The second model, on the other hand, associated particularly with Kant, assigns a dynamic, indeed a *creative* role to the human mind: through such activities as synthesis, interpretation, inference, judgement, even perception itself, the mind imposes its own order and meaning on what Kant called 'the raw material of sensible impressions'. And inherent in this conception is a natural tendency towards idealism, which culminates in the Kantian claim that 'the order and regularity of appearances, which we call *nature*, we ourselves introduce'.[15]

Brentano rejects both these accounts outright, developing in their place a theory of mental phenomena which, he hoped, would nevertheless combine all that was worth salvaging from either of them. Accordingly, for Brentano, *mental phenomena are simply acts which have contents*. We will see shortly what is involved in the notion of 'having a content'; for the moment we can note that all mental phenomena are, for Brentano, mental *acts*. Indeed, he uses the terms 'mental phenomenon' and 'mental act' synonymously.[16]

Now this latter fact ought to alert us to an oddity in Brentano's philosophy of mind. If mental phenomena are, without exception, mental

7

acts or activities, it should follow that the contents of those acts – impressions, ideas, images etc. – are *not* mental phenomena, precisely because they are not acts or activities. And if, as Brentano believed (p.77), all phenomena divide into those that are mental and those that are physical, it will follow that things like sensations, ideas, impressions, concepts, and thoughts are in fact *physical* phenomena. This seems implausible. Whether or not it is finally defensible will turn in large part on how we understand the term 'phenomenon'.

One of the major tasks undertaken in *Psychology from an Empirical Standpoint* is, precisely, the establishment of a clear 'distinction between mental and physical phenomena', and it would be natural to take Brentano's goal here as the introduction of a sharp distinction between mental and physical entities in general – where the term 'entity' is intended to range indiscriminately over all ontological categories, including objects, acts, events, properties, states of affairs, and so on. In which case Brentano, like Descartes, would be dividing all that there is in the world into two primitive ontological categories. This reading would be natural, but it would be wrong. Brentano begins his discussion by asserting: 'All the data of consciousness are divided into two great classes – the class of physical and the class of mental phenomena' (p.77); and here at the outset he states explicitly that it is 'the data of consciousness', not things in general, which are to be partitioned. Shortly afterwards he objects to an alternative theory on the grounds that 'it turns out that the so-called physical phenomenon does not actually appear to us, and, indeed, that we have no presentation of it whatsoever – certainly a curious misuse of the term "phenomenon"!' (p.78). Phenomena, in other words, are appearances, things which are 'given to consciousness as such'; and for Brentano they are utterly distinct from physical objects. In short, then, physical objects are not physical phenomena. Far from attempting, like Descartes, a global partition of all that there is, under the two categories of the mental and the physical, Brentano's distinction is one made entirely *within* the traditional, intuitive category of mental entities. He calls mental acts and activities 'mental phenomena', and he calls all other *phenomena* 'physical'; but the only other things given to consciousness as such, the only other 'phenomena', are the contents of those acts.[17]

What needs to be noted at this point is that in this series of stipulations and definitions the external, material world has quietly slipped away. It may be an exaggeration to claim that Brentano's phenomenology depends essentially upon a 'bracketing' of the natural world, or that it requires a modification of the 'natural attitude' so that the focus of one's attention shifts from the external world to facts about subjectivity – but it is clear that within his phenomenology there is no reference to, and no philosophical use of denizens of the natural world. There is, in other words, a pronounced solipsistic tendency in Brentano's early thought, a tendency which, as we shall see, exercised a profound influence on Husserl's philosophy, both early and late.

Intentionality, primary and secondary

In spite of its central importance in Brentano's thought, its massive influence on Husserl's phenomenology, and, indeed, the considerable amount of disagreement between critics and commentators as to exactly what he meant by it, I believe that Brentano's early notion of *intentionality* can in fact be dealt with quite briefly. So far we have seen that Brentanian phenomenology has a strictly circumscribed subject matter: it restricts itself to a consideration of mental and physical phenomena, that is, to mental acts and their contents. 'Intentional in-existence'[18] is merely the name – or rather, one of the names – which Brentano gives to the relation in which, for example, phenomena of these two kinds stand to one another: physical phenomena, that is, intentionally in-exist in mental phenomena. Unfortunately, Brentano does not provide a theoretical account of the nature of this relation; instead he merely gives a number of examples of it, and a number of approximate synonyms for it. Amongst the latter are a content's 'mental in-existence', 'immanent objectivity', 'existence as an object . . . in something', and '[existence] immanently as an object'. The converse relation, of a mental to a physical phenomenon, is called an act's 'reference to a content', 'direction toward an object', 'inclusion of an object within itself', and '[containment of] an object intentionally within itself.' (pp.88–9).

As these phrases suggest, and as the rest of *Psychology from an Empirical Standpoint* amply confirms, Brentano is at no great pains to distinguish the notions of *the object* as against *the content* of a mental act; Brentano is indeed happy to identify them. To take a simple example: one might wish to distinguish in the case of an act of visual perception between the object perceived (a Bugatti, let's say), and the content of consciousness present in that act (namely whatever percepts, images, sensations, impressions and what not, of which the perceiver is directly aware). Crudely speaking, *we* might say that the object is, but the content is not, immanent to the mind: a Bugatti is not a mental item; and a visual percept is certainly not the sort of thing capable of winning the Targa Florio. But even though Brentano uses the expressions 'object' and 'content' interchangeably throughout *Psychology from an Empirical Standpoint*, he is guilty of no confusion;[19] for he uses them both to mean the immanent content existing *in* a mental act. As for the notion of an external object, on the other hand, he has simply no use for it: because external objects are not phenomena there is no room for them in a phenomenology.

The notion of intentionality with which we have been concerned up to this point we can call that of *primary intentionality*; it is the relation between a mental act and the content of that act, in so far as the content is not that act itself. Primary intentionality is thus essentially non-reflexive, and it is paradigmatically – though not uniquely – the relation in which a mental phenomenon stands to a physical phenomenon when the latter is the content of the former. With the notion of primary intentionality come also the corresponding notions of *primary object* (or *content*), and *primary consciousness*. If the relation between an act (*a*) and its content (*c*) is one of primary intentionality (ie. if $a \neq c$), then we can also say that *c* is the primary content (or object) of *a*, and that *a*'s relation to *c* is one of primary consciousness.

The relation of primary intentionality is not, however, restricted to terms one of which is a physical phenomenon; for mental acts themselves can be the primary objects of mental acts. Suppose, for instance, that I remember seeing a certain colour. In this case the colour is a physical phenomenon and the seeing of it was a mental act – but it is precisely that mental act which in turn now makes up the content of another mental act, namely my act of memory. Likewise, one can imagine hearing a tone, expect to taste a certain taste, think of feeling a certain sensation, and so on. Intentional acts, it appears, can unproblematically comprise the primary objects of intentional acts – as long, that is, as the intending and the intended acts are numerically distinct. But why do we need the stipulation that in primary consciousness, act and object shall be distinct? Why can't an act straightforwardly intend itself? Indeed, isn't it precisely in the identity of an act with an object of consciousness that the possibility of *self consciousness* resides? As a first step towards an answer to these questions, we can invoke a widespread intuition. The intuition, which Brentano certainly shared, is this: a mental act or conscious state can never have *itself* as its sole and entire content because consciousness is, in Ryle's apt phrase, systematically elusive: 'like the shadow of one's head it will not wait to be jumped on'.[20] Every time I try to make some conscious act, *a*, the direct object of my consciousness, I find that my consciousness has, so to speak, taken a step backward and it is now a different act, a_1, which has *a* as its object. And in so far as I can focus my awareness on a_1, this will be because it has in turn become the object of another act, a_2, and so on.

We are now faced with a dilemma. On the one hand we have accepted, in Brentano's name, that the relation of primary intentionality has no reflexive form, that an act cannot have itself as its primary object. And yet, on the other hand, as Brentano himself observes: 'there are undoubtedly occasions where we are conscious of a mental phenomenon *while it is present in us*; for example, while we are having the presentation of a sound, we are conscious of having it' (p.126; my italics). In which case, 'the presentation of the sound is connected with the presentation of the presentation of the sound', and in this sense synchronous, reflexive consciousness *does* seem possible.

Brentano resolves this dilemma by discerning a more complex structure within intentional acts than that captured in his account of primary consciousness. This structure makes possible the possession by one and the same mental act, at one and the same time, of more than one intentional object. The primary object of an intentional act is the immanent 'content' of that act, in the sense we have already indicated. The *secondary object* of an intentional act, according to Brentano, is that very act itself. And so, in the case of the example we have been examining, 'we can say that the sound is the *primary object* of the act of hearing, and that the act of hearing itself is the *secondary object*' (p.128). Brentano then advances a number of theses concerning primary as against secondary objects:

(1) Physical phenomena can only be primary, never secondary objects.
(2) Inner consciousness is always of secondary, never of primary objects.
(3) Primary objects can be observed, attended to, and concentrated upon – secondary objects cannot.
(4) Awareness of secondary objects is incorrigible and self-verifying – that of primary objects is always defeasible.

These theses together act as the foundation for Brentano's account of evidence, truth, and knowledge, and will be dealt with on pp. 23–8 below.

In summary at this point we can say that the overall picture of intentional acts and relations which Brentano endorses is the following. Mental phenomena are acts and activities which possess an immanent content, or are directed to a primary object. Any phenomenon, mental or physical, can be the primary object of an intentional act, *a*, – with the sole exception of act *a* itself. Provisionally we might represent primary consciousness (where *a* is an act, *c* is its content, and *a* is not identical with *c*) as:

(i)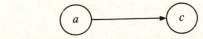

In addition to its possessing a primary object, a mental act may also possess a secondary object, namely itself, which is intended along with (*nebenbei*) the primary object.[21] The reflexive element is sometimes called a piggy-back element, in that it is dependent upon the presence of primary consciousness on which it supervenes. The resulting structure might, though again merely provisionally, be represented as:

(ii)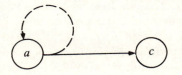

(Here the broken line represents secondary, the continuous line primary consciousness.) The structure which Brentano explicitly rules out as impossible (where '*a*' in both occurrences names the same act) is:

(iii)

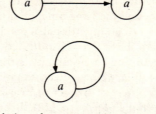

or, equivalently:

(iv)

Some reasons for doubting the appropriateness of these representations, and indeed the coherence of Brentano's theory, will be presented on pp. 20–3 below.

Presentations

I turn now to another aspect of Brentano's early philosophy of mind, namely his account of the different species of mental phenomena. First, then, the Brentanian taxonomy in outline:

> Three main classes of mental phenomena must be distinguished, and distinguished according to the different ways in which they refer to their content. . . . In the absence of more appropriate expressions we designate the first by the term 'presentation' (*Vorstellung*), the second by the term 'judgement' (*Urteil*), and the third by the terms 'emotion', 'interest', or 'love'. (p.198)[22]

The three kinds of mental phenomena identified here are of course species of acts or activities: 'It is hardly necessary to mention', Brentano writes, 'that by "presentation" we do not mean that which is presented, but the presenting of it' (p.80).

What is a Brentanian 'presentation'? It is an episode of awareness or consciousness in which a given item, its content, is neutrally and disinterestedly 'present'. A presentation, in other words, involves no intellectual, emotional, volitional, aesthetic or other attitude to the presented content on the part of the subject: it is not judged, estimated, evaluated, wanted, hated or the like; it is simply and neutrally *there*. Were I ever to experience a totally disinterested visual perception, say, then amongst other things certain individual colours would be presented – and the perceiving of them would be a presentation.[23]

Bertrand Russell claimed that the converse of presentation is acquaintance, in that for an object, *O*, to be present to a subject, *S*, is just for *S* to be acquainted with *O*. And this provides (albeit unintentionally on Russell's part) a nice gloss on Brentano's doctrine. Russell writes:

> I am *acquainted* with an object when I have a direct cognitive relation to that object, i.e. when I am directly aware of the object itself. When I speak of a cognitive relation here, I do not mean the sort of relation which constitutes judgement, but the sort which constitutes presentation. In fact . . . the relation of subject and object which I call acquaintance is simply the converse of the relation of object and subject which constitutes presentation.[24]

Russell's doctrine of knowledge by acquaintance stands, needless to say, in contrast to his theory of propositional knowledge, or 'knowledge by description'. Acquaintance (or presentation) is a relation between a subject and an object or object-like entity. The latter, however, though it may be complex – in the sense that it may be composed of a number of distinct parts – has no syntactic or grammatical articulation: its parts, if it has any, are not related one to another in anything like the ways in which the parts of a sentence or proposition are. So knowledge by acquaintance has the schematic form: X knows A, where 'A' is potentially a syntactically structureless singular term. Knowledge by description, on the other hand, is schematically of the form: X knows *that p*, where 'p' is essentially sentential.[25] Now perhaps the most striking characteristic of Brentano's account of mental phenomena is that he categorically denies the existence, not only of propositional knowledge, but of all propositional attitudes whatsoever: no mental act can properly be said to have a content which is of the form: '*that p*'. All mental acts, in other words, either are or are based upon and incorporate, acts of presentation/acquaintance.

Judgements

Brentano argues as follows for this somewhat implausible conclusion. A judgement and a presentation may possess the same content: 'In fact, with regard to content, there is not the slightest difference between them . . . every object which is the content of a presentation can also be . . . content of a judgement' (p.221). And again, 'nothing is an object of judgement which is not an object of presentation' (p.201). But as the contents of presentations, the objects of direct acquaintance, are non-propositional and non-predicative, it follows that the contents of judgements must be non-propositional and non-predicative too.

Not surprisingly this theory creates a number of intractable problems. For instance, if the content of a judgement is an object-like entity, the sort of thing that corresponds to a singular term, how can judgements (or their contents) be either true or false? For there is no clear sense in which singular terms (or objects) can be said to possess truth-values (they

13

don't *say* anything). Moreover, if the content of a judgement is an object, how can one distinguish between affirmation and denial, between an assertion that such-and-such is the case and the corresponding assertion that it is not the case? Indeed this last difficulty is merely a special case of a wider problem confronting Brentano, namely, how can non-propositional, syntactically unarticulated entities stand to one another in *logical* relations? Singular terms (or objects) are not related to each other by entailment, implication, compatibility, relevance or the like.

Fortunately we do not need to follow Brentano into the details of the 'complete overthrow and . . . reconstruction of elementary logic' (p.230) which he rightly believed were required by his adoption of a non-propositonal theory of judgement; for this aspect of his philosophy had little influence on Husserl, and what little it had (e.g. in *The Philosophy of Arithmetic*) was short-lived.[26] From a Husserlian point of view there are, however, two issues which we should note. The first concerns Brentano's distinction between presentations (*Vorstellungen*) and judgements, and his related use of the claim that all judgements are, in the last analysis, existential. The second concerns the form which Brentanian content analysis takes – given, that is, that the sort of syntactic analysis familiar in the analytic tradition since Frege, Russell, and Wittgenstein is clearly not available to an advocate of a non-propositional theory of judgement and thought.[27]

Frege expressed succinctly the distinction in which we are interested:

> We can grasp a thought without acknowledging its truth. To think is to grasp a thought. Once we have grasped a thought we can acknowledge it as true – make a judgement – and give expression to this acknowledge-ment – make an assertion. . . . Assertoric force is to be dissociated from negation. To each thought there corresponds an opposite; and to make a judgement *is* to make a choice between opposite thoughts: accepting one of them and rejecting the other is one act. So there is no need for a special sign for [or act of] rejecting a thought.[28]

According to Frege – and his view seems to have become, with few exceptions, the dominant one amongst analytic philosophers – there are just two kinds of propositional act: on the one hand one can neutrally grasp, entertain, contemplate or simply *have* a thought, in a way which is without commitment to the truth or falsity of that thought. And more positively, on the other hand, one can judge, believe, assert, or affirm that the thought is true. Now at first sight it might well appear, as it indeed appeared to Brentano, that there is in addition to the foregoing a third kind of act, comprising those which are essentially negative, which doubt, deny, or reject the truth of a thought. Frege, however, has two powerful reasons for rejecting such a tripartite division. In the first place, as the above quotation suggests, the positive act of accepting, asserting, or judging *that p* is the very same act as, negatively, rejecting or denying *that not-p*. Every thought has a unique contradictory, and to make a judgement just *is* to make a choice between a given thought and its negation. There is, in other words, no possibility that one can successfully judge that *p* is the case, and at the same time remain quite uncommitted as to the truth or falsity of *not-p*. But in this case the distinction between positive acts of acceptance, and negative acts of rejection simply collapses. Frege's second reason for distinguishing only between grasping a thought and judging it to be true is this: affirmation and denial stand in *logical* relations one to another (for example, it is logically inconsistent to affirm and to deny one and the same proposition). Logical relations, however, hold primarily between propositions, and only derivatively between acts and activities: psychological acts are logically related only in so far as their contents are logically related to each other. If this is the case, then the difference between affirmation and denial ought to be represented in a perspicuous notation, not as a difference between acts of judgement, but as a difference between their respective contents. So, for Frege, the difference between (i) *judging that p* and (ii) *denying that p* is not a difference between act types, but a difference in content; in which case this difference can be less misleadingly expressed as that between (iii) *judging that p* and (iv) *judging that not-p*. This is precisely what Brentano's theory denies.

According to Brentano there are just two basic forms of judgement, two forms, that is, which the mental act of judging can take: one can affirm *A*, or one can deny *A*. Of course this theory remains unintelligible in the absence of any account of what it is to affirm or deny something non-propositional. What can it mean to 'affirm the colour red', say, or to 'deny the taste of honey'? Brentano's account, in outline, is as follows. First, and in stark contrast to Frege, he denies that there is any philosophical relevance whatsoever in the fact that the sentence is the linguistic form in which we typically converse, communicate, and express thoughts and judgements. On the contrary, he claims, the belief that 'the compounding of several elements [is] . . . essential for the nature of judgements' is a straightforward consequence of our having taken the accidental and superficial forms of utterance, which 'are in fact *nothing but* a matter of linguistic expression', to mirror the underlying forms of the judgements themselves. This is a mistake; for the rules which govern the formation and significance of sentences apply exclusively at the level of language; and the rules governing the formation and significance of judgements are prior to, and entirely independent of them. So while it is certainly the case that everyday linguistic utterances are typically sentential, are syntactically complex, and contain elements belonging to different categories (e.g. subject and predicate; function and argument;

noun-phrase and verb-phrase, or whatever), none of this is true of the contents of judgements. And, in particular, the content of a judgement does not require, does not even permit, anything corresponding to the articulation into subject and predicate which Brentano thought characteristic of linguistic utterances.

The second element in Brentano's account of how non-propositional judgement is possible is his subscription to the thesis that existence is not a property or attribute of things, that 'existence' is not a predicate. And so, he claims, a sentence such as '*A* exists', in spite of its superficial and misleading form, does not express a judgement involving 'the conjunction of an attribute of "existence" with *A*; rather it is *A* itself we affirm'. Some light is thrown on this analysis by Brentano's remark that

> Aristotle had seen that [the concept of existence] is one we acquire
> through reflection on the affirmative judgement. . . . One may say that
> an affirmative judgement is true, or one may say that its object is
> existent; in both cases one would be saying *precisely the same thing*.[29]

In other words the expression 'exists' in the sentence '*A* exists' serves only to indicate that one is claiming to speak truly – but to claim to speak truly is simply to make an assertion or affirmation. So the linguistic expression 'exists' serves merely to express assertoric force; and a judgement which affirms *A* is true if and only if *A* exists: 'The concepts of existence and non-existence are correlatives to the concepts of the truth of (simple) affirmative and negative judgements'.[30]

The third element in Brentano's theory is his doctrine that 'every categorical proposition can be translated without change of meaning into an existential proposition' (p.213); indeed 'the reducibility of all propositions which express a judgement to existential propositions is . . . indubitable' (p.218). Fortunately the details of this reductionist programme need not concern us here.

If we put these three elements together we arrive at a theory according to which all judgements are either affirmations or denials of things. The things in question are the intentional objects of presentations, and are without syntactic structure. An affirmation of a thing is true just in case the thing exists; a denial of a thing is true just in case that thing does not exist.

Finally, and in summary, we can note a number of outstanding features of Brentano's theory of judgement, virtually every one of which is in diametrical opposition to the corresponding element in Frege's theory of thought and judgement. First, the contents of presentations, i.e. sense qualities, are for Brentano none other than the contents of judgement: the things we see, feel, and taste are identical with the contents of the judgements we make. Two points are perhaps worth stressing: (1) this doctrine reverses a trend initiated by Kant and epitomized by Frege, which insists on a sharp, categorial distinction between the sensory and the intellectual; between, on the one hand, such things as sensations, perceptions, impressions, sense data and the like, and, on the other hand, such things as concepts, judgements, thoughts, inferences, and so on.[31] And (2) the Brentanian doctrine that one and the same thing can now be presented to sensibility, now the content of judgement, is an important ingredient of Husserl's theories of 'evidence', 'self-evidence', and 'fulfilment'.

Second, in order to allow that the contents of presentations are also the contents of judgements, Brentano was forced to adopt a radically non-propositional account of thought and judgement; for it is clear that the contents of presentations, the deliverances of sensibility for example, are not syntactically articulated.

Third, because of his analysis of the concept of truth, which makes it a correlative of the concept of affirmation, mental phenomena which are without affirmative or negative force (i.e. presentations) are without truth-value: 'there is . . . no knowledge, no error in presentations' (p.223).

Fourth, a consequence of Brentano's doctrine that the concept of existence, like that of truth, is a correlative of affirmation, is that mere presentations, without affirmation, are without ontological commitment. This doctrine, it will turn out, is a significant ingredient in Husserl's account of the phenomenological reduction.

Fifth, the last characteristic of Brentano's theory of judgement and thought that I wish to highlight here is its virtually total dissociation from issues – whether methodological, conceptual or doctrinal – to do with language. Language, for the early Brentano, is not merely irrelevant to, it actually entirely misrepresents the structure and content of our discursive conceptual acts and abilities.[32] If, as Dummett has suggested, one of the hallmarks of the analytic tradition in philosophy is that

> the philosophy of thought is to be equated with the philosophy of language: more exactly (i) an account of language does not presuppose an account of thought, (ii) an account of language yields an account of thought, and (iii) there is no other adequate means by which an account of thought may be given,[33]

then Brentano manifestly belongs outside that tradition. And so too, in so far as he followed Brentano in this matter, does Husserl.

The analysis of phenomena

'Our investigation has shown', Brentano writes, 'that wherever there is mental activity there is a certain multiplicity and complexity' (p.155). Now, as we have already noted, Brentano's analysis of the possible forms which this complexity can take is determinedly non-syntactic: neither judgements nor presentations are articulated in anything even remotely resembling the ways in which the sentences of natural languages are articulated. So far, however, we have failed to indicate how Brentano does propose to analyse the contents of such acts. The major constraint within which such an analytic procedure must work is, however, already in place: whatever form of analysis we adopt, it must apply univocally not only to 'intellectual' presentations (concepts and thoughts) and to judgements, but to 'sensory' presentations as well.

The key notions in terms of which Brentano conducts his analysis are those of *proper part, integral whole, aggregate, dependence,* and *containment.* His analytic procedures belong, therefore, within whole-part theory or mereology; and this theory is applied to two separate aspects of phenomenological analysis. The relations between an act and its content are construed by Brentano as the relations of a whole to its parts; and the relation of a whole to its parts is also the model for the complexity possessed by the contents themselves. But before examining these applications of the theory we need to know in outline what the theory is.

At the centre of the theory adumbrated in Brentano's early writings is a distinction between two kinds of complex whole or unity: I shall call them strong and weak wholes (Brentano calls them 'real things' and 'collectives' respectively). The distinction rests ultimately on the intuition that there are degrees of intimacy or tightness with which the various elements that make up a complex unity can be united or bound together. In a weak unity or whole the elements are only loosely grouped together: the trees that make up a wood, the sheep that form a flock, the people that together comprise a crowd, for example, do so merely in virtue of their spatial proximity. A flock, we can say, is just a lot of sheep together. The same is not however true of an individual sheep. A sheep is not just an aggregate, collection, or heap of organs (or cells, or molecules, or bits and pieces of whatever sort) which just happen to be at the same place at the same time; for it is easy to imagine precisely those organs (cells, molecules, etc.) rearranged in such a way that we would no longer say that they constituted a sheep – even though the original aggregate would still be present. And in so far as one can destroy the sheep while preserving the aggregate of its parts, aggregate and sheep cannot be one and the same thing. The sheep, we might say, is a strong unity, whereas the totality of its parts, like the flock of which it is a member, is only a weak one. This has tempted some philosophers to say that, unlike a weak unity, a strong unity is a whole greater than the sum of its parts. The intuitions I have alluded to are, needless to say, at their clearest when one takes as examples of strong unity so-called organic wholes, organisms like trees, sheep, or people, and of weak unity mere aggregates based on spatial proximity. But the distinction between these two kinds of whole is by

18

no means restricted to cases such as these. As we shall see, Brentano believed that (non-spatial) mental phenomena can comprise both strong and weak unities; and Husserl applied the distinction to (non-spatiotemporal) abstract objects.

So much for the intuitive basis of Brentano's distinction. What theoretical account can we now give of it? What, we need to ask, are the general laws governing the relations of parts to wholes? And, more specifically, what is the difference between whole-part relations as they characteristically obtain in a strong unity, as against those which obtain in a mere aggregate or 'collective'? In answer to the first, general question, the following seems to be the minimal Brentanian apparatus. First we require a distinction between a wide notion of *part*, according to which it is possible for a given thing to be a part of itself, and a narrower notion of *proper part* which is incompatible with such self-containment. In this sense, if x is a proper part of y, then x is not identical with y. Second, with Brentano, we can invoke the principle that whatever is a part of a part is therewith a part of the whole: if x is a part of y, and y is a part of z, then x is *eo ipso* a part of z. Third, and more contentiously, Brentano subscribes to the so-called principle of mereological essentialism which asserts that the parts of a given whole are essential to that whole: if x has y as a part, then x necessarily has y as a part.[34] Finally, and most contentiously of all, there is Brentano's advocacy of what I shall call the principle of mereological adequacy, namely, that *all* analysis is part-whole analysis, that there can be nothing more to a complex unity, of whatever sort, than its comprising certain elements which are related as parts are to wholes. This may not sound contentious – after all, what else could 'analysis' be but the reduction of a complex whole into its constituent elements; what else could a complex consist in, if not in its parts? The principle is given teeth, however, by Brentano's restriction on the possible ways in which a part *can* be related to a whole. There are just two such ways, depending on whether the whole in question is strong or weak.

If we take the notion of a strong whole as primitive, we can define a weak whole as any whole which has at least one strong whole as a proper part. So in effect we are construing a strong unity or whole as one none of whose proper parts is itself a strong unity or whole. But why should we do this?

There is a distinction between strong and weak unity which shows up grammatically in the fact that one can always ask, concerning a collective whole W: W of what? Aggregates, crowds, flocks and the like are essentially wholes *of* certain items.[35] Weak wholes, I shall say, have members. Strong wholes, on the other hand, have no members, though they do have proper parts. And so, while one can significantly ask what a flock is a flock of, it makes no sense to ask what a sheep is a sheep of. The animals which form a flock are its proper parts, and they are its members; the proper parts of a strong whole are not its members – in his early works Brentano calls them its 'divisives' (p.157), later he calls them its 'moments'. The difference between a member and a divisive, he claims, is that members are 'things in their own right' or 'things in and of themselves', whereas divisives are not. Strong wholes, it appears, have parts (divisives or moments) which are not independent or self-subsistent entities, but which depend or are adjectival on the wholes which contain them. In the case of weak wholes, on the other hand, the relation of dependence seems to run in the opposite direction: a weak whole is dependent or adjectival on the parts which are its members.

If we now, finally, add to the foregoing the principle of mereological essentialism, that a whole of any sort depends essentially on its parts, then we obtain the following result. A strong whole depends on its proper parts, and they in turn depend on it: a strong unity involves the *mutual* dependence of whole and parts. In a weak whole, however, although the whole depends on the parts, the parts are themselves strong wholes, and as such are independent of it. The relation of a member to a weak unity Brentano later called 'one-sided detachability'.[36] The notion of dependence at work here is one of fully-fledged metaphysical or ontological dependence. The claim that x is dependent on y, in the sense in which we are interested, is never a causal or contingent claim, neither is it a mere formal truth of logic nor a trivial truth by definition; it is a claim which, if justified, has as its basis the essential natures of the items involved.[37]

In summary, the concepts we have so far been examining can be elucidated thus:

– a strong whole is a complex unity which stands in a relation of mutual or 'two-sided' dependency to its divisives.
– a weak whole, or aggregate, is 'one-sidedly' dependent on its members: the members are independent of the whole.
– a divisive is a dependent part of a whole.
– a member of a whole is independent of that whole.

How might we represent this? I shall adopt the following conventions. A weak unity or aggregate of things will be signified by an ellipse; a strong whole by a circle. A flock of five sheep, or indeed any weak unity comprising five members can be unproblematically represented as

(1)

If we continue to employ a circle to represent an independent or self-subsistent thing, then we can adopt the convention that concentric circular sub-figures are to signify dependent parts of the whole:

(2)

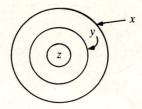

Here (2) as a whole represents a strong unity (x) with two proper parts or 'divisives' (z and y). The figure has the advantage of showing that if z is a part of y and y is a part of x, then z is a part of x. And finally, by way of stipulation, I shall distinguish pictorially between physical and mental phenomena by using, respectively, shaded and clear areas to represent them. Our next task is to investigate how this theory applies to the analysis of mental acts and their contents.

Brentano's early theory of intentionality has it that an intentional object or content is a component part of the mental phenomenon which possesses it. Thus if a content c intentionally in-exists in an act a, then c is a proper part of a. We can represent the case in which, say, I have direct acquaintance with a physical phenomenon (itself simple) as:

(3)

Of course Brentano denies that there ever actually occurs an act of such simplicity, for, in the first place, presentation or acquaintance is always accompanied by judgement, in which case 'the object is present to consciousness in a twofold way, first as an object of presentation, then as an object held to be true or denied' (p.201). In the second place, moreover, 'there is a special connection between the object of inner perception and the presentation itself, [such that] both belong to one and the same act' (p.127). In other words, in addition to the primary consciousness represented by (3), there is also the secondary consciousness or inner perception whose object is the whole act which (3) represents: 'Every act, no matter how simple, has a double object, a primary and a secondary object' (p.153).

Can we capture these two kinds of structural complexity? For as Brentano insists 'This lack of simplicity is not a lack of unity' (p.155). The unity here is indeed a strong unity. When I have a presentation of an object and simultaneously judge that it exists, there are not two independent mental phenomena present. The representation, say,

(4)

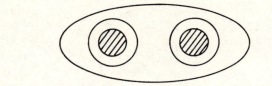

would be quite inadequate, for two reasons: it fails to show that the two acts have one and the same object; and it fails also to show that the judgement is dependent on the presentation. Rather, using the conventions already introduced, we can represent an act of judgement whose content is a simple physical phenomenon with which I am acquainted (i.e. which is an object of presentation) by:

(5)

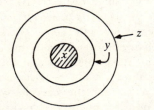

Here x is the physical phenomenon, y the presentation of x, and z the judgement of x. As far as primary consciousness is concerned, embeddings of any degree of complexity can in principle be represented in this way, by the inclusion of ever more concentric circles. The representation of secondary consciousness is not, however, such an easy matter.

Brentano explicitly asserts that secondary consciousness is a *part of* an act of primary consciousness: 'The presentation which accompanies a mental act, and which refers to it, is part of the object on which it is directed' (p.128; cf. p.256). And again: 'The consciousness of the primary object and the consciousness of the secondary object are not each a distinct phenomenon but are two aspects of one and the same unitary phenomenon' (p.155). Now clearly the resources to hand are inadequate to picture the structure of secondary consciousness, which can be represented neither as a physical phenomenon, nor yet as still one more mental phenomenon containing other phenomena as proper parts (i.e. not as still one more concentric circle). The problem is indeed precisely that secondary consciousness does *not* contain its object as a proper part, but is, rather, itself its own object. And this is why it is not simply our system of representation that is incapable of modelling Brentano's theory; it is the theory itself which is incoherent.[38] On the one hand Brentano maintains that the relation of a mental phenomenon to its content is that of a whole to a proper part: the content intentionally in-exists in the mental phenomenon, but cannot be identical with it. On the other hand, however, the mental phenomenon of secondary consciousness is said to possess a content which is identical with itself. This is a straighforward contradiction.

Self-evidence, self-knowledge, and self-perception

The opening words of *Psychology from an Empirical Standpoint* are these:

> My psychological standpoint is empirical; experience alone is my teacher. Yet I share with other thinkers the conviction that this is entirely compatible with a certain ideal intuition (*ideale Anschauung*). (p.xv)

The tension noticeable here, between a desire to rely exclusively on what experience can teach us, and yet at the same time to admit the possibility of some sort of 'ideal intuition' characterizes Husserl's phenomenology just as it does Brentano's. Both philosophers intended their investigations to result in a body of *laws*, that is, in a connected system of *a priori*, universal, necessary, apodictic, and immutable philosophical truths; yet both believed that knowledge can ultimately concern only items given in experience, the home of contingency and particularity. Indeed, both of them subscribed ultimately to a perceptual, or quasi-perceptual model of human knowledge: in the last analysis one genuinely knows only what one actually and directly perceives (in some sense or other of the term 'perceives'). The attempt to resolve the tension between these broadly 'rationalist' and 'empiricist' tendencies, and so to harmonize the demand for infallible knowledge with the requirement that such knowledge should in no way transcend the evidence of actual experience, was one to which Husserl devoted his life's work. And in this he followed Brentano.

He followed Brentano too in the broadly Cartesian nature of the resolution proposed: self-evident knowledge is ultimately self-knowledge. It is in the mind's experience of itself that one is presented with evidence which, on the one hand, is 'given directly in experience', but which, on the other hand, none the less warrants claims to infallible, non-trivial knowledge. And according to Brentano, 'inner perception' is the unique source of such knowledge.

The claims which Brentano makes concerning the role and the reliability of inner perception can appear – especially to those who find Wittgenstein's treatment of such issues convincing – to be quite extravagantly naive: 'inner perception possesses these distinguishing characteristics', he asserts, 'it is immediate, infallible, and self-evident' (p.91). And then, as if to add insult to injury, he claims that this is itself a truth which we know on the basis of immediate, self-evident, inner perception (cf. p.140). Clearly we need to know exactly what an inner perception is, and how it differs from a so-called 'outer' perception.

In a sense the question is easily answered: '[what] all mental phenomena have in common is the fact that they are only perceived in inner consciousness, while in the case of physical phenomena only external perception is possible' (p.91). In other words, it might appear, we have a two-part taxonomy of acts of presentation: an act is an inner perception if and only if its intentional object is a mental phenomenon, and an act is an outer perception if and only if its object is a physical phenomenon. The appearance here is, however, misleading in a number of respects. In the first place, remarks of the kind just quoted can easily create the impression that what Brentano has in mind is something like the familiar distinction between, on the one hand, perception that is 'outer' in that it comprises sensory awareness of material objects in the external world, and on the other hand some form of introspective awareness directed towards the acts and contents of consciousness. This cannot be right, however, for as we have already seen Brentano does not allow the possibility of perceptual access to the denizens of the external world, and his distinction between mental and physical phenomena *is* in effect the distinction between acts and their contents. Second, moreover, Brentano's remarks too often create the impression that he employs merely a twofold classification of presentations: outer perceptions (of physical phenomena) stand contrasted only with inner perceptions (of mental phenomena). In fact, however, his taxonomy is tripartite.

We need to distinguish the following three sorts of consciousness or awareness. (1) There are mental acts whose primary content is a physical phenomenon or sensory quality. These are called acts of outer perception, though they are not therewith perceptions of an 'outer' world. (2) There are mental acts whose *primary* object is itself a mental act. Brentano calls them acts of 'inner observation' or 'introspection', and a prime example is an act of remembering whose content is some previous mental act. I indulge in inner observation, in other words, when I remember wanting something: my earlier act of wanting is the primary object of my present act of remembering. Finally, and in sharp contrast to the foregoing, there is (3) the synchronous, reflexive awareness of a mental act as a *secondary* object – the awareness, that is, which a mental phenomenon has of itself. Now it is exclusively consciousness of the latter sort which Brentano calls 'inner perception' and about which he makes extravagant epistemological claims concerning infallibility, self-evidence and the like. Terminologically, then, we shall need to keep distinct *outer perception*, *introspection* (both of which are forms of observation), and genuine *inner perception*.

Epistemologically the important point is that observation of any sort 'is to a great extent subject to illusion. Inner perception, on the other hand, is infallible and does not admit of doubt' (p.35). Now we can readily agree that memory and outer perception are less than totally reliable; but with what right does secondary consciousness lay claim to infallibility? Brentano's fundamental, and very Cartesian intuition seems to be this: for me there is logical space for error, for illusion, misconception, mistaken judgement and the like, only in so far as it is possible for there to be a real distinction between how I take things to be, and how they actually are. I *can* only be wrong if it is possible that things are not as I conceive (perceive, judge) them to be. If it could somehow be guaranteed that, however things might seem to me, *that* is necessarily the way they in fact are, then my beliefs and judgements would necessarily be true.[39] But what could conceivably act as guarantor here? What could, even in principle, close the gap between how I take things to be and how things really are, so as to seal off all logical possibility of error? The only candidate would seem to be the strict identity, the complete coincidence of, in Brentano's terms, the act and the object of judgement (belief, conception, presentation, or whatever). My taking something to be thus-and-so becomes logically indistinguishable from its actually being thus-and-so in the limiting case in which the actuality exclusively *consists in* my taking it to be thus-and-so. And this is of course precisely the form which secondary consciousness or inner perception takes, with the result that 'the phenomena of inner perception . . . are true in themselves. As they appear to be, so they are in reality' (p.20).

We have here, in this odd use of identity, I believe, the source of the persistent reflexivity which permeates the thought of Brentano – and, indeed, of Husserl – and which results in the foundational role ascribed by both of them to such notions as self-presentation, self-evidence, self-knowledge, self-consciousness, self-verification, reflection, and the like. One of the well-known slogans of Husserlian phenomenology is '*Zu den Sachen selbst!*' – 'Back to the things themselves', and inherent in the programme this implies is, crudely speaking, the intention to set aside mere appearances and to deal directly with the reality as it is in itself. There are two requirements here: first, the objects of investigation should be such that the distinction between appearance and reality does not apply; they must be just what they seem to be. And, second, these items must be *given*, and this can only mean given in experience. A long philosophical tradition, to which both Brentano and Husserl belong, has it that the only items satisfying both these requirements, the only things which enjoy complete coincidence of appearance and reality but which are such that there are experiences of them, are those very experiences themselves.

This train of thought, in all its naivety, is explicitly present in Brentano's writings. He says for example that 'whenever a mental act is the object of an accompanying inner cognition *it contains itself as presented*' and it is 'this alone [which] makes possible the infallibility and immediate self-evidence of inner perception' (p.139, my italics). The claim that a mental act can contain itself as it is in itself is equivalent to the claim that 'as they appear to be, so they are in reality'. And this identity within inner perception of appearance and reality, of the merely phenomenal with the real, is repeatedly stressed by Brentano: 'mental phenomena are those which alone possess real existence as well as intentional existence' (p.92); 'we define [mental phenomena] as the only phenomena that possess *actual existence* in addition to intentional inexistence' (p.98; cf. *Ideas* §49/p.153).

The picture which has emerged of Brentano's early theory of knowledge can be summarized as follows. Knowledge of the objects, properties, and facts which belong to the material world is, to say the least, problematic. We have no perceptual access to them, and any inference about their nature we might make, on the basis of the perceptions which we do in fact have, will be ultimately unwarranted: 'We have no right . . . to believe that the objects of so-called external perception really exist as they appear to us' (p.10). For 'the phenomena of so-called external perception cannot be proved true and real, even by means of indirect demonstration' (p.91). It is possible in principle, however, for a person to acquire knowledge of his own mental states and activities through introspection or inner observation. But although it is possible for true beliefs to be obtained and justified in this way, Brentano believes that the method is inherently difficult to employ and so unreliable in its results that a belief acquired in this way is more likely to turn out to be false than true (cf. pp.29–36). The exclusive source of reliable, indeed infallible, knowledge is inner perception – the simultaneous reflexive awareness of itself which is a part of every mental phenomenon. The knowledge is infallible, I have tried to indicate, not because it is knowledge of the self, or knowledge restricted to the sphere of subjectivity (though it is incidentally both those things), but because it is literally reflexive. And the epistemological reflexivity involved here is nowhere more apparent than in the use to which Brentano puts his notion of *Evidenz*, a term which is usually and rightly translated as *self-evidence*.

Brentano's claim that genuine inner perception presents us with things that are self-evident and indubitable must be understood, so to speak, in a logical rather than a psychological sense. There are, that is, many things which sane people normally, perhaps even inevitably, take to be self-evident and which, as a matter of contingent psychological fact, they are incapable of doubting. I personally cannot bring myself genuinely to feel any doubt about the fact that I have never been on the moon, say, or that I presently have two hands which I can see in front of me. But such autobiographical asseveration is beside the point. When Brentano claims that a belief justified by inner perception is indubitable, he means that it is by its very nature such that the concept of falsity is incapable of applying to it. And likewise, a belief of this sort is self-evident in the sense that it is, conclusively, *evidence for itself*. Appearance and reality – that which acts as evidence and that which it is evidence for – are, within inner perception, one and the same.

Empiricism in its classical form is, *inter alia*, a doctrine concerning the origin of the contents of consciousness according to which every such content, every item of which the mind can be aware, originates in sensibility. Without sensory experience the mind would remain, in Locke's words, 'white paper devoid of all characters'. Brentano's theory of knowledge, however, because of the crucial role it assigns to inner perception – the mind's non-sensory awareness of itself – can seem to be only marginally a form of 'empiricism', in which the notion of sensory experience has little or no part to play. In fact, however, this is far from being the case. Every mental phenomenon possesses an intentional object or content; and every mental phenomenon either is, or incorporates as a proper part, a presentation. Presentations, we have already seen, are either of physical or of mental phenomena; and the latter are presented either as a primary or a secondary object. Although this is not emphasized in *Psychology from an Empirical Standpoint*, it is none the less the case that each of these three kinds of presentation necessarily has as its kernel a physical phenomenon.[40] But as a physical phenomenon is for Brentano a *sensory* content, and as every mental act whatsoever has as its kernel a presentation, it follows that every mental act whatsoever is ultimately founded on an item which originated in sensibility. What needs to be shown at this point, then, is that all three kinds of presentation contain as their ultimate element a *physical* phenomenon. The case in which the primary object of a presentation is a physical phenomenon of course conforms trivially to our requirement. But what of the case in which, through an act of inner observation, a, I am acquainted with a mental phenomenon, c? If it is possible to represent this situation thus:

(6)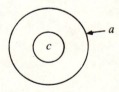

then we have a form of knowledge which is devoid of sensory content, that is, whose origin is independent of outer perception. No mental phenomenon, however, can finally have the form represented in (6); for the content c is itself a mental phenomenon, and so must itself possess an intentional content, c_1. This content in turn can be either a mental or a physical phenomenon; but, if mental, it must again possess an intentional content, c_2, . . . and so on. The only sort of item which is capable of bringing to an end this regressive infinity of conditions on the possibility of act *a* is one which itself has no intentional content. And that is, by definition, a physical phenomenon, or sensory quality:

(7)

In principle – we might say figuratively – there is no upper bound to the number of concentric circles representing acts of presentation (one can remember wanting to hope to expect to hate . . . and so on indefinitely); but the *last* term in this series must be a physical phenomenon; the innermost area must be shaded.

The third and final case, that of secondary consciousness of a mental phenomenon, likewise poses no threat to Brentano's empiricism. In so far as the object of secondary consciousness is a mental act whose primary object is ultimately a physical phenomenon, the secondary consciousness or inner perception also has that physical phenomenon as its most basic element; for the parts of an act of secondary consciousness are the parts of the mental phenomenon which is its object.

If this is right, then Brentano's empiricism is unqualified: every act of awareness and every judgement has as its ultimate constituent a 'physical phenomenon', that is, a content which originated in outer sense. This serves, however, only to intensify the incompatibility, noted above, between Brentano's empiricism and the opposing 'rationalistic' tendencies in his thought. He never successfully resolved these tensions – but their resolution was to become one of the ultimate goals of Husserl's philosophical enterprise.

Part I
Naturalism

I

The Philosophy of Arithmetic

Introduction

Husserl's earliest philosophical work, his *Habilitationsschrift* entitled *On the Concept of Number. Psychological Analyses*,[1] appeared as a booklet in 1887; and four years later he published the first (and, as it turned out, the only) volume of an exhaustive study on the same topic entitled *Philosophy of Arithmetic. Psychological and Logical Investigations*.[2] Of these two works we need here consider only the latter, however, for it in fact incorporates, 'virtually verbatim' (p.8),[3] almost all of the earlier study.

As a rough initial characterization we might say that the *Philosophy of Arithmetic* has as its overall aim the solution of Fregean problems via the application of Brentanian procedures and techniques: Husserl sets out, that is, to give an account of the general concept of number; of the individual numbers themselves; of the logical form both of ascriptions of number and of assertions of arithmetic; and, more generally, of the nature of arithmetical truth, knowledge, and understanding.[4] And to this end he employs, for example, the techniques of whole-part analysis and 'descriptive psychology', as well as Brentanian doctrines concerning presentations, intuitions, mental acts, intentional in-existence, and the like. On the one hand, then, Frege and Husserl share a common goal: to provide a philosophically rigorous analysis of, and warrant for, the most basic concepts, assertions, and methods whose employment is constitutive of objectively valid arithmetical practice. For Frege, however, the objectivity of arithmetic is only possible on the assumption that intuition (perception, sensation, imagination, or feeling, for example) plays no constitutive role whatsoever in our arithmetical knowledge; and so the central question he addresses in *The Foundations of Arithmetic* is: 'How are the numbers to be given to us when we can have no presentation (*Vorstellung*) or intuition (*Anschauung*) of them?'[5]

31

For Husserl, in contrast, working from within the framework of a Brentanian empiricism, the task is rather to demonstrate that arithmetical knowledge is sound precisely *because* it can ultimately be traced back to concrete presentations and intuitions. 'No concept can be grasped,' Husserl states categorically, 'which lacks a basis in concrete intuition (*in einer konkreten Anschauung*)' (p.79).

In the introduction to Part I of the *Philosophy of Arithmetic* Husserl says that the analysis of the concept *number* is by no means of exclusively mathematical interest:

> The interrelated concepts of *unity*, *multiplicity*, and *number* are concepts fundamental to human knowledge in general, and as such are of particular philosophical interest in spite of the considerable difficulties which attend an understanding of them. . . . These difficulties are intimately connected with *certain peculiarities in the psychological constitution of these concepts*, and with the elucidation of these psychology too is especially concerned. (p.13; my italics)

The discipline of psychology to which Husserl here refers, and to which the *Philosophy of Arithmetic* was intended at least in part to be a contribution, is the descriptive psychology or 'phenomenology' of Brentano.[6] And Husserl simply takes it as axiomatic that:

(i) *Phenomena* (i.e. mental acts and their contents) exhaust the subject matter of this discipline (cf. p.22).

(ii) Mental acts or mental phenomena have immanently in-existent contents (or 'objects') (pp.68, 70).

(iii) All mental phenomena are ultimately founded on sensory data, i.e., on concrete intuitions (p.79).

(iv) Aggregates or collectives are weak wholes: they depend on their proper parts, but their parts are themselves independent of such wholes.

(v) A thing is a strong whole: it depends on its proper parts, and they in turn depend on it. A thing therefore cannot be a mere aggregate, and its proper parts cannot themselves be objects (cf. pp.131, 159).[7]

The one major issue on which Husserl and Brentano part company concerns what I earlier called the doctrine of sensory-intellectual collapse. Brentano's empiricism, as we have seen, combines with his theory of whole-part analysis to rule out not only the need for, but also the possibility of, any irreducible distinction between particular sensory intuitions on the one hand, and general discursive concepts on the other. Or, to put it another way, the category which Brentano calls 'presentations' (*Vorstellungen*) is a genuinely homogeneous category. Husserl, however, rejects this doctrine entirely, and reverts to the Kantian usage according to which the term 'presentation' is allowed to range over two quite heterogeneous kinds of phenomena. Husserl, that is, wishes to distinguish between particular items of sensory awareness – he calls them 'intuitions' (*Anschauungen*) – and mental contents which are in principle general and, therefore, non-sensory – i.e. concepts (*Begriffe*).

Clearly much more needs to be said about the precise nature of Husserl's understanding and use of principles (i) to (v) above, and of their associated terminology, but the introductory function of the present section can be better served if for the moment we postpone that task and concentrate instead on the general nature of the philosophical programme Husserl attempts to implement in the *Philosophy of Arithmetic*.

He takes as his ultimate goal the clarification and legitimation of the concept *number*, specifically of the concept of a cardinal number (*Anzahl*), which he construes as a general concept whose instances are the positive whole integers 2, 3, 4, etc. (cf. pp.82, 139). According to Husserl the procedure for clarifying a concept can have two distinct phases. If the concept in question is complex, that is, if it contains one or more concepts as its proper parts, then the first phase will be 'analytic' and will consist in a mereological decomposition of the concept. The analytic phase, when carried out completely, results in a number of classically analytic statements concerning the concept in question and the part-whole relations between it and the simple concepts which it comprises. So, for example, 'The concept *bachelor* contains the concept *man*', and 'The concept *bachelor* contains the concept *unmarried*' will be analytic statements resulting from conceptual analysis; and the totality of such statements are said to define the concept *bachelor*. (Of course the concept *man* is not itself simple – it can be taken to include the concepts *male, human, adult*, and so on. But because parts of a part are also parts of the whole, these latter concepts, along with their parts, if any, will also be parts of the concept *bachelor*.) As Husserl himself observes, on this view of definition

> we can only define that which is logically complex, and as soon as we come up against ultimate, elementary concepts all definition comes to an end. . . . In such circumstances our only course is to exhibit the concrete phenomena from which the concepts have been abstracted, along with the nature of that abstractive process. (p.119)

The second or 'genetic' phase in the process of conceptual clarification is thus the attempt to throw light on simple, unanalysable component concepts by tracing them back to the concrete intuitions from which, by abstraction, they emerged.[8] Because Husserl believes that the concept *number* is simple – in the particular sense that it has no concepts as proper parts – its elucidation can only be genetic; for in its case

> little is to be achieved by way of definition. The difficulty lies rather with the *phenomena*, and with their correct description. . . . Only by

33

considering the phenomena can we gain any insight into the nature of
the concept of a number. (p.129)

The 'phenomena' to which Husserl here refers, and to which his
descriptive psychology restricts itself, are the immanent contents of so-
called 'outer' perception, along with the reflective awareness which we
have in inner perception of our own mental acts. And the greater part of
the *Philosophy of Arithmetic* is explicitly devoted to a genetic investigation into the phenomenal origins of the concept of *number*.

At the beginning of this section I quoted Husserl's allusion to certain
difficulties with, and peculiarities in, the psychological constitution of the
concepts which form the basis of arithmetical knowledge. Not
surprisingly, these difficulties and peculiarities alike stem from the apparent elusiveness of any adequate intuitive foundation for those concepts.
If concepts originate via abstraction, then what precisely are the intuitions
from which we abstract the concept *number*? In the most straightforward
cases we presumably abstract a simple concept from a number of intuitions of items which then become the concept's instances. So we abstract
the concept *redness*, for example, by ignoring the differences between,
and by concentrating on what is common to, a number of individual,
concrete colour sensations. But if the instances of the concept *number* are
the specific numbers 2, 3, 4 etc., then either abstraction does not in this
case proceed from an intuition of a concept's instances, or we urgently
need an account of what an intuitive, sensory presentation of an individual number is supposed to consist in.[9] And we can say in advance that,
even if it should turn out to be possible to provide an acceptable doctrine
concerning intuitive presentations of the numbers 2, 3, 4 and the like, it
looks extremely unlikely that any such account will be available for large
numbers. What concrete intuition could we possibly have of a number
like 12^6, say, or of a transfinite cardinal?

Husserl proceeds to untangle these issues as follows: He distinguishes
between, on the one hand, those (small) numbers the concepts of which
are abstracted from direct concrete intuitions of their instances, and on
the other hand, those (larger) numbers of which there is simply no
authentic (*eigentlich*) intuitive awareness, and of which we can therefore
have at best an indirect, merely symbolic presentation. We can, he
maintains, have authentic intuitive presentations of no numbers greater
than about 12; beyond this point our grasp can only be inauthentic,
indirect, and symbolic (pp.192, 222). The text of the *Philosophy of
Arithmetic* is accordingly divided into two roughly equal parts; the first is
entitled 'Authentic Concepts of Multiplicity, Unity, and Number'; the
second is called 'Symbolic Concepts of Number and the Logical Origins
of Cardinal Arithmetic'. To summarize: an authentic concept is one
which, if simple, has been directly abstracted from concrete intuitions of

items which thus become its instances, or which, if complex, contains only authentic concepts as its simple parts.

What, then, are the concrete bases from which we abstract the authentic concepts of particular (small) numbers? Husserl's answer is indirect, and it is not in fact until Chapter IV that he finally formulates an 'analysis of the concept of number according to its origin and content' – the first three chapters are concerned, rather, with the origin and content of the concept of a multiplicity (*eine Vielheit*).[10] This oblique approach is motivated by two considerations: in the first place the concept of a multiplicity is related in interesting and illuminating ways to the concepts of specific numbers; and secondly, the intuitive basis of the concept of a multiplicity is far more easily identified than those of the number concepts:

> There is no doubt about the concrete phenomena which comprise the basis for the abstraction of [the concept] in question. They are aggregates (*Inbegriffe*), multiplicities of determinate objects. And what is meant by the expression ['aggregate'], everybody knows. (p.15)

The concepts of multiplicity and number are related, for example, in that whenever a multiplicity of things is given it is appropriate to ask 'How many things?' – a question which will be answered by the provision of a particular cardinal number: 'Wherever one can talk of a specific number one can also talk of a multiplicity, and *vice versa*' (p.14). The reason, Husserl suggests, is that the concept of a particular number is related to the concept of a multiplicity as a determinate concept is related to an indeterminate one, where *both are concepts of the same sort of thing*. Indeed, the colloquial expression in English for 'a multiplicity' just is 'a number', as when one says, e.g., 'I am presently feeling a number of emotions', or 'I can hear a number of sounds.' Now while talk about a sensory or intuitive awareness of *a number, simpliciter*, looks unappetizing, it is certainly possible, indeed it is perfectly normal to talk of a perception or sensory awareness of *a number of things*: as in the above examples, one can properly claim direct awareness of multiplicities both in inner and in outer perception.

In short, then, Husserl's overall programme is determined by his belief that an account of the conceptual complexity and the intuitive basis of the concept *multiplicity* (or indefinite number) can be formulated relatively unproblematically, and, moreover, that this account can subsequently be made to yield, with minimal modification, an account of the determinate number concepts. This entire programme has, however, to be implemented twice: once for the 'authentic' concepts of number (Part I), and then again for the 'inauthentic' or symbolic concepts of number (Part II).

The intuitions to which our numerical concepts are finally to be traced back are, according to Husserl, intuitions whose contents are determinate *aggregates* of things. Indeed, because a given, determinate numerical concept is abstracted from concrete phenomena in more or less the standard way,[11] numbers turn out on Husserl's analysis to be *properties of aggregates*. An ascription of number ('There are five windows on the ground floor') is an assertion about a particular aggregate of things (p.166); and a statement of arithmetic ('5+5=10') is a general assertion about the formal properties of aggregates of certain kinds (p.182).

So much for our preliminary overview of the Husserlian programme in the *Philosophy of Arithmetic*. Two tasks now face us. The first is to examine more closely the general philosophical – and especially the epistemological – foundations on which this programme rests. And here we especially need an account of exactly what Husserl meant by such crucial terms of art as 'intuition', 'concept', 'abstraction', 'moment', 'aggregate', 'authentic', 'symbolic', and the like. This is no easy matter, however, as the text is neither explicit about, nor consistent in its use of these notions. The second task involves identifying and evaluating the aggregative theory of number which Husserl erects on those foundations.

Powers of the mind

The following picture of what it is to be a sentient, rational being emerges from, and is, I believe, presupposed by the doctrines explicitly defended in the *Philosophy of Arithmetic*.[12]

Intuitions

The human mind is in one respect passive, in that it has the capability of simply receiving or registering certain items. The items in question, in so far as the mind is genuinely passive and plays no role whatsoever in constituting or modifying them, are exclusively contents of intuitions which belong to outer sense, i.e., Brentanian 'physical phenomena'. Strictly speaking, an intuition is an act or state of consciousness which necessarily, therefore, possesses an in-existent, immanent content or object. The major distinguishing feature of intuitions, which separates them from other forms of presentation such as concepts, is that their content or object is directly or immediately present to consciousness – present, Husserl likes to say, 'in person'. And he takes this to imply two things: first, that the content of an intuition is present as it really is, that for such contents there is no distinction between appearance and reality; and second, that the contents of intuitions are, so to speak, inert. Considered in their own right, that is, such contents are functionless and perform no work: it makes no sense to ask what the content of an intuition as such means, represents, signifies, or refers to.

In other respects, however, the mind is active – albeit to a rather limited extent. Indeed, there are just three primitive forms of mental activity to which Husserl appeals in the *Philosophy of Arithmetic*. They are:

(i)   ignoring, disregarding, or neglecting parts or aspects of a given complex whole
(ii) noticing, concentrating on, or attending to parts or aspects of a given complex whole
(iii) combining, unifying, or amalgamating parts or aspects of given complex wholes.

Outer sense presents us with intuitions that are complex. Now suppose that I am immediately and directly aware in visual intuition of two coloured circular areas, one red, the other yellow. By an act of will (the nature of which Husserl does not further specify) I can bring myself to ignore or neglect one of the coloured circles so that it is no longer an object of my attention; and conversely, I can focus my concentration on the other circle (the yellow one, let's say) to the exclusion of all else. That I *can* focus my attention on one isolated element of my original intuition, that that element *can* in and of itself comprise the sole content of a subsequent intuition – this provides us with the beginnings of an account of whole-part relations as they apply to and, more importantly, as they originate in, purely sensory phenomena. (Cf. *LU* III, §§2–4/pp.437–42; *LU* VI, §52/p.800; and *Ideas* §92/p.268.) And in this matter Husserl's debt to Carl Stumpf, under whose auspices much of the research for the *Philosophy of Arithmetic* had been conducted, was immense. According to Stumpf, complex presentations will possess '*independent* contents' if 'the elements of the complex presentation are, by virtue of their nature, capable also of being separately presented'.[13] A complex intuition may, in other words, have a content that is an aggregative whole, in that its component parts may themselves be capable, in isolation, of comprising the sole content of an intuition. Although my initial visual presentation was in fact of two adjacent coloured circles, I *could* have had an intuition of the yellow circle by itself – and this possibility is revealed, phenomenologically, by the possibility of my concentrating my attention on that circle, to the exclusion of all the other elements in my original intuition.

Attention can, however, be focused on contents of a quite different sort. Suppose, for instance, that I am concentrating on the yellow circle, and that I successfully ignore its shape, its location in my visual field, and so on, and that I attend only to its colour. Now the particular phenomenal colour of which I am directly aware does not seem to be an aggregative whole; for it possesses no proper parts which could themselves be intuitively presented in isolation. The phenomenal colour is not, however, for that reason simple: I can concentrate on its hue, for example, or on its intensity, or its saturation. But none of these is something which could possibly by itself comprise the content of an intuition. Certainly I can *notice* the intensity of the colour, concentrate my attention on it, perhaps even observe it changing – but not in isolation from, say, its hue. Stumpf writes of a similar case:

> From this it follows that both are in their nature inseparable, and that in some sense they together comprise a total content of which each is merely a partial-content. . . . [But these partial-contents] cannot be independent contents, for their nature forbids them to have isolated and mutually independent existence in a presentation.[14]

So the ability to neglect or ignore certain elements presented in intuition, and correlatively to focus attention on others, yields an intuitive awareness of items belonging to two radically different sorts: on the one hand there are *independent* contents, capable of being presented by themselves; and on the other hand there are essentially *partial* contents (*Teilinhalte*) which are dependent (*unselbständig, abhängig*), in that their existence as phenomena is necessarily bound up with the existence of some other phenomenon. Husserl calls such dependent phenomena 'moments' (*Momente*).

So far, then, on the basis only of mental activities (i) and (ii), and without leaving the sphere of mere intuitions, we have in outline an account of three distinct categories of content. There can be intuitive awareness of 'things' (*Dinge, Einzeldinge*), of aggregates of things (*Inbegriffe, Menge, Sammlungen*, etc.), and of so-called 'moments'. As with Brentano, a 'thing' is any phenomenal entity which is a strong whole: there is, Husserl says,

> a particular sense in which we speak of the *unity* of a thing. What we mean by this is that the attributes which there are in the concept of a thing are not put together like the elements of a mere aggregate, but rather that they constitute a whole whose parts are substantively combined together (which mutually permeate one another). (p.159, cf. pp.131, 195)

An aggregate, on the other hand, is a weak whole whose proper parts are themselves things. Aggregative contents can be either given (as when I simultaneously intuit a red and a yellow circle), or made (as when, by engaging in mental activity (iii), I create for myself a complex image of, say, the colours in the spectrum). The third category, that of moments, contains no wholes of any kind. Incapable of self-subsistence, moments are ineluctably *partial* phenomena.

Finally, under the present heading, we need to ask exactly what Husserl meant by a 'concrete' intuition – and we need, moreover, to take certain precautions against a number of possible misunderstandings of this notion. Because descriptive psychology is restricted to a study of phenomena – either mental acts or their immanent contents – 'concrete' entities cannot be identified with material, physical objects, or indeed with any other denizens of the external world.[15] Furthermore, Husserl's distinction between *concreta* and *abstracta* is not at all the common distinction between, respectively, those entities which can be perceived or intuited (perhaps because they possess causal properties), and those which cannot (perhaps because they are causally inert): Husserl is quite clear that abstract entities can be directly intuited (cf. pp.119, 194 etc.). And again, Husserl's distinction between abstract and concrete phenomena is independent of his distinction between inner and outer sense: despite the strong temptation to think that a concrete intuition must be an intuition of a 'physical phenomenon', Husserl straightforwardly allows there to be concrete intuitions of mental acts and states (cf. pp.16, 69, 80 etc.). And, finally, a concrete intuition is not necessarily an intuition of a 'thing' (in Husserl's unusual sense of the term).

So what, in general, *is* a concrete phenomenon? And what, more specifically, are the concrete intuitions in which all conceptual activity – indeed our entire conscious life – has its foundation and origin? The distinction is defined mereologically: a concrete phenomenon is anything which, *qua* phenomenon, can comprise either a strong or a weak whole; and an abstract phenomenon is any mental or physical phenomenon which cannot. An abstract phenomenon, that is, is one which is intrinsically and inescapably partial, which can only be presented as a dependent part or aspect of some more encompassing whole. So something is to count as a concrete intuition if it is a mental act or state whose content is (a) directly and immediately presented, and (b) either a thing or an aggregate of things. In which case there can, for example, be a concrete intuition of a sound, or of a collection of sounds, of a judgement, an emotion, or an act of imagination, or of an aggregate made up of such mental acts and contents; but there can only be an abstract intuition of such '*abstrakte Momente*' as (via outer sense) the hue of a colour, the timbre of a note, the redness of a phenomenal surface, or (via inner sense) of the intensity of an emotion, the assertoric force of a judgement, or the unity of a complex mental act.

In short, then, Husserl's basic thought seems to have been this: an intuition is to be classified as concrete if it possesses a content of a certain sort. Contents, in turn, are classified ultimately by appeal to their actual or possible origins: some contents are such that they could have originated in an isolated intuitive whole, whereas other contents could only have originated *in abstraction from* some ineliminable, encompassing intuition on which they are dependent. Intuitive contents which necessarily originate via abstraction are called abstract; all others are concrete. And abstraction is just the combination of processes (i) and (ii), the neglecting of certain items given in consciousness, and the concentration of attention on others (cf. p.79). 'To "abstract" from something merely means to pay no special attention to it' (*HSW* p.116).

Concepts

Later in life, Husserl wrote of the *Philosophy of Arithmetic*:

> How immature, how naive, how almost childish this work seems to me; and not without reason did its publication trouble my conscience. . . . [For] I was a mere beginner, without proper knowledge of philosophical problems, and with insufficiently trained philosophical skills.[16]

Now these inadequacies are nowhere more manifest than in Husserl's treatment of concepts, their content, their nature, and their origin. On these matters the text of the *Philosophy of Arithmetic* remains profoundly obscure, and it is quite clear that in 1891 Husserl had hardly even begun to develop a coherent account of human conceptual abilities. It was, above all others, to precisely this task, however, that he devoted the greater part of his subsequent intellectual life. Such crucial Husserlian doctrines and procedures as those concerning the eidetic reduction, the intuition of essences, the phenomenological reduction, intentionality, noematic sense, horizons, fulfillment, and much else besides, are in large part responses to, or modifications of the naive and inchoate theory of concepts adumbrated in the *Philosophy of Arithmetic*. And through such subsequent works as 'Psychological Studies of Elementary Logic', *Logical Investigations, Ideas, Formal and Transcendental Logic, Cartesian Meditations*, and *Experience and Judgement* we can trace in Husserl's thought a continuous process of development whose motivation and starting point were the perceived inadequacies of his earlier treatment of problems concerning, amongst other things, the generality, the content, the significance, the acquisition, the expressibility, and the structure of concepts.

In the *Philosophy of Arithmetic* Husserl distinguishes between two different kinds of concept. He calls them 'abstract' and 'general' concepts – and as the latter are the least problematic of the two, we can begin with them.

A general concept is a species of presentation, and as such, therefore, consists of a mental act or state which possesses an immanent, intentionally in-existent content. To avoid confusion I shall refer to the mental act or state as a *conceiving* (or an act of conception), and to its immediate, immanent content as a *concept*. One crucial characteristic possessed by the content of a conceiving – and one which distinguishes such an act from an intuition – is that the content itself has a content. An intuition is necessarily an intuition *of* something (its content); and an act of conception is necessarily *of* something (its content, i.e. a concept); but while the content of an intuition is inert, in that it has in turn no content of its own, a conceiving has a content which, far from being inert, plays a complex representational role: concepts themselves are necessarily concepts *of* something or other.

Now we have here, I believe, an explanation of the confused contrast which Husserl attempts to draw between the 'direct' or 'immediate' relation of an intuitive presentation to its content, as opposed to the 'indirect' or 'mediate' relation in which a concept stands to *its* content. The confusion is caused by the fact that the word 'content' is here being abused: as applied to intuitions it expresses the old Brentanian notion of an immanent, in-existent, intentional object of an act; but as applied to concepts it expresses a new and as yet uninvestigated notion – something akin to meaning, sense, or significance. It is important to get clear about this confusion, for out of it was to emerge one of Husserl's greatest philosophical contributions, his non-Brentanian doctrine of intentionality. The situation is this: for the author of the *Philosophy of Arithmetic*, the relation in which an intuition stands to its content (a thing, say, or a moment) is the same as the relation in which an act of conceiving stands to a concept: both are instances of straightforward intentional containment. But the relation between a concept and that which it is a concept of is clearly not a relation of a whole to one of its parts – though Husserl remained at this time entirely unclear as to just what this relation might be. The notion of intentionality which he inherited from Brentano is, because of its exclusive concern with immanent in-existence, simply incapable of providing the basis of an account of how one thing can represent *another*, of how 'a presentation can have an intention which *reaches out beyond* the immanent content of the act' (*HSW* p.131, my italics). But even though Husserl had no model in terms of which to analyse and explain how concepts work, how one thing can mean another, he had nevertheless begun to see that the notion of an immanent content was inadequate to the task; and in his confused distinction between the 'direct' presence of intuitive contents and the 'mediate' presence of conceptual contents there is a tension that was subsequently to be resolved, more coherently, into the contrast between the *real content* and the *intentional object* of an act, and, later still, into that between *noeses* and *noemata*.

Intuitions are distinguished from general concepts in two ways: not only in terms of the (confused) distinction between direct and mediated presentations, but also in terms of the contrast between *particular* and *universal* presentations. A general concept is the content of a presentation capable in principle (i.e. irrespective of the number of instances that it contingently happens to possess) of applying to more than one thing (p.342). And this capacity, according to Husserl, results directly from the nature of the abstractive process by which such concepts are created.

As we have already seen, in one of its forms abstraction is a process which, when applied to concrete intuitions yields an intuitive awareness of abstract moments. Now it is important to note that a moment is a particular, *singular* item of sensory awareness. Let us suppose, to return to the earlier example, that by ignoring the size, shape, and location of a yellow patch in my visual field, I successfully concentrate my visual attention on its colour. Unfortunately the expression 'its colour' is ambiguous – and in the present context perniciously so. It can (and indeed would normally) be taken to mean a property or attribute which a number of different items might each possess; but on the other hand it might mean an unshareable attribute whose identity conditions make ineliminable appeal to the identity of the particular item which has it. Wittgenstein brings out this distinction clearly:

> We use the phrase 'two books have the same colour', but we could perfectly well say: 'They can't have the *same* colour, because, after all, this book has its own colour, and the other book has its own colour too.' This would be stating a grammatical rule – a rule, incidentally, not in accordance with ordinary usage. . . . (Here it will be useful if you consider the different criteria for what we call 'the identity of these things').[17]

According to Husserl an abstract moment is a part – albeit an inseparable part, incapable of independent existence – discernible within some given phenomenal whole. And as a part it is by its very nature specific to that whole: it is a particular item, not a shareable feature. But now let us further suppose that in my visual field there are in fact two similarly coloured patches. Without invoking any powers of the mind other than those already introduced, that is, by appealing only to my ability to (i) ignore or disregard parts or aspects of a given whole, and (ii) concentrate or focus on parts or aspects of a given whole, I can now abstract from the particularity of the two numerically distinct moments of yellowness. Ignoring all aspects in which they differ, I can concentrate on their similarities; indeed I can straightforwardly *see* the similarity between the yellowness of the one patch and the yellowness of the other.[18]

As yet we have not left the realm of intuitions, that is, of specific, particular sensory items; for even the similarity between the two abstract moments of colour is itself merely a particular abstract moment of the complex content of my visual perception as a whole. At this point, however, the transition to *general* presentations can be made: my awareness of the similarity of the two colour moments is an awareness of of an equivalence relation, and this relation can be transformed into an identity, holding between the corresponding abstract concepts.[19] Frege's *Foundations of Arithmetic* is the *locus classicus* of this account of abstraction. Frege writes:

> The judgement 'line *a* is parallel to line *b*', or, using symbols,
> $$a \mathbin{/\mkern-5mu/} b,$$
> can be taken as an identity. If we do this, we obtain the concept of a direction, and say:
>   the direction of line *a* = the direction of line *b*.
> Thus we replace the symbol // by the more generic symbol =, through removing what is specific in the content of the former and dividing it between *a* and *b*. We carve up the content in a way different from the original way, and this yields us a new concept . . . . The concept of a direction is only discovered at all as a result of a process of intellectual activity which takes its start from the intuition.[20]

In the case of the example we have been using, if I call one of the yellow patches '*a*' and the other one '*b*', then it is impossible for the yellow colour-moment of *a* to be numerically identical with that of *b* (unless, of course, contrary to hypothesis, *a* and *b* are themselves identical). The two colour-moments can, however, be similar; and their similarity can, moreover, be perceived. The abstract concept of a quite determinate shade of yellow is abstracted from this intuitive similarity by transforming it into an identity, i.e. in the move from

(1) *a*'s yellow colour-moment is similar to *b*'s,

to

(2) *a*'s yellowness = *b*'s yellowness.

Although the two sentences have the same truth-conditions, they can be used to express different mental acts: (1) would function appropriately as an expression of my purely intuitive awareness of a specific relation holding between particular items, while (2) might express my conceptual grasp of a relation that holds between general concepts.

This whole business is bedevilled by the fact that such expressions as '*a*'s colour', '*a*'s yellowness', 'the yellow colour of *a*' and the like are ambiguous, depending on whether we take the mention of *a* to be ineliminable. If such expressions are construed as referring to an attribute which *a*, and only *a*, can possess, then the attribute is an individual moment. But if we take them to refer to an attribute which, although in fact possessed by *a*, can nevertheless be identified independently of any appeal to *a* (e.g. as '*b*'s yellow colour', or even less specifically, as, say, 'chrome yellow'), and which therefore can have instances other than *a*, then the attribute is an abstract concept.[21]

The genealogy of concepts, as we have it so far, is this. All experience begins with concrete intuitions. By selectively disregarding certain parts of the content of a concrete intuition we can come to have a direct sensory awareness of an abstract moment, which is a particular, individual part or aspect of the original concrete whole, but one that is incapable in isolation of comprising the entire content of an intuition. We might call this *intuitive abstraction*. A second process of abstraction, call it *conceptual abstraction*, is then applied to a number of abstract moments: the process consists in abstracting from (i.e. ignoring) the identity of the particular items which incorporate the moments in question. This yields a presentation that is, like a moment, attributive, but which, unlike a moment, is shareable – in that nothing in its content restricts it to the possession of one and only one bearer. The immediate result of conceptual abstraction Husserl calls an abstract concept; and the final stage in the genealogy of concepts is the introduction of so-called 'general concepts'.

The distinction between abstract and general concepts, presupposed but nowhere explained in the *Philosophy of Arithmetic*, amounts, I think, to this. In conceptual abstraction one's attention is selectively focused on the content of a presentation, on an abstract moment of some given whole presented in inner or in outer sense. One then ignores certain aspects of this moment and others similar to it, and as a result one achieves an awareness of a new mental content, *viz*: an abstract concept. Now, at least in the first instance, this concept is itself simply an object of contemplation; *it* comprises the in-existent content of a mental act. But concepts are by no means merely items upon which we can focus our attention – indeed, in the normal course of events it is only rarely that we indulge in such reflective concentration on abstract concepts. To put it crudely, the concept 'chrome yellow', say, is for most people rarely if ever something they think *about*; more usually they think *through* it, of things in so far as they are, or are not, that shade of yellow. Just as one can either look at a telescope, treating it as a visual object, or look through it at other things, treating it as a visual aid, so one can either (metaphorically speaking) look at a concept, treating it as an object of thought, or look through it to the objects to which it applies (its *Begriffsgegenstände*), thus treating it as a medium rather than as an object of thought. A more familiar analogy might make this clearer. We distinguish between the mention and the use of a linguistic expression: on the one hand I can refer to, or mention, the linguistic expression 'the capital of England', and on the other hand I can use that expression to refer to a certain city. It would appear (e.g. pp.19, 137, 195, 340) that for Husserl an abstract concept is one which is, so to speak, mentally mentioned, in that it itself is the direct object of an act of presentation. A general concept, on the other hand, is an abstract concept *used* to refer to its instances (see pp. 136–9, 180 etc.). If these two analogies are to the

44

point, then Husserl's way of distinguishing abstract from general concepts in the *Philosophy of Arithmetic* would seem to correspond closely to the traditional distinction between, respectively, concepts interpreted in intension, and concepts interpreted in extension.[22] In the last analysis, however, the text is insufficiently explicit, and the matter remains indeterminate.

If the foregoing account is right, then in diagrammatic form Husserl's earliest account of presentations, their different types, the relations between them, and their origins, can be summarized as follows:

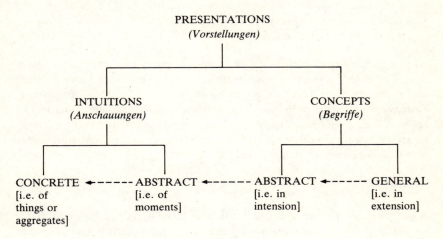

Fig. 1

Here the dotted arrows represent the direction of dependence or 'foundation' – read backwards they represent the direction of the abstractive process.

Now if this reading is accepted, it appears that two of the doctrines heralded in the *Logical Investigations* as radical new discoveries are in fact already present – though only in a tacit and inchoate form – in the *Philosophy of Arithmetic*. One such doctrine concerns the need for a sharp distinction between two different processes of abstraction, the one yielding an intuitive awareness of abstract moments, the other yielding a grasp of general concepts:

> The theory of abstraction since Locke has confused the problem of abstraction in the sense of *the emphatic attention to 'abstract contents'*, with the problem of abstraction in the sense of *the formation of concepts* . . . . [The latter process yields] abstract presentations whose intention is directed to the species, and not to any dependent or abstract content. If such an intention is intuitively fulfilled, then it will rest on a foundation of concrete intuitions which have, so to speak,

45

accentuated partial-contents [i.e. moments]; but the intended species is distinct from these partial-contents themselves. (*LU* II, §40/p.426; cf. *PdA* pp. 78, 138, 194, etc.)

The second doctrine concerns the possibility of 'categorial intuition', the direct awareness of a 'universal object', or 'species'. In the *Logical Investigations* Husserl writes:

> In an act of abstraction . . . the universal *itself is given to us*; we do not think of it merely in significative fashion as when we merely understand general names, but we apprehend it, *behold* it. Talk of an *intuition*, and more precisely of a *perception of the universal* is in this case, therefore, well justified. (*LU* VI, §52/p.800)

Although both the later theory of categorial intuition, and the still later theory of eidetic reduction and the intuition of essences are more detailed and more sophisticated than anything to be found in the *Philosophy of Arithmetic*, it is nevertheless the case that both have their roots in the account which that work suggests of our awareness of abstract concepts, an account according to which we can indeed have 'an authentic presentation of a determinate species' (p.194).

Authentic presentations of number

A recursive definition typically consists of three parts: the first comprises an explicit list of (one or more) elements that together make up the definitional *base*; the second introduces a *rule* or procedure which, when applied to the elements in the base, can be used either as a means of generating new elements, or as a means of testing whether something not already present in the base is to be counted as a new element. And the third part contains a *closure* specification, limiting admissible elements to those that are either already in the base or are generable from them. We can, for example, give a recursive definition of the concept *bishop*.[23] The first clause of the definition specifies that certain individuals (the Apostles) were bishops. The second clause then introduces a procedure (apostolic succession, via the laying on of hands) by which, on the basis of those mentioned in the first clause, new bishops can subsequently be generated – and new bishops on the basis of them, and so on indefinitely. The definition looks like this:

(a) Andrew, Bartholomew, James, John (etc.) are bishops.
(b) If *x* is a bishop, then so too is an immediate apostolic successor of *x*.
(c) Nothing is a bishop, unless in virtue of clauses (a) and (b) above.

The rule implicit in the procedure of generation can be used to test whether or not some arbitrary person is in fact a bishop: *x* is a bishop if and only if *x* is related, ultimately, to one of the Apostles via an unbroken chain of apostolic successors.

A particularly elegant example of a recursive definition is that of the concept *natural number*. Today this would typically be expressed as follows:

(a') Zero is a natural number.
(b') If *x* is a natural number, so too is the successor of *x*.
(c') Nothing is a natural number, unless in virtue of clauses (a') and (b') above.

Here we can use (b') to test whether or not some arbitrary object *x* is a natural number: *x* is a natural number if and only if *x* is related to zero via an unbroken chain of numerical successors. So, for instance, we can establish that 3 is a natural number because it is the successor of 2, which is a natural number because it is the successor of 1, which in turn is a natural number because it is the successor of 0, whose status as a natural number is simply given, by clause (a').

Husserl was ignorant of the formal properties of recursive definitions and, anyway, would have rejected the specific terms in which the foregoing is couched.[24] Nevertheless, the distinction between numbers which are *given*, as such, and those which are then recursively *generated* on the basis of them lies at the very heart of his empiricist philosophy of arithmetic. And it is this distinction which, perhaps more than any other, entitles his philosophy of arithmetic to claim a significant advance on that of his great empiricist predecessor John Stuart Mill.

According to Mill the axioms and definitions of arithmetic are alike 'inductive truths . . . known to us by early and constant experience'. The definitions of arithmetic are, in other words, real propositions, known *a posteriori* on the basis, ultimately, of enumerative induction.[25] And it is of course for just this doctrine and its consequences that Frege in *The Foundations of Arithmetic* reserves his most withering polemic and his most devastating objections. One of Frege's strongest points against such Millian empiricism in the foundations of arithmetic is the utter implausibility of the account which it offers of large numbers. As Frege observes; 'Mill seems to hold that we ought not to form the definitions $2 = 1 + 1$, $3 = 2 + 1$ . . . and so on, unless and until the facts he refers to have been observed'. But, he then asks incredulously, 'who is actually prepared to assert that the fact which, according to Mill, is contained in the definition of an eighteen-figure number has ever been *observed*?'[26] The claim that, if it is to have an intelligible content, a statement like '$3494872197 = 3494872196 + 1$' must be an expression of the result of enumerative induction on directly observed matters of fact can, surely, be dismissed out of hand.

Husserl, who was thoroughly familiar with Frege's objections to

Millian empiricism, avoids this unacceptable consequence by adopting something at least analogous to a recursive procedure: he distinguishes, that is, between those numbers which are given as such (those of which, he says, we possesss an *authentic* concept), and those that are not genuinely given at all, but which are somehow ('symbolically') generated on the basis of those that are. Of course, if Husserl's theory as a whole is to remain, as he intended it should, a form of empiricism, then both parts of his theory must conform to the appropriate empiricist constraints: not only must our epistemic access to the 'base' numbers be accounted for in purely empirical terms, but the mode of symbolical generation of the other numbers must, in turn, involve nothing unacceptable to an empiricist. In the remainder of the present section I shall examine the account he provides of the genuine concepts of numbers; and in the following section I shall turn to the symbolic presentations of number which, he claims, can be generated on that base.

The concrete intuitions which form the foundation of our numerical concepts are intuitions of aggregates – or, to speak more precisely, they are intuitions whose contents are aggregates *as such*. And according to Husserl there are four stages on the road that leads from concrete intuitions to an abstract, authentic concept of a determinate number.

Step 1. I have an intuition, in inner or outer sense, of a determinate aggregate.
The aggregate must be determinate in two senses: first, it must contain only members that can be individuated unequivocally. I might, for example, have an intuition whose content was (as if of) a bank of clouds; but because it is quite unclear where one component cloud in the formation ends, and where another begins, my intuition, although complex, would fail to qualify as an aggregate in Husserl's semi-technical sense of the term. Aggregates must be determinate, second, in that they must possess sharp boundaries: for any aggregate A, and any thing x, it must be determined whether x is a member of A or not. If either of these conditions were to fail, then of course no determinate number would be assignable to an aggregate.

At this point we need to ask: What exactly is involved in my having 'a concrete intuition of an aggregate as such'? We already know that an aggregate is a weak whole, that is, a complex entity whose proper parts are themselves strong wholes or 'things'. Aggregates, in other words, have two general characteristics: as weak wholes they are, precisely, *wholes* – and as such possess a unity or integrity of some sort. On the other hand, however, they are merely *weak* wholes, and so are composed of a multiplicity of distinct, independent component 'elements. Now according to Husserl, if the phenomenal content of my intuition is to be accurately described as an aggregate, then both the unity and the diversity must be phenomenally present: I must be aware of each of the elements individually, and yet aware at the same time of their making one aggregative whole. Only if both conditions are met can we talk of intuiting an aggregate *as such*. In terms reminiscent of Russell, we might say that awareness of an aggregate as such necessarily involves awareness of the aggregate as many, and also of the aggregate as one.[27] But now we seem to be faced with the following difficulty:

> It is evident that comparison of the individual contents that we discover in a given aggregate will not by itself result in the concept of a . . . determinate number . . . . Indeed, it is not these individual contents themselves that are the basis for abstraction, but rather the concrete aggregates as *wholes*, into which they are united. And yet even comparison of such aggregates as wholes does not seem to yield the desired result. But if aggregates consist *merely* of individual contents, and if these constitutive parts may be entirely heterogeneous, then how can aggregative wholes ever manifest a common characteristic? (p.18)

The difficulty, in other words, is this: an aggregate is made up of its individual component elements, so in a sense there is nothing more to an aggregate (a, b, c), say, than a, b, and c themselves. Aggregates are, moreover, arbitrary, in that there is no requirement of homogeneity on their members: *any* two phenomena can be members of one and the same aggregate. But in that case, what account can we possibly provide of our intuitive awareness of an aggregative whole – that is, over and above the account which we give of our intuitive awareness of its individual elements? Husserl writes:

> This difficulty is, however, only apparent. It is in fact wrong to say that aggregates consist merely of individual contents. Although one can easily overlook the fact, there is nevertheless something there, over and above the individual contents; it can be noticed; and it is necessarily present whenever we speak of an aggregate or a multiplicity. It is the *combination (Verbindung)* of the individual elements into a whole. (p.18)

Clearly Husserl does not mean to imply the incoherent thesis that an arbitrary aggregate containing n things will always in fact contain $n + 1$ things; for the additional 'something' he claims to discover here is not a thing but, rather, a *moment*.[28] It is in fact a moment of unity which attaches to the elements, not individually but, so to speak, *en masse*:

> The presentation of an aggregate of given objects is a unity in which the presentations of individual objects are contained as component presentations. Of course this combination of parts, as present in any arbitrary aggregate, is merely loose and external in comparison with

other kinds of combination – to such an extent, indeed, that in this case one might doubt the wisdom of talking about 'combination' at all. Be that as it may, there *is* however a particular unity there, and the unity must, moreover, be noticed as such; for otherwise the concept of an aggregate . . . could never arise . . . . From now on I shall use the term 'collective combination' (*kollektive Verbindung*) to signify the kind of unity which characterizes an aggregate. (p.20)

Step 2.   I concentrate my attention on this peculiar collective combination. On the basis of such an awareness is built one's grasp of the concept *aggregate*, and this in turn provides the basis for one's grasp of the authentic concepts of number. But what are we to make of 'collective combination'? The following requirements set out, I believe, the major constraints within which a Husserlian answer to this question must be formulated:

(i)   Appeal may only be made to phenomena, that is, to mental acts and their contents in so far as we are conscious of them.
(ii)   All concepts must ultimately be abstracted from concrete intuitions.
(iii)   Aggregates are arbitrary wholes: any two things can participate in one and the same aggregate.
(iv)   Aggregates are complex wholes: an aggregate must have at least two things as its proper parts.
(v)   Aggregates are, nevertheless, unary: an aggregate is a whole and as such possesses a principle of unity or combination.
(vi)   That in virtue of which a number of different things are united cannot itself be just another thing. Unity is, rather, a *relational* phenomenon.

Now our goal is to shed light on (v); but requirements (ii), (iii), and (iv) seem to present considerable obstacles in the way of achieving this. Requirement (ii) is problematic because a concrete intuition is one whose content is either a thing or an aggregate. But as the phenomenon under investigation is, precisely, the nature of our awareness of aggregates, clearly no appeal to the latter can be made here, without immediately begging the very question at issue. So, according to requirement (ii) our account may ultimately appeal only to our intuitive awareness of *things*. Yet an aggregate is not a thing; its unity is not reducible to, or explainable in terms of, the unity of a thing; and, moreover, by (iii), its unity is not to be explained by appeal to the nature of the things that are its elements or members. Because an aggregate may be an arbitrary whole, 'it would be obviously futile to look for a relation or combination amongst the presented contents which it encompasses' (p.69). In trying to account for the unity of an aggregative whole,

since we know that the most heterogeneous contents can be united in an aggregative manner, all relations whose range of application is restricted by the nature of the particular contents can be discarded without further ado. (p.65)

But if not to the things which form aggregates, and if not to any of the relations which hold between those things in virtue of their various properties and attributes, then where are we to look for the concrete intuitions which underlie our concept of an aggregate? Taking his lead from Kant,[29] Husserl's answer is that aggregative wholes are not in the last analysis given or discovered; they are created. Although the individual elements may be given in passive intuition, 'they are united only by an act; and so their union can only be noticed by means of a special reflection on that act' (p.69).

> An aggregate is produced when an undivided interest, containing within it also a unitary act of noticing, brings into relief and grasps various different contents. The collective combination can thus only be grasped through reflection on the mental act by which the aggregate comes into being. (p.74)

In short, then, our concept of an aggregative whole originates, as we would expect, via abstraction from concrete intuitions. But the concreta in question are not – and indeed on pain of vicious circularity, cannot be – aggregates. Rather, they are mental acts of a quite specific sort, namely acts of aggregation or, as Husserl calls them, acts of 'collective combination': 'By reflecting on the mental act that produces a unity out of the contents . . . in an aggregate, we acquire the abstract presentation of collective combination' (p.77). Husserl then immediately adds that 'by means of this, we form the concept of a multiplicity, as that of a whole whose parts are united solely by collective combination'. This is in fact the next, and crucially important step.

Step 3. *I abstract the concept of multiplicity (or indeterminate number) from concrete intuitions of acts of collective combination.*
To see how this occurs, we need to take a still closer look at acts of collective combination themselves. Suppose, for example, that I am intuitively presented with three arbitrary and unrelated things, *a*, *b*, and *c*. Now it may well be that I have, initially, an intuition of *a*, another intuition of *b*, and yet another of *c*; in which case my awareness is in no sense aggregative; for here there are three presentations whose contents are singular things, rather than a single presentation whose content is an aggregate of three things. The possibility of a presentation (*P*) of the latter sort requires that presentation is, so to speak, distributive; in other words, that we can in principle move from

(1) $P(a)$ and $P(b)$ and $P(c)$ . . . etc.,

to

(2) $P(a$ and b and c . . . etc.).

Here (2) represents the form of a concrete intuition of an aggregate; the abstract concept of *multiplicity* is gained, according to Husserl, as follows:

> singular contents, each determinate in one way or another, are given in collective combination. We then proceed via abstraction to the general concept by ignoring their particular determinations, and concentrating our attention principally on their collective combination, while they themselves are regarded and considered only as contents in general: each one is regarded simply as a *something or other*, as a mere *single thing*. (p.79)

We might represent this as the move from

(2) $P(a$ and b and c . . . etc.)

to

(3) $P(x$ and y and z . . . etc.)

where the determinate content of the former presentation is transformed into a general content by transforming its constant elements into variables. (3) as a whole represents an act of conceiving a multiplicity; its content (represented by the matter in parentheses) is the concept *multiplicity* itself; and 'the linguistic expression of collective combination is the conjunction "and"' (p.80). In which case,

> multiplicity in general . . . is nothing more than: something and something and something . . . etc.; or one thing and another and another. . . etc.; or one [thing] and one and one . . . and so on. (*ibid*)

Step 4. *I acquire the concept of a determinate number by resolving in a certain way the indeterminacy in the concept of a multiplicity.*
The concept of a multiplicity of things is just the notion of one thing, and another, and another, and so on indefinitely; but the determinate concept of precisely *one thing, and another, and another* (and no more) is the very concept with which we associate the word 'three':

> By suppression of that indeterminacy just noted, there arises out of this general concept [i.e. of multiplicity] the particular multiplicity concepts, or *numbers*. The more general concept of multiplicity encompasses all concepts of the same sort as *one and one, one and one and one* . . . etc. as its particularizations, which are . . . given the names 'two', 'three', 'four', and so on. Every concrete multiplicity falls under one and only one of these concepts. (p.336, cf. *HSW* p.116)

Symbolic presentations of number

In so far as our possession and application of numerical concepts require that we have a distinct but simultaneous presentation of each of the particular elements in an aggregate, the account is clearly incapable of generalization so as to cover all numerical concepts: there is simply a limit to the number of distinct items that one can simultaneously and explicitly notice, or on which one can at one and the same time focus one's attention. Husserl puts the number at about twelve. How then do we acquire numerical concepts of greater cardinality? 'How can we even talk of concepts that we don't authentically possess? And isn't it absurd that arithmetic, the most certain of the sciences, should be founded on such [inauthentic] concepts?' (p.192, cf. p.340).

Husserl's answer is that there is nothing untoward in this situation, because there is nothing illegitimate about so-called 'inauthentic' concepts:

> An inauthentic or *symbolic* presentation is, as the name suggests, a presentation via signs. If a content is not directly given to us, as what it in fact is, but is only given indirectly via signs that uniquely characterize it, then our presentation of that content is not an authentic but, rather, a symbolic one. (p.193)

Or, at least, they are legitimate just as long as they conform to the overall requirements governing the legitimacy of concepts in general, the most important of which is that 'no concept is thinkable which lacks a foundation in concrete intuition.' The problem to which Part II of the *Philosophy of Arithmetic* is addressed is: How *can* inauthentic concepts of number be grounded in concrete intuitions? An inauthentic concept, after all, is precisely one that is not abstracted from concrete intuitions of items which then become its instances. Husserl's solution to this problem has two major components: the first is an account of our intuitive awareness of large aggregates, that is, of aggregates whose members are too numerous to be collectively combined in the way outlined in the last section. This provides us with an epistemological theory concerning our symbolic grasp of inauthentically presented multiplicities or aggregates. The second component is an account of how such numerically indeterminate multiplicities are rendered numerically determinate; for it is in just this process of numerically determining symbolically presented multiplicities that our grasp of large numbers is grounded. And the legitimacy of our concepts of individual numbers greater than, say, twelve, is a consequence of the fact that, in the last analysis, their origin depends only on concrete intuitions – either concrete intuitions of large aggregates, or concrete intuitions of number-words, numerals, and other arithmetical signs.

We know already not only that an aggregate is a unity made up of diverse elements, but also that the most difficult epistemological task is to account for our awareness of this unity; our awareness of the individual elements themselves, we can agree, is relatively straightforward and unproblematic. In the case of small aggregates our grasp of their unity is a function of our awareness of collective combination; but collective combination is precisely what is ruled out when we are presented with more than about a dozen distinct items. So what is the nature of our grasp of a large aggregate as a whole? How can we have an intuitive presentation of a substantial group *as one*?[30]

> Only one answer is possible here: in the intuition of a sensible group
> (*Menge*) there must be *immediately comprehensible signs* in which this
> group character can be recognized . . . The name and concept of a
> group can then be immediately associated with these signs. (p.201)

The signs in question here are variously called 'second-order sensible qualities', 'quasi-qualitative characteristics', 'figural moments', and '*Gestalt* qualities'. They are second-order qualities and relations in the quite literal sense that they are qualities and relations whose terms are themselves qualities and relations. Some concrete examples might help to make clear what Husserl has in mind. We are often presented with large aggregates or groups which have, as such, a distinctive character: we talk for example, of a stand (of trees), a crowd (of people), a swarm (of bees), a medley (of notes), a range (of mountains), a constellation (of stars), or a pattern (of dots).[31] And the differences between the respective collective nouns are, according to Husserl, a linguistic reflection of the phenomenal differences in our experiences of the various kinds of groups. A group or aggregate as a whole, we might say, can possess sensible properties which are not possessed by any of its members. But here is the problem: we cannot at this point simply invoke the notion of a property possessed by 'a group as a whole'; for our aim is precisely to explain how we so much as come to possess this notion in the first place. We require, in other words, an account of intuitions whose contents are *Gestalt* qualities or figural moments, but which does not merely assume either (i) that such contents are presented *as* qualities or moments of an aggregative whole, or (ii) that the qualities or moments are possessed by any of the individual members of the aggregate in question. Moments, it should also be remembered, are contents that result from abstraction, and so themselves require a foundation in concrete intuition.

Husserl meets these various requirements by insisting that figural moments are second-order moments whose bearers are first-order moments whose bearers, in their turn, are things. The concept of a figural moment, in other words, is directly abstracted neither from an aggregate or group as such, nor from the individual things that are the aggregate's

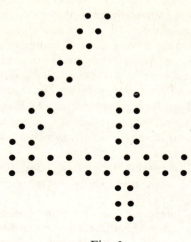

Fig. 2

members. Again, a concrete example may help. The group (Fig. 2) of some fifty dots has, as a whole, a quite particular physiognomy: we see it as the numeral '4'. But some care is needed here in identifying precisely *what* is seen as '4'. It is not the aggregate or collection of dots, for that remains unchanged when the dots are reorientated or rearranged; and it is obviously not the dots themselves, none of which looks in the least like the numeral '4'. It is, rather, according to Husserl, the dots' *relational properties* that possess the quasi-qualitative characteristic in question, that is, which give rise to the particular physiognomy or *Gestalt* present in Fig.2.

In summary, then, Husserl believes that we can come to possess a legitimate (though not an authentic) general concept of a *group*. We do this by abstracting from some figural moment given in intuition. The sole immediate foundation of this figural moment is the complex of relational moments possessed by the members of the group; and it is these members, or things, which in turn are the sole foundation of those relational moments. In this way our concept of a group has, ultimately, a 'foundation in concrete intuition.' The concept, however, remains inauthentic because the figural moment is merely a *sign* for the group: the groups themselves, as such, play no part in our acquisition of the concept of a group, and so the general concept is *not* in this case abstracted from items which then comprise its instances.

One point can be noted here in passing as it will be significant later. Husserl's epistemological theory of the nature and origin of our concept of a group (or large aggregate) has tacitly dispensed with the earlier requirement that aggregates in general be arbitrary, that is, that an aggregate can be composed of utterly heterogeneous elements. Although we can have in mind a four-membered aggregate made up, say, of a person, a planet, an emotion, and an equation, it seems that *Gestalt* properties are only possessed by groups of things *of the same sort* (cf. pp.203, 209). But as (large) numbers are merely determinations of (large) multiplicities, it would seem that a number will be ascribable to a group only in so far as the members of the group are homogeneous, that is, only in so far as they all fall under a given concept. As Frege himself noted,[32] this makes Husserl's theory, in spite of initial appearances to the contrary, not dissimilar to that according to which an ascription of number involves an assertion about a concept.

So much for symbolic presentations of large (but indeterminate) numbers of things. I turn now to the symbolic presentations of determinate numbers.

Although 'symbolic presentations of groups comprise the basis for symbolic presentations of number', and indeed although numbers are merely 'the different species of the general concept of multiplicity' (p.222), nevertheless 'our investigation is by no means at an end':

> The remote symbolizations that we have so far achieved are, because of
> their vague generality, inadequate for purposes of counting and
> calculating. For these we require contentful symbolical constructions
> which, though sharply distinguished from the true . . . concepts
> of numbers 'in themselves', are nevertheless specifically adapted
> to represent them. (p.223)

In outline Husserl's theory is this: we invent a system of signs, or *numerals*, which has three essential properties. (1) The signs themselves are perceptible items – whether written or spoken they are possible contents of concrete intuitions. (2) They comprise a recursive progression, so that any possible combination of numerals has a unique place in this series, and so that the series of numerals is recursively generable, in that there is an effective procedure which enables us to formulate 'every subsequent item in the series on the basis of the earlier ones' (p.225). (3) One or more of the earliest signs in the series must be correlated with an *authentic* concept of number. Our understanding of this series of numerals is then taken to consist in our ability to employ it in calculation; and this understanding in turn is taken to be *constitutive of* our grasp of numerical concepts. Calculation, according to Husserl, is in essence nothing more than 'a *sensory* operation that derives signs from signs via fixed rules grounded in the system of numerical signs' (p.257).

In the normal, decadic system of numerals the signs '2','3', '4', etc. up to '9' (or thereabouts) are correlated with authentic concepts of number that have been abstracted from intuitions of small aggregates. Complex numerals are then generated by the familiar conventions – the familiar rules of concatenation which enable us to form signs for units, tens, hundreds, thousands, and so on. These conventions determine a unique series of signs in which every element has exactly one immediate predecessor and one immediate successor.

So what, for example, is involved in my grasp of the numerical concept signified by the sign '50'?

> The concept 50 is given to us via the construction 49+1. But what is 49? 48+1. What is 48? 47+1 . . . and so on. Each answer signifies a reduction of the question to a new level; and only when we finally reach the realm of authentic numbers can we remain satisfied with an answer. (p.229)

Of course, as Husserl elsewhere admits, an inauthentic concept like that of the number 50 is not given to us exclusively as equivalent to 49+1; it might equally be construed as $100 \div 2$, as $21+29$, as $41+3^2$, and so on. The point still remains, however, that our grasp of the concept is essentially symbolic in the sense that our only epistemic access to it is *as* what the sign '50', *or any numerically equivalent sign* signifies. And here the notion of a 'numerically equivalent sign' is to be understood purely formally as (roughly): 'a sign that is intersubstitutible solely as a consequence, ultimately, of the conventional rules governing the sequence of numerals'.

Abstracting, for the moment, from the obscurity and naivety of some specific parts and aspects of Husserl's theory, the overall account that he provides of the nature and origin of our numerical concepts seems to me profoundly plausible. In the first place there is, I believe, a massive qualitative difference between my grasp of a number like 3, say, and my grasp of a number like 12^6. The former represents something with which I can, so to speak, have intuitive contact: perceptual experience can be articulated in such a way that the concept *three* applies within it as directly and immediately as does, for example, the concept *red*. Under certain circumstances I can *see* that something is a threesome, or a trio, or that it is tripartite – without inference, criteria, calculation, counting, or the manipulation of signs. Echoing Wittgenstein we might ask: How do I know there are three things here? It would be an answer to say: 'I have learnt English'.[33] On the other hand, however, and in stark contrast, my conceptual grasp of a concept like that of 12^6 is, it seems, exclusively constituted by my understanding of the place of '12^6' in the system of arithmetical signs: nothing in my experience corresponds to this concept; and my understanding of it reaches no further than my ability correctly to identify and manipulate numerals and other arithmetical signs. Thus I can be said to have grasped what '12^6' signifies if I am able to calculate that it signifies the same thing as '2985984', as '$12^5 + 2737152$', and the like. But, as Husserl says, the notion of calculation relevant here is merely that of 'a rule-governed method of deriving signs from signs in some algorithmic sign-system, in accordance with the "laws" peculiar to that system; or better, in accordance with the conventions of union, separation, and transformation' (p.258).

It is worth noting, in passing, that Paul Benacerraf's influential article, 'What Numbers Could Not Be',[34] concludes with an account of 'what arithmetic . . . is all about' that is quite strikingly Husserlian. He argues, with considerable plausibility, that any attempt to identify a given number with a particular object (e.g. a set) is doomed to failure, if only because there cannot in the nature of the case be good reasons to say of any particular set, or indeed of any particular object, that *it* is the number in question: if one set can be made to do the job, then so too can an infinite number of other ones. For example, whatever reasons justify identifying the number 3 with, say, the particular set $\{\{\{\emptyset\}\}\}$, also and equally justify identifying it with the different set $\{\emptyset, \{\emptyset\}, \{\{\emptyset\}\}\}$. Benacerraf concludes that it is not 'any condition on the *objects* (that is, on the sets) but rather a condition on the relation under which they form a progression', that is the crucial consideration in attempting to account for what goes on in arithmetic: '"Objects" do not do the job of numbers singly; the whole system performs the job or nothing does'.[35] But in this case the objects themselves are, within limits, arbitrary:

> To *be* the number three is no more and no less than to be preceded by 2, 1, and possibly 0, and to be followed by 4, 5, and so forth. . . . *Any* object can play the role of 3; that is, any object can be the third element in some progression.

There are, however, *some* formal and epistemological constraints on the objects capable of playing this role within an abstract structure. Benacerraf identifies three. (1) 'It must be possible to individuate these objects independently of the role they play in that structure', and this is achieved by making the objects perceptible, that is, by identifying them with number *words*. (2) The objects must comprise 'a recursive sequence'; and this requirement 'is most easily explained in terms of a recursive *notation*. After all, the whole theory of recursive functions makes most sense when viewed in close connection with notations rather than with extralinguistic objects'. (3) 'In counting we . . . correlate sets with the initial segments of the sequence of number words.' And so 'we learn the elementary arithmetical operations as the cardinal operations on small sets, and extend them by the usual algorithms. Arithmetic then becomes cardinal arithmetic at the earlier levels in the obvious way, and the more advanced statements become easily interpretable as *projections* via truth functions, quantifiers, and the recursive rules governing the operations.' These three requirements are, to all intents and purposes, the same as those identified by Husserl in the *Philosophy of Arithmetic.*

In this way Husserl is able to provide a coherent *empiricist* account of the nature and origin of our concepts of number. It avoids the implausibility of the Millian theory, especially as that applies to our grasp of large numbers; but equally it avoids the implausibility of an extreme formalism,[36] according to which the subject matter of arithmetic consists exclusively in arbitrary signs and the rules for their transformation and substitution. According to Husserl, in contrast, arithmetic has a substantive subject matter – the formal properties of *aggregates* – and even though most of these aggregates are presented only symbolically, via perceptible numerical signs, and even though our understanding of these signs consists largely in our ability to employ them in a formal calculus, nevertheless in the last resort the entire edifice of our arithmetical understanding rests on, and is articulable solely in terms of, elements acceptable to an empiricist: the contents of concrete intuitions, along with the mental acts of attending, ignoring, and uniting that are directed towards them.

The nature of numbers

Up to the present point our concerns have belonged more or less exclusively within epistemology and the philosophy of mind. We have examined the account provided by Husserl of such notions as *presentation, intuition, concept, content,* and *abstraction;* of the distinction he draws between presentations of things, moments, and aggregates, between authentic and symbolic presentations, between presentations of first- and second-order moments, and so forth – in so far, that is, as these comprise the elements in terms of which he attempts to elucidate the nature of our arithmetical knowledge and understanding. At this point, however, we require a change of discipline, so to speak, in order to answer some of the questions still outstanding in the philosophy of arithmetic. There are, in other words, a number of problems whose import is not primarily epistemological, which belong, rather, to semantics, logic, and ontology, but a solution to which is required of any adequate theory of the foundations of arithmetic. Such problems concern, for instance, the nature of numbers themselves; the logical form of ascriptions of number and of assertions of arithmetic; the notions of *truth, reference, necessity* and the like that apply to sentences containing number words, and so on.[37] Merely so as to have a pair of convenient labels to hand, I shall call the former 'subjective', and these latter 'objective' issues and problems.[38]

Now it is no easy matter to identify, even in a most general way, the position that Husserl adopts with respect to these 'objective' issues. In the first place, his dominant and overriding concern throughout the first volume of the *Philosophy of Arithmetic* is to contribute to Brentanian descriptive psychology and, in terms available within that discipline, to provide a satisfactory theory of numerical intuitions and concepts. The 'logical' investigations mentioned in the sub-title of that work were to have comprised the subject matter of the second volume, but this of course was never completed.[39] There is thus an inevitable indeterminacy in Husserl's text: on a number of issues it is simply unclear what he would have said. Indeterminacy, however, is not the only, and is certainly not the greatest problem to confront the reader; for, in the second place, elements of Husserl's Brentanian inheritance produce a great deal of interference and distortion that make it difficult to discern what he has to say about the objective aspects of the topics with which he deals. Indeed, for some critics, amongst whom the most notable and influential was Frege, this interference was so strong that it effectively drowned out all of Husserl's contributions to such topics, with the result that, in Frege's view, 'everything is transposed into the subjective mode'.[40] On Frege's mistaken (but entirely understandable) reading of Husserl, that is,

> it is clear enough that . . . numbers are supposed to be ideas; . . .
> but where is the objective something *of which* a number is an
> idea? . . . . This mingling of the subjective and the objective spreads
> such an impenetrable fog that the attempt to get clear on this point is
> doomed to failure.[41]

But Frege's verdict, and the interpretation on which it is based, are not secure; and our first task will be to dispel some of the 'impenetrable fog' which supposedly results from Husserl's failure to keep the subjective and the objective apart.

The major source of this interference is the doctrine of intentionality tacitly assumed in the *Philosophy of Arithmetic*, according to which the 'object' of a mental act is no more than an immanent content of consciousness. If one adopts this frame of reference, and if one conforms to the consequent limitation of one's domain of discourse to mere 'phenomena', then clearly the sorts of questions that Frege wishes to raise cannot even be consistently formulated; for their whole purpose is to instigate an investigation into the nature of non-phenomenal, extra-mental, non-intentional entities (objects, properties, numbers, functions, truths, and the like, *as such*). It is vitally important, however, that we correctly identify the status of the self-imposed constraints which, for Husserl and Brentano, determine the content and limits of descriptive psychology.

The doctrine known as methodological solipsism is, in one of its forms, an attempt to delimit the considerations that can have genuine explanatory value within, say, a discipline like cognitive psychology. The doctrine asserts, roughly, that no mental act or state can presuppose the existence of any individual other than the subject to whom that state is ascribed. In short, 'how the world is makes no difference to one's mental states'.[42] But one can be a methodological solipsist without being a solipsist *tout court*. The decision to adopt, in a given context, a certain frame of reference, and to withhold in that context assignment of an explanatory role to entities of a certain sort commits one to a denial neither that such entities actually exist, nor indeed that such entities may have a perfectly proper explanatory function in some other context. The situation is directly analogous where the context in question is the discipline of descriptive psychology, and where one's theoretical goals are largely epistemological: one can, in the pursuit of *those* goals, limit one's universe of discourse to 'phenomena' and eschew all reference to physical objects, without thereby being under the slightest obligation either to deny that physical objects exist, or to adopt those limits in the pursuit of quite other goals.

If these considerations are germane,[43] then we can reject, as misconceived, one of Frege's most fundamental objections to Husserl's programme in the *Philosophy of Arithmetic*. Frege writes:

> If a geographer was given an oceanographic treatise to read which gave a *psychological* explanation of the origin of the oceans, he would no doubt get the impression that the author had missed the mark . . . . [Husserl's *Philosophy of Arithmetic*] has left me with exactly the same impression.[44]

But Husserl does not attempt to give a psychological explanation of the nature and origin of the numbers themselves, but rather an epistemological theory of our *concepts and intuitions of* numbers; and in that attempt adoption of the methodological constraints which in part determine the nature of descriptive psychology is entirely well motivated. Frege could hardly have objected in this way to a treatise that gave a psychological explanation of the origins of *our knowledge and understanding* of the oceans. On the other hand, when we turn, as we do now, to consider the numbers themselves, such constraints can and must fall away; for the methodology they impose is simply inappropriate to the study of the more 'objective' issues in the foundations of arithmetic.[45]

There are two major kinds of context in which numerals and number words occur.[46] On the one hand there are those that Husserl calls '*Zahlenaussagen*' or 'predications of number'; they characteristically provide answers to the question 'How many?', and employ a number word in an attributive or adjectival role. The following sentences, for example, express empirical ascriptions of number: 'There are three broken windows on the ground floor'; 'Five people came to dinner last night'; 'There are a dozen flowers in the garden', and so forth. But as Husserl remarks: 'not every determination of number belongs as such to arithmetic. Arithmetic has nothing to do with a determination like "the number of flowers in the garden"' (p.408). On the other hand, and in contrast to predications of number, there are the genuine propositions of arithmetic. An arithmetical proposition is, typically, one in which number words play a substantival rather than an attributive role: an arithmetical proposition, we might say, predicates something of a number, rather than predicating a number of something. And so 'Two is an even prime', '2 = 5 − 3', and '5 < 2', say, are elementary propositions of arithmetic.[47]

Ascriptions of number

If number words play an adjectival role in ascriptions of number, one of the first questions to which we need an answer is this: What sort of thing is it that numbers are predicated of? What exactly do we ascribe numbers *to*? Or, to put it in Husserl's terms: What sort of thing is the subject of a numerical predication, the bearer of a numerical property? The gist of his answer is that

> the subject of a numerical predication is *an aggregate* (multiplicity, group, etc.). Formally speaking, a number stands to a concrete group as a concept stands to one of its instances. Numbers thus relate, not to the concept of the counted objects, but rather to the aggregate of them. (p.166, my italics)

This answer is hardly helpful, however, until we know in rather more detail how a concept stands to its instances, how an aggregate is related to its members, or how, in general, predication works. The existing text of the *Philosophy of Arithmetic* remains largely uninformative on such matters; but fortunately there are two posthumously published pieces, 'On the Logic of Signs (Semiotics)' and 'On the Theory of Aggregates', which date from about this time and which shed considerable light on these issues.[48]

Husserl's early semantic theory is articulated in terms of two fundamental distinctions, namely between direct and indirect signs, on the one hand, and between singular and plural terms on the other. The former contrast, which bears a striking resemblance to that drawn by Russell between logically proper names and so-called 'denoting phrases', is motivated by the intuition that while some signs are merely arbitrarily correlated with, and do not describe or in any way characterize what they stand for, other signs successfully pick out their designata in virtue of the latters' possession of some identifying property or attribute. And so, according to Husserl, a direct sign

> is one which has to do neither with a particular concept of the thing designated, nor with its content, nor with its particular characteristics. The proper name of a person, for example, stands in this relation to the

person whose name it is; it designates but it does not characterize him. (p.341)

An indirect sign, on the other hand, functions only 'via the mediation of certain conceptual marks':

> With respect to indirect signs it is necessary to distinguish between what the sign *means* (*bedeutet*) and what it *designates* (*bezeichnet*), whereas in the case of a direct sign these two things coincide. The meaning of a proper name, for example, consists merely in this: that it stands for just this particular object. Indirect signs, however, require intermediaries between sign and thing: the sign designates the thing through those intermediaries which, for that very reason, constitute its meaning. (p.343)

The second contrast on which Husserl relies is considerably less familiar than the first – at least within the so-called analytic or Anglo-American tradition in philosophy. Within that tradition, as Peter Simons has recently emphasized, there is 'a remarkable prejudice in favour of the singular', and as a consequence '*plural* terms are the Cinderellas of philosophical grammar, and few philosophers have recognized them'.[49] One symptom of this is the use that philosophers in the tradition of, say, Frege, Russell, and Carnap have made of abstract entities like truth-values, numbers, concepts, propositions, and (especially) sets. This proliferation of abstract entities results, at least in part, from a felt pressure to find a *single* entity that will perform a given logical or semantic task, or that can be correlated with a given expression type.[50] But as we will see, the pressure to invoke a single abstract object (i.e., in circumstances where no suitable single concrete object is available) can to some extent be reduced if we allow, instead, the possibility of appeal to pluralities of concrete objects. Another, more obvious symptom of the prejudice in favour of the singular is the existence of a straightforward lacuna in received semantic theory: we simply have no account of plural reference, of how sentences containing plural referring expressions function.[51]

Husserl's two distinctions combine to yield a four-fold classification of terms into

(i)   *Direct singular*: 'Paul McCartney', 'Sheffield', 'this', 'me', 'it'.
(ii) *Indirect singular*: 'the largest planet in the solar system', 'my car', 'that tree', 'the person now talking'.
(iii) *Direct plural*: 'John, Paul, Ringo, and George', 'these', 'us', 'the aggregate of John, Paul, Ringo, and George'.
(iv) *Indirect Plural*: 'the Beatles', 'the inhabitants of Sheffield', 'our cars', 'those trees', 'the aggregate of people who live in Sheffield'.

Our present concern is primarily with expressions belonging to categories

(iii) and (iv); for it is they that are most relevant to a Husserlian theory of numerical ascriptions. I shall call expressions of kinds (iii) and (iv) plural terms, and those belonging to kinds (i) and (ii) singular terms. And I shall say that plural terms (if they designate at all) designate aggregates of individuals. Here the term 'individual' is intended to range over both phenomenal things and physical objects. An aggregate, however, is not an individual of any sort, but is, precisely, a *plurality* of individuals:

> If 'A', 'B', 'C' . . . etc. designate arbitrary objects that . . . are compatible one with another, i.e. such that the being of one does not exclude the being of another, then the expression 'A and B and C . . . etc.' provides a definition . . . of the term 'aggregate of objects A, B, C . . . etc.'. (p.385)

Now if we agree, as I think we must, that the expression, or list

(1)   John, Paul, Ringo, and George

designates exactly four individuals, and if we then introduce a new expression

(2)   the aggregate of John, Paul, Ringo, and George

by stipulating that it shall designate all and only the individuals designated by (1), then it will follow trivially that (2) designates exactly four individuals. Likewise if we introduce another new term

(3)   the Beatles

by stipulating that it too be co-designative with (1), then, again trivially, (3) will designate exactly four individuals.[52]

This is not very exciting; but at least in this way we can begin to combat the temptation to think that (2) is a *singular* term, and hence that we need to countenance, over and above the four individuals mentioned in (1), a fifth thing called an aggregate. Unlike both set-theoretic talk and talk of mereological sums, aggregate talk does not provide us with a way of substituting *one* thing in the place of many – on the contrary, the entire purpose of aggregate talk is to give us a manageable way of preserving the *plurality* which, Husserl claims, underlies the possibility of numerical predication. The nature of aggregates, and of plural reference in general, can be brought out if we compare some of the more striking features of aggregate theory with those of its closest rival, set theory.[53] I shall employ the following shorthand:

$$xMy =_{df} x \text{ is a member of aggregate } y$$
$$A(x) =_{df} x \text{ is an aggregate}$$
$$I(x) =_{df} x \text{ is an individual}$$
$$[x, y, z] =_{df} \text{ the aggregate of } x, y, \text{ and } z$$
$$\{x, y, z\} =_{df} \text{ the set of } x, y, \text{ and } z$$

$$[x : F(x)] =_{df} \text{ the aggregate of all F's}$$
$$\{x : F(x)\} =_{df} \text{ the set of all F's}$$

According to the dominant conception of a set, the set whose members are, say, John, Paul, Ringo, and George, *viz* $\{j, p, r, g\}$, is an abstract object. In other words it is a unitary, non-spatio-temporal entity that has no causal powers or material properties, and is, hence, imperceptible. A set is not made up of its members; rather the relation is that the identity of the set is determined solely by the identity of its members. By contrast, the aggregate $[j, p, r, g]$ is actually composed of its members and so is as concrete, as spatio-temporal, and as material as they are. Unlike the set, the aggregate can for example fly into Los Angeles, be photographed, and sing off-key. (It should not be thought, however, that in order to comprise an aggregate the individuals that are its members need to be in the same place: an aggregate is just a plurality of individuals, and a plurality of individuals can perfectly well be dispersed in space and/or in time.)

The formal, and in particular the arithmetical properties of aggregates differ conspicuously from those of the 'corresponding' sets. Because parts of a part are also parts of the whole, aggregates do not iterate. In other words there can be no aggregate of aggregates distinct from the aggregate of the individuals involved, in the way that there can and must be classes of classes that are distinct from the class of members of those classes. Aggregates collapse:

$$[[j, p], [r, g]]$$

is an aggregate of four individuals, that is,

$$[[j, p],[r, g]] = [j, p, r, g].$$

Moreover,

$$[[j, p, r]]$$

is an aggregate of three, identical with $[j, p, r]$. On the other hand, and in sharp contrast, the set

$$\{\{j, p,\}, \{r, g\}\}$$

has exactly two members, and the set

$$\{\{j, p, r\}\}$$

has exactly one. And finally, although the null set, $\{\emptyset\}$, is a set, the expression 'the null aggregate' means nothing at all.

Some of the formal properties of Husserlian aggregates can be expressed as follows:

(H1) $A(x) \ \& \ A(y) \supset (x = y \equiv (z)(zMx \equiv zMy)).$

65

This principle provides us with identity conditions for aggregates according to which two aggregates are identical if and only if they have all their members in common. This is hardly surprising as aggregates are *composed* of their members.

(H2) $$xMy \supset I(x) \mathbin{\&} A(y).$$

Only individuals can be members of aggregates; and only aggregates can have members.

(H3) $$A(x) \supset (\exists y)(\exists z)(yMx \mathbin{\&} zMx \mathbin{\&} y \neq z).$$

In other words aggregates are genuine *pluralities* of individuals: no aggregate can have less than two distinct members. And so it follows not only that

(H4) $$\sim (\exists x)(x = [y\colon F(y) \mathbin{\&} (z)(F(z) \supset z = y)]),$$

but also that

(H5) $$\sim(\exists x)(x = [y\colon y \neq y]).$$

There is neither a singleton nor a null aggregate.[54]

How does this help us to understand what goes on when we ascribe a number to something – as when, for example, we say 'There are three coins in the fountain'? According to Frege, this is an assertion of second-level, ascribing a property to a first-level concept. The subject of the assertion is the concept

(ξ_1) *is a coin in the fountain,*

and the predicate is, in effect,

(ξ_2) *is a concept with three instances.*[55]

The motive for this analysis is, in part, that there simply *is* no object, no entity of level-0, to which the numerical property can plausibly be ascribed: neither the individual coins themselves, nor the set of them, nor the mereological sum of them can be said to be *three*; for of course all of these are *single* things. And if there are no suitable bearers of numerical properties at level-0 in the type hierarchy, then clearly we must look for them at some higher level. But this argument is based on a false dilemma. It proceeds by offering either (i) a single item of level-0 (an object), or (ii) a single item of level-1 (a concept) as the only possible bearer of a numerical property, and by then suggesting that because there cannot be any appropriate candidates of the first sort, an ascription of number must be an assertion about an item of the second kind – a concept. The choice between options (i) and (ii) is not, however, exhaustive. It seems plausible only because of our prejudice in favour of the singular – and it is certainly true, of course, that no *one* thing can as such be that which is three. The option that has been overlooked, however, is that the bearer of the number property is, precisely, a plurality of objects. A plurality, an aggregate, is essentially a *many* – and an ascription of number merely tells us *how many*.

On what grounds might we decide between the Fregean and the Husserlian analyses of the logical form of ascriptions of number – assuming for the moment that both are equally internally coherent? Amongst the questions that will need to be answered here, the most obviously relevant are the following: Which theory conforms most closely to our pre-theoretical use and understanding of numerical ascriptions? Which is ontologically the most parsimonious? Which is epistemologically the least problematic? Which is formally the simplest and most elegant? And, finally, which of the two analyses yields a superior account of arithmetical propositions? Surprisingly, perhaps, given their respective reputations as philosophers of mathematics, Husserl's account turns out to be as defensible as Frege's in virtually all of these respects.

An everyday ascription of number typically expresses the result of an act of counting, or of a calculation which has its basis in acts of counting, and typically conforms to the schema:

(4)   There are n F's,

where 'F' is a count noun or count noun phrase, 'n' is a numeral or number word other than 'zero' or 'one',[56] and the verb is in the plural. I shall take as paradigmatic the sentence:

(5)   There are three coins in the fountain.[57]

Now according to the Husserlian analysis of a sentence like (5), logical form differs from surface grammar minimally if at all. Such sentences seem to be about a number of objects, and seem to specify what that number is; and on Husserl's theory, unlike Frege's, the appearance is not misleading. The logical subject is indeed plural, as both the plural verb ('are') and the number word ('three') strongly suggest. The logical subject, in other words, is an aggregate designated by an indirect plural term ('coins in the fountain') that we would translate into our notation as '$[x:$ coin in the fountain $x]$'. Moreover the aggregate is in this case composed of concrete, material, perceptible objects of a reassuringly familiar and accessible kind, *viz*: coins. To this aggregate the predicate ascribes a property, the property of *being three*. Now although an aggregate is composed of its members, the property of being three is, of course, not ascribed to these members individually. None of the coins is itself three. To understand how we can assert that an aggregate may possess a property that is not possessed by any of its members, without thereby being committed to the existence of aggregates over and above their members, we need to introduce some distinctions.

I shall call a property, $\emptyset$, *distributive* if, given that it is possessed by an aggregate as a whole, it is possessed by every member of the aggregate:

$$\emptyset[x\colon F(x)] \supset (x)(F(x) \supset \emptyset(x))$$

Most common-or-garden empirical properties are distributive in this sense. So, for example, if Tom, Dick, and Harry are pale, then Tom is pale, Dick is pale, and so too is Harry. On the other hand I shall say that a property, $\emptyset$, is *collective* if, given that it is possessed by an aggregate, it is possessed by none of the individual members:

$$\emptyset[x\colon F(x)] \supset (x)(F(x) \supset \sim \emptyset(x)).[58]$$

We most often encounter collective properties (and the corresponding collective predicates) when our concern is with the nature, the composition, or the performance, as a whole, of some team, group, crew, committee, or other body composed of people. The following sentences, for instance, are most naturally construed as involving collective predication:

(6)   The Beatles are about to disband.

(7)   The Cabinet is (are) in session.

(8)   Tom, Dick, Harry, and Bill are a famous string quartet.

(9)   The team is (are) known for its (their) teamwork.

Disbanding, say, or *being a string quartet*, are simply not things of which a single individual is capable – which is partly why sentences involving collective predication resist straightforward translation into quantifier notation. But to say that a property is collective and does not distribute to the members of an aggregate does not entail a repudiation of our thesis that an aggregate is literally composed of its members; for to say that a given property does not distribute is by no means to say that there is no *other* property which does this. More specifically, we do not need to deny the possibility that there exist one or more distributive properties in terms of which the collective property can be explained. Indeed, if aggregates are not, properly speaking, individuals, then there must always be some property or complex of properties which is possessed by the individual members of an aggregate, and which comprise what Black calls the 'retrieval conditions' for any collective property of the aggregate:

Suppose that π is some plural referring expression occurring in the context $f(\pi)$ and referring there to objects $a_1, a_2, ..., a_n$. Then, in order to understand $f(\pi)$, I must know the retrieval conditions for referential descent, for the use of π in this context. That is to say, I must know how to pass from the assertion f to the assertions g_i that are explicitly about the a's.[59]

As long as we can in principle provide such retrieval conditions, we can explain the possibility of collective predication, without invoking 'individual' aggregates as their ineliminable subjects – indeed, specification of its retrieval conditions will comprise an analysis of a given instance of collective predication.

These considerations are relevant to our overall topic because on a Husserlian theory of number, ascriptions of number turn out to be collective predications whose subjects are aggregates. Sentence (5), for example, asserts that the aggregate of coins in the fountain has the property of being three. And this is to be construed neither as making ineliminable reference to a single thing called an aggregate, nor as predicating the property of being three of each individual coin, i.e., distributively. How, then, is it to be understood? What are the retrieval conditions here? I suggest that the account which makes most sense, and which conforms most closely to both the letter and the spirit of principles (H1) to (H5) above, is this: sentence (5) is to be understood in terms of the retrieval condition

(10) $F(a)$ & $F(b)$ & $F(c)$ & $a \neq b$ & $b \neq c$ & $a \neq c$

where 'F' designates the property of being a coin in the fountain, and 'a', 'b', and 'c' are arbitrary names. This contrasts favourably with the more familiar alternative:

(11) $(\exists x)(\exists y)(\exists z)(F(x)$ & $F(y)$ & $F(z)$ & $x \neq y$ & $y \neq z$ & $x \neq z)$.[60]

The contrast is favourable in a number of respects. First because (10) does, while (11) does not capture in a satisfying way the pre-theoretical grasp which someone has of the meaning of an assertion like 'There are three coins in the fountain'. One is surely saying of the physical coins that they are three, and not saying of some first-level concept that it falls within a second-level concept. Second, the Husserlian analysis is ontologically more compact: there is no need to introduce concepts as the unsaturated, abstract entities that bear numerical properties. And as a result, third, the analysis is epistemologically less problematic than its Fregean rival; for it simply fails to raise the familiar difficulty concerning abstract entities, *viz*, if they are without causal powers and are thus imperceptible, how can we have any acquaintance with them or acquire any knowledge about them? As we would expect, Husserl's theory is, but Frege's is not, compatible with epistemological empiricism. And finally, Husserl's theory is formally more simple than Frege's; for ascriptions of number turn out to involve only objects and their properties, and not, with Frege, first-level concepts and their second-level properties.

There remains one problematic area with which we must now deal: How can a Husserlian aggregative theory of number explain zero and one? As we noted earlier, principle (H3) rules out the possibility not only of an aggregate with no members, but also of an aggregate with only one member. Frege writes:

> The easy way out is to say: 'These are not numbers at all'. But this raises the question: What, then, are they? [According to Husserl] they are negative answers to the question 'How many?' They are like the answer 'Never' to the question 'When?' . . . . But it is really asking too much to ask us to regard the answer 'One' to the question 'How many moons has the earth?' as a negative answer. In the case of zero, however, the matter is inherently more plausible . . . . [But even so] the answer 'Zero' to the question 'What is the number of predecessors of Romulus on the throne of Rome?' is no more negative than 'Two' would be. In answering 'Zero' we are not denying that there is such a number: we are naming it.[61]

Now this last remark of Frege's is simply disingenuous, for it was Frege himself who had already provided the most plausible account of ascriptions of zero: 'existence is analogous to number. Affirmation of existence is in fact nothing but the denial of the number nought';[62] and conversely, ascription of the number nought is just a denial of existence. To say that *the number of people in the room = 0* is to say no more and no less than that *there aren't any people in the room.* And if this is right, then when we answer the question 'How many F's are there?' by 'There aren't any', we are not forced to conclude that there is something of which the number zero is being predicated. We need only deny that '[x: x is a person in the room]' has a designation. Husserl's point, to which Frege alludes dismissively, is that negative answers like 'None', 'Zero', 'There aren't any' and the like stand to the question 'How many?' in the same relation in which negative answers like 'Nowhere' and 'Never' stand to the questions 'Where?' and 'When?' (see pp. 130–1). And the point has a great deal of force; for we can and do handle negative answers to questions about place and time without any compulsion to conclude that there exist things designated by the expressions 'nowhere' and 'never' – the zero-place and the zero-time, so to speak. Analogously, we can take 'None' to be a negative answer to the question 'How many?' without construing it as designating an object called 'the number zero.'[63] In this way we can consistently deny that zero is a number, and that there is any need to countenance null aggregates, while at the same time providing a plausible account of so-called 'ascriptions of zero'.

I do not intend to spend much time on the number one; for it seems to me that Husserl is simply wrong to deny that it is a number, and wrong to claim that to the question 'How many?' the answer 'One' is a *negative* answer. On any plausible account the positive whole numbers are 1, 2, 3 etc., and not, as Husserl has it, 2, 3, 4, etc. Although this is not a disaster for his aggregative theory, it does require us to give up principles (H2) and (H3) and those they imply. But there seems no good reason why we should not adopt in their place principles which allow, as a limiting case, an aggregate to possess just one member. Unlike set theory, which distinguishes sharply between a singleton set and its only member, and which acknowledges the existence of the null set, aggregate theory will now identify a one-membered aggregate with its only member, but will still refuse to countenance any such thing as an aggregate with no members. So (H5) remains, and (H3) might be replaced by the principles

$$I(x) \supset (xMx \& (y)(yMx \supset y = x)),$$

and

$$A(x) \supset (\exists y)(yMx).[64]$$

Propositions of arithmetic

According to Husserl, 'in arithmetic numbers are not abstracta':

> Arithmeticians generally operate, not with numerical concepts as such, but rather with generally presented objects of these concepts; the signs that they combine in calculating have basically the character of . . . general signs. Thus '5' does not mean the concept (the abstractum) five; rather '5' is a general name . . . for each aggregate (*Menge*) which as such falls under the concept five. '5 + 5 = 10' means just: any aggregate that falls under the concept five, when united with any other aggregate that falls under the same concept yields an aggregate that falls under the concept ten. (p.182)

Which is to say that numbers are *species of aggregates*, and that numerals in arithmetic are not proper names but general terms. As employed in arithmetic, that is, a numeral functions as an indirect plural term that designates every aggregate of a given cardinality.

We can represent in diagrammatic form the semantic properties of the four categories of term that Husserl employs:

(i) Direct Singular Term

('Paris')

O_1

(ii) Indirect Singular Term

('The capital of France')

Property

O_1

71

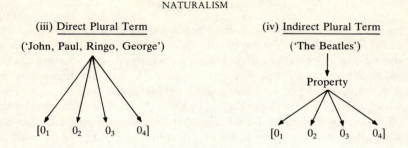

(iii) Direct Plural Term

('John, Paul, Ringo, George')

(iv) Indirect Plural Term

('The Beatles')

Property

$[O_1 \quad O_2 \quad O_3 \quad O_4]$

Numerals, it appears, are to be assigned to category (iv). But there is a complication: numerals, we are told, designate aggregates of a given cardinality, and as we already know, an aggregate is just a plurality of objects. The picture which emerges is thus:

(v) Indirect Plural Numerical Term

('4')

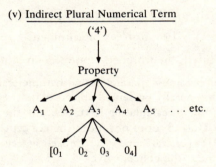

Property

$A_1 \quad A_2 \quad A_3 \quad A_4 \quad A_5 \quad \ldots$ etc.

$[O_1 \quad O_2 \quad O_3 \quad O_4]$

Here A_1, A_2, etc. are the aggregates possessing the property which secures them the cardinality in question; O_1, O_2, etc. are the individual objects comprising one such aggregate.

Now it seems clear that Husserl regarded the relation of designation as univocal and transitive. He says, for example, that 'an indirect sign is a complex sign whose parts are stratified one above another, and not side by side . . . S is a sign for object O by being a sign for S_1 which in turn is a sign for object O; or by being a sign for S_1 which is a sign for S_2, which is perhaps a sign for S_3, and so forth, until finally the sign S_n designates O directly' (p.343). This might seem immediately objectionable, for it leads to the bizarre conclusion that Paul McCartney (say) is one of the things designated by the term '4' – given, that is, that there are four Beatles. But although the conclusion is bizarre, certainly, it is not I think objectionable, and indeed much of its oddity stems merely from the starkness of the contrast between it and the more familiar set-theoretic accounts of number. It must be borne in mind, however, that for Husserl the concept of number is related to acts of counting, where what gets counted are individual things; that numerical properties are properties of concrete things (albeit collectively not distributively); and that one of the key concepts on which his theory is based is precisely that of *plural* reference. Understood aright, the claim that Paul McCartney is one of the things designated by '4' is no more contentious than the (true) claim that Paul McCartney is one of the things that would be included in an itemization of all foursomes. The claim in no way implies either that Paul McCartney himself has the property of being four, or that he is identical with the number four. To think otherwise is to misunderstand the nature of plural reference and the distinction between collective and distributive properties.

We have as yet no explanation of the 'property' alluded to in (v), which picks out all and only aggregates of like cardinality, in this case, all aggregates with just four members. And this is important, for there is more than a whiff of circularity about the attempt to explain a given cardinal number in terms of aggregates of a given cardinality. Husserl himself has little to say about this matter; but it is possible to provide an account based on, and largely compatible with, his other doctrines.

The text of the *Philosophy of Arithmetic* contains a rambling series of arguments (pp.96–125) intended, apparently, to show that the notion of a one-to-one correspondence, and the notion of numerical equivalence defined in terms of it, are 'completely useless and a matter of indifference' (p.117) when it comes to explaining the nature and origins of number. His objections are, however, largely *ad hoc* and unpersuasive, and in fact he soon came to change his mind; for within a year he could write:

> In my chapter on definitions of number via equivalence I was decidedly in error. To be sure, I was there concerned with authentic presentations of number, and for them such definitions are unnecessary. I failed to notice, however, that inauthentic presentations of number are in need of a principle of characterization and the notion of equivalence performs this role admirably. (p.403)

Indeed it does; and Husserl's own explanation of symbolic presentations of number can itself be used to provide the raw materials for an account of numerical equivalence in terms of one-to-one correlations. A given number, we said, is not a single object of any sort but a species of aggregates, namely those of a given cardinality. And correspondingly, a numeral is not a singular term but a plural term that designates indirectly all aggregates of that cardinality. How does it do this? And, in particular, what non-circular account can we give of the property *being of cardinality n*, where non-circularity involves supposing neither that we already understand what numbers are, nor that we already possess signs that have been given a numerical interpretation. As Husserl clearly saw, the solution lies in an appeal to a two-stage introduction of numerical signs: they are introduced first as an arbitrary, uninterpreted series of perceptible marks whose only essential property is formal: they must comprise a recursive progression, so that the composition of the sign itself determines its unique place in the series. Any such series will do. Suppose we invent one that runs

'*a*', '*b*', '*c*', '*aa*', '*bb*', '*cc*', '*aaa*', '*bbb*', . . . etc.

The second stage is the provision of a pragmatic interpretation for the signs by assigning them a use: one determines what we now call 'the cardinality of an aggregate' by correlating one-to-one the members of the aggregate with elements from the series of signs, starting from the beginning of the series and proceeding in order. This is called counting; and an aggregate will have a cardinality X, just in case there is no other sign after 'X' in the series which can be correlated in this way. In terms of our invented sequence of signs, for example, we determine the cardinality of the Beatles by mapping the signs, in order, into the individual members of that aggregate. And its cardinality is *aa* because '*aa*' is the last element in the sequence that correlates one-to-one with a Beatle. So '*aa*' is just another sign for what we call '4'. Moreover, in this notation it will be the case that $a + a + a + a = aa$, because once we are *given* a particular recursive progression of signs, along with the rules governing one-to-one correlations of signs with things, it then becomes possible to map the sequence of signs into itself:

It is worth noting that we can begin to extract elementary truths of arithmetic (in this case, that $1 + 1 + 1 + 1 = 4$) on the basis merely of an appeal to perceptible signs and the correlations governing (i) their place in a recursive sequence, and (ii) our use of them in one-to-one correlations with things, including themselves.[65] There is nothing here that an empiricist could not accept. But note that, in sharp contrast with the Millian theory, elementary truths of arithmetic are *not* contingent, inductive generalizations about the observed behaviour of 'pebbles and gingersnaps'. They are, rather, *formal, a priori* truths about the behaviour of recursive progressions. It is necessarily the case that $4 = 1 + 1 + 1 + 1$ because (informally) '4' is the unique value yielded when '1' is mapped four times onto the determinate sequence of signs that runs '1', '2', '3', '4', etc.

To describe the procedure by which we determine the cardinality of an aggregate is not yet to explain what the cardinality of an aggregate *is*: after all, there are uncounted and even uncountable aggregates which nevertheless have a determinate number of members. Here we say that an aggregate has a cardinality *n* if its members *can* be mapped one-to-one into the sequence of numerals beginning with '1' and ending with '*n*'.

Numerals lead a double life, according to Husserl, and in neither life are they names of objects, or singular referring expressions. On the one hand they function as indices of cardinality, and in this sense they are indirect plural terms designating numerically equivalent aggregates. On the other hand they are also elements in a recursive progression, and as such they possess all the *formal* properties belonging to the members of any such progression. It is in virtue of the latter that the system of numerals can be used as a calculus; but it is in virtue of the former that this calculus has an application to non-mathematical reality. Speaking loosely, we can say that it is because of the formal properties of the numeral sequence (determined by the particular conventions we have adopted) that $4 = 3 + 1$ is a necessary truth of arithmetic; but it is because of our practice of one-to-one correlations of numerals and objects (other than numerals) that '$4 = 3 + 1$' can be used to tell us about the behaviour of, amongst other things, pebbles or gingersnaps, molecules or units of time, and so forth.

At this point, admittedly, many aspects and consequences of Husserl's philosophy of arithmetic remain indeterminate, perhaps even suspect; a resolution of all such indeterminacies and doubts is, however, a task far beyond the scope of the present work. But there is justice in the demand that before finally quitting this topic we provide some defence of the Husserlian theory – at least, that is, against the more familiar criticisms that have been levelled against it. In conclusion, therefore, and very briefly, I shall try to estimate the extent to which that theory is vulnerable to the sorts of objections raised against it, influentially, by Frege and others. There are a number of these, but they fall under three broad headings: (I) objections to any theory according to which numbers are properties of 'external things'; (II) objections to aggregate theories of number; and (III) objections to 'psychologism'.

(Ia) That number is not a property of 'external things'.

In a justly famous passage, Frege inveighs against any theory according to which 'the concept of number can be classed along with, say, that of colour', as a property of material objects like tables, chairs and trees:

> Is it not in a totally different sense that we speak of a tree as having 1000 leaves and again as having green leaves? The green colour we ascribe to each single leaf, but not the number 1000. If we call all the leaves of a tree taken together its foliage, then the foliage too is green, but it is not 1000. To what then does the property 1000 really belong? It almost looks as though it belongs neither to any single one of the leaves, nor to the totality of them all; is it possible that it does not

really belong to things in the external world at all?[66]

This polemic has seemed cogent, I believe, largely because Frege's readership has shared his prejudice in favour of the singular, with its consequent emphasis on distributive as against collective properties of things. The polemic simply collapses, however, if one allows the possibility that objects in the external world can possess not only distributive properties like colour, but also collective properties like number.

(Ib) That number is not restricted to external things.

Perhaps as a result of Mill's influence it is often thought that on an aggregate theory number properties must be restricted to aggregates of empirical or concrete objects, and hence that the theory fails to capture the universality of arithmetic. 'Another reason for refusing to classify number along with colour and solidity,' Frege writes, is that number 'is applicable over a far wider range' (*ibid* p.30). As well as being able to count cabbages and kings, he points out, we can equally well count such non-physical, non-sensible things as concepts, figures of the syllogism, judgements, and the like.

Husserl in fact agreed wholeheartedly; for he himself wrote of Mill's restriction of numerical properties to 'physical things' that 'this opinion is so palpably false that one can only wonder how a thinker of Mill's stature could rest content with it' (p.17). And Husserl goes on to insist that we can number not only physical objects but also such things as judgements, possibilities, imaginary objects, and so on. On the reading of Husserl's theory presented above, that is, entities of any kind whatsoever can be numbered, just so long as it is possible to correlate individual such entities one-to-one with the series of numerals. And this means, ironically, that Frege's criticism can be turned back on him; for it is Frege rather than Husserl who fails to do justice to the universal applicability of number. If, with Frege, we take the analysis of ascriptions of number to involve objectual quantification, so that 'The number of F's is two' is read as '$(\exists x)(\exists y)(F(x) \;\&\; F(y) \;\&\; (z)(F(z) \supset z = x \vee z = y))$', then it becomes impossible to provide a plausible analysis of many actual ascriptions of number that we make, apparently unproblematically, in everyday life. For instance, we have no difficulty in understanding, and if we have the appropriate knowledge we have no difficulty in answering, questions like the following: 'How many years was Robinson Crusoe marooned on his island?' 'How many officers came to arrest Joseph K.?' 'How many daughters had King Lear?' or 'The Ancient Mariner stoppeth one in every how many?' On Frege's theory the only true answer to these questions is: zero. And intuitively that seems to be the wrong answer.

An important point emerges from this. An analysis along Fregean lines involves two kinds of ontological commitment: ascriptions of number commit us to the existence of objects of the kind numbered; and assertions of arithmetic commit us to the existence of abstract objects (numbers or sets). A Husserlian analysis, however, commits us to neither: we can number imaginary, even impossible entities – as long as we can distinguish them one from another (in the way in which, for example, we have no difficulty in distinguishing Goneril, Regan, and Cordelia) – and we can assert that $4 = 3 + 1$ without assigning '4' an abstract, singular referent. This does not imply, however, that we cannot number abstract objects. On the contrary, one of the great virtues of Husserl's theory is that it is ontologically *neutral*: what there is is not a matter to be decided by arithmetic. And this is just as it should be.

(Ic) That ascriptions of number involve concepts, not objects.

Frege writes:

> If I give someone a stone with the words: Find the weight of this, I have given him precisely the object he is to investigate. But if I place a pile of playing cards in his hands with the words: Find the number of these, this does not tell him whether I wish to know the number of cards, or of complete packs of cards, or even say honour cards at skat.
> To have given him completely the object he is to investigate, I must add some further [concept-]word: cards, or packs, or honours. (*ibid* p.28)

Frege concludes that it is not to the *object* that a number is ascribed, but to the *concept*, for 'an object to which I can ascribe different numbers with equal right is not the real bearer of a number' (*ibid*). Frege's general point can be granted entirely, but it requires no modification of Husserl's theory; for although that theory asserts that the bearers of numerical properties are aggregates, it allows that aggregates are typically picked out via (what Frege would call) a concept. The assertion that there are three coins in the fountain ascribes to the plurality of objects that fall under the concept *being a coin in the fountain* the property of being three.[67] Husserl must, however, deny that because an ascription of number 'involves' a concept, we have to infer that an ascription of number is 'about' a concept – in other words, that the concept itself is therefore the subject of numerical predication. This he does (p.166); and rightly, for the inference is invalid.

(IIa) That aggregate theory cannot account for 0 and 1.

We have already dealt with this objection: Husserl's analysis of so-called 'ascriptions of zero' is defensible. But his analysis of ascriptions of the number one, as *negative* answers to the question 'How many?', must be abandoned. This, however, can be accomplished with only minor disturbance to his overall philosophy of arithmetic.

(IIb) That no unique number can be assigned to an aggregate.

The following looks like a powerful objection to any aggregate theory of number:

> There are various ways in which an aggregate can be separated into parts, and we cannot say that one alone would be characteristic. For example, a bundle of straws can be separated into parts by cutting the straws into half, or by splitting it up into single straws, or by dividing it into two bundles . . . . The number word 'one' [moreover], in the expression 'one straw', signally fails to do justice to the way in which the straw is made up of cells, or of molecules. (*ibid*, p. 30)

In other words, if the members of an aggregate are parts of that aggregate, and if parts of a part are therewith parts of the whole, then the aggregate as such can have no determinate number of members – indeed it will possess incompatible number properties. The bundle of ten straws will be at one and the same time one bundle (of ten), two bundles (of five), ten straws, twenty half straws, 10^5 cells, 10^8 molecules, and so on indefinitely. To the question 'How many parts has this aggregate?' there is simply no answer. Frege is surely right in the observation we have quoted already, that 'an object to which I can ascribe different numbers with equal right is not the real bearer of a number'. So aggregates are not the real bearers of numerical properties.

The objection is cogent if one construes ascriptions of number as assertions that an aggregate has a certain number of *parts* – in an undifferentiating sense of the term 'part' according to which molecules, cells, sub-bundles, straws and so on would all be parts of a bundle of straws. But there is neither good reason, nor any tendency on Husserl's part, to construe ascriptions of number in this way. On the contrary, a numerical property attaches to an aggregate in virtue of its having just so many *members,* and not in virtue of any facts concerning its parts; and while all the members of an aggregate are parts of the aggregate, it is simply not the case that all the aggregate's parts are its members. A bundle of straws can have a unique, determinate number of member straws, even though the question 'How many parts has this bundle?' is senseless. This is because on Husserl's theory an aggregate can only be specified in two ways: it is given either by listing its members or, more usually, by identifying those members as the instances of a certain concept. Now Frege imposed an important constraint on the kind of concept that can perform this role: 'Only a concept which isolates what falls under it in a definite manner, and which does not permit arbitrary division of it into parts, can be a unit relative to a given number' (*ibid* p.66). This is right; but nothing in Husserl's doctrine is inconsistent with it. Aggregates are specified in ways which provide identity conditions for their members – typically in the form [x: F(x)], where 'F' is a count noun or count noun phrase expressing a sortal concept that, indeed, 'does not permit an arbitrary division into parts'.

(IIc) That aggregate theory wrongly characterizes the notion of arithmetical truth.

There is, it might be thought, an objection to Husserl's theory of number along the following lines. If number words refer (amongst other things) to properties possessed by aggregates of physical objects, and if propositions of arithmetic make assertions about the behaviour of these aggregates, then, as Mill argued, those propositions can at best be empirical, contingent claims based on induction. The assertion that 3 + 1 = 4, say, can surely claim no more than that when we unite an aggregate with three members with an aggregate with one member, the result will (probably) be an aggregate with four members. (Cf. Husserl's own remarks at p. 182.) This conclusion seems unacceptable, however, if only because the empirical generalization about what happens when we unite or divide aggregates is often false, whereas the arithmetical assertion that 3 + 1 = 4 never is.

Now although Husserl himself has little to say about the notion of truth which applies to propositions of arithmetic, it seems clear that he intended that they should be at least necessary truths, knowable *a priori*.[68] Husserl's is indeed, like Mill's, an aggregate theory of number formulated within the constraints of an overall empiricism. But, unlike Mill's, it includes an essentially *formalist* component, and it is this (as we saw above, pp. 73–5) that enables Husserl to avoid the implausible conclusion that arithmetical assertions are based on induction and allow of exceptions. At the heart of his analysis of arithmetical practices and procedures, that is, lies his account of how we manipulate signs forming a recursive progression, and how we correlate one-to-one elements of this progression both with elements in the progression, and with items outside it. In this way Husserl manages to allow that the truths of arithmetic are necessary truths while at the same time explaining the possibility of their application to non-mathematical reality.

(IIIa) That Husserl identifies numbers with ideas.

Husserl's greatest crime in the *Philosophy of Arithmetic*, according to Frege, is his attempt to provide a 'psychological' foundation for arithmetic. This attempt supposedly rests on Husserl's identification of numbers with 'ideas', and it is from this source that there flow all the evils which Frege devoted his life's work to fighting. Frege argues powerfully that such a doctrine will be quite unable to provide any cogent explanation (a) of large numbers, (b) of the objectivity of arithmetic, (c) of the universal applicability of number, (d) of the necessity of arithmetical truths, (e) of the nature of arithmetical proof, or (f) of the relation between arithmetic and logic.[69] Frege's attack on psychologism, on the relevance of subjectivity, introspection, intuition, or the appeal to what is 'private' has indeed been vastly influential within the so-called analytic tradition in philosophy; and many of his arguments and objections are cogent and totally persuasive. But in the present context they are simply irrelevant; for Husserl does not identify numbers with subjective 'ideas', and does not attempt to provide a 'psychological' foundation for logic or arithmetic.

The shortest rebuttal of the claim that Husserl transposes everything into the subjective mode by identifying numbers with ideas is to point out that, as a matter of fact, Husserl did not identify numbers with *any* sort of object: numbers are not objects for Husserl; they are not individual, self-subsistent entities of any sort, whether material, mental, phenomenal, abstract, or any other. They are, rather, *formal properties* of aggregates. Arithmetic is the formal science of these properties, and Husserl can consistently maintain that, where valid, its results are objective, necessarily true, applicable universally, and knowable *a priori*.

We have already seen that Husserl's philosophy of arithmetic was intended to comprise two major, complementary investigations. The first was epistemological, and concerned the ('subjective') origin and nature of *our grasp of* arithmetical concepts. The second was to have been a 'logical investigation' dealing with the 'objective' aspects of arithmetic. And nothing but confusion has resulted from the misguided attempt to construe Husserl's remarks about intuitions, concepts, presentations, and mental acts as if they were intended to comprise an explanation of such notions as *objectivity*, *truth*, *reference*, *proof*, and *existence* in arithmetic.[70]

Grounds for dissatisfaction

The first volume of the *Philosophy of Arithmetic* appeared in 1891. Some three years later Husserl was still optimistic that he could complete the second volume, and provide therewith an account of the 'logical' or objective aspects of the foundations of arithmetic.[71] But at some point in 1895 he changed his mind, coming to believe that the project was unworkable and that it would have to be abandoned. It is by no means immediately clear, however, exactly why Husserl came to this conclusion, or precisely which elements of his original programme he now found objectionable. Moreover his own occasional pronouncements on this matter are often profoundly misleading: his next major work, the *Logical Investigations* (1900–1), for instance, hints strongly that the earlier programme was contaminated by something called 'psychologism', and that it was abandoned for that reason. 'As regards my [present] explicit criticism of psychologistic logic and epistemology', he wrote in the *Logical Investigations*, 'I would recall the saying of Goethe: There is nothing on which one is more severe than the errors one has just abandoned' (*LU* Foreword (first ed.)/p.43). But this remark is doubly misleading. In the first place the *Philosophy of Arithmetic* is nowhere guilty of the 'psychologism' Husserl subsequently found so objectionable; and in the second place, psychological investigations of the sort *actually* carried out in that work (investigations belonging to Brentanian descriptive phenomenology) far from being repudiated, are explicitly endorsed and further developed in the *Logical Investigations*.

But if not for its supposed psychologism, then why was the *Philosophy of Arithmetic* shelved? There are, I think, four reasons.

First, and at the most general level, Husserl came to see that the perspective within which the project as a whole had originally been conceived was too narrow. An investigation of the logical, symbolic, and objective aspects of *arithmetical* knowledge, he realized, must remain unacceptably naive in the absence of an antecedent understanding of (say) the nature of logic, language, knowledge, meaning, existence, and truth *in general*; and in 1895 it was precisely this understanding that Husserl lacked. The *Logical Investigations* is the direct result of his attempt to fill this need, to provide, that is, an entirely general account of the most fundamental concepts required in *any* theory of objective, rational knowledge. As Husserl himself puts it: 'I was eventually compelled to lay aside my philosophical–mathematical investigations until I had succeeded in reaching a certain clearness on the basic questions of epistemology and in the critical understanding of logic as a science' (*LU* Foreword (first ed.)/p.43).

Second, as Husserl began to broaden the scope of his inquiry he came to see that the relations between arithmetic, mathematics in general, and logic are more intimate than he had at first suspected, indeed that arithmetic is ultimately merely a part of a *mathesis universalis*.[72] In the first volume of the *Philosophy of Arithmetic*, that is, Husserl had proceeded on the assumption, inherited from his teacher Weierstrass, that 'pure arithmetic (or pure analysis) is a science based entirely and exclusively on the concept of cardinal number. It needs no other kind of presupposition . . .'.[73] But as Husserl's investigation into the logical aspects of arithmetic progressed, it became clear, as he wrote to Stumpf, that

> the opinion by which I was still guided in [volume one of the *Philosophy of Arithmetic*], to the effect that the concept of cardinal number forms the foundation of general arithmetic, soon proved false.

. . . The fact is that 'general arithmetic' (including analysis, theory of functions, etc.) finds *application to* the cardinals (in 'number theory'), as well as to the ordinals, to continuous quantities, and to *n*-fold extensions (time, space, colour, force continua, etc.).[74]

And in the same letter he adds that '*arithmetica universalis* is no science, but rather a segment of formal logic.' To put it crudely, then, the movement in Husserl's thought concerning the foundations of arithmetic during the period 1890 to 1900 began with the assumption that arithmetic was a special science with its own unique subject matter, comprising the cardinal numbers and all that could be constructed on their basis; and it concluded in the view that arithmetic has no substantive subject matter of its own, and is ultimately indistinguishable from pure logic. (We shall see in the next chapter how Husserl's conception of formal logic itself also underwent considerable concomitant change during this period.)

A third reason for the abandonment of the programme of the *Philosophy of Arithmetic* concerns Husserl's increasing disenchantment with the form of empiricism adopted in that work, and in particular with the inability of 'sensualism' to account adequately for our knowledge of abstract, purely formal, *a priori* truths. Following Brentano, Husserl had assumed that all presentations and concepts originate ultimately in concrete intuitions belonging to outer sense. But, as indeed Kant had long since argued, such a view tends to '*sensualize* all concepts of the understanding, i.e. interpret them as nothing more than empirical or abstracted concepts of reflection'.[75] We can only guess as to the motives which led Husserl to modify his earlier account of how intuitions are related to concepts – especially to formal concepts or 'categories' – but in any event the *Logical Investigations* advances a theory of categorial intuition that goes beyond anything to be found in the *Philosophy of Arithmetic*.

The fourth, and I think by far the most significant failure of Husserl's first project, is its inherent inability to reconcile claims concerning subjectivity (about intuitions, presentations, concepts, judgements, abstraction etc.) with claims concerning objectivity (about numbers, objects, existence, truth, validity, and the like); and the root cause of this inability lies in the doctrine of intentionality that Husserl had taken over from the young Brentano, and according to which the object of a mental act is merely an in-existent, immanent *content* of consciousness. For if a state of consciousness is only ever *of* its own immanent contents, then clearly the possibility of any intelligible relation between consciousness and an external, non-mental reality becomes remote. In the Foreword to the *Logical Investigations* Husserl writes that, in moving from the 'psychological' to the 'logical' part of the *Philosophy of Arithmetic*, he realized that 'no true continuity or unity could be established':

I became more and more disquieted by doubts of principle, as to how to reconcile the objectivity of mathematics, and of all science in general, with a psychological foundation for logic . . . and I felt myself more and more pushed towards general critical reflections on the essence of logic, and on the relationship, in particular, between the subjectivity of knowing and the objectivity of the content known. (*LU* Foreword (first ed.)/p.42)

And elsewhere he wrote that, after the completion of the *Philosophy of Arithmetic*,

I was tormented by incomprehensible new worlds: the world of pure logic, and the world of act-consciousness . . . . *I did not know how to unite them*, yet they had to have some relation to one another, and form an inner unity.[76]

In his earlier work, in other words, Husserl had provided a theory of 'the subjectivity of knowing' involved in arithmetical knowledge, and also, at least embryonically, a theory concerning the objectivity of the content of arithmetic. What he very soon came to realize, however, was that 'no true continuity or unity could be established' between these two theories – as long, that is, as intentionality remained an exclusively intra-mental relation holding between mental acts and their 'subjective' contents.[77] One of the major contributions of the *Logical Investigations* is a new account of intentionality specifically designed to overcome this defect.

The perceived inadequacies in Husserl's early project for a philosophical investigation of the foundations of arithmetic comprise together a set of interlocking problems to whose solution Husserl devoted the next thirty years of his life; but chief amongst them is the problem of reconciling the subjective and the objective aspects of rational knowledge, by the provision of a theory of mind, on the one hand, and a theory of truth on the other, and by showing how each is related to and compatible with the other. Throughout the rest of his career Husserl struggled to reconcile what, in the *Philosophy of Arithmetic*, he had called the 'psychological' and the 'logical' aspects involved in all knowledge. In the *Logical Investigations* he asked:

How *can* that which is intrinsically objective become a presentation, and thus, so to speak, something subjective? What does it mean to say that an object exists both 'in itself' and 'given' in knowledge? How can the ideal nature of what is universal, [for example] a concept or a law, enter the stream of real mental events and become an item of knowledge for a thinking person? . . . Now clearly these and similar questions are inseparable from . . . those concerning the clarification of pure logic; for the task of clarifying logical ideas like *concept, object, truth, proposition, fact, law*, and the like itself leads ineluctably to the former questions. (*LU* Introd. to Vol II, §2/p.254)

And in 'Philosophy as Rigorous Science' he asked, again,

> How can experience as consciousness give or contact an object? How
> can experiences be mutually legitimated or corrected by each other,
> and not merely replace each other, or confirm each other subjectively?
> How can the play of consciousness whose logic is empirical make
> objectively valid statements, valid for all things that exist in and of
> themselves? . . . How is natural science to be comprehensible . . .
> to the extent that it pretends at every step to posit and to know a
> nature that is in itself – in itself, in contrast to the subjective flow of
> consciousness? (*PRS*, in *HSW* p.172)

Husserl eventually came to believe that the reconciliation of the objectivity
and the subjectivity of knowing could never be effected within a purely
naturalistic framework, and that any final reconciliation would necessitate
the adoption of a transcendental point of view. For the moment, however,
our concern remains with Husserl's naturalistic philosophy, the most
complex and sophisticated expression of which is to be found in the
Logical Investigations.[78]

II

Logical Investigations

Introduction

At this point, before turning to an examination of Husserl's thought in the *Logical Investigations*, the text of that work itself requires some introductory comment; for amongst other things it is appallingly long (in the definitive Husserliana edition, for instance, it comprises over 1,000 pages), it is badly written, poorly organized, and not always obviously consistent.

As a rough initial guide to this labyrinth we can, I think, see it as made up of three distinct book-length studies. The first, entitled *Prolegomena to Pure Logic*, presents and defends a particular conception of the nature of formal logic. The science of logic studies 'the laws of rational thought', but, according to Husserl, this entails neither that it is a mere empirical science resulting in contingent generalizations about how rational thought in fact proceeds, nor that it is at bottom a practical discipline resulting in normative laws governing how rational thought should proceed. Rather, Husserl claims, logic is a purely formal science whose subject matter comprises abstract, non-spatio-temporal entities, and whose results are *a priori*, timeless, and entirely general truths.

Taken together Investigations I–IV make up the second 'sub-work' discernible within the *Logical Investigations* as a whole, in so far as each of these investigations addresses problems concerning the *objectivity* of logic as Husserl conceives it. It is here, for example, that he introduces and defends a theory of syntax, of semantics, of abstract entities, of wholes and parts, and so forth. Here, in other words, Husserl's primary focus is on 'the objectivity of the content known' (cf. *Crisis* §68/p.234).

The third 'sub-work' encompasses Investigations V and VI, respectively entitled 'On Intentional Experiences and their "Contents"' and 'Elements of a Phenomenological Elucidation of Knowledge', in which Husserl turns to problems concerning 'the subjectivity of knowing'. The most important of these are (i) the problem of accounting for the intentionality of consciousness without thereby restricting its access merely to its own in-existent contents, and (ii) the problem of reconciling the claim that logic deals with abstract and hence non-sensible entities, with the claim that, nevertheless, objective knowledge of such entities is possible. Clearly the solution of (i) requires that some modification be made to the earlier theory of intentionality, while the solution of (ii) equally clearly requires modification of Husserl's earlier brand of empiricism, and in particular of his early account of abstraction.

It is important to recognize, however, that such specific doctrinal modifications as these nevertheless take place within an overall theoretical and methodological framework that remains constant throughout the *Philosophy of Arithmetic* and the *Logical Investigations*; for both are essentially works of Brentanian descriptive psychology or phenomenology. In the first edition of the *Logical Investigations*, for example, Husserl is quite explicit about this:

> Phenomenology *is* descriptive psychology. Epistemological criticism is, therefore, in essence psychology, or at least is only capable of being built on a psychological basis. *Pure logic therefore also rests on psychology.* (*LU* Introd. to Vol II, §6/p.262. My italics)

Now this is confusing. On the one hand Husserl's *Prolegomena* is devoted, above all else and at very great length, to the refutation of psychologism: to showing the incoherence of any attempt to provide either an interpretation or a justification of logical theory that is couched in ineliminably psychological or mentalistic terms. And yet, on the other hand, the following six investigations are intended to vindicate the claim that the *only* adequate understanding and justification of pure logic is that provided by psychology. No wonder Husserl's earliest critics were baffled.[1]

In fact the resolution of this apparent contradiction is a straightforward matter: we have merely to note that Husserl continues, infuriatingly, to use the term 'psychology' in two quite different senses. On the one hand, as we saw earlier,[2] it is the name of an empirical science similar to botany, zoology, or anthropology, while on the other hand it is the name of a distinctively philosophical inquiry which takes its starting point in 'phenomena'. And no contradiction arises from Husserl's rejecting the former while at the same time accepting the latter as integral to any adequate explanation or justification of logical theory.

What is not in the least a straightforward or simple matter, however, is the status of the assertions made *within* descriptive psychology or phenomenology. For if that discipline restricts its domain of discourse to *phenomena*, then clearly assertions made within it about objects and states of affairs existing in the external world, as indeed about the objectivity of our reference to and judgements about them, will remain ultimately as problematic as they were for the author of the *Philosophy of Arithmetic*, and for precisely the same reason. The issue is a complex and sensitive one, but I postpone explicit treatment of it for the moment; for first we need to know something of Husserl's doctrines concerning the nature of logic and the concepts constitutive of it.

The nature of logic

For us, now, in the last quarter of the twentieth century, the nature of logic – that is, of the discipline of formal, deductive logic – is very largely unproblematic: it is a pure science devoted to the investigation and codification of relations of deductive consequence holding between sentences, or perhaps between the thoughts or propositions they express. And in this connection we understand the need to distinguish (proof theoretic) relations of syntactic consequence and (model theoretic) relations of semantic consequence; there is a general consensus as to how issues concerning, say, formal schemata, calculi, interpretation, truth, validity, consistency, and completeness are related one to the other; and today we can be clearer than ever before about how, if at all, the subject matter of logic is related to that of other disciplines like psychology, mathematics, set theory, ontology, epistemology, or linguistics.

This was not, however, the situation in which philosophers like Schröder, Peirce, Husserl, Frege, and Russell found themselves – philosophers, that is, who concerned themselves with logical theory and the foundations of mathematics around the turn of the century. On the contrary, for them logic was still in the melting pot: not only its proper scope, subject matter, concepts and methods, but also its standing with respect to mathematics, psychology and (what today we would call) the theory of meaning were all problems yet to be solved, some of them even problems yet to be recognized. It is to the formulation and solution of just such problems as these that Husserl addresses himself in the *Logical Investigations*.[3] His investigations, in other words, belong, not within deductive logic itself, but to a second-order discipline that coincides, more or less, with what is known today as the philosophy of logic.[4]

Husserl employs the term 'logic' and its cognates in a wide and confusing variety of senses. At one extreme, for example, he uses it to refer to something as specific as traditional syllogistic, or the formal study of linguistic patterns of valid inference, while at the other extreme the term seems to encompass nothing less than a full-blown Kantian 'critique of the possibility of knowledge in general'.[5] We can begin to make some sense of this diversity if we introduce, on Husserl's behalf, a distinction between a discipline called 'formal' or 'pure' logic, and something called 'philosophical' logic.[6]

Pure logic

This investigates what we might call *the formal conditions of rationality as such*, and for Husserl this means that it studies formally the necessary conditions of any rational thought whatsoever, irrespective, that is, of what such thought might be about. But, we need to ask, what does 'rationality' or 'rational thought' mean in this context? The question is embarassing in its generality. Still, without attempting anything like a definitive answer, we can perhaps say as a working hypothesis that one approaches an ideal of discursive rationality in so far as one aims at the acquisition of beliefs all of which are true and to each of which one is justified in subscribing. On this conception, then, rationality is an intentional notion: it is not whether one's beliefs are in fact true, but whether one intends them to be true, taking every appropriate means to ensure that they are, that is the final measure of one's degree of rationality. So in certain circumstances it can be entirely rational to believe something that is actually false, to discount evidence that is in fact pertinent, to trust a proof that eventually turns out to be invalid, and so on.

Now broadly speaking the formal constraints which a set of beliefs, thoughts, or judgements must meet if it is to be rational in this sense are of three kinds. First, the individual judgements themselves must be well-formed and significant. And according to Husserl the first task of pure logic is the discovery and codification of 'the pure forms of possible judgements':

> This theory of the pure forms of judgement is the intrinsically first discipline of formal logic . . . . It concerns *the mere possibility of judgements, as judgements*, without inquiry whether they are true or false, or even whether they are compatible or contradictory. (*FTL* §13(a)/p.50)

There are two complementary and, ultimately, inseparable aspects to this branch of logical theory. On the one side there are considerations concerning the forms of possible judgements or assertions: Husserl calls this aspect of logic the investigation of the *formal categories of meaning* (i.e. such concepts as proposition, concept, variable, name, sense, reference, and so forth); today we might call it a syntactico-semantic investigation. And, on the other side, there are considerations to do with, not the possible forms of significant judgement as such, but rather with the formal properties of items to which they might apply. This aspect of logic studies the *formal categories of objects* (i.e. such notions as object, state of affairs, aggregate, property, continuum, moment, number, and the like); we can follow Husserl in calling it 'formal ontology'.

The second major constraint on the rationality of a set of beliefs, considered formally, is that they should each be *grounded*. And in the present context this means that the beliefs should conform maximally to the appropriate formal laws governing notions like evidence, verification, and proof. One such species of formal law, corresponding to the categories of meaning, is the traditional law of thought, like the Law of Excluded Middle or the Law of Contradiction. Other such formal laws, corresponding to the formal ontological categories, are those relating parts to wholes, objects to aggregates, aggregates to numbers, dependent to independent objects, and so forth. While some of these laws are analytic (e.g. 'no judgement of the form *p and not-p* is true'), others, according to Husserl, are synthetic (e.g. 'if *a* and *b* are independent parts relative to some whole *W*, then *a* and *b* are independent relative to each other'); all, however, are *a priori*.

The categories of meaning and the corresponding categories of formal ontology together determine what it makes sense to say, or to think; they rule out sheer nonsense or gobbledygook (*Unsinn*). Conformity to the formal laws at the next level, on the other hand, rule out formal inconsistency or absurdity (*Widersinn*). Thus the judgements expressed by the sentences 'All *F*'s are *G*'s and some *F*'s are not *G*'s', say, or '2 + 4 = 7', although formally absurd are nevertheless significant and intelligible, the sentences themselves 'as genuine as any' (*LU* IV, §12/p.517). In contrast, nothing intelligible is expressed by an *unsinnig* string of signs like '2 > + +', or 'Some all is are'.[7]

According to Husserl, then, the first, most basic branch of formal logic isolates and clarifies the 'categories of meaning' along with the corresponding 'categories of objects' that are involved in the very possibility of significant judgement or meaningful language. At the second level, pure logic formulates those *a priori* laws conformity to which is a necessary and sufficient condition for the avoidance by meaningful judgements of formal absurdity or self-contradiction. Third, and finally, pure logic deals with the formal properties of *theories* or systems of beliefs considered as wholes; for there are constraints on rationality that impinge, not on individual beliefs considered in isolation, their well-formedness, significance, internal coherence and the like, but rather on entire sets of beliefs and the relations in which they stand to one another. The most obvious constraint here is that of consistency: one clearly falls short of at least one, traditional ideal of rationality to the extent that one can face with equanimity the existence of contradictory or incompatible elements within one's system of beliefs.

Husserl himself, however, has a stronger conception of rationality than the one we have employed so far. While it is, for him, a necessary condition of rationality that one's beliefs and judgements be significant, well-formed, grounded, and consistent, this is not yet a sufficient condition. His intuition seems to be that, at its highest level, rationality also requires *systematization*. In other words rational thought ultimately expresses itself in the achievement of a theoretical understanding of things, and not simply in the adoption of a mere unordered aggregate of beliefs about them, no matter how true or justified those beliefs may be: 'More is plainly required, namely *systematic coherence* in the theoretical sense, which means finding grounds for one's knowing, and suitably combining and ordering the sequence of such groundings. The essence of science therefore involves, not merely isolated pieces of knowledge, but unity in the whole system of grounded validations' (*LU Prol.*, §6/p.62). Theoretical understanding is of course expressed in *theories*, and for Husserl the ideal of rationality is most clearly and adequately realized in a complete, consistent, axiomatic theory. He later wrote of the *Logical Investigations*:

> Since the concept of theory was [there] intended to be understood in the pregnant sense – in conformity with the nomological or deductive sciences – that is to say, as a systematic connection of propositions in the form of a systematically unitary deduction, a beginning was found there for a theory of deductive systems, or, in other words, a logical discipline relating to the deductive sciences as deductive and considered as theoretical *wholes*. The earlier level of logic had taken for its theme the pure forms of all significant formations that . . . can occur *within* a science. Now, however, *judgement systems in their entirety* become the theme. (*FTL* §28/p.90)

Finally, then, pure logic culminates, at what Husserl calls 'its highest level', in the investigation of the formal properties of possible theories. Logic becomes, in other words, 'the theory of theories' or 'the purely formal theory of science as such'. It is the science that studies the possible forms of any systematic, rational knowledge whatsoever, regardless of the material content of that knowledge.[8]

The distinction between categories of meaning and formal ontological categories is carried forward to this final level, where it appears as a distinction between, on the one hand, the formal properties of a theory, and, on the other hand, the formal properties of any *field* for which that theory is valid:

> The objective correlate of the concept of a possible theory, determined exclusively in terms of its form, is the concept of *a possible field of knowledge over which a theory of this form will preside*. But such a field is known to mathematicians as *a manifold*; a manifold is thus a field which is uniquely determined by falling under a theory of such a form, i.e., by the fact that its objects are capable of *certain* combinations that fall under *certain* basic laws of such-and-such a *determinate* form (which is here the sole determining factor). The

objects remain entirely indeterminate as regards their matter . . . .
These laws, then, as they determine a *field* and its *form*, likewise
determine the theory to be constructed, or more correctly, *the
theory's form*. (*LU Prol.*, §70/p.241)

Although the matter is not entirely clear, it does appear that Husserl here
at least anticipates the modern distinction between proof theoretic and
model theoretic investigations of formal systems. At the highest level of
generality pure logic is, it seems, the metalogical study of the formal
properties, both syntactic and semantic, of formal logical systems. And if
this is right, then Husserl's conception of logic was more sophisticated
and modern than those of his contemporaries Frege and Russell.[9]

Philosophical Logic

All the syntactic, semantic, logical, and metalogical laws and principles
that together comprise pure, formal logic are, Husserl writes, 'the merely
negative conditions of the possibility of truth':[10]

> An act of judgement which violates these conditions can never result in
> truth . . . . But on the other hand, even if it satisfies the require-
> ments of these laws it does not *thereby* attain its goal . . . . Accord-
> ingly, this insight compels us to ask what must be added, over and
> above these formal conditions of the possibility of truth, if a cognitive
> act is to reach its goal.

He then immediately adds:

> These supplementary conditions lie on the subjective side, and concern
> the subjective characteristics of intuitability, of self-evidence, and the
> subjective conditions of its attainment . . . . The problems of logic
> are determined from the outset as *two-sided* . . . . On the one side
> we have the question of the constitution of forms and their laws and,
> on the other, that of the subjective conditions of the attainment
> of self-evidence.

Now it is perhaps not immediately clear why Husserl takes the fact that
formal logic supplies merely necessary conditions of rational thought to
imply the need for an investigation into the subjective characteristics of
self-evidence. Why the turn to subjectivity here? And whence the sudden
importance of 'self-evidence'? There are a number of different trains of
thought that converge at this point.

Logic in general, we have said, investigates the conditions of the
possibility of rational thought; and pure logic is concerned with the
constraints which thoughts (judgements, assertions, theories, etc.) must
meet, in respect of their form, if they are to be rational. Rationality is not,
however, an exclusively formal matter: one can have a set of consistent

beliefs, each of which conforms to the formal laws governing structure, internal coherence and the like, and yet remain quite beyond the bounds of reason. For instance, I contravene no formal law of logic if I have a straightforward, unproblematic perception of a green object and judge that it is red. So some exploration is needed here of the notion of rationality as it concerns the *material content* of our beliefs and judgements, rather than their mere logical form:

> it is not sufficient that, in some way, some objects or other are given in advance and that the act of judgement is directed towards them . . . merely in conformity with the rules and principles prescribed by logic with respect to their *form*. Rather, the success of the cognitive performance also makes demands on the modes of pregivenness of the objects themselves, with respect to their *content*. (*EU* §4/p.19)

This exploration will concern 'subjectivity' in so far as it necessarily addresses problems to do with perception, intuition, experience and the like, as the sources and as the justifying grounds of such material content.

A second, closely related train of thought is this: the concept of rationality is intimately connected to the notion of *evidence* – construed for the moment broadly enough to encompass whatever grounds, reasons, arguments, and proofs we validly appeal to in the justification of our beliefs. Evidence, in general, can be either transitive or, so to speak, reflexive: in the first case the obtaining of one state of affairs is evidence for that of another; in the second case, a state of affairs is said to be self-evident. Now as we saw earlier,[11] there are pressures to construe the possibility of transitive evidence as itself dependent on the prior availability of self-evidence. The pressure comes from two directions. On the one side there is the need – not universally, but very widely felt – to provide an absolute rather than a merely 'internal' grounding for one's system of beliefs. In the absence of genuine self-evidence, it is felt, the unpleasant possibility opens up that no matter how great the amount of evidence we possess for our beliefs, those beliefs will still be ultimately groundless. The obtaining of some state of affairs, a, may be conclusive evidence for that of another, b; but the judgement 'b obtains because a obtains' itself can provide no stronger grounds for the belief in b's obtaining than the strength of the grounds we have, quite independently, for believing that a obtains. As for this latter belief, we as yet have *no* grounds for it; it in turn requires evidence of its own; and so too does anything adduced in evidence of *it*, and so on. Only something that is evident but whose evidence is *independent*, can put a stop to this regression, and thereby make intelligible the possibility of a system of beliefs that is genuinely grounded.[12] And on the other side, there is the familiar pressure to emphasize the fundamental importance of self-evidence when one considers the nature and utility of formalized theories:

> However formal a proof procedure may be, the trustworthiness of the
> theorems that it generates still depends ultimately upon our conviction
> that each of the axioms is logically valid.[13]

The utility of a formalization of some branch of (putative) knowledge
depends in part upon the assumptions, axioms, postulates, and
presuppositions on the basis of which proof proceeds, but whose truth is
incapable of proof within the system itself. In the last resort, it is felt, the
only possible warrant for the adoption of such axioms and assumptions is
their *self*-evidence. But 'self-evidence' is itself an epistemological notion;
and 'for this very reason the . . . work of the special sciences . . . is in
need of a continuous "epistemological" reflection and critique which only
the philosopher can provide' (*LU Prol.*, §71/p.245). For Husserl, then,
the 'objective' and exclusively formal discipline of pure logic stands in
need of a complementary investigation into the 'subjective' and also the
material aspects of rational thought. If we call this latter discipline
'philosophical logic', then the greater part of the *Logical Investigations*
belongs within it – as indeed does the vast majority of Husserl's subsequent work.

Formal ontology

According to Eugen Fink, throughout Husserl's writings 'the concept of
"ontology" is to be taken in a narrow sense in relation to the contemporary [i.e. Heideggerian] use of the word, in as much as it does not mean
a philosophical determination of being *qua* being, but rather an *a priori*
eidetic of object realms and, more particularly, an eidetic in the naively
thematic "straightforward attitude"'.[14] If we take the phrase 'an *a priori*
eidetic of object realms in the naively thematic "straightforward attitude"'
to mean an investigation, from a naturalistic point of view, of possible,
purely formal categories and structures of objects, then Fink's remark
accurately characterizes one of the aims of the *Logical Investigations* , and
in particular the aim of Investigation III. The aim characterizes 'formal
ontology'.[15]

The term 'object' is unfortunate here, however, for it can carry suggestions, on the one hand, of materiality – objects it might be thought are
paradigmatically such things as tables and chairs, molecules and planets –
and it can suggest, on the other hand, a quite specific ontological category
that stands over against other ontological categories like *function,
property, event*, or *state of affairs*. Both suggestions should, however, be
resisted; for in Husserl's hands *object* is simply the ontological *summum
genus*, the broadest, least specific ontological category there is. An object
is just an entity of some sort, a something-or-other, an
anything-whatsoever.[16] And this means, in the absence of any further

specification or limitation, that the results of formal ontology will encompass material, mental, abstract, theoretical, intentional, and even fictional 'objects'. It should perhaps be stressed that formal ontology, 'the pure (*a priori*) theory of objects', is an integral part of formal logic, and not, as some recent commentators have suggested, an independent discipline whose canons and commitments differ radically from those of formal logic.[17] For Husserl, that is, formal logic as a whole comprises both formal apophantics (which we can say, albeit anachronistically, would include essentially the propositional and predicate calculi, and perhaps modal logic), and formal ontology (which includes number theory, set theory, aggregate theory, abstract geometry, mereology, and the like). These last mentioned sub-disciplines are formal in the sense that they abstract from all empirical, material or contingent characteristics of objects; but they are nevertheless ontological, not apophantic, in that they concern fields of *objects* rather than the judgements we make about them. The pursuit of formal ontology, like that of formal logic as a whole, is thus a task that falls properly to the mathematician or mathematical logician, and not at all to the philosopher whose dominant concerns are epistemological (*LU Prol.* §71/p.244). The question arises, therefore, as to why, in a work explicitly addressed to philosophical and epistemological problems, Husserl should feel the need, in Investigation III, to embark upon an inquiry of a quite different kind – one whose results belong *within* formal logic. In this respect Investigation III is clearly the odd man out.[18]

The Introduction to Investigation III is in effect an explanation of, and an apology for, this excursion into pure logic. Husserl explains there that the digression is necessary because there are a number of concepts and laws properly belonging within formal ontology that he will require in his subsequent attempts to solve genuine philosophical problems. Now normally when one needs to employ results belonging to some formal science, that need is met by the availability of an already established body of theory concerning the concepts and laws in question: if one needs to employ notions like *number*, *set*, or *n-dimensional space*, for instance, then one can simply turn to arithmeticians, mathematical logicians, or geometers, who can supply from stock, so to speak, sophisticated, abstract theories concerning such things. There exists, however, (or existed when Husserl wrote)[19] no such body of results concerning the formal relations of dependence and independence in which parts and wholes stand to one another. And yet Husserl intended to use the machinery of whole-part analysis – just as he had in the *Philosophy of Arithmetic* – as his main analytic tool. So, in spite of the fact that, as Husserl says, 'we are not here engaged on a systematic exposition of logic, but on an epistemological clarification', at this point we nevertheless need to do some logic; for as Husserl somewhat testily remarks:

we cannot here allow our analytic investigation to await the systematic development of our subject matter . . . . Difficult notions employed by us in our clarificatory study of knowledge . . . cannot be left unexamined until such time as they emerge within . . . logic itself. (*LU* III, Introd./p.435)

There is thus no alternative: concerning the difference between dependent and independent objects, and the formal relations of parts and wholes, 'we cannot avoid going into these questions in some detail' (*ibid*).

Husserl's formal ontology, like Frege's, allows of just two primitive ontological categories: there are entities that are self-sufficient or complete (*selbständig*), in the sense that they are intrinsically capable of existing alone; and there are those entities that are ontologically dependent or incomplete (*unselbständig*) and which thus require completion by, or in, something else in order to exist. But in contrast to Frege, whose ontological taxonomy was in the last analysis merely a reflection of the categories in terms of which he had articulated his logical-syntax, Husserl appears at this time to have formulated his ontological theory as a direct expression of brute ontological intuition.[20] One way to illustrate the force of such pre-theoretical ontological intuitions concerning relations of dependence and independence between entities is to consider certain suppositions of the form: *the universe might have consisted in a single such-and-such*. Many suppositions of this form, though no doubt empirically false, are at least intelligible. One can coherently conceive of a so-called 'pocket universe' consisting of nothing but an ashtray, say, or of nothing but two spherical objects of equal mass and equal diameter having equal but opposite angular momentum. But it is unintelligible to suppose that the universe might have consisted of nothing but a size, a similarity, a husband, or a surface. 'You can't *just* have a size,' one wants to say, 'there has to be something of which it *is* the size.' Likewise, for there to be such a thing as a husband there has to be something, a wife, whose husband he is; for a similarity to exist there must exist whatever it is between which the similarity obtains, and so on. When God created the universe he could not, so to speak, have *begun* by creating just a size, or a husband, or a surface. Of their very nature certain things, it seems, can only exist in (or between, or in relation to) one or more other things.

The foregoing distinction between dependent and independent entities is, according to Husserl, 'absolute'. He means that it is primitive, exhaustive, and exclusive: everything whatsoever falls under one, and only one, of those irreducible categories. The distinction between *wholes* and *parts*, on the other hand, is a 'relative' one: there are circumstances in which we are free to consider certain parts as themselves wholes having parts, and certain wholes as themselves parts of some larger whole.

It is important in this context to note that Husserl's use of the term 'part' is, like his use of the word 'object', as inclusive and indiscriminate as possible. Just as an object is anything whatsoever, regardless of its nature or category, so a part of an object is *'anything* that can be distinguished in an object . . . or that is present in it . . . or that truly helps to make it up' (*LU* III, §2/p.437). Husserl's determination to 'interpret the word "part" in its *widest* sense' is both explicit and well motivated. The enterprise in which he is engaged is formal ontology, that is, the *a priori* investigation of the relations of dependence and independence in which anything can stand to anything else. And if that enterprise is to be genuinely formal, then it must abstract entirely from all material constraints and determinations. This means that we must, for example, resist the temptation to think of the relations of constitution – the relations in which a complex whole can stand to its constitutive elements – exclusively or even predominantly in terms of the quite specific relation in which a material object stands to the material bits of which it is made. 'Not every part is included in its whole in the same fashion, and not every part is woven together with every other, in the unity of a whole, in the same way' (*LU* III, §15/p.465).

If we now combine the distinction between dependent and independent entities with that between wholes and parts we obtain a fourfold classification, into (i) things that are *independent wholes*, that is, complex, unitary entities capable in principle of existing alone. Husserl calls such things 'concreta' or 'concrete objects'. There are (ii) *dependent wholes* or complex parts; entities, that is, which are ultimately partial because they lack ontological autonomy, but which can be considered as wholes in so far as they allow analysis into parts. There are (iii) *independent parts*, entities which go to make up some whole, but which do not depend for their existence on their participation in that whole. As Husserl points out, in everyday talk the word 'part' is normally reserved for use in this sense – the sense in which, for example, a particular brick is a part of a wall, or the earth is a part of the solar system. Husserl employs the term 'piece' (*Stück*) for a part of this kind. And finally (iv) there are *dependent parts* or *moments*, that is, entities which contribute to the constitution of some complex unity but which, unlike 'pieces', are intrinsically incapable of existing in isolation:

> Each part that is independent relatively to a whole W we call a piece (portion); each part that is dependent relatively to W we call a moment (an abstract part) of W. It makes no difference here whether the whole itself, considered absolutely, or in relation to a higher whole, is independent or not. Accordingly, abstract parts can in their turn have pieces, and pieces in their turn abstract parts.
> (*LU* III, §17/p.467)

So much for the formal categories that comprise the kernel of Husserl's ontology. At this point it remains, of course, an open question, a question of *applied* ontology, whether any (and if so, exactly what) objects fall under them. Nevertheless we can now use those categories to define a number of derivative notions. An aggregate, for instance, is merely a whole, all of whose proper parts are independent; and what we earlier called a strong whole, or individual 'thing', [21] is a whole all of whose parts are dependent – either reciprocally, one on another, or each on the whole that they constitute – and none of which is dependent on anything but that whole or its proper parts. Husserl calls this 'the pregnant concept of a whole' (cf. *LU* III, §21/p.475). Finally, the important relation of ontological *foundation* can be defined as follows: '*x* is founded upon *y*' means the same as '*x* is ontologically dependent on *y*'; and '*x* is founded' means '*x* is ontologically dependent' (*LU* III, §14/p.463). Any given whole is, trivially, founded on its parts: it would not be *that* whole if it were not made up of just those parts. More interestingly, however, as we will see, there are foundational relations that run in the opposite direction, between the parts and the whole they comprise, as also between the various parts themselves.

The foregoing contextual definition of a foundation is, however, almost entirely unhelpful; for although it provides a means of translating sentences containing terms like 'foundation' and 'founded upon' into synonymous sentences that do not contain those terms, we have as yet only the vaguest pre-theoretical grasp of what those elucidatory sentences are themselves supposed to mean. We have, moreover, as yet no idea whether there is any restriction, and if so, what, on the terms that can be substituted for '*x*' and '*y*' above. It is fortunate, therefore, that Husserl also provides at least the beginnings of a theoretical analysis of the notion.

The relation of ontological foundation holds, in the first instance, between kinds or 'species' of objects, and does so in virtue of *a priori* laws governing 'necessities of coexistence', that is, laws to the effect that the members of two species 'stand in relations of necessary association' (*LU* III, §14/p.463).[22] In other words it is only in a secondary, derivative sense that we can speak of an individual object as founding, or as founded upon, another: it is only in so far as an object is of a certain *kind* that it is capable of standing in foundational relations to another object of some kind (whether the kinds at issue are the same or different). According to Husserl: 'there is always an *a priori* law governing what is dependent [i.e. governing foundational relations], having its conceptual roots in what is universal in the whole and the part in question' (*LU* III, §10/p.453). And again: 'the necessities or laws which serve to define given types of dependent contents . . . rest on the species-essence of the contents, on their peculiar nature' (*LU* III, §11/p.455). So, for instance, Henry – just Henry, considered independently of any kind to which he might belong – cannot be said to stand in any foundational relations at all. But in so far as Henry is a husband, a father, an employer, or a murderer, there must exist certain other kinds of thing (a wife, an offspring, an employee, a victim) to which he is related foundationally. And as a human being, say, or again, as a spatio-temporal object, Henry may well be foundationally related in more complex, less obviously 'analytic' ways to such things as internal organs, pairs of parents, mental events, portions of space-time, and so forth.

In general, then, and at the most basic level, the goal of Husserlian formal ontology is the formulation of entirely general laws governing foundational relations that hold between certain kinds of objects, that is, objects in so far as they belong to certain species.[23] As a direct result a pre-eminent importance is assigned to the formal notion of *a φ as such*, or, equivalently, to the notion of *an object in so far as it belongs to a certain species*.[24] Now this notion is by no means of merely local interest because of the role it plays within the whole-part theory advanced in the *Logical Investigations*. On the contrary, the notion assumes a considerably wider significance as a consequence of Husserl's adoption, not only elsewhere in the *Logical Investigations* but throughout his philosophical career, of analytical procedures articulated in terms of, and justified by appeal to, that very theory of wholes and parts.

Perhaps the most important point to note here is that although the concept of *an object in so far as it belongs to a certain species* is indeed fundamental to Husserl's ontological theory, it is not itself an ontological category: there are no such things as 'objects-in-so-far-as-they-belong-to-certain-species'.[25] Substitution instances of the schema: *x qua* φ ('Henry, *qua* murderer', say, or 'The Pope, *qua* head of state') cannot be construed as singular referring expressions; for they create irreducibly intensional contexts in which co-extensional expressions cannot in general be exchanged *salva vertate*. If we take sentences of the form: *x, qua* φ *is*, ψ, as primitive, intersubstitution fails at both the φ and ψ places. Thus from

(1) Henry, *qua* husband, is entitled to a married man's tax allowance,

and

(2) All husbands are men,

we cannot infer

(3) Henry, *qua* man, is entitled to a married man's tax allowance.

And likewise,

(4) George, in so far as he is a bachelor, is an adult human being,

and

(5) Every adult human being has lungs,

do not together validly yield

(6) George, in so far as he is a bachelor, has lungs.

It appears, as a consequence of this, that expressions of the form '*x qua* φ' are best construed, not as genuine syntactic units, but rather as complex sentential fragments whose apparent unity breaks down under analysis. Simons has suggested, as an informal elucidation, that expressions of the form 'x qua φ' should be taken to have the force of: 'x is a φ, *and it is in virtue of being a φ that x . . .*'. This suggestion has the double virtue of indicating clearly the presence, and scope, of the intensional context, and of minimalizing the temptation to think we are here countenancing a strange, hybrid sort of entity called 'an-object-in-so-far-as-it-belongs-to-a-certain-species'.

Husserl believes that the discipline of formal ontology should ultimately yield 'a complete, law-determined survey of all the possibilities of complexity in the form of wholes and parts, and an exact knowledge of the relations possible in this sphere'; though he insists that his third Investigation represents nothing more than 'a small beginning' to such an enterprise. Nevertheless that Investigation does contain Husserl's attempt to formulate six basic theorems of whole-part theory.

Theorem I: If a φ as such needs to be founded on a ψ, then every whole having a φ, but not a ψ, as a part requires a similar foundation.[26]

Husserl adds: 'This proposition is axiomatically self-evident. If a φ cannot *be* except when completed by a ψ, a whole including a φ but no ψ cannot satisfy φ's need for supplementation, and must itself share that need.' But far from being axiomatically self-evident, as it stands Theorem I is simply false. It implies, for example, that if a married man cannot exist as such without there being someone who is his wife, then any whole that has a married man as a part depends for *its* existence on the existence of that man's wife. Fortunately this is very far from being the case: for otherwise every team, group, institution, committee, crew, or other whole containing a married man as a member would necessarily and instantaneously cease to exist the moment that man ceased to be married.

I think we must assume, charitably, that this is not what Husserl intended. Perhaps the most defensible suggestion as to how Theorem I might be modified, so as to render it both informative and true, is this: we add to it the requirement that the φ is, *as such*, a part of some whole – in other words, that it is in virtue of being a φ that the object in question belongs to a given whole. So the modified theorem runs:

Theorem I*:   If a φ as such needs to be founded on a ψ, then every whole having a φ as such as a part requires a similar foundation.

This suggestion blocks the formulation of counter-instances of the foregoing kind; for those counter-instances depend upon there being an absence of connection between an object's participation in some whole, and that object's belonging to a certain species – a form of independence ruled out by Theorem I*. As thus modified, however, the theorem is less interesting and more trivial than might at first appear. Because a whole is founded on its parts, Theorem I* asserts no more than that the relation of dependence is transitive. If a φ as such requires foundation in a ψ, and if some whole W has a φ as such as a part (i.e. if W requires foundation in a φ), then W will also require foundation in a ψ.

Theorem II: A whole which includes a dependent moment without including, as its part, the supplement which that moment demands, is likewise dependent – and is so relatively to every subordinate independent whole in which that dependent moment is contained.

This, as Husserl remarks, is merely a corollary of Theorem I, and adds nothing new to it.

Theorem III: If x is an independent part of y, then every independent part, z, of x is also an independent part of y.

Husserl claims that this theorem is entailed by Theorem I, and that it asserts the transitivity of the relation *being an independent part of*. I can make no sense of the proof Husserl himself provides of Theorem III; but in fact the theorem follows from Theorem I*, together with the claim that a whole depends upon its parts, whether dependent or independent.

Theorem IV: If x is a dependent part of a whole, y, it is also a dependent part of any other whole of which y is a part.

This asserts the transitivity of the relation *is a dependent part of*, and its proof is similar to that of Theorem III.

Theorem V: A relatively dependent object is also absolutely dependent, whereas a relatively independent object may be dependent in an absolute sense.

Although hardly a theorem, this proposition provides a useful gloss on the account we provided earlier of the distinction between dependent and independent parts of a given whole. A part that is independent relative to some whole may nevertheless not be independent *tout court*, for it may depend for its existence on some other whole. In contrast, a part that is dependent relative to some whole is absolutely dependent.

In this context it is worth noting that Husserl's ontological distinction between concrete and abstract objects is couched in terms of the distinction between dependent and independent parts. Indeed the notion of an abstract object is identified with that of a dependent part: 'An *abstractum simpliciter* is . . . an object in relation to which there is some whole of which it is a dependent part' (*LU* III, §17/p.468; cf. *LU* II, §41/p.428). And, correspondingly, an absolute *concretum* is just an object that is absolutely independent: 'Since the proposition holds that each absolutely independent content possesses abstract parts, each such content can also be looked on, and spoken of, as an absolute concretum.' Now these remarks of Husserl's serve to introduce a conception of the difference between abstract and concrete objects quite different from that (fundamentally Fregean) conception which has predominated within so-called analytic philosophy, and according to which an object is abstract in so far as it is causally inert – in so far, that is, as it is capable of neither causal agency nor causal sensitivity. In this latter sense abstract objects are imperceptible, immutable, and non-spatio-temporal. There is, however, nothing intrinsic to the Husserlian notion of an abstractum, or essentially non-selfsubsistent object, to prevent abstracta from entering into causal relations with other things, including perceivers, from undergoing change, or from possessing temporal and spatial properties. (Cf. *LU* II, §40/p.427).

Theorem VI: If x and y are independent parts of some whole, z, then they are also independent relative to each other.

Husserl's proof by *reductio* is succinct: 'if x required supplementation by y, or any part of y, there would be, in the range of parts determined by z certain parts (those of y) on which x would be founded. But in that case x would not be independent relative to its whole, z.' (*LU* III, §14/p.465). Like Theorems I*, II, III, and IV, Theorem VI is entailed by the transitivity of the part-whole relation. Indeed each of Husserl's mereological theorems (with the sole exception of V, which is merely an informal elucidation) is a consequence of the following two fundamental principles:

(1) If x is a part of y, and y is a part of z,
     then x is a part of z

and

(2) If x is a part of y, then y is founded on x.

What is, for present purposes, important about these principles and theorems is not so much the explicit treatment they receive in Investigation III, but rather the use to which Husserl puts them throughout the rest of the *Logical Investigations* and, indeed, throughout the rest of his subsequent works.

Meanings as objects

With the exception of the topics examined in the previous section, and which belong to formal ontology, a branch of pure logic, Husserl intended the *Logical Investigations* as a whole to provide a phenomenological clarification of the most basic notions upon which the

101

discipline of pure logic itself depends. He offers, that is, 'a series of analytic investigations that will deal with the constitutive ideas of a pure or formal logic' (*LU* Introd. to vol.II, §5/p.259). And in these investigations one concept stands out as both more fundamental and more problematic than any other: the concept of *meaning*.

The importance of meaning for Husserl's enterprise is signalled by his observation that 'pure logic, wherever it deals with concepts, judgements, or syllogisms, is exclusively concerned with the *ideal* unities that we here call "meanings"' (*LU* I, §29/p.322). To understand this we need to know, amongst other things, what 'ideal unities' are (the topic of Investigation II), and what solutions Husserl offers to problems concerning both the 'subjective' and the 'objective' aspects of meaning (matters dealt with in Investigations V and VI, and in Investigations I and IV, respectively). In the present section I shall be concerned with the claim that meanings are 'ideal unities' or 'ideal objects'.

As we noted earlier, Husserl employs the term 'object' in the widest possible sense; a sense in which anything whatsoever is an object – whether it be, for instance, an act, a state of affairs, a property, a material thing, a moment, or a meaning. Now throughout the *Logical Investigations* there is presupposed a taxonomy of objects that we need to get clear about at this point. Its major categorial articulations are as follows:

Concrete vs. abstract objects

This distinction is unique in belonging to *formal* ontology, and is based on the distinction between those objects which by their very nature can, as against those which by their very nature cannot, exist independently of other objects. Moments are abstract objects; all other objects are concrete.[27]

Physical vs. mental objects

Husserl inherits this distinction, with minimal modification, from Brentano. A mental object or phenomenon is anything that either has an intentional content, or is a proper part of something that has an intentional content; a physical object or phenomenon is simply anything that is not a mental object. (Cf. *LU* VI, §8/p.868.) A mental *act* is always an intentional phenomenon. Such things as sensations and sense data, on the other hand, are not mental acts, though they are mental phenomena; for although they themselves lack intentional content, they are nevertheless proper parts of genuinely intentional phenomena. (Cf. *LU* V, §10/p.556.)

The theoretical account of intentionality that Husserl provides in the *Logical Investigations* differs markedly not only from that implicit in

Brentano's *Psychology from an Empirical Standpoint* but also from that which he had himself assumed in the *Philosophy of Arithmetic*. Nevertheless one commitment is shared by all three of these works: the distinction between things mental and things physical is essentially a distinction between kinds of *phenomena*. As a result, so-called 'physical' objects should under no circumstances be taken to include such material denizens of the external world as tables and chairs, viruses and galaxies. In the context of the *Logical Investigations*, physical entities are a species of appearance; and the discipline that studies them is phenomenology, not physics.

Real vs. ideal objects

Real objects are those that possess temporal properties and which are thus in principle capable of change. Ideal objects, on the other hand, are atemporal or 'timeless': they can neither come into existence, nor go out of existence, nor undergo any form of alteration. (Cf. *LU* II, §8/p.351.) Under this heading we can also note in passing that 'the sphere of *real* objects . . . is in fact no other than the sphere of *objects of possible sense perception*' (*LU* VI, §44/p.782). Moreover, the distinction between real and ideal objects coincides exactly with that between individual and universal objects.

Individual vs. universal objects

A universal object, or species, is one that is in principle capable of having instances; an individual object is in principle incapable of this (*LU* I, §32/p.331). In Husserlian terminology, then, the notions of *atemporal object*, *species*, *universal*, *ideal object*, and *specific object* are coextensive. (I will, however, avoid using the misleading term 'specific object', for it is all too easily taken to be synonymous with 'individual object' – a term with which, however, it should stand in the sharpest contrast.)

Actual vs. merely intentional objects

Husserl sometimes distinguishes between objects that enjoy 'actual existence' and those that have 'merely intentional existence' (cf. *LU* VI, Appendix §8/p.869). This can all too easily be misconstrued as equivalent to the common sense distinction between an existing person or thing, like Margaret Thatcher, and a non-existent, merely fictional or imaginary one like Sherlock Holmes. But this is not at all what Husserl has in mind. Under Brentano's influence, not that of common sense, Husserl ascribes 'actual existence' to whatever elements are present in an experience as its component parts; the intentional object of an experience, on the other hand, is not a *part* of that experience, and is said to exist merely intentionally. Husserl's distinction is thus one made within descriptive psychology or phenomenology, and one that concerns two kinds of *phenomenon*. As Husserl explicitly warns us: 'One must *not* forget, of course, that "actual" does *not* here mean the same as "external to consciousness"' (*ibid*; my italics).

Phenomenal vs. external objects

This is a distinction that is highly problematic, but about which, unfortunately, Husserl has next to nothing to say in the *Logical Investigations*. As a work of descriptive psychology or phenomenology the *Logical Investigations* naturally restricts its purview to *phenomenal* objects, that is, to mental acts and their contents in so far as these are directly given in experience. But this restriction inevitably rules out any reference to, or investigation of, transcendent, non-phenomenal, mind-independent objects existing in the external world. It is worth stressing, therefore, that (in spite of strong terminological suggestions to the contrary) neither 'concrete', nor 'physical', nor 'real', nor 'individual', nor 'actual' objects should be taken to coincide with non-phenomenal or mind-independent objects, with *real* objects in the more usual sense of that term.

Husserl's system of classification, with its attendant terminology, can be summarized by the following diagram:

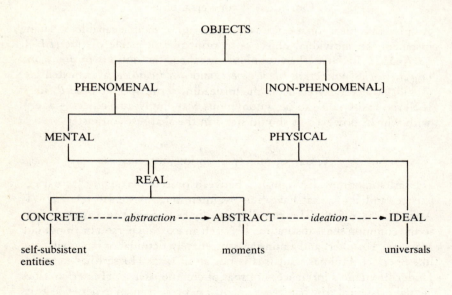

Fig. 3

104

From within the phenomenological perspective of the *Logical Investigations* Husserl can make no appeal to the nature or the existence of what we would normally call the real, external world – I have therefore, so to speak, bracketed it here.[28]

What Husserl has to say about species *per se* is limited – though, as we will see, he has a great deal to say both about the nature of the awareness we have of species, and about the role that that awareness plays in accounting for the possibility and nature of human knowledge. A species, we are told, is a single, complete, self-identical object capable of having instances. Strictly speaking, the instances of first-level species are individual abstract moments; but Husserl allows that there is little or no harm to talk that assigns to a species, as its instances, the individual wholes that have the moments in question as their dependent parts. (Cf. *LU* II, Introd./p.337.) Suppose, for example, that I have a visual presentation of a circular red patch, r. The colour moment of r is an abstract, though real, individual part of r. And as such it is unshareable: no object distinct from r may have *that* moment as a part. Clearly, however, there is a sense in which it is possible for another patch, p – indeed, for indefinitely many other patches – to be of 'exactly the same colour' as r. Husserl construes the judgement that 'p has exactly the same colour as r' as an assertion of numerical identity, equivalent to 'the colour of p = the colour of r'. And, *ex hypothesi*, the colour of r = red. The occurrence of the word 'red' in the last sentence cannot be taken to designate the moment of redness that is a proper part of r; and as the notion of numerical identity evidently applies to whatever it is that that occurrence of the word 'red' *does* designate, Husserl concludes that it designates a concrete object, but one that is universal rather than individual, and ideal rather than real. The abstract individuals that are the instances of this universal are the individual moments of redness belonging to r, to p, and to every other real individual that possesses a qualitatively similar colour moment.

The application of the foregoing considerations to the case of *meanings* is straightforward:

> The essence of meaning is seen by us, not in the meaning-conferring experience, but in its 'content', the single, self-identical intentional unity set over against the dispersed multiplicity of actual and possible experiences of speakers and thinkers. The 'content' of a meaning experience in this ideal sense is not at all what psychology means by 'content', *viz*: any real part or moment of an experience.
>
> What, e.g., the statement 'π is a transcendental number' says, what *we* understand when we read it, and mean when we say it, is no individual feature in our thought-experience, which is merely repeated on many occasions. Such a feature is always individually different from case to case, whereas the sense of the sentence should remain *identical*

... the selfsame element [is] expressed in them all, 'selfsame' in the very strictest sense.

The genuine identity that we here assert is none other than the *identity of the species*. As a species, and only as a species, can it embrace in unity, and as an ideal unity, the dispersed multiplicity of individual singulars.

The ideality of meanings is a particular case of the ideality possessed by species in general. (*LU* I, §§31–2/pp.329-31).

The appeal to meanings as species is intended to render intelligible the great diversity of individual phenomena that can yet be said to have one and the same content or sense. These individual phenomena include, amongst others, different expression tokens of the same type; expressions belonging to different but synonymous types; different utterances of one and the same sentence, either by one person on a number of occasions, or by a number of speakers; different mental acts or states of the same type; and also mental acts and states of different types. So, for example, what is meant by the sentence token 'π is a transcendental number' is also meant by any other sentence of that type, by any sentence synonymous with it, and by any utterance of that sentence, irrespective of when, where, or by whom the utterance is made. Moreover, that very meaning is also what is grasped by anyone who entertains the thought that is π a transcendental number, or by anyone who judges, doubts, expects, or hopes that this is so.

Unlike a number of philosophers belonging within the analytic tradition in contemporary philosophy, Husserl rejects the claim that there is an essential or explanatory relation between the nature of linguistic expressions, or linguistic phenomena in general, and the nature of 'meanings in themselves'. Echoing Brentano, Husserl writes at the end of the first Investigation: 'We have so far preferred to speak of meanings which, as the normal, relational sense of the word suggests, are meanings of expressions. There is, however, no intrinsic connection between the ideal unities which in fact operate as meanings, and the signs to which they are tied' (*LU* I, §34/p.333). Husserl maintains that there is, however, an integral connection between meanings as species, on the one hand, and certain mental acts on the other. The connection is this: the instances of such a species (if it in fact has any instances) are necessarily abstract moments of concrete, individual acts of meaning:

The manifold singulars for the ideal unity *meaning* are of course the corresponding act-moments of meaning, the *meaning-intentions*. Meaning [*in specie*] is related to varied acts of meaning . . . just as redness *in specie* is to these slips of paper which . . . all 'have' the same redness. (*LU* I, §31/p.330)

106

The claim that meanings are species whose instances are moments of meaning-intentions stands, of course, in urgent need of further clarification – to the provision of which pp. 114–42 below are devoted. That clarification, in so far as it is phenomenological, cannot, however, come from an examination of 'meanings in themselves'. As Husserl rightly remarks: 'it lies in the nature of our subject matter . . . that we cannot separate vexed issues concerning the nature of universal objects from issues concerning the nature of universal presentations' (*LU* II, §7/ p.351). And in particular we need to examine the epistemic role played by meaning, not only in so far as meanings function as direct *objects* of awareness, but also in so far as they function as the bearers of intentionality – as that in virtue of which there can be such things as direct objects of awareness in the first place.

Categorial intuition

Wittgenstein begins Part II, Section xi of the *Philosophical Investigations* with the following remarks:

> Two uses of the word 'see'.
> The one: 'What do you see there?' – 'I see *this*'. (And then a description, a drawing, a copy.) The other : 'I see a likeness between these two faces' – let the man I tell this to be seeing the faces as clearly as I do myself.
> The importance of this is the difference of category between the two 'objects' of sight.[29]

These remarks serve to introduce a series of investigations in which Wittgenstein argues, on largely phenomenological grounds, for the need to distinguish two quite different notions of *seeing* (or of *perception* in general), and, corresponding to them, two quite different notions of *object perceived*. The case that particularly concerns Wittgenstein is not so much one in which I enjoy a straightforward perception of a given concrete object, but rather one in which 'what I perceive [is] . . . an internal relation between it and other objects' (p.212) – as, for instance, when I see the similarity between two faces, or when I suddenly come to see an ambiguous figure like the duck-rabbit *as* a rabbit.

Wittgenstein argues, first, that in such cases what I undergo is a genuinely perceptual experience: in the sentence 'I see a likeness between those two faces' the verb should be construed literally, as a verb of perception, and not metaphorically, as expressing a judgement I have made, or a conclusion that I have reached. This is particularly clearly the case when I experience what Wittgenstein calls 'the dawning of an aspect,' that is, the sudden change in perception which can occur in contemplation of a systematically ambiguous figure. Phenomenologically, the experience consists in the apparent jump or switch from the figure's being a representation of one object (a duck, say) to its being a representation of a quite different object (a rabbit), there being, of course, no material change in the figure itself. When I experience a change of aspect, it is not that I, as it were, change my mind, revise my opinion, or come to a different judgement about what I see. Rather, it is my perceptual experience itself which undergoes radical alteration: I *see* the figure differently. And as Wittgenstein observes: 'the *concept* of seeing is modified here' (p.209). The modification, I take it, consists in extending the primitive or primary concept of seeing – a concept which, for example, can unproblematically be applied to cats and dogs, as well as to human beings – so that it applies to cases in which the object seen is not a concrete object at all. The justification for calling the one a 'primary', the other an 'extended' or 'secondary' notion of perception is simply that the applicability of the former is a necessary condition of the applicability of the latter: one cannot experience a change of aspect without perceiving that to which the aspect belongs, just as one cannot perceive a likeness without perceiving the things that are alike.

Wittgenstein argues, second, with respect to the dawning of an aspect, that 'the substratum of this experience is the mastery of a technique' (p.208); for it is 'only if someone *can do*, has learnt, is master of, such-and-such, that it makes sense to say he has had *this* experience' (p.209). If the object is an ambiguous drawing, say, then besides being familiar with the conventions of representation therein employed, one would also have to be able to recognize objects of the kind represented: 'What I perceive in the dawning of an aspect is not a property of the object, but an internal relation between it and *other objects*' (p.212; my italics).

> But how queer for this to be the logical condition of someone's having such-and-such an *experience*! After all, you don't say that one only 'has toothache' if one is capable of of doing such-and-such. – From this it follows that we cannot be dealing with the same concept of experience here. It is a different though related concept. (p.208)

In short, there are certain 'secondary' perceptual experiences, like the dawning of an aspect, which are available only to someone who has had the relevant primary experiences and who, moreover, is master of a technique on the basis of which the object of those experiences is taken to be internally related to other objects of the same kind.

Although his terminology and style are utterly different from Wittgenstein's, Husserl is, I believe, advancing a series of structurally exactly similar considerations in the following passage, which appears in the section entitled 'Phenomenological analysis of the distinction between sensuous and categorial perception':

> It is said of every percept that it grasps its object *directly*, or grasps this object *itself*. But this direct grasping has a different sense and character according as we are concerned with a percept in the narrower or the wider sense, or according as the directly grasped object is *sensuous* or *categorial*, or, in other words, according as it is a *real* or an *ideal* object. Sensuous or real objects can in fact be characterized as objects of the lowest level of possible intuition, categorial or ideal objects as objects of higher levels.
>
> In the sense of the narrower, 'sensuous' perception, an object is directly apprehended . . . if it is set up in an act of perception in a straightforward manner. What this means is this: that the object . . . is not constituted in relational, connective, or otherwise articulated acts, acts founded on other acts which bring other objects to perception.
>
> Each straightforward act of perception . . . can serve as basic act for new acts which . . . in their new mode of consciousness likewise bring to maturity a new awareness of objects which essentially presupposes the old . . . . We are here dealing with a sphere of objects which can only show themselves 'in person' in such founded acts (*LU* VI, §46/p.787f).

Like Wittgenstein, Husserl wishes to distinguish, on the one hand, primary or 'straightforward' perceptual experience, the appropriate objects of which are real individuals, and on the other hand, a kind of perceptual experience which, although founded on experiences of the first kind, goes beyond them in providing an awareness of objects that are not spatio-temporal individuals. The ability to 'go beyond' primary perceptual experience requires mastery of a technique; and the two terms Husserl uses for the technique in question are *abstraction* and *synthesis*.

In the *Logical Investigations* Husserl is considerably more careful than he had been in the *Philosophy of Arithmetic* to keep clearly distinct two quite different notions of abstraction.[30] On the one hand, that is, 'abstraction' can mean the process whose basis is a perception of something concrete, and an application of which yields a perception of something abstract (i.e. of a moment). The other, contrasting notion is that of a procedure which, when applied to experiences of real objects, yields an awareness of an ideal object (i.e. of a species). And, with respect to the claim that 'our perception of *ideal* objects depends on abstraction', Husserl notes that 'naturally I do not here mean "abstraction" merely in the sense of a setting-in-relief of some dependent moment in a sensible object, but ideational abstraction, where no such moment, but its idea, its universal, is brought to consciousness and achieves actual givenness' (*LU* VI, §52/p.800).

Given that all of the second Investigation, and much of the sixth, are devoted to an examination of ideational abstraction, it is surprising, and not a little disappointing, to find that Husserl nowhere specifies in detail precisely what he takes such ideational abstraction to be. We know, of course, that the procedure begins with a sensory awareness of individual moments, and that it terminates in the direct, non-sensory awareness of an ideal species; but exactly how this is to be done, or exactly what techniques and procedures one is to employ, remain largely a mystery. The closest that Husserl comes to an explicit statement on this issue is this:

> We must presuppose such an act [i.e. of ideational abstraction] in order that the *very sort*, to which the manifold single moments 'of one and the same sort' stand opposed, may *itself* come before us, and may come before us as *one and the same*. For we become aware of the identity of the universal through repeated performance of such acts upon a basis of several individual intuitions, and we plainly do so in an overreaching act of identification which brings all such single acts of abstraction into one synthesis. (*LU* VI, §52/p.800)

We noted earlier that a significant element in Husserl's acceptance of species as concrete (but not, of course, as real) objects is the fact that a species possesses identity conditions that make ineliminable appeal neither to the existence or identity of any item belonging to that species, nor, indeed, to the existence or identity of any other item whatsoever. That identity conditions can be provided at all warrants the claim that species are bona fide *objects*; and that those conditions are, so to speak, free-standing, warrants the claim that species are *concrete* (i.e. self-subsistent, independent) objects. This train of thought naturally leads to the notion of identity being placed at the centre of the philosophical stage. But the theory in which this notion is then embedded by Husserl is so obscure that even Findlay, in his otherwise uncritical introduction to the *Logical Investigations*, is forced to concede that it is 'immensely tangled' and 'unbearably complex'.

One symptom of this tangle is as follows. The last quoted passage is an attempt by Husserl to answer the question: How do we become aware of a species, given that, as an ideal object, there can be no sensory awareness of it? This question is then tacitly exchanged for another, namely: How do we become aware of the identity of a species? This, in turn, is then in effect exchanged for a third: How do we bring about the identity of the species? And it is only this latter question that is, finally, answered. The answer, we are told, is *via* 'an overreaching act of identification which brings . . . single acts of abstraction into one synthesis'. At issue here, according to another formulation, are 'the characters of founded acts that give form to acts of straightforward . . . intuition, and *transform them into new presentations of objects*' (*LU* VI, §61/p.819; my italics).

I have been unable to find evidence in Husserl's text that is clear enough to enable me to say with any confidence just what his theory on these matters is; and the remainder of the present section is accordingly an attempt merely to outline a train of thought that might have been in Husserl's mind, and which is at least suggested by the text at a number of points.

The foregoing talk of 'identification', 'acts', 'unity', 'synthesis', 'presentations', 'intuitions' and the like sounds Kantian – and, in particular, it calls to mind the famous passage in which Kant concludes that 'of all presentations, *combination* is the only one which cannot be given through objects':

> the combination . . . of a manifold in general can never come to us through the senses, and cannot, therefore, be already contained in the pure form of sensible intuition. For it is an act of spontaneity of the faculty of presentation; and all combination – be we conscious of it or not, be it a combination of the manifold of intuition . . . or of various concepts – is an act of the understanding. To this act the general title 'synthesis' may be assigned, as indicating that we cannot present to ourselves anything as combined in the object which we have not ourselves previously combined, and that of all presentations, *combination* is the only one which cannot be given through objects.[31]

In contemporary analytic philosophy *identity* is typically construed as a relation, that is, as a reflexive relation in which every object stands to itself and to nothing else. In that tradition, moreover, one of the most important contexts in which the notion of identity is employed is in talk of the identity-conditions of members of a given class of objects – or, equivalently, of the truth-conditions of identity statements concerning members of that class. Historically, talk of this kind has its origin in the writings of Frege; and in so far as Husserl was influenced by those writings, he too at times indulges in such talk. There is, however, an older tradition within which the importance of the notion of *identity* is taken to lie in its contrast with notions like *multiplicity*, *diversity*, and *plurality*. And in this tradition, the concept of identity is most intimately linked with that of *unity*.[32] In the passages quoted above, the considerations adduced by both Kant and Husserl belong within this latter, non-Fregean tradition, central to which is the epistemological problem of accounting

111

for the nature and origin of our awareness of complex unity, of any unity, that is, which stands over against, but which yet encompasses, the diversity and multiplicity of different experiences, mental acts, mental states, and the like. Now characteristic of the Kantian response to such problems is the claim that unity-in-complexity or identity-in-diversity is never merely given in experience, but is always created. It results, that is, from acts of 'synthesis' which, as the name implies, are acts in which a number of diverse elements are combined together to yield a presentation that is a single, unified, complex whole.

The fundamental intuition that underlies these considerations is perhaps this: in so far as we are aware of complex unities, of self-identical objects whose integrity transcends the complexity and diversity of the given experiences which constitute the basis of that awareness, that unity cannot itself be an item which is straightforwardly given in experience. For if it were, it would necessarily be just one more item constitutive of the very diversity whose unity requires explanation. One cannot, so to speak, explain the unity possessed by a given sequence of experiences merely by adding yet another member to that sequence.

Intuitions of this broadly Kantian kind are present in Husserl's early thought, and were, indeed, to assume an even greater importance in such subsequent writings as *Ideas* and *Cartesian Meditations*. In the *Logical Investigations* there is, however, one respect in which Husserl's view is clearly and radically non-Kantian. According to Kant, all complex unity whatsoever – 'be we conscious of it or not, be it a combination of the manifold of intuition, sensory or non-sensory, or of various concepts' – is a result of synthetic, higher-level acts. Kant, in other words, has a univocal account of the origin of unity-in-diversity according to which such unity is never simply given in experience but is always constructed. Husserl, on the other hand, distinguishes between the unity possessed by a manifold of sensory intuition, and the unity possessed by any other sort of manifold.[33] When a manifold of intuition is sensory it *can*, according to Husserl, possess a unity that is simply and straightforwardly given in experience, even though it is undoubtedly a manifold in the sense that it contains a number of distinct parts, both pieces and moments. In contrast, when a manifold of intuition is non-sensory, its unity must result from 'founded' or 'higher-level' acts of synthesis. In Husserl's words:

> The manner in which . . . a thing appears [in sense perception] is *straightforward*: it requires no apparatus of founding and founded acts. . . . The unity of [sense] perception does not therefore arise through our own synthetic activity, as if only a form of synthesis, operating by way of founded acts, could give unity of objective reference to part-intentions. (*LU* VI, §47/p.788–9)

But on the other hand, concerning non-sensory or categorial intuitions, it is essential . . . that they be achieved in stages . . . . This excludes from synthetic acts that immediate unity of representation which unites all representative contents of straightforward intuitions. The complete synthetic intuition therefore arises . . . in so far as the mental content which binds the underlying act itself sustains *interpretation* as the objective unity of the founded objects. (*LU* VI, §57/p.812)

The picture which emerges from remarks such as these is, I think, as follows. In a straightforward or primary act of sense perception one is typically presented with a unitary, real object that is nevertheless complex, in that it comprises a number of distinguishable concrete parts and abstract moments. These latter are as individual and real as the perceived object as a whole; and although there may initially be no explicit awareness of them, attention can subsequently be turned towards them, so that they in turn become objects of straightforward sensory intuition. When such an act of selective concentration is focused on a dependent part of the object, i.e. on an abstract moment, the act of selective concentration is itself a form of abstraction (though not one of 'ideational abstraction'). Suppose, for example, that I have a visual presentation of three objects. I concentrate my attention on their colour moments, and I have visual presentations of three distinct, real, but abstract individuals, m_1, m_2, and m_3. If these three moments stand to one another in the equivalence relation of *being chromatically alike*, and if I am aware that this is so, then I am in a position to see one and the same colour, C, which has the property of being instantiated in three different places. The colour term 'C' is now a name for what m_1, m_2, and m_3 have in common; it is the name of a species which, as such, is not a possible object of sensory or straightforward perception. My awareness of C is nevertheless a perceptual awareness: I can *see* the colour that the three moments have in common – but not in the same sense in which I can be said to see those moments themselves. And, as Wittgenstein observes, 'if this sounds crazy, you need only reflect that the *concept* of seeing is modified here' (p.209). C is a synthetic whole, the result of synthetic activity; and only a being possessed of certain intellectual abilities is capable of perceiving a synthetic whole.[34] The most important such abilities, in the absence of which perception of non-spatio-temporal objects would be impossible, are those involved in the formulation of judgements of identity: 'we become aware of the identity of the universal . . . in an act of overreaching identification which brings acts of [non-ideational] abstraction into one synthesis' (*LU* VI §52/p.800).

But what exactly is it that gets synthesized? What precisely are the diverse elements whose similarity is transformed into an identity the terms of which are species? The sentence quoted at the end of the last paragraph implies that it is *acts* of a certain sort (acts of selective

113

concentration on abstract moments) that comprise the ingredients for synthesis; and, indeed, this was precisely the position which Husserl had adopted earlier, in the *Philosophy of Arithmetic*, where ideational abstraction proceeds from a basis of acts whose suitability lies in their possession of qualitatively similar in-existent contents. In spite of appearances to the contrary, however, this doctrine is jettisoned in the *Logical Investigations*, in the first place because the content of an intentional act is no longer taken to be a real, in-existent part of that act; and, second, because the bases of ideational abstraction are no longer taken to be mental phenomena at all. Abstraction or synthesis proceeds, rather, from the *meanings* or 'intentional materials' of acts:

> The categorial moment of the synthetically founded act . . . connects, in all circumstances, the *intentional materials* [of the underlying acts], and is in a real sense founded upon them . . . . The material of the founded acts is founded *in the materials* of the underlying acts . . . . Categorial formation rests phenomenologically on what is universal in an objectifying act, or is a function essentially bound up with the generic element in objectifying acts. Only experiences of this class permit categorial syntheses, and such synthesis directly connects their intentional essences. (*LU* VI, §77/p.811)

Remarks such as these are difficult, certainly; but they may also appear to be objectionable in a much stronger sense, for they seem to imply that an awareness of meanings is a necessary pre-condition of any awareness we may have of ideal objects or species. This would, of course, be blatantly incoherent, given that meanings are themselves a subclass of ideal objects. If Husserl is to be saved from this incoherence we must find a way of construing claims to the effect that 'categorial formation . . . rests on what is universal in an objectifying act' in such a way as to avoid commitment to the thesis that categorial formation rests on awareness of what is universal, or in other words that awareness of what is universal is founded on a prior awareness of what is universal. But given that, according to Husserl, the elements which are synthesized to yield an intuitive awareness of what is universal are themselves meanings (i.e. universals), escape from this incoherence effectively requires that there be some other mode of epistemic access to meanings that is prior to, and independent of, any direct intuitive awareness we may have of them. To see how this is indeed the case we must turn to Husserl's account of intentionality, and the role meanings play within it.

Meanings and intentionality

The analysis of intentionality provided both by Brentano in *Psychology from an Empirical Standpoint*, and by Husserl in the *Philosophy of*

Arithmetic was, as we saw earlier, essentially mereological. The characteristic property of a mental phenomenon, that it is 'directed towards an object', was explained by appeal to the immanent in-existence of a content of that phenomenon. And here the notion of a content is to be taken literally: the intentional object is *contained in* the phenomenal whole as one of its proper parts.

Perhaps the greatest single doctrinal innovation to emerge in the *Logical Investigations* is Husserl's rejection of the principle of mereological adequacy, and his consequent adoption of a radically new account of intentionality. Far from allowing the content and the object of a mental act to coalesce, the hallmark of the new theory is that, with respect to any particular mental act, content and object never coincide. The intentional object of an act, in other words, is under no circumstances a *part* of that act.

This immediately creates a challenge, however, to which Investigation V is largely a response, namely that of showing *how* the elements actually present within an act can possibly enable that act to aim at, refer to, or mean something that, by its very nature, is no part of it.

One point is worth bringing out explicitly at the beginning of our examination of this topic. Husserl's theory of intentionality is entirely general and, to a large extent, purely formal. It is an attempted solution to the problem of how in general *something*, in virtue solely of its internal constitution (its various parts and moments), can succeed in establishing even putative reference to *something else*, to something, in other words, that is identical neither with it nor with any of its parts or moments. I stress this way of formulating the problem, with its absence of any material constraints on something's being an intentional object, so as to avoid all temptation to think that Husserl builds into his theory, from the very beginning, any assumptions or specifications concerning the kinds of things that, either in practice or in principle, intentional objects are. And in particular I want to avoid the temptation to assume at the outset that 'the object intended in an act . . . is usually some ordinary sort of thing like a physical individual or a natural state of affairs'.[35] With an assumption like this in place, it is all too easy to misconstrue Husserl's theory of intentionality as yet another attempt to solve 'the problem of our knowledge of the external world', by establishing how subjective mental acts are capable of referring to physical objects and natural states of affairs.[36] And, in consequence, it is all too easy to misconstrue the very nature of Husserl's enterprise as a whole. This is, precisely, a *phenomenological* enterprise within the constraints of which the role assigned to notions like *external reality, ordinary physical object*, and *natural state of affairs* is, to say the least, problematic.

For the time being, therefore, and so as to avoid begging a number of questions at the outset, I shall leave the material nature of intentional

115

objects unspecified, and adopt instead a merely formal definition: an intentional object is any object (in Husserl's wide sense of the term) that is meant, or intended, or referred to, by something with which it is not identical and of which it is neither a part or a moment.

Although Husserl gives no initial specifications as to what categories of things can function as intentional objects, the situation is entirely different with respect to the sorts of things that can *have* intentional objects. As part of his unquestioned inheritance from Brentano, Husserl takes it that wherever there is intentionality, the mind has been at work. In the last analysis only one kind of entity can have an intentional object – namely, a mental act.

So our problem (call it *P*) is now: *How is it possible for a mental act, solely in virtue of its internal constitution, to have as an object something distinct from any part or aspect of itself?* And it is a constraint on any adequate solution to *this* problem that appeal be made only to the internal constitution of the mental acts in question. Husserl is explicit about this:

> We take intentional relation, understood in purely descriptive fashion, as *an inward peculiarity of certain experiences*. (*LU* V, §10/p.555; my italics)
>
> Intentional experiences have the peculiarity of directing themselves . . . to presented objects, but they do so in an *intentional* sense. An object is 'referred to' or 'aimed at' in them . . . . This means *no more than* that certain experiences are present, intentional in character . . . . Only one thing is present: the intentional experience whose essential descriptive character *is* the intention in question . . . . If this experience is present, then, *eo ipso* and through its own essence (we must insist) the intentional 'relation' to an object is achieved . . . . And of course such an experience may be present in consciousness together with its intention, although its object does not exist at all. The object is 'meant', i.e. 'to mean' it is an experience, but it is then merely entertained in thought, and is nothing in reality. (*LU* V, §11/p558; my italics)

Husserl's problem is thus set up, *ab initio*, in such a way that only an adverbial, and not any genuinely relational theory of intentionality *can* possibly count as a solution to it.

Now problem *P* has every appearance of being an intelligible and interesting problem; but one possibility which cannot be ruled out at this point is that, as formulated above, the only defensible answer will turn out to be: It is *not* in fact possible for an act to have such an object solely in virtue of its internal constitution. Perhaps it will turn out that intentionality is not, or is not exclusively, an '*inward* peculiarity' of certain mental acts and states. A decision on this matter must, however, await a verdict on that acceptability of the theory Husserl offers as a solution to *P*. It is not the case, therefore, that for us any question is begged if we follow Husserl in his adoption of a framework within which only an adverbial theory of intentionality can be acceptable; for the question which remains open is precisely whether such a theory *is* acceptable and, if so, whether Husserl has one.

The problem then, in Husserl's words, is to account for the fact that 'something non-existent or transcendent can be the intentional object in an act in which it has no being' (*LU* V, §20/p.587). And the solution, in the last analysis, will turn out to be that it is 'the *matter* of acts . . . which gives them their determinate objective reference' (*LU* V, §22/p.598):

> The matter . . . [is] that element in an act which first gives it reference to an object, and reference so wholly definite that it not merely fixes the object meant in a general way, but also the precise way in which it is meant . . . . It is the act's matter that makes its object count as this object and no other. (*LU* V, §20/p.589)

As a first step towards making sense of this answer we need to introduce, albeit briefly and provisionally, some of the more important terminology in which Husserl couches his general theory of mental acts, of which his theory of 'act material' or 'matter' is a part:

Consciousness: a primitive term used in more or less the usual way to refer to whatever belongs within the so-called 'stream of consciousness', i.e., within 'the entire, real, phenomenological being of the empirical ego' (*LU* V, §1/p.535).

An experience: a particular episode of consciousness. Experiences are real (i.e. temporal) events and, when complex, possess real parts and moments. Having a sensation, an itch for example, is an experience, as is suddenly remembering that one has left the front door unlocked.

A content of experience: a real part or moment that goes to make up an experience. A content of experience is therefore present *in* an experience in the way that any part is present in a whole of which it is a part. *The* content of an experience is the totality of the parts and moments that together comprise it.

An act: a specific type of experience, namely one that is intentional. All acts are, by stipulative definition, intentional experiences; but not all experiences are acts. 'That not all experiences are intentional is proved by [the existence of] sensations and sensational complexes' (*LU* V, §10/p.556). Having an itch, for example, is an experience which (unlike remembering that the front door is unlocked) involves no direction towards an object that is not part of that experience.

An objectifying act: an act whose quality is essentially such as to consist in the presentation of an object. (Cf. *LU* V, §§37–41.)

117

The matter of an act: that in virtue of which an experience has an intentional character. The matter or material of an act is part of the content – is, in fact, an abstract moment – of an act.

The quality of an act: roughly speaking, the mood or force or attitude that characterizes an act's relation to its matter. One and the same matter can, for instance, be part of an act of *desire*, or of *doubt, fear, judgement*, or *expectation* – and the italicized terms here are names of different act qualities. An act's quality, like its matter, is a moment of that act. (Cf. *LU* V, §20/p.589.)

The intentional essence of an act: the matter of an act taken together with its quality.

The semantic essence of an act: the same as an act's intentional essence. (Cf. *LU* V, §21/p.590.)

A concrete example may help to bring these notions to life. Suppose that while on holiday in France I suddenly remember having left unlocked the front door of my house in Sheffield. The experience will doubtless be a complex one. It may involve a variety of feelings, of surprise, say, or of dismay, anxiety, or anger. I may have certain physical sensations associated with tension or agitation. A number of mental images, more or less determinate, may pass through my mind – of a front door, of a set of keys on a kitchen table, of a man in a black mask making off with a television set, and so on. In addition there may be certain thoughts that occur to me, or judgements that I make; I may, for instance, explicitly think 'the front door is unlocked'. And I may expect the house to have been burgled on my return. Present in this complex experience are a number of component experiences of which some, perhaps all, are themselves complex. The most general, initial way of sorting this complexity, according to Husserl, is to distinguish between those experiences which are, and those which are not, intentional. To the latter sort belong the sensations, the feelings, and the emotions I undergo, in so far as these are merely 'lived through' or experienced, and are not taken to refer to anything beyond themselves. To the former sort, on the other hand, belong the presentation of my front door, say, and the expectation that the house will have been burgled. As Husserl repeatedly insists, while sensations and feelings are things I 'live through' or undergo, in that they are items that exist exclusively within my stream of consciousness, the same cannot be meaningfully said of the objects of intentional acts. It makes no sense to say that I undergo my front door, or that I live through that my house will have been burgled. Although an intentional *act* is always an experience, its *object* is typically neither an experience nor a proper part of one.

Amongst intentional experiences Husserl next distinguishes between those that are 'nominal' and those that are 'propositional'. The objects of nominal acts are 'things', or are at least 'thing-like' (e.g. *my front door*, which I can perceive, visualize, remember, imagine to be different from the way it actually is, and so on); whereas the objects of propositional acts are states of affairs (e.g. *that the door is unlocked*, which is something I can entertain, assert, doubt, expect to be the case, and the like). Propositional acts are, acording to Husserl, higher-order or founded acts involving categorial synthesis – so we can postpone investigation of them for the moment. In contrast, the most basic category of act, to which all acts of sensory intuition belong, and upon which all acts of higher-order are ultimately founded, are nominal acts (*LU* V, §§42f.). We can take as an example the presentation that I have of my front door, a presentation which is a distinguishable part of the complex experience of remembering that it was left unlocked.

Let us assume that the presentation is vivid. In that case we can distinguish a number of different aspects and ingredients that go to make it up. There are, in the first place, the sensations, qualia, data, or raw feels that constitute the irreducible content of my experience. These will be characterizable in terms, say, of colour, tone, intensity, relative size, shape, and so on. In addition to these there are those aspects which characterize the quality of the act – did the experience for instance have the quality of a genuine perception, of a memory, of a dream, or was it an exercise in creative imagination? Was the experience merely contemplative, or was it one in which an assumption of the reality of the object was active? Under this head Husserl's most important distinction is that between nominal acts that are *positing*, in the sense that the object of the presentation 'is referred to as existing', and those that are *non-positing* and which 'leave the existence of their object unsettled' (*LU* V, §38/p.638).[37] And, finally, there is whatever it is in my presentation that makes it, precisely, a presentation *of my front door* – its so-called matter.

Now the trouble is that there doesn't seem to be anything left, anything contained in my experience over and above its sensory components and its quality, to which this latter role could be assigned. Viewed in one way, my experience is just an awareness, possessing some quality, of certain colours and shapes, arranged in certain ways. There is not, in addition to these, some further immanent content of my presentation. Viewed in another way, of course, my experience is a presentation of my front door, and that object is certainly not an immanent content of my experience.[38] How, then, do we account for the one solely on the basis of the other? Husserl simply does not say. Although he devotes the greater part of Investigations I, IV, V, and VI to the examination of issues concerning meaning, intentionality, reference, content, matter, and the like, and although he asserts more than 150 times that it is the matter of an act (or, derivatively, the meaning of an expression) which is responsible for its direction towards an object, he nowhere so much as attempts to explain in detail *how* the matter of an act is supposed to accomplish this feat. At this point, therefore, we need to construct an explanation using whatever materials we can glean from the text, or infer from other theses to which Husserl does subscribe.

One of the constraints within which this explanation must function is already clear: something *in* an act must function in such a way as to make that act a presentation of a determinate intentional object. So this explanation will be essentially adverbial; for 'to represent an object . . . to oneself is, we said, to be minded in this or that descriptively determinate fashion'; it is no more than to have 'a particular experience, or a particular mode of mindedness' (*LU* V, §11/p.559). Another constraint is that the theory must be general – general enough, that is, to explain the intentionality of an arbitrary act, whether it be either nominal or propositional, positing or non-positing, perceptual, emotional, intellectual, imaginative, or volitional, and regardless of whether the object intended is concrete, abstract, ideal, or fictional. And, third, the theory must be capable of participating in an overall account of mental acts, on the one hand, and of meaning, on the other. In this respect a theory of intentionality is not an isolated matter, but something that must ultimately play a crucial role both in the philosophy of mind and in the philosophy of language.

The texts which perhaps come closest to suggesting the lines along which such a theory should be developed are these:

(A)   Matter [is] . . . that moment in an objectifying act which makes the act present *just this object in just this manner*, i.e., in just these articulations and forms, and with special relation to just these properties and relationships. Presentations which agree in their matter do not merely present the same object in some general fashion: they mean it in the most complete fashion *as* the same, as having exactly the same properties. (*LU* VI, §25/p.737)

(B)   It is clear . . . that the concept of 'matter' must be defined by way of the unity of total identification, as the element in our acts which serves as a basis for identification. (*LU* VI §25/p.738)

There are two different questions that one can ask concerning intentional matter, as a means of getting clear about its nature. One is: Under what circumstances is it the case that two or more different acts have one and the same matter? The other is: What function does intentional matter perform, what does it *do*? In effect the two passages quoted above are, respectively, answers to these questions; and, fortunately, the answers converge.

According to (A) we say of two different acts that they have the same matter, not merely when they have the same intentional object, but when that object is presented in the same way. Both, that is, must possess the same *Art des Gegebenseins*. Of course one must be careful here: the matter of a given act is a dependent part of, and so is unique to, that particular act. It makes no sense to say of two disjoint acts that they have the same matter. Or rather, in so far as it *does* make sense to say of two non-overlapping acts that they have the same matter, that cannot be to claim that they have an abstract part in common, but only that their respective individual matters are of the same type. In that permissible sense, however, it is clearly the case that we typically say of two people that they have had the same intentional experience (the same image, say, or thought, or desire) when their experiences are not only directed to one and the same object, but also characterize that object in the same way. Husserl even borrows Frege's example to illustrate this very Fregean line of thought: to imagine, or think of, or otherwise refer to someone *as* the victor of Jena is to do something different from imagining, or thinking, or referring to that same person *as* the vanquished at Waterloo. 'The meaning expressed in our pair of names is plainly different, though the same object is meant in each case' (*LU* I, §12/p.287f.). The matter of an act, in other words, is responsible not only for there *being* an intentional object, and for *which* intentional object it is, but also for what that object is presented *as*.

In the last analysis these are not, however, different roles; for none can be performed without the simultaneous performance of the others. Why this is so becomes clear when we turn to our second question and the answer to it suggested by (B). An intentional experience is one which has an object that is no part of that experience. For this to be possible, something in the experience must be such as *to determine which particular object is in question*. And this italicized phrase, I take it, means no more and no less than *to pick out or identify the object meant*. Given that the object is not itself present in the experience, this can only mean: *to provide an identity condition of the intentional object* – a procedure that would seem to require appeal to the distinguishing attributes and characteristics possessed by the intentional object.

The attributes and characteristics of an intentional object are themselves, however, intentional, non-immanent objects; and so clearly no direct appeal to them can be made in explaining how, in general, an act can achieve direction towards something that is not immanent to that act. Equally clearly, it is not the quality of an act that is responsible for its intentionality; for the quality can be varied at will while the identity of the intentional object remains constant. The only remaining candidate for what Husserl calls 'the element in our acts which serves as a basis for identification' would seem to be the acts' sensory or intuitive contents. As both Hume and Kant long since pointed out, however, not every sensory impression is capable of participating in this procedure: feelings of pleasure and displeasure, sensations of pain and the like 'must always remain purely subjective' and are never 'capable of forming a representation of an object'.[39] Those sensory or intuitive contents of an act that are capable of forming a representation of an object Husserl, not unreasonably, calls its *intuitively representational contents* (*LU* VI, Introd./p.669; VI, §22/p.730).

So how do representational contents represent? The answer suggested at a number of points by Husserl is that these immanent contents of an act perform a representative function by being subject to an 'interpretation' (*Auffassung*), and that this consists in their being taken to comprise a set of conditions that together determine the identity of something – something which then comprises the intentional object of that act. When I perceive or vividly imagine something – my front door, say – then according to Husserl, this means no more phenomenologically than that I undergo a

> certain sequence of experiences of the class of sensations, sensuously unified in a particular serial pattern, and informed by a certain act-character of 'interpretation', which endows it with an objective sense. This act-character is responsible for the fact that an *object* [e.g. my front door] is perceptually apparent to me. (*LU* VI, §6/p.688)[40]

And, most explicitly, Husserl writes:

> I see a thing, e.g. this box, but I do not see my sensations. I always see *one and the same box*, however *it* may be turned and tilted. I always have the *same* . . . perceived object. But each turn yields a *new* 'content of consciousness'. Very different contents are therefore experienced, though the same object is perceived . . . . In the flux of experienced content we imagine ourselves to be in touch with one and the same object; and this itself belongs to the sphere of what we experience. For we experience a 'consciousness of identity', i.e. a claim to apprehend identity. On what does this consciousness depend? [We must] reply that the different sensational contents are given, but that we apperceive or 'take' them 'in the same sense', and that *to take them in this sense is an experienced character through which the 'being of the object for me' is first constituted*. (*LU* V, §14/p.565)

In the simplest cases of straightforward sensory presentation this can only mean, I think, that some of the sensory elements in an experience are themselves taken to be properties which are co-instantiated. (Cf *LU* I, §23/pp.309-310. This reading gets some indirect support from the development Husserl's views on this topic subsequently receive in *Ideas*; see pp.173–84). Whatever it is that my sensations of colour, shape, and size, my visual impressions of movement, my tactile awareness of hardness, coolness, and so forth present me with – considered as various quite distinct contents of my consciousness – I must take as in some sense belonging together, as presenting me, in other words, with a *single* instance of something large, green, rectangular, cold, hard, moving, and so forth. And here we at least begin to get conditions on something's being, say, my front door as I perceive it at a certain time. But it is only a beginning, and a rather shaky one at that.

These last remarks, it must be admitted, are speculative; but the text of the *Logical Investigations* simply fails to provide any explicit account of how the intentional relation is established, or what exactly it consists in. We know of course that it consists in our doing *something* to, or with, the immanent and ultimately sensory contents of experience. But as to precisely what this something is we are left in the dark. Detailed criticism of this theory would be pointless at the present stage of our investigation, however, because the theory is taken up again, modified, extended, and to some extent improved in Husserl's subsequent works, and especially in *Ideas*. Nevertheless certain aspects of the theory, as we have it so far, are disturbing. In the first place it is distressingly unoriginal, consisting of little more than a series of borrowings from Kant. In the second place, the theory is not obviously consistent; for Husserl wants to say, on the one hand, that in a straightforward sensory intuition of an intentional object one is aware of a non-synthetic unity, but, on the other hand, he seems committed to there being *some* form of synthetic activity in even the most rudimentary and primitive kinds of intentional act. And third, the theory conspicuously fails to address the issue of how one's representation-of-an-object is related to *that object*; of how, for instance, my perception (which has 'the inward peculiarity' of being a my-front-door sort of experience) is related to my front door.

So far we have looked at the notion of intentionality only in so far as it applies to those primitive acts that are both nominal and sensory, such as 'straightforward' acts of sense-perception or imagination. Husserl is quite clear, however, that it is exclusively within such objectifying acts that intentionality originates and that, therefore, all other kinds of acts whatsoever receive their intentional character by being founded on the matter of sensory, nominal, objectifying acts:

each simple 'matter', involving no further material foundations, is nominal, and . . . therefore each ultimately underlying objectifying act is nominal. But since all other act-qualities are founded on objectifying acts, this last foundation upon nominal acts carries over from objectifying acts *to all acts whatever*. (*LU* V, §43/p.38; my italics)

And nominal objectifying acts must be sensory because, as we saw on pp.112–13, all intuitive awareness of non-sensory items like species or states of affairs is founded on 'straightforward' acts of sense-perception:

ideal objects 'can only be "perceptually" given in acts which are founded on other acts, and in the last resort, on acts of sensibility' (*LU* VI, Introd./p.670; cf. VI §48/p.795). The influence of Brentano is still very strong here, not only in relation to Husserl's retention of a fundamentally non-propositonal account of intentionality, but also in his insistence that all 'higher-level' acts involving awareness of what is abstract or what is ideal are founded on acts of presentation that are sensory, and whose objects are thus both concrete and real. In this respect, then, the *Logical Investigations* continues to defend not only the claim earlier expressed in the *Philosophy of Arithmetic* by the slogan: 'no concept is graspable that lacks a foundation in concrete intuition', but also that which characterized much of Brentano's early phenomenology, namely that every act either is a presentation or is founded on a presentation.

We need, now, to return to the problems concerning categorial intuition and presentations of meaning that we left unresolved on pp.112–14. The most outstanding problem was this: there seems to be no coherent way of specifying the bases from which ideational abstraction or categorial synthesis proceed. On the one hand, that is, Husserl is committed to the claim that an awareness of the ideal objects called 'universals', 'species', and 'meanings' is only possible as a result of the application of a process of synthesis to items that are given in 'straightforward' acts. On the other hand, however, he also appears to claim that those very items are themselves meanings, or universals, or 'intentional materials' of objectifying acts. Consequently, Husserl seems to be faced by the following dilemma: either 'straightforward' awareness of meaning is possible, in which case the whole apparatus of founded, synthetic, higher-level acts is simply otiose; or 'straightforward' awareness of meaning is not possible, in which case there appears to be no appropriate material to which synthesis can be applied in the first place.

The considerations examined on pp.114–23, however, suggest a way in which Husserl might escape this dilemma and the incoherence it threatens. Expressions like 'the matter', 'the meaning', 'the sense', and 'the intentional matter' of an act are systematically ambiguous. They can either be used to refer to an individual, real, abstract moment of some particular concrete experience, or they can be used to refer to a universal, ideal species that a number of such concrete experiences have in common. Given that an awareness of the former is independent of, and prior to, any awareness of the latter, the one is in principle capable of acting as the foundation of the other. And this is, indeed, precisely what Husserl maintains is the case: 'to meanings *in specie* correspond acts of meaning, the former being nothing but ideally apprehended moments of the latter' (*LU* V, Introd./p.533). 'The manifold singulars for the ideal unity *meaning* are naturally the corresponding act-moments of meaning, the *meaning-intentions*' (*LU* I, §32/p.330). And this doctrine enables Husserl to avoid the potential incoherence noted above precisely because 'in the act of meaning we are not conscious of meaning *as an object*' (*LU* I, §34/p.332).

To learn more about these acts of meaning intention we must investigate the use to which Husserl puts them in the account he provides of linguistic meaning.

Meanings and language

Although there is, needless to say, a great variety of problems, some specific and at times even esoteric, to the solution of which a theory of linguistic meaning can be addressed, perhaps the most general and the most fundamental is that intimated by Wittgenstein's question about what it is that breathes life into a sign: 'Every sign *by itself* seems dead. What gives it life?'[41] Husserl confronts this problem directly; and his answer is unequivocal: 'what makes an expression *an expression* are . . . the acts attaching to it' (*LU* V, §19/p.583). Meaning, or content, or significance, in other words, 'only pertain to an expression in virtue of the mental acts which give it sense' (*LU* I, §12/p.287): 'a peculiar act-experience relating to the expression is present . . . it shines through the expression, lending it meaning and, thereby, relation to objects' (*LU* I, §18/p.302). (A preliminary caveat is, however, in order: no matter how intimately linguistic meaning and mental acts may be related, the two are not the same. As we will see, Husserl does not subscribe to any crude form of psychologistic theory according to which meanings and mental acts are identified.)

In addition to providing an account of how, in general, linguistic expressions come to possess any significance whatsoever, a theory of meaning is also called upon to perform a number of other, more specific tasks. Amongst these are, first, the task of analysing the *concept* of meaning, of isolating and explaining whatever subsidiary notions go to make up our intuitive, pre-theoretical notion of an expression's significance. (And here one would expect to find an investigation into the nature of, and the relations between, such notions as sense, reference, content, syntactic form, connotation, mood, expressive power, and the like.) On the other hand there is, second, the task of identifying and analysing the various different kinds of linguistic expression capable either of possessing a meaning in isolation, or of occurring as a part of some other expression which, as a whole, possesses a meaning. (Under this head one would expect to find an account of complete and incomplete expressions, of proper names, definite descriptions, predicates, quantifiers, connectives, demonstratives, sentences, and so on – as well as an explanation of how these various kinds of expression function within modal contexts, and contexts of direct quotation and *oratio obliqua*.)

Although Husserl has something to say on virtually all of these topics, he does not have a systematic and comprehensive semantico-syntactic theory of the kind one associates with, say, Frege, Carnap, or the author of the *Tractatus*. Nevertheless he does employ a number of *ad hoc* distinctions between categories of expression, the respective members of which function syntactically or semantically in interestingly similar ways. One of the most basic such distinctions is that between independent or categorematic expressions, on the one hand, and dependent or syncategorematic expressions on the other. Roughly speaking, sentences and singular terms ('proper names') comprise those expressions that are independently meaningful, whereas all other sorts of expression – connectives, adverbs, predicates, relational expressions, variables, etc. – have a meaning only in so far as they are capable of participating in other, complex, independently meaningful expressions. As Husserl himself remarks, we have here a straightforward application of the 'general distinction between independent and dependent objects, within the special field of meanings' (*LU* IV, Introd./p.493). And in conformity with his overall view that meaning only attaches to a sign in virtue of certain mental acts, Husserl maintains that

> A meaning, accordingly, may be called 'independent' when it can constitute *the full, entire meaning of a concrete act of meaning*, 'dependent' when this is not the case . . . . [Such] dependence of meaning *qua* meaning . . . determines, on our view, the essence of syncategorematica. (*LU* IV, §7/p.506)

Proper names or singular terms can express an independent nominal meaning because that meaning can comprise the matter of an act of objectifying presentation, such as an act of sense-perception or imagination. Likewise a sentence can be independently meaningful because of the intimacy of the relation in which its meaning stands to that of a complete, independent thought or judgement. But there is no such complete concrete act the entire meaning of which is what words like 'and', 'less than', 'simply', or 'is green' express. This seems to me right; and it provides an interesting *phenomenological* justification of the syntactic distinction that Frege draws (and which Husserl adopts) between sentences and proper names as complete expressions, as against predicates, connectives and the like as 'unsaturated' and 'in need of completion'.[42]

The major structural components of Husserl's theory of meaning can be presented most clearly if, for the moment, we restrict ourselves to a consideration of that theory as it applies to complete expressions and – more particularly, in the first instance – to sentences. We can take, as a concrete example, someone's utterance of the sentence: 'Einstein invented the general theory of relativity'. Depending on the circumstances in which it is uttered, and on the tone of voice, utterance of this sentence might serve to express and to communicate to a hearer a variety of different states of mind. The speaker might, for instance, be expressing his conviction that a certain state of affairs obtained, or he might be expressing incredulity, indifference, or admiration. Utterance of a sentence can, in other words, stand to a state of mind in the relation of sign to thing signified – but it would be quite wrong to say that the sentence had that state of mind as its *meaning*. Husserl consequently introduces a useful distinction that helps to resolve an ambiguity in the notions of a *sign* and an *expression*. On the one hand, that is, the utterance of a sentence can serve as a sign of some 'inner experience', it can express that experience, and in this way inform a hearer of its existence. But here 'being a sign of something' is equivalent to 'being evidence for the existence of something', in the way in which, say, volcanic phenomena are signs that the earth's interior is molten (*LU* I, §2/p.270). The relationship in which one thing is a sign of, or circumstantial evidence for, the existence of something else Husserl calls 'indication', and in the particular case where a linguistic utterance is evidence for the existence of the speaker's mental state he calls the relation one of 'intimation'. On the other hand, however, utterance of a sentence can serve as a sign, or as an expression of something in a radically different way: it can make an assertion, or express a meaning or sense. And what a sentence intimates is, typically, independent of what it asserts or expresses: the meaning or content of the sentence 'Einstein invented the general theory of relativity', for example, does not in the least concern the mental states of its users or hearers. This distinction is used by Husserl to separate neatly two traditional notions of 'judgement' that are easily confused: 'one tends to confuse the evidently grasped ideal unity with the real act of judging, to confuse what an utterance intimates with what it asserts.' (*LU* I, §11/p.286).

Henceforth, therefore, I shall follow Husserl in distinguishing terminologically between what an expression *intimates* (e.g. a mental state), and what it *means* or *expresses* (its meaning or sense); and it is in problems connected with the latter that our interest ultimately resides. But before leaving the topic of 'intimation' it is worth noting briefly the sophistication of the account that Husserl provides, *en passant*, of its phenomenology, of how one is conscious of what linguistic and other sorts of behaviour intimate about a person:

> To understand an intimation is not to have a conceptual knowledge of it, not to judge in the sense of asserting anything about it: it consists simply in the fact that the hearer *intuitively* takes the speaker to be a person who is expressing this or that, or as we certainly can say, *perceives* him as such . . . . The hearer perceives the intimation in the same sense in which he perceives the intimating person – even though the mental phenomena which make him a person cannot fall, as such,

within the intuitive grasp of another . . . . The hearer perceives the
speaker as manifesting certain inner experiences, and to that extent he
also perceives these experiences themselves: he does not, however,
himself experience them. (*LU* I, §7/p.278)

This is an important use of the notion of intimation, and one not unrelated to the insights that, for example, lie behind Wittgenstein's remarks
concerning the nature of the cognitive relations in which I stand to
another person. 'My attitude towards him', Wittgenstein writes, 'is an
attitude towards a soul. I am not of the *opinion* that he has a soul'.[43] Now
in the *Logical Investigations* Husserl's treatment of problems connected
with intimation is brief; but that treatment was, in effect, to furnish the
nucleus of the phenomenological account he subsequently provided,
most famously in the fifth *Cartesian Meditation*, of the consciousness we
have of other conscious beings.

Putting issues to do with the intimatory functions of language to one
side for the moment, we can turn now to the central problems concerning
linguistic meaning: How are we to account for the fact that linguistic
expressions are significant; and in what does their significance consist?

The form that Husserl's answer to this question takes is at first, perhaps, rather surprising, and seems to involve the implausible claim that
expressions of every sort function as names, that is, by referring to, or
standing for, objects:

> Each expression not merely says something, but says it *of* something: it
> not only has a meaning, but refers to [one or more] objects. (*LU* I,
> §12/p.287)
>
> Our examples entitle us to regard the distinction between an ex-
> pression's meaning, and its power to direct itself *as a name* to this or
> that objective correlate . . . as well-established. (*LU* I, §13/p.289;
> my italics)
>
> In meaning, a relation to an object is constituted. To use an ex-
> pression significantly, and to refer expressively to an object . . . are
> one and the same. (*LU* I, §15/p.289)
>
> Every expression . . . names or otherwise designates something.
> (*LU* I, §14/p.290)

We can begin to make these claims somewhat less implausible by setting
them within a broader context that takes account not only of Husserl's
philosophical views, but also of his terminology. And in that context we
should note, first, that the term 'object' covers anything whatsoever,
including properties, relations, facts, and states of affairs. In which case
the bizarre claim that sentences, say, are names of objects (cf. *LU* I,
§14/p.290) can perhaps be given a sympathetic reading, to the effect that
an indicative sentence typically picks out or stands for some state of

affairs – and this sounds considerably less implausible. We should note, second, that the only expressions that are in question here are complete or categorematic expressions; for they are, by definition, the only expressions that *can* be assigned a meaning in isolation. So Husserl is not at all committed to the thesis that incomplete expressions like 'or', 'incidentally', 'is green' and the like are names of anything. And third, we need to note that the term 'object' does not mean anything like *independently existing denizen of the external world*; it means, rather, *intentional object*. Only if this is so can any sense be made of Husserl's numerous remarks to the effect that, although every significant expression essentially 'refers to an object', nevertheless 'it makes no difference whether the object exists' (*LU* I, §15/p.293).

It is worth pausing over this last point, the point, namely, that an expression may be said to possess a reference (or an object, or an objective correlate), simply in virtue of being meaningful, and irrespective of whether there actually exists any such thing. On Husserl's conception of reference, then, the following three sentences must be capable in principle of being simultaneously true. Concerning some expression E:

(1) E is meaningful
(2) E is a name of an object, O, which is its 'objective correlate',
and yet
(3) There is no such thing as O.

Sentences (1) and (2) are related (amongst other ways) in that the truth of (1) is sufficient for the truth of (2). On the other hand, both (1) and (2) are entirely independent of the truth or falsity of (3). This, by itself, is enough to ensure that Husserl does not, and cannot, have a relational theory of reference. And this, in turn, makes any assimilation of Husserl's theory of linguistic meaning to Frege's potentially highly misleading. Frege's notion of reference contains elements that are unequivocally relational: the reference of an expression is an entity (i) whose existence and identity are independent of its being referred to by that, or by any other, expression, and (ii) in the absence of which the expression straightforwardly fails to *have* a reference. For Frege, to say that an expression refers to a fictional or a non-existent entity can only be an unacceptably confused way of saying that the expression doesn't refer at all. The point of calling the Fregean notion of reference 'relational' is to stress that its applicability essentially depends upon the existence of two terms – one of which is the entity referred to. By contrast, Husserl's notion of reference is 'adverbial': an expression may be said to have a reference (*eine bestimmte Richtung auf eine Gegenständliches*) even though there in fact exists no entity to which it is appropriately related. In which case the misleading phrase 'having a reference' (along with equally misleading equivalents like 'being directed towards an object', 'possessing an objective correlate' and the like) must be understood to mean something *intrinsic* to an expression's meaning, a role that an expression can perform, so to speak, intransitively, irrespective of what the world may or may not contain. 'To use an expression significantly, and to refer expressively to an object . . . are one and the same. [And] *it makes no difference whether the object exists*' (*LU* I, §15/p.293; my italics). This family of issues needs to be examined in some detail.

It has recently become commonplace, if not virtually obligatory, for writers on Husserl's theory of meaning to assimilate Husserl's distinction between a sign, its meaning, and its object to Frege's distinction between an expression, its sense, and its reference. Mohanty's treatment of these issues, for example, is typical in suggesting that Husserl's theory differs only terminologically, and not at all doctrinally, from Frege's: 'Husserl's terminology is different from Frege's. What Frege calls "*Sinn*", [Husserl] calls "*Bedeutung*"; for Frege's "*Bedeutung*" [Husserl] uses "*Gegenstand*".' Mohanty then adds: 'I shall render Frege's *Sinn* (and Husserl's *Bedeutung*) as "sense", and Frege's *Bedeutung* (and Husserl's *Gegenstand*) as "reference"'.[44]

This orthodoxy strikes me as utterly wrong. Frege's notion of *Bedeutung* is a notion of genuine, full-blooded, relational reference; and it is in terms of *that* notion that his theory of linguistic *Sinn* is articulated. Roughly speaking, an expression's *Sinn* is the condition which anything must meet in order to be the *Bedeutung* of that expression.[45] And the *Bedeutung* of an expression (if it has one) is that in virtue of whose identity expressions can be intersubstituted *salva veritate* for the expression, throughout any context of the appropriate kind. The following eight propositions represent, I believe, some of the consequences of these doctrines, and some of the commitments implicit in a broadly 'Fregean' theory of meaning.

F1) An expression may have a *Sinn* even though it lacks a *Bedeutung*.

F2) To any determinate *Sinn* there can correspond at most one *Bedeutung*.

F3) The *Bedeutung* of a sentence is a truth-value.

F4) The *Bedeutung* of a proper name is the object that is the bearer of that name.

F5) The *Sinn* of a declarative sentence is a thought.

F6) Thoughts are singular, individual entities.

F7) Thoughts are only contingently and externally related to mental acts.

F8) Linguistic meaning is fundamentally a sentential phenomenon.

Just how un-Fregean Husserl's theory is can be gauged from the fact that his theory entails the falsity of every one of these Fregean propositions. The following claims (H1–H8), that is, represent the central tenets of Husserl's theory of meaning; and each is incompatible with the corresponding Fregean claim.

H1)   An expression may not have a sense if it lacks an object.
On Husserl's account of sense, as he himself says, for an expression to have a sense just *is* for it to have direction towards an object. These two conditions are one and the same (*LU* I, §15/p.293). The consequent need to distinguish between (Fregean) 'reference' and (Husserlian) 'direction towards an object' is examined in connection with H4, below.

H2)   An expression with a determinate sense may have intentional direction towards more than one object.

This can happen in either of two ways, according to Husserl. On the one hand there are expressions that belong to what we earlier called the category of 'plural referring expressions', such as 'the twins', 'us', 'those elephants', and 'Benelux' (see pp. 62–4). This is a category which Frege refused to acknowledge; for him *Bedeutung* was always and essentially a one–one relation between an expression and an entity. There seems, however, no good reason why we should accept Frege's prejudice on this matter: expressions can be provided with a determinate, constant sense that enables them to pick out, say, *two* objects, quite as straightforwardly as they can be provided with a sense that gives them a unique reference. On the other hand – so Husserl claims – it can happen that an expression has a constant sense, and yet that it is now directed towards one object, now towards a quite different one:

> The expression 'a horse' has the same meaning in whatever context it occurs. But if on one occasion we say 'Bucephalus is a horse', and on another 'That cart-horse is a horse', there has been a plain change in our sense-giving presentation in passing from the one statement to the other. The expression 'a horse' employs the same meaning to present Bucephalus on the one occasion and the cart-horse on the other. It is thus with all general names. (*LU* I, §12/p.288)

There is, I think, nothing worth saving in this confused and inconsistent set of ideas. For one thing, it is simply false that the expression 'a horse' presents Bucephalus on the one occasion and the cart-horse on the other: *those* roles are performed, if by anything, by the expressions 'Bucephalus' and 'that cart-horse', respectively. Second, the theory that common names or concept-words (like 'a horse') function by referring to or naming all the objects in the extension of the term (i.e. all horses) is objectionable for precisely the reason that Frege communicated in his first letter to Husserl: 'There seems to be a difference of opinion between us', Frege wrote, 'about how a concept-word (common name) is related to objects.' Frege then presents his own view in diagrammatic form, the relevant part of which is this:

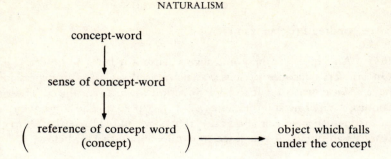

'Now it seems to me', Frege goes on, 'that for you the schema would look
like this:

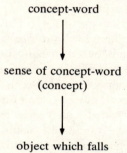

So that, for you, it would take the same number of steps to get from
proper names to objects as from concept words.' But in that case, Frege
objects, 'a concept-word whose concept was empty would then have to
be excluded from science just like a proper name without a corresponding
object'.[46] Frege's point, in other words, is that a concept-word is not
related to its instances as Husserl seems to suggest; for if it were, then
concept-words that lack instances would be semantically deviant – but
this is simply not the case. And, third, Husserl's remarks at *LU* I,
§12/p.288 are objectionable because they are inconsistent with his theory
of intentionality, and in particular with his account of the determination
of an act's object by its matter. It is an essential element of that account
that 'identical matters can never yield distinct objective references' (*LU*
V, §20/p.589).

H3)   The intentional object towards which a sentence is directed is a state
        of affairs (not a truth-value).
Husserl is explicit: 'What plays the part of object to judgement and
opinion we call *the state of affairs* judged' (*LU* V, §28/p.611; cf. *ibid*
§17/p.579).

H4) The intentional object towards which a proper name is directed is not the actual bearer of that name.

Now as part of an interpretation of Husserl's theory of linguistic meaning in the *Logical Investigations* this statement will perhaps be thought controversial – and certainly it contradicts a very widely held opinion amongst Husserlian commentators and critics, namely, that in the *Investigations* the intentional object of an act, or the reference of an expression, is identical with a real object (at least, in those cases where an appropriate real object exists).[47] This is a crucially important issue; for, in it, there come to a head a number of problems – to do with intentionality, meaning, objects, reference, the nature of phenomenology, the degree of Husserl's commitment to methodological solipsism, and the nature of his commitment (if any) to realism – problems the solutions we provide to which will in large part determine what, in general, we make of Husserl's early philosophy as a whole.

Anyone who concerns themselves with the issue of intentionality will doubtless sooner or later have to face the following dilemma: either intentionality is a genuinely relational phenomenon, in which case it requires the actual existence of the intended object, or intentionality is only pseudo-relational, in which case it can be said to characterize a mental act even if no appropriate real object exists. These alternatives represent a dilemma, rather than, say, merely a matter for straightforward choice, because *prima facie* neither alternative seems acceptable. If, on the one hand, we take intentionality to be genuinely relational, then although we are well placed to account for the possibility of objective thought and experience – that is, roughly, thought about and experience of the real world – we seem unable to account smoothly for thought and experience that *doesn't* concern objective reality. When I think about Sherlock Holmes, when I suffer a visual or auditory hallucination, or when I dream, I stand in *no* relation to an item in reality such that that item is what I am thinking about or experiencing. But equally it is clear that in such circumstances I am thinking about or experiencing *something*; and it is this latter state of affairs that a genuinely relational theory seems badly placed to explain. It looks, in other words, as though a relational theory will have to give two radically different accounts of the nature of singular thought, according to whether the object thought about actually exists or not.[48] And what makes this implausible is the widespread and strong intuitive conviction that, when I think a singular thought, there is no specifiable, significant difference between what I do when the object about which I am thinking exists, and what I do when when it doesn't. My thinking that Saint Nicholas has a beard, and my thinking that Santa Claus has a beard, regarded as acts of thinking, do not appear to differ essentially, and deserve to be treated as acts of the same type, explainable by appeal to one and the same theory.

Accounting for singular thoughts and experiences concerning non-existent objects is not an embarrassment for a non-relational or 'adverbial' theory of intentionality: to think about an object is merely to be 'minded' in such-and-such ways, to have such-and-such a configuration within mental space; and that is clearly something one can do irrespective of whether or not the object actually exists. I can be minded in a Santa-Claus-directed-sort-of-way; and to this possibility the non-existence of Santa Claus poses no threat at all. The embarrassment for adverbial theories is, rather, that they are not well placed to account for the objective aspects of intentional mental acts and states. If those acts and states are merely *mental* configurations, if all their essential characteristics are, so to speak, intransitive, then it is quite unclear in what sense they can be said to make contact with reality, or in what sense an extra-mental item and an intentional object can ever be one and the same.[49]

Perhaps the most natural first suggestion as to how this dilemma might be resolved is this: we reconcile the adverbial and the relational accounts of intentionality by identifying the intentional object and the real object (when there is a real object), but we provide an essentially adverbial account in cases where the intended object does not exist. In this way, it is hoped, we can allow not only for the fact that we sometimes think about and perceive the real world, but also for the fact that we sometimes have thoughts and undergo experiences that fail in this respect. This hodge-podge theory is objectionable, however, in part because it simply fails to provide any unitary, single explanation of intentionality, of what it is to have something in mind. Rather it provides two explanations, the choice between which, in any given case, depends on matters extraneous to the intentional act itself. More importantly, however, the attempt at reconciliation is objectionable because it requires the possibility that an intentional object (adverbially understood) can be identical with a real item in the external world. This, however, is not an intelligible application of the notion of identity; for it makes no sense to assert that anything intrinsic to my being minded in a Saint-Nicholas-directed-sort-of-way is identical with the real Saint Nicholas.

But if identity is too strong and intimate a relation, perhaps the overall strategy of reconciliation can still be salvaged if we construe the relation as a weaker and more distant one – say, one of 'correspondence' – so that when I am minded in a certain intentional way, there will be *some* (as yet unspecified) relation between my intentional object and the 'corresponding' real object, if there is one. Schematically this is, I believe, the form of theory that Husserl adopts in the *Logical Investigations* . But note that within a theory of this sort the nature, the identity, and the existence of whatever real object happens to 'correspond' to a given intentional mode of mindedness has no relevance to the nature, the identity, or the existence of that state of mindedness itself. In other words, a real object is at best externally and contingently related to an intentional act or state to which it corresponds. It follows, therefore, within Husserl's frame of reference, that questions to do with the existence or the nature of such real objects, as also questions concerning the relation of 'correspondence' in which they stand to mental acts and states, cannot even be posed within the constraints constitutive of descriptive psychology or naturalistic phenomenology. From *within* those constraints, the assumption of the existence of an external world that is independent of our cognitive states, but which is nevertheless largely as we believe it to be, and is, moreover, such as to contain entities which we sometimes successfully pick out by our intentional acts – assumptions such as these have the status of massive, unjustified, unnecessary, and even 'metaphysical' prejudices and presuppositions. And Husserl is quite clear that, as such, they must be put to one side; for naturalistic phenomenology restricts its purview to *phenomena* and its assertions to those that have the property of being self-evident. This means that in the last analysis naturalistic phenomenology of the kind practised in the *Logical Investigations* can have nothing to say about the relation, if any, in which intentional acts stand to reality as it is in itself. It is not so much that that work attempts, but fails, to offer a theoretical explanation of how reference to the real world is possible, it is more that this problem cannot even be raised without contravening the self-imposed methodological and doctrinal constraints involved in phenomenology from a naturalistic point of view.

Given, however, that Husserl's ultimate concern in the *Logical Investigations* is to reconcile 'the subjectivity of knowing and the objectivity of the content known', the adoption of that point of view turns out to be manifestly, and perhaps inevitably, unsuccessful. And this failure is, I believe, the single most significant factor leading Husserl to take the 'transcendental turn' away from a naturalistic phenomenology towards a form of transcendental idealism, and away from mere methodological solipsism towards a form of transcendental solipsism. (See pp. 153–7.)

If these admittedly rather general and schematic considerations are acceptable, they indicate not only that Husserl did not, indeed could not, identify the intentional object of an act with a real, objective item existing in the external world, but also that such an identification would be of dubious coherence given what he does say about intentional objects. If we call any theory of the sort usually attributed to Husserl, and according to which the intentional object of an act can be a real object, a *realistic* theory of intentionality, then two questions arise at this point: What textual evidence is there that Husserl was a non-realist? And, if that evidence is available, why have realistic readings of the *Logical Investigations* been so widespread?

An answer to the second question is not hard to find. The fact is that

Husserl's text is replete with suggestions, hints, and even apparently explicit endorsements of a realistic theory of intentionality. Many of the hints and suggestions are merely terminological: Husserl seems to talk, for example, of 'objective reference', and 'objectivity', of 'real objects', 'actual objects', 'concrete objects' and the 'objectifying acts' that 'refer to' or 'name' them. And all this has undoubtedly a realistic ring to it. The following four points, however, have a tendency to counteract this misleading impression.

First, we noted earlier that, although not entirely consistently, Husserl's dominant use of terms like 'real', 'actual', 'physical', 'concrete' and the like is a technical use, suitable for employment in the descriptive characterization of psychological phenomena (see pp. 102–7). As such his dominant use of these terms carries with it no tacit realistic commitments; and certainly that use should not be interpreted to mean anything like 'existing independently in the external world'.[50]

Second, there is Husserl's potentially highly misleading employment of a notion that is rendered in English by the words 'objectivity', 'objective correlate', and 'objective thing'. Husserl's words are '*Gegenständlich*', and '*Gegenständlichkeit*' – and his use of them, to talk, for instance, about the 'objective relation' in which an intentional act stands to 'something objective' (e.g. *LU* V §20/p.589) is easily construed as an endorsement of a realistic theory according to which the objects of intentional acts are *objective* entities existing independently of our mental acts and states. And in this, the normal sense of the word, 'objectivity' contrasts of course with 'subjectivity' – understood to signify, roughly, whatever is dependent for its existence or its nature on the thinking or experiencing subject. This is not, however, the sense in which Husserl typically employs the notion of *Gegenständlichkeit*. On the contrary, his understanding of it belongs to a tradition that takes it to mean, not *objective* in anything like the normal sense, but rather *object*-ive or object-directed, that is, having an object, an intentional object.[51] And doubtless Husserl inherited this notion directly from from Brentano, who had, famously, written:

> every mental phenomenon is characterized by what the mediaeval schoolmen called the intentional (or mental) inexistence of an object, and by what we . . call the relation to a content, the direction to an object (by which a reality is not to be understood), or *an immanent objectivity. (PES* p.88; my italics. Quoted by Husserl in *LU* V, §10/p.554)

Brentano's phrase is '*die immanente Gegenständlichkeit*', and on pain of obvious incoherence, this can have nothing to do with 'objectivity' as normally understood – after all, Brentano is talking here about things that are paradigmatically subjective: the immanent parts and moments of mental phenomena. Husserl too adopts this way of using the term *Gegenständlichkeit* to signify presence or possession of an intentional object – but he explicitly dissociates himself from the Brentanian theory according to which the *Gegenstand* in question is an immanent part of an act: 'The "immanent", "mental" object is not therefore part of the descriptive (real) make-up of the experience; it is thus in truth neither immanent nor mental. But equally it does not exist outside the mind (*extra mentem*), it does not exist at all' (*LU* V, §11/p.559).[52]

Another merely terminological factor that has doubtless encouraged a belief – especially amongst readers of the English version of the *Logical Investigations* – that Husserl's is a realistic theory of intentionality is his apparent adoption of a Fregean, that is, a realistic, theory of '*reference*'. This is, indeed, a merely terminological matter; for although the appearance in the English translation of the term '*reference*' (especially in a context where it stands contrasted with a notion of 'sense') has almost inescapable Fregean overtones, the German that Husserl himself employs has no such realist connotations whatsoever. Indeed, given that Husserl mentions Frege just once in the *Investigations*, and then solely in order to criticize his choice of terminology, it is unfortunate that the English translation of that work should make the two philosophers appear in this respect much more in agreement than in fact they are. One example of the Fregeanization of Husserl's text will have to suffice. Section 13 of the first Investigation is entitled '*Zusammenhang zwischen Bedeutung und gegenständlicher Beziehung*', and Husserl writes there:

> es sei der Akt des Bedeutens die bestimmte Weise des den jeweiligen *Gegenstand Meinens* – nur dass eben *diese Weise des bedeutsamen Meinens* und somit die Bedeutung selbst bei identischer Festhaltung *der gegenständlichen Richtung* wechseln kann. (p.289)

The three italicized phrases in this passage are rendered, respectively, as 'we refer to our object', 'this mode of significant reference', and 'the objective reference'. The section title itself is translated as 'Connection between meaning and objective reference'. This is all potentially misleading because, quite simply, Husserl is not talking about '*reference*' at all – not, at least, as that word is standardly understood in contemporary discussions in the theory of meaning. *That* notion of reference is extensional, genuinely relational, and brings with it ontological commitment to whatever items comprise its terms. Husserl's notion of '*gegenständliche Richtung*', in sharp contrast, is intentional, pseudo-relational, and is specifically designed to be applicable in cases where 'the object does not exist':

> In der Bedeutung konstituiert sich die Beziehung auf den Gegenstand.
> Also einen Ausdruck mit Sinn gebrauchen und sich ausdrückend auf

den Gegenstand beziehen (den Gegenstand vorstellen) is einerlei. Es kommt dabei gar nicht darauf an, ob der Gegenstand existiert. (*LU* I, §15/p.293)

The intentional object to which an expression has *gegenständliche Richtung* can never be the same as the object (if any) that would be assigned to that expression as its Fregean *reference*, if only because that which a given expression has necessarily and as such can never be identical with that which that expression may very well lack altogether.

Finally, and much more compellingly, there is one passage that has seemed to many to constitute irrefragable proof of the realistic character of Husserl's notion of intentionality. He writes:

It is a serious error to draw a real distinction between 'merely immanent' or 'intentional' objects, on the one hand, and 'transcendent', 'actual' objects, which may correspond to them, on the other . . . . It need only be said to be acknowledged that *the intentional object of a presentation is THE SAME as its actual object, and on occasion as its external object, and that it is* ABSURD *to distinguish between the two.* The transcendent object would not be *the object of this presentation* if it were not ITS *intentional* object. (*LU* V, Appendix to §§11 and 20/p.595; Husserl's italics)

This passage seems to be saying, and in no uncertain terms, that the intentional object of an act and a real, actual, transcendent, external object are, indeed, capable of being one and the same. And this appears to be an unqualified endorsement of a realist view of intentionality. Before drawing this conclusion, however, it is worth noting how the passage continues. With respect to the claim that transcendent and intentional objects are identical, Husserl immediately adds:

This is plainly a merely analytic proposition. The object of the presentation, of the 'intention', *is* and *means* the presented, the intentional object. If I have a presentation of God, say, or an angel, or an intelligible being-in-itself, or a physical thing, or a round square, etc., I mean the transcendent – in other words the intentional – object named in each case. And here it makes no difference whether this object exists, or is imaginary, or absurd. That the object is 'merely intentional' of course means neither that it *exists*, but only in the *intentio* of which it forms a real component part, nor that there exists some shadow [or sign] of it. It means, rather, that what exists is the intention, the '*meaning*' of an object thus constituted, but *not* the object itself . . . . But enough of these truisms. (*ibid.*, Husserl's italics.)

Now, no matter how one construes it, the claim that intentional acts successfully make contact with mind-independent items that exist in an objective, external world is not an 'analytic' claim or a mere 'truism'. On the other hand, a number of the propositions Husserl advances here *are* genuinely analytic – for example: 'The object of the presentation, of the "intention" is and means what is presented, the intentional object'; and again, 'The transcendent object would not be the object of this presentation if it was not its intentional object'. The former claim is a truth of logic, and tells us no more than that the intentional object of an act is the intentional object of an act. The latter claim is true by definition; it is an instance of the general truth that *nothing* can be 'the object of a presentation' if it is not its 'intentional object' – these two phrases being of course synonymous. And Husserl is quite right to insist that it would be logically inconsistent (*widersinnig*) to deny such claims as these.[53] It is likewise an analytic truism, a trivial and merely formal truth that, say, *if the Schloss in Berlin is my intentional object, then the Schloss in Berlin is my intentional object.* Not only are such empty tautologies intrinsically incapable of providing substantive grounds for subscription to realism, however, but they are also clearly taken by Husserl himself to be entirely compatible with an account of intentionality according to which 'to represent an object, e.g. the Schloss in Berlin, to oneself is . . . to be minded in this or that descriptively determinate fashion'. And this is so even though this mental act can only be described adequately 'by saying that the Schloss is perceived, imagined, represented . . . etc.' (*LU* V, §11/p.559). Those tautological truisms are, moreover, intended to be compatible with the claim that 'to be an object (*Gegenstand-sein*) consists phenomenologically in certain acts in which something appears or is thought of as an object' (*LU* V, §8/p.550). To have an intentional object, phenomenologically speaking, is merely to undergo 'a particular sort of experience or particular sort of mindedness' (*ibid.*). And in a phenomenological account of this 'sort of mindedness', this 'inward peculiarity of certain experiences', actual objects in the external world play no part whatsoever; 'for the intentional object . . . is only in question *as intentional*, and not as an external reality' (*LU* V, §15(a)/p.572; my italics).

There remains an unanswered question at this point, as to why Husserl should feel any need to assert what, by his own admission, are trivialities that one cannot even consistently deny. What precisely was his intention in the passages quoted above? There are two mistaken views about intentionality that Husserl is there concerned to discredit. One is any theory that implies that the object of an intentional act is always an image, a sign, an idea, or a 'shadow' of something. When I am thinking about the Schloss in Berlin then (*trivially*) I am thinking about the Schloss in Berlin – and not about something else, like an idea, an image, or a representation of the Schloss. According to Husserl, naive representational theories of intentionality are guilty of an incoherence in denying this truism. The second, not unrelated, view of intentionality that Husserl wishes to combat here is, familiarly, the Brentanian theory according to which the intentional object is taken to be an immanent, real *part* of a mental act. Husserl explains, in summary, that to say an intentional object exists 'means of course neither that it exists, but only in the *intentio* of which it forms a real component part, nor that there exists some shadow [or sign or image] of it'. Husserl attempts to discredit both these views by showing that 'it is a serious error', an error of logic, to deny assertions of the form: *If A intends object x, then A intends object x*. Now one manifestation of this error is the substitution for the first '*x*' of something designating an external or transcendent object, and the simultaneous substitution for the second of something designating an immanent or mental one. To this Husserl responds that it is *analytic* that 'the intentional object of a presentation is the same as its actual object'; for to deny this is to commit oneself to the *Widersinn* that the object I intend is distinct from the object I intend. There is nothing here, however, that warrants attribution to Husserl of a realistic or genuinely relational theory of intentionality, and little or no reason to assimilate his theory of *gegenständliche Beziehung* to Frege's theory of *Bedeutung*.

H5)   The sense of a declarative sentence is not a thought but a species.

H6)   The contents of thoughts are universal objects.

H7)   Thoughts are mental acts.
A thought, according to Frege, is an abstract individual that one grasps when one performs an act of thinking; and this abstract object is identical with the sense of the sentence that expresses that act. Husserl, by contrast, took a thought to be a mental act; and he took the sense of a sentence to be, not an individual object, but a universal or species. Given also the contrast between the roles assigned by the two philosophers, respectively, to truth-values and to states of affairs as the correlates of thoughts, one must conclude that there is no simple or illuminating way to map the one theory onto the other.

H8) Linguistic meaning is fundamentally nominal.
The outlines of Husserl's theory of meaning follow the outlines of the account he provides of intentional acts; and, as we saw above, the most primitive intentional acts, whose role it is to provide the foundation for all subsequent, higher-level acts, are non-propositional or nominal acts. States of affairs are higher-level objectivities (*LU* VI, §48/p.795), the awareness of which is constituted on the basis of 'straightforward', ultimately intuitive experience. Linguistic understanding necessarily mirrors such relations of dependence, so that grasping the meaning of a name or nominal expression is something that may occur prior to and independently of the understanding of any sentence whose *Gegenstand* is a state

of affairs (cf. *LU* V, §42/p.650). The contrast with Frege's theory – according to which 'a word only means something in the context of a sentence' – is sharp.

In final summary, the overall structure of Husserl's theory of linguistic meaning can perhaps best be presented in diagrammatic form. There are four major and irreducible relations in terms of which that theory is articulated, represented as follows:

$X \longrightarrow Y$: X is instantiated in Y

$X \Longrightarrow Y$: X is indicated or intimated by Y

$X \dashrightarrow Y$: X is intentionally directed towards Y
  or: Y is the intentional object of X

$X \rightarrow Y$: X is expressed by Y;
  or: X is the sense of Y.

We can take, first, the case of a common name or concept-word, e.g. the word 'green'. The situation is this:

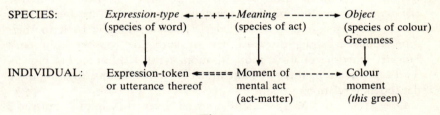

Fig. 4

What, as it were, breathes life into this situation are the mental acts, and in particular the moments of those acts called their act-matters, which are the source of all intentionality, which are intimated by certain speech acts, and whose species constitute the meaning or sense of linguistic expression-types.

· The structure is only slightly different when the expression in question is a proper name or a sentence. The difference is occasioned merely by the fact that the object intended is not itself a species:

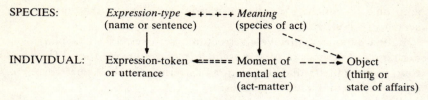

Fig. 5

Here again, the engine at the centre of this machinery is the act of meaning-intention which, in virtue of its matter, is capable of having an intentional object, a sense or meaning, an adequate expression in language, and so on. Such acts of meaning-intention do not, however, exhaust the kinds of acts to which Husserl assigns a role in his theory of meaning. We have yet to examine acts of meaning-fulfilment – the topic of the next section.

Fulfilment and objectivity: experiencing the truth

One part of his inheritance from Brentano that Husserl never relinquished was a commitment to an overall framework of priorities and dependencies within which, for example, the concrete is always more basic than the abstract, the sensory is always the foundation of the conceptual and the intellectual, the real is prior to the ideal, and nominal phenomena are more primitive that propositional ones. In the *Logical Investigations* much effort is devoted, as indeed it had been in the *Philosophy of Arithmetic*, to tracing phenomena that are intellectual, conceptual, categorial, abstract, ideal, and/or symbolic back to their foundations in 'straightforward' acts of 'authentic' sensory intuition.[54] Husserl's theories of abstraction, ideation, synthesis, founded or higher-level acts – even his theory of intentionality – are attempts to bring these dependency relations to light.

One item in this programme that we have yet to examine is Husserl's attempt, using only resources available within naturalistic phenomenology, to provide an explanation of our objectivity concepts – concepts such as *truth*, *being*, *knowledge*, *rationality*, and *reality*. Husserl's aim is to explain the nature and the applicability of such concepts, and to do so, moreover, solely in terms of our sensory intuitions and the various mental operations that we apply to them. The goal, in other words, is a naturalistic, phenomenological explanation of objectivity, or, in Husserl's words, 'a phenomenological elucidation of knowledge'. And that explanation is intended to comprise the nucleus of a solution to the problem which, above all others, exercised Husserl in the *Logical Investigations*, the problem, namely, of reconciling 'the subjectivity of knowing and the objectivity of the content known.' The task which faces Husserl in the sixth Investigation, in other words, is to build a bridge that will link, on the one side, the analysis of subjectivity and the mind that he has already provided in Investigations I to V – an analysis directed towards mental phenomena, intentionality, intuition, abstraction, conception, judgement, and the like – and, on the other side, the fact that some subjective mental phenomena can also, correctly, be characterized as objectively 'rational', 'justified', 'valid', or 'true'.

If we are to understand some of the more idiosyncratic features of Husserl's treatment, it is important to note that the materials available to him in attempting to build this bridge are severely circumscribed. In so far as the attempt is to belong to naturalistic phenomenology, the only items to which appeal can be made are such phenomena as can be consistently acknowledged from within the framework of a naturalistic methodological solipsism – that is, mental acts along with their real and intentional contents. So the bridge between subjectivity and objectivity, and indeed the account of what objectivity consists in, must be constructed entirely from materials to be found on the subjective side of the divide.

The theory of intentionality, as we have it so far, aims to explain how a mental act can have the intrinsic property of *Gegenständlichkeit*, or 'object-directedness'. The theory is quite general in that it applies to any intentional act whatsoever – irrespective of any type or sort to which that act might belong and, in particular, irrespective of whether the act in question is an intellectual act of thought or a sensory act of intuition. What the theory does not yet tell us, however, is how two or more acts are related to one another when they, so to speak, share the same intentional object. This is a substantive problem for Husserl precisely because 'object-directedness' is an intrinsic property of acts, and one which they can possess without there actually being an object to which they are directed.[55] This problem can be intensified, slightly, if we introduce the added complication that one act may be a merely signitive, conceptual act, whereas the other may be an act of sensory intuition. So the problem is this: how can we account for the fact that I can not only conceive of an object or a state of affairs, but that I can also perceive *that very same thing*? How must the two acts be related to enable this to happen? In Husserlian terminology this is the problem of 'the relation of significant intention to fulfilling intuition', that is, of how 'the intentional essence of the intuitive act fits in with, or *belongs to*, the semantic essence of the significative act' (*LU* VI, §16/p.719). And it is a constraint on any acceptable phenomenological solution that no role be assigned by it to the existence or the identity of non-phenomenal objects.

We cannot here appeal to the identity of the actual objects intended by the two acts, because the acts may still be related in this way even though there *is* no actual object that they both intend. Likewise the explanation cannot concern the respective qualities of the two acts, which can be varied at will without making any significant difference to the situation at issue. Husserl holds, therefore, that 'the identification is based solely on their materials'; it is the acts' respective material or matter which explains the possibility of the one being fulfilled by the other.

There is a complication that we must notice here. The concept of fulfilment is itself a phenomenological, indeed an *intentional* notion: the relation in which two acts of mine stand to one another when one is said correctly to be a fulfilment of the other is not a relation that can hold whether I am aware of the fact or not. 'Fulfilment' is the name of an experience – the experience that I have when I become aware that two different intentional acts correspond or fit together in certain ways. (As we shall see, it is this characteristic of fulfilment, above all others, that prevents it from performing the central role Husserl assigns it in his theory of knowledge.)

Consequently, any situation in which fulfilment occurs necessarily involves three acts: the signitive or 'empty' act of meaning-intention; the intuitive act whose content is what fulfils the first act; and, finally, the act whose function it is to match the contents of the first two acts one with another, and the outcome of which is an awareness of fulfilment:

> This means that not only signification and intuition, but also their mutual adequation, their union of fulfilment, can be called an act, since it has its own peculiar intentional correlate, *ein Gegenständliches*, to which it is 'directed'. (*LU* VI, §8/p.696)

The peculiar intentional correlate of an act of fulfilment is: *the identity of the objects of the other two acts*. 'In all cases [of fulfilment] an intention comes into coincidence with the act which offers it fulness; i.e. the object which is meant in it is the same as the object meant in the fulfilling act' (*LU* VI, §14/p.715). And Husserl calls the experience of such an intentional identity an act of 'recognition'.

To what sorts of concrete situation is this analysis intended to apply? Husserl gives as an example the case in which, initially, I understand the meaning of an expression like 'my inkpot' (or, equivalently, in which I have in mind a concept like the concept of *my inkpot*) 'in merely symbolic fashion'.[56] This means that I perform an act of meaning-intention, the intentional object of which is my inkpot, but that I enjoy no simultaneous perception or sensory intuition of that object. I am, as it were, *merely* thinking about it, in its absence. Suppose next that I subsequently come to be in a position in which 'my inkpot stands before me: I *see* it' (*LU* VI, §6/p.688). The ensuing situation may belong to either of two quite different kinds. On the one hand I may simply remain unaware of the identity or coincidence that holds between what I am conceiving and

144

what I am perceiving: while thinking of my inkpot my eyes may wander idly over my room, and they may alight on something black and shiny, lying on the floor, half covered by discarded sheets of manuscript. Although I see it, and although I am indeed thinking about it, I simply fail to recognize it. On the other hand, however, it may be the case that my meaning intention, as it were, suddenly seems to hit its target: what I am thinking about and what I am seeing coincide for me, and I say: 'That's *it*! That's my inkpot!' Here, Husserl says, my empty act of meaning-intention achieves fulfilment in my act of perception. 'But how does this happen?' Husserl asks (*LU* VI, §6/p.688). 'What brings these acts into unity?'

> The answer seems clear. The relation, as one of naming, is mediated, not merely by acts of meaning, but by acts of recognition which are here acts of classification. The perceived object is recognized as an inkpot, [and so is] *known* as one. (*Ibid.*; my italics.)

And in this way *knowledge* enters the scene. Indeed it turns out that, for Husserl, 'talk of knowledge *refers to* a relationship between acts of thought and fulfilling intuitions' (*LU* VI, §67/p.837).

At a naively intuitive level there are, I think, three main ingredients in this view of knowledge, and together they make it seem plausible – to Husserl's eyes at least. One concerns the nature of intentionality; another, the nature of truth; and the third, the nature of perception. They can be summarized briefly as follows.

With respect to intentionality Husserl takes seriously the claim that insofar as one can *aim* at an object, or perform an act that has 'direction towards' something, then it must make sense to talk of *hitting* what one aims at, or actually *reaching* that towards which one is directed. This feeling is intimately related to the next.

With respect to perception, Husserl believes that its defining characteristic, that which makes it unique and which thus sets it apart from all other intentional acts whatsoever, is its power to present its intentional object 'in person'. What distinguishes a genuine perception from a memory, say, or an expectation, an act of imagination, or a merely intellectual grasp of a thing is that, while a non-perceptual act essentially involves some image, likeness, sign, or representation of its object, in a genuine perception 'the object itself is actually present, and in the strictest sense present *in propria persona*' (*LU* V, §5/p.542). 'Perception is characterized by the fact that in it . . . the object "itself" appears, and does not merely appear "in a likeness"' (*LU* VI, §14/p.712). 'The perfection of an imagination, however great, still leaves it different from a perception: it does not present the object itself, not even in part. . . . It offers only its image which . . . is never the thing itself. *That* we owe to perception' (*LU* VI, §36/p.761). In some sense or other, it would seem, perception

145

puts us into direct, immediate contact with the thing itself. It is in a straightforward perceptual act, apparently, that an intentional aim can hit its target.

And finally, concerning truth, Husserl took seriously, and quite literally, the view expressed in the traditional adage that truth requires an *adequatio rei ac intellectus*. On this view, for there to be such a thing as truth there must be (i) an intellectual commitment of some kind, a conception, or thought, or judgement; (ii) something, a *res*, that is conceived or judged; and (iii) a relation of 'correspondence' between (i) and (ii) in virtue of which (i) is an *adequate* conception or judgement of (ii). To this Husserl adds a fourth requirement that, in a phenomenological theory of truth, all three elements must be given in experience – and in particular there must be direct awareness of the correspondence between (i) and (ii).

These three intuitions come together to yield a theory according to which a given complex act counts as a *knowing*, as an experience of truth, just in case it incorporates:

(a) an intellectual act of meaning-intention, A, with an intentional object, O_1;
(b) an act of perception, P, which presents an object, O_2, itself and in person;
(c) an act of synthesis or identification, S, that brings to awareness the fact that O_1 and O_2 are numerically identical.

Truth, according to Husserl, is 'the correlate of an identifying act', in other words it is 'the full agreement of *what is meant* with *what is given as such*. This agreement we experience in self-evidence, in so far as self-evidence means the actual carrying out of an adequate identification' (*LU* VI, §39/p.765).

In the act of meaning intention (A) we have the *intellectus*; the perceptual act (P) gives us the *res* itself; and the act of identification (S) gives us a direct awareness of the *adequatio*. What we have here is truth, Husserl believes. And, because there is also awareness of every relevant element in the situation, it also constitutes a case of awareness of truth, or knowledge:

> When a presentative intention has achieved its last fulfilment, the genuine *adequatio rei et intellectus* has been brought about. The object is actually 'present' or 'given', and present precisely as intended . . . . And so also, *eo ipso*, the ideal of every fulfilment, and therefore of a signitive fulfilment is sketched for us. The *intellectus* is in this case the thought-intention, the intention of meaning. And the *adequatio* is realized when the object meant is in the strict sense *given* in our intuition, and given just as we think it. (*LU* VI, §37/p.762)

146

Perhaps the single most crucial condition that must obtain, if a theory of this kind is to provide a feasible account of objectivity, is that in perception we should be presented with an object itself, as it is in itself.[57] If this condition fails, then the theory can provide no account of genuine – but at best only of merely apparent – knowledge and truth. And of course an account of apparent objectivity is not an account of any sort of objectivity at all: merely apparent objectivity is a species of subjectivity.

Strangely, Husserl himself unwittingly provides precisely the reasons why this condition cannot be met, and why perception cannot in general be said to present 'the object itself, as it is in itself':

> Perception, so far as it claims to give us the object 'itself', really claims thereby to be no mere intention, but an act, which may indeed be capable of offering fulfilment to other acts, but which itself requires no further fulfilment. But generally, and in all cases of 'external' perception, this remains a mere pretension. The object is not actually given, it is not given wholly and entirely as that which it itself is. It is only given 'from the front', only 'perspectivally foreshortened and projected' and so on. (*LU* VI, §14/p.712)

This is an early appearance of the doctrine of the *perzeptive Abschattung des Gegenstandes*, of the adumbrative or perspectival nature of the objects of perception. We shall hear more about this important doctrine in subsequent chapters; at this point, however, it is enough to note that its truth is incompatible with the theory of objectivity presented in the *Logical Investigations*. For in so far as objects are only ever presented partially and perspectivally in sense perception, they are never presented 'adequately' or 'in person'. As Husserl came to realize, if a perception of an object is to be 'adequate' in the way that his theory of knowledge and truth requires, the object must be presented entirely and transparently in that perception: it must possess no areas of opaqueness, no properties, or parts, or aspects that are not themselves given 'in person' in the perception of it. And this condition is never fulfilled in sense perception, which on the contrary always presents certain *aspects of* an object, rather than the object as it is in and of itself.

The theory also fails in so far as it makes essential use of a number of objectivity concepts whose applicability it is supposedly the purpose of that theory to explain. For example, it is not enough that the objects O_1 and O_2 should merely seem to me to be identical, what is required is that they actually *be* identical: their identity must be an objective fact of which I become aware. But it is the very possibility, in general, of my being aware of an objective fact, and also the nature of the relation in which mere subjective seemings stand to genuinely objective knowledge, that are precisely what need to be explained in the first place.

Even if we allow that certain phenomena can properly be characterized as self-evident, and even if we accept that certain experiences are capable of fulfilling other experiences, we nevertheless lack the resources with which to explain how such subjective, intentional experiences can ever make contact with reality, or can ever be related to things which are not subjective or intentional in such a way as to constitute objective knowledge of them. And so, as Günther Patzig puts it, in the *Logical Investigations* 'the daring bridge called evidence, intended to connect judgement with fact, had the drawback, rather unfortunate in a bridge, that it ended on the same side of the river from which it began'.[58] Given the naturalistic perspective that informs the phenomenology of the *Logical Investigations*, Husserl found it impossible to escape the domain of seemings, or to provide an acount of objective truth and knowledge using only the materials available within descriptive psychology. In the last resort, therefore, that work fails in its overall aim at precisely the point, and for just the reason, that the *Philosophy of Arithmetic* had earlier done so. Neither work could satisfactorily explain, in naturalistic terms, how 'the psychological' and 'the logical' were to be reconciled, how 'that which is intrinsically objective [can] become a presentation, and thus, so to speak, something subjective' (*LU* Introd. to vol.2, §2/p.254).

This failure was, I believe, inevitable, given the combination in Husserl's early thought of two Brentanian commitments. One was to a methodological solipsism according to which the workings of the mind can be investigated and understood in complete isolation from any facts concerning the nature, or even the existence, of non-mental reality. The other commitment was to a naturalism which viewed mental phenomena as merely one species of natural occurrence amongst many others – albeit one that could be investigated independently of all the others. These two points of view combine to yield a programme according to which, on the one hand, the properties of a certain class of natural occurrences (mental acts) are to be analysed and explained in isolation, but according to which, on the other hand, the members of that class possess properties (being true, referring to reality, constituting knowledge, etc.) which can only be analysed or explained by appeal to the relation in which they stand to items outside that class. In short, the programme is unworkable because it simultaneously requires and prevents an explanation of mental phenomena considered in isolation.

As we shall see subsequently, Husserl came to see that no adequate phenomenological explanation of the possibility of knowledge or truth could be formulated so long as he remained committed to a programme that involved both naturalistic and solipsistic elements. Within a few years of writing the *Logical Investigations*, that is, he had renounced his naturalism, adopting instead a transcendental point of view – though one that nevertheless remained essentially solipsistic. Towards the end of his life, however, he also abandoned his transcendental solipsism in favour of a philosophical explanation of objectivity couched in terms of the inter-subjective agreements in responses and judgements obtaining amongst the various members of a given community.

The nature of Husserl's transcendental solipsism is the subject of the following chapter; and in Chapter IV we will examine the final phase in the evolution of Husserl's thought, from solipsism to intersubjectivity and the possibility of objective truth.

Part II
Transcendental Idealism

III

Solipsistic Idealism

Introduction

The first edition of the *Logical Investigations* appeared in 1901, and largely on the strength of this work Husserl was invited, almost immediately, to take up the post of *ausserordentlicher Professor* at the University of Göttingen. He moved from Halle to Göttingen in September of that year, remaining there, first as an *Extraordinarius* and later as an *Ordinarius*, for the next fifteen years. During this period he published only one book, entitled *Ideas Concerning Pure Phenomenology and Phenomenological Philosophy. First Book: General Introduction to Pure Phenomenology*, (or *Ideas* for short).[1] This appeared in 1913. By general consent this work is one of the most central and influential texts of Husserlian phenomenology; and in the present chapter we will be largely concerned to come to terms with the doctrines it contains.

It seems that for some four or five years after he arrived in Göttingen Husserl's philosophical activity was directed predominantly towards defending, expanding, and modifying theories that belonged essentially to the same naturalistic point of view that had characterized his thought in the *Logical Investigations*. At some point during 1905 or 1906, however, Husserl's philosophical orientation underwent a radical and permanent change, as a consequence of which he came to believe that no merely naturalistic framework could ever yield acceptable solutions to problems of the kind with which he was concerned. It is unclear whether Husserl's sudden and intense interest in Kantian thought was a contributory cause, or merely a subsequent symptom of this disenchantment with naturalism – during the winter semester of 1905–6, for instance, he taught courses on Kant's philosophy every day of the week except Sunday – but in any case in 1907 he delivered a series of five lectures which, for the first time, made public the fact that his philosophy had taken a 'transcendental turn' away from naturalism.[2] The vision that Husserl tentatively and incompletely articulates in these lectures was to receive its definitive expression in *Ideas*.

Now it is no simple matter to identify with any degree of precision the respects in which Husserl's philosophy changes, and the respects in which it remains constant, between, say, 1901 and 1913. One factor which presents even the best intentioned and most sympathetic reader with an initial obstacle that can prove, in this respect, all but insurmountable, is the fact that at some point during this transitional period, and for no good reason, Husserl invented and introduced an entirely new set of technical terms, and of conventions governing their use. After 1907 we hear less and less of 'acts', their 'matter', 'quality', or 'sensory content', or of 'abstraction', 'species', or 'categorial perception'. We are presented instead with texts that concern things called 'noemata', 'noeses', 'thetic characteristics', 'doxic syntaxes', 'hyletic data', 'protodoxic posita', 'the noematic object in the How', and worse. It has to be said that this terminology is nothing short of barbaric: it is ugly; it is unnecessary; for the greater part is neither precisely defined nor, even, informally explained; and, moreover, it is not always used consistently.

Having said this, the problems still of course remain, of how we should overcome the obstacle this terminology presents, and of how we should characterize the changes that Husserl's thought underwent after completion of the *Logical Investigations* . In a sense it will take us the rest of the present chapter to provide anything like an adequate response to these issues. But, by way of anticipation, it can be said now that the massive changes in terminology will turn out to mask a very considerable degree of specific doctrinal continuity. Husserl's particular theories concerning wholes and parts, foundational relations, ideal objects and our intuitive awareness of them, the relations between the content, the object, and the force of a mental act, the nature and role of 'fulfilment', and much else besides, remain recognizably the same beneath their new terminological disguises. What changes radically, however, is the nature of the overall philosophical framework within which these theories are developed and put to use. It is, to adopt a musical analogy, as though Husserl had left the themes of his earlier composition largely unaltered, but had transposed the whole thing into a radically different key. One way to describe this change is to say that Husserl moves from a naturalistic point of view to a transcendental one; another is to say that he relinquishes mere methodological solipsism for a full-blooded transcendental idealism. Both ways of talking require explanation.

A philosophical theory is naturalistic to the extent that it is committed to the view that the universe contains nothing but natural phenomena – a natural phenomenon being any object, event, property, fact, or the like, whose explanation can in principle be couched exclusively and without remainder in terms acceptable within the natural sciences. So not only does naturalism exclude all ineliminable supernatural or theological elements from a proper explanation of things; it excludes all such metaphysical or philosophical elements as well. A naturalistic philosopher will hold, with Quine, that 'knowledge, mind, and meaning are part of the same world that they have to do with, and that they are to be studied in the same empirical spirit that animates natural science. There is no place for a prior philosophy.'[3]

In the present context, the most important ingredient in naturalism is the thesis that the human mind is just a common-or-garden part of the natural order of things. And in this regard the obvious secular opponent of naturalism is transcendental idealism, which is precisely the view that the mind is *not* ultimately just a part of the natural world, but on the contrary must be assigned some foundational or constitutive role with respect to the natural world as a whole – a role that therefore inevitably places some aspects or functions of the mind beyond the explanatory reach of the natural sciences.

It is important to note, however, that it is not idealism *per se* that is incompatible with naturalism. Certain forms of empirical or subjective idealism, for example, can coexist peacefully with, are indeed sometimes the expression of, a consistently naturalistic outlook. Thus there is just as little threat to naturalism from a reductivist theory according to which all phenomena (including physical ones) are reducible to mental phenomena, as there is from a naturalistic materialism according to which all phenomena (including mental ones) can be explained entirely by appeal to facts concerning matter in motion – just as long, that is, as the base class itself is naturalistically construable. In other words both 'materialism' and 'mentalism' (i.e. one kind of empirical idealism) can take the form of reductive strategies in which one set of natural phenomena are identified with or reduced to another. And clearly this strategy would not require the abandonment of a naturalistic perspective. It is, rather, *transcendental* idealism that is in diametrical opposition to naturalism; and it is so because (in a sense that has yet to be specified) it requires us to transcend the realm of natural phenomena entirely, in order to achieve a point of view from which it can be seen that certain mental phenomena are not – or are not merely – elements within the natural world. 'Transcendental subjectivity', according to Husserl, is 'a subjectivity antecedent to all objective realities' (*FTL* §65/p.169). It is of course the notion of a transcendental, non-worldly, or supra-scientific perspective that is anathema to the naturalistic philosopher: 'naturalism', Quine writes, is 'the abandonment of the goal of a first philosophy. It sees natural science as an inquiry into reality, fallible and corrigible but not answerable to any supra-scientific tribunal, and not in need of any justification beyond observation and the hypothetico-deductive method'.[4] Husserl's rejection of naturalism in philosophy was unwavering after 1907.

The term 'solipsistic' I shall use in a weak sense, to describe any theory in which ultimate primacy, or priority, or independence is ascribed to the mental acts, states, or abilities of individuals considered in isolation. I shall not be concerned with, and I shall not use the term 'solipsism' to mean, the stronger and more specific doctrine that 'I alone exist or am known to exist; the theory that there are no other minds or persons.'[5]

Solipsistic theories come in two radically different kinds. Methodological solipsism has been identified by Putnam with the assumption that 'no psychological state, properly so-called, presupposes the existence of any individual other than the subject to whom that state is ascribed'.[6] Putnam adds: 'Making this assumption is, of course, adopting a *restrictive program* – a program which deliberately limits the scope and nature of psychology'. It is a restrictive programme, minimally, in that it accords the mental states of an individual the capacity for independent treatment, in total isolation not only from facts about the inanimate environment of the individual, but also from facts about other psychological subjects. The author of the *Logical Investigations* was a methodological solipsist – a position that is entirely compatible with a naturalistic point of view.

The second kind of solipsistic theory is transcendental solipsism – and by this I shall understand any form of transcendental idealism in which a non-natural explanatory role is assigned to the mental acts, states, or abilities of individuals considered in isolation. The author of *Ideas* was a transcendental solipsist in this sense – as too were the authors of *The Critique of Pure Reason* and the *Tractatus Logico-Philosophicus*. As a species of transcendental idealism, solipsism of this kind contrasts with those other forms of idealism according to which a non-naturalistic theory is to be articulated by appeal, not to individuals considered in isolation, but rather to individuals considered as comprising an intersubjective community, or as participating in some social whole. Arguably both Husserl's *Crisis* and Wittgenstein's *Philosophical Investigations* are works written from the standpoint of such a non-solipsistic, transcendental idealism. Just as solipsistic idealism is naturally expressed using the singular form of the first person pronoun, as concerning 'I', 'me', and what is 'mine', so, on the other hand, non-solipsistic idealism is inherently plural, invoking 'us', what is 'ours', and the things 'we' do and share.[7]

Finally, in the matter of terminology, something needs to be said about the word 'transcendental' itself. Kant originally introduced it as follows:

> I entitle *transcendental* all knowledge which is occupied not so much with objects as with the mode of our knowledge of objects in so far as this mode of knowledge is to be possible *a priori*. A system of such concepts might be entitled transcendental philosophy.[8]

I take this to mean that in its primary sense the term 'transcendental' designates a kind of knowledge or understanding – namely such as concerns the *a priori* conditions which govern the possibility of our knowledge of objects. Something is transcendental, in other words, in so far as it involves reflection on the necessary conditions for the possibility of any objective knowledge whatsoever. And this seems to be just the sense in which Husserl uses the term. For instance, he justifies calling the phenomenological reduction 'transcendental' by appealing to the fact that 'we have here the ultimate source of the only conceivable solution to the deepest problems in epistemology, problems that concern the nature and possibility of objectively valid knowledge' (*Ideas* §97/p.285). We might say that transcendental matters concern the relation in which the mind, consciousness, meaningful experience, and the like stand to the natural world, in so far as this relation is not itself taken to be a natural relation obtaining *within* that world. As we will see, many of Husserl's most striking and most problematic theories – concerning for example intentionality, synthesis, constitution, evidence, reason, horizons, and so on – are attempts to characterize precisely this relation. And Husserl's ultimate aim is to do this in a way which will enable him to reconcile the subjectivity of knowing and the objectivity of the content known, and so 'clear up the relations in which knowledge and object stand to each other in conscious life itself' (*Ideas*, Author's Preface/p.26).

From 'naturalism' to 'rigorous science'

The present section concerns Husserl's changing conception of the nature and function of philosophy itself. In the *Logical Investigations*, by and large, Husserl had adopted a modest and piecemeal approach to philosophical problems: specific problems were dealt with individually and on their own terms, and conceptual clarity was pursued for its own sake. In an article entitled 'Philosophy as Rigorous Science', which he published in 1911, and which acted in effect as his manifesto for the next decade, Husserl refers, ominously, to 'the "system" for which we yearn' (*PRS* in *HSW* p.167). And he claims that philosophy can never be either rigorous or scientific as long as it lacks a single 'system of doctrine'. In *Ideas* and the works that follow it, Husserl attempts to formulate just such a single system of doctrine – an integrated, unique, self-subsistent, and self-warranting set of methodological and doctrinal commitments; in short a fully-fledged *philosophia prima*.

This enterprise has a number of distinguishable characteristics which, for Husserl, are interrelated in the most intimate ways. There is, for instance, the ideal towards which his philosophy, towards which indeed any philosophy worthy of the name, aspires – namely, to become 'a rigorous science'. There is, too, the function that such philosophy must fulfil: to provide 'a transcendental grounding of knowledge' or 'a firm foundation for science'. There is, further, the requirement that philosophy be essentially 'self-responsible' or 'self-warranting', which is to say that, although the claims made within philosophy must be entirely justified and rational, their justification and rationale cannot come from or depend upon anything external to that discipline itself. There can in principle be no *other* discipline whose task it is to investigate the foundations, or warrant the assumptions on which philosophy rests. As Husserl says, rather darkly, 'the intrinsically first criticism of cognition, the one in which all others are rooted, is transcendental self-criticism on the part of phenomenological cognition itself' (*FTL* §107(d)/p.289). In general this demand is tantamount to the well-known Husserlian requirement that philosophy should be literally 'presuppositionless', that it should aim at 'pure and absolute knowledge' (*PRS* in *HSW* p.167). And, finally, there is the requirement that, to be defensible, philosophy must eschew all forms of naturalism and – what is the same thing for Husserl – embark upon a 'critique of reason' which is 'the foremost prerequisite for being scientific in philosophy' (*PRS* in *HSW* p.169).

In order to understand how these elements combine to determine the nature and purpose of philosophy, as Husserl now sees it, we must distinguish between two different conceptions of science to which he appeals.[9] There are, on the one hand, the natural and human sciences, such as physics, astronomy, and chemistry, or psychology, history, and anthropology. These sciences are characterized individually by the fact that each has its own well-defined domain, or field, comprising items of a certain kind which it is the responsibility of the science in question to explore, codify, and describe. It is possession of such a well defined 'region' (*Gebiet*, *Region*, *Sphäre*, *Feld*, etc.) that enables the natural and human sciences to have a 'doctrinal content' which is stable over time, which is accepted unquestioningly by the majority of scientists working within a given discipline, and which is objective in that 'there is, by and large, no room for private "opinions", "notions" or "points of view"'. And conversely, as Husserl points out, to the extent that there *is* widespread disagreement, or room for private opinions and the like within a science, 'the science in question is not an established one, but is in the process of becoming a science, and is generally so judged' (*ibid*).

On the other hand, however, no natural or human science is what Husserl calls a *rigorous* science. 'All natural science', he writes, 'is naive in regard to its point of departure. For it, the nature it is to investigate is simply *there*' (*PRS* in *HSW* p.171). The natural and human sciences, in other words, are philosophically naive: they have an unquestioned commitment to the adequacy of a naturalistic standpoint, according to which the world is such that the truth about it can be established by normal scientific methods of inquiry. In contrast to such naive science there stands rigorous science, which is precisely science that is *not* philosophically 'naive in regard to its point of departure', and which does not make unexamined and questionable assumptions about the existence and nature of reality, the possibility of objective knowledge, the adequacy of scientific procedures, and so forth. Rigorous science is rigorous, negatively speaking, in that it has expunged all uncritically accepted assumptions from amongst its commitments, whether tacit or explicit. More positively, it is rigorous in that it contains no claims or assertions that are not absolutely grounded, or fully justified. The claim that all assertions are to be 'absolutely' grounded means that each assertion is to be entirely justified, but that its justification is not to be relative to any antecedently accepted premise, presuppositon, or prejudice. 'Rigorous science' is clearly just first philosophy under a different name.

Husserl thought that the possibility of stability, agreement, collaboration, objectivity, and genuine progress in any given science depends upon there being some set of entities, some ontological region, the investigation of which is the responsibility of that science. Without such a field there could never emerge what he called 'scientifically strict doctrinal systems' – what we might call stable bodies of scientific knowledge. Now, when Husserl advocated that philosophy itself should aspire to the status of a rigorous science, he also imposed upon it the requirement that there should be some specific and unique 'region of being', some particular set of entities which would comprise its distinctive subject matter. Only if such a region could be found and isolated, he believed, could philosophy ever be 'scientific', and so look forward to enjoying the stability, the internal agreement, and the steady progress which (he thought) had characterized the development of the mature natural sciences. And only if the entities inhabiting that region of being were prior to, and in some way explanatory of, whatever natural entities comprise the subject matter of normal science could philosophy claim to be 'rigorous'. What ultimately distinguishes philosophy from any other discipline, then, is neither its method, nor its function, but simply the particular species of *thing* which it is its task to investigate and describe.

There is no doubt much that is defensible in Husserl's analysis of the philosophical naivety underlying the assumptions inherent in everyday natural science. But this ought not to blind us to the simple-minded nature of the assumptions inherent in Husserl's own account of the nature, the methods, and the goals of that science. According to him, for example, science is essentially descriptive; and he takes this to mean that, for a given, established scientific discipline there must exist some 'region of being' whose denizens are simply *there*, and whose nature is both determinate and investigation-independent. The task of the natural scientist is then to explore the region in question, and to describe whatever he discovers in it. The methods, procedures, and concepts employed in this

159

endeavour, if they are appropriate and 'objective', will just 'spring from' the nature of the objects under investigation:

> We do not and cannot bring method to any field from beyond its boundaries . . . . Determinate method is a norm which springs from the fundamental nature and universal structures of the region in question. (*Ideas* §77/p.215)

Husserl shows not even a tacit awareness of any of the difficulties which attend this primitive picture – difficulties concerning, say, the under-determination of theory by data, the applicability of the notion of a theory-independent observation statement, the difference between exploring something and understanding it, or between a descriptive assertion and an explanatory hypothesis. But although Husserl's philosophy of science is too unsophisticated to be of any intrinsic interest to us, it is nevertheless important because of its consequences. For when Husserl claims that philosophy itself should be a rigorous science, he takes this to mean that it should conform to the simple model of science as a descriptive enterprise whose concepts and methods will just 'spring from' the intrinsic nature of the objects to be described, and whose goal is the exhaustive characteriza-tion of an ontological region that is just *given*, and all of whose properties are determinate and investigation-independent. For Husserl, philosophy as rigorous science is none other than transcendental phenomenology – the science of an ontological region called 'transcendental subjectivity'. The items comprising this region are simply given, and the goal of the science is their exhaustive description.

There is an attractive misconception of Husserlian phenomenology which was at one time widely endorsed, and against which we should perhaps protect ourselves here. Many of the themes and concerns of transcendental phenomenology can, rightly, be seen as Cartesian; and there is no denying the massive influence that Descartes' thought had on Husserl's philosophical development. There is one crucial respect, how-ever, in which it would be wrong to assimilate Husserl and Descartes too closely: although both are, in a sense, concerned with what we might call 'the foundations of objective knowledge', Husserl clearly distances him-self from the Cartesian project when he writes: 'The point is not to *secure* objectivity, but to understand it' (*Crisis* §55/p.189). Husserl's aim is not to isolate 'a premise, or set of premises, from which the rest of knowledge [can be] deduced' and so 'absolutely secured' (*ibid.*). His aim, in other words, is not to prove that scepticism is false, or to show that we are, after all, justified in some or all of the knowledge claims we normally make. Rather, he aims to explain what, in the last analysis, those claims *mean*. And here, he maintains, 'the only true way to explain something is to make it transcendentally understandable' (*ibid.*). This is not, however, a process that is supposed to make that thing certain, or less doubtful. The

phenomenological method, and the phenomenological reduction in particular, are not intended primarily as weapons in the fight against
scepticism. Husserl never doubted that we possess objective knowledge,
and he never attempted to rebut a scepticism intended to induce such
doubt. His problem was, rather, to make intelligible our possession of
such knowledge, given the apparent subjectivity of the mental processes
that it rests upon.

The phenomenological reduction, as we will see in later sections, has
nevertheless a great deal of work to do. Amongst the tasks that it will be
asked to perform are the following. First, it is to enable us to escape the
commitments of naturalism, and to attain a transcendental point of view.
Second, it is to be, at least in part, the guarantor of 'rigour', in that
performance of it will put us in a position to make 'absolutely grounded'
assertions. Finally, and perhaps most importantly of all for Husserl, the
reduction is to open up the *region* whose denizens it is from now on to be
philosophy's task to explore. Performance of the reduction, it is claimed,
will reveal to us 'a new region of being, never before delimited in its
peculiarity' (*Ideas* §33/p.112); 'a region of being which is essentially
unique and which can in fact become the field for a new science – the
science of phenomenology' (*Ideas* §33/p.113).

The transcendental reduction: preliminaries

Before we even begin to outline the nature of the transcendental or
phenomenological reduction, there are some difficulties of principle that
must be faced at the outset.

The reduction is not a theory or claim, it is a procedure; it is not
something that Husserl would have us believe, it is something he would
have us *do*. In its purest form it would, therefore, be expressed, not in
declarative sentences purporting to be true, relevant, justified, or logically
consistent, but rather in *imperatives*. And this makes it difficult to
evaluate philosophically.

How in general does one evaluate a set of instructions? Directions to
the achievement of some goal are, obviously, efficient or adequate to the
extent that they facilitate or make possible the achievement of that goal
without at the same time preventing the attainment of any other ends
whose realization is assigned a priority no less than that assigned to the
realization of the former goal. And if one has the ability to recognize
whether or not the state of affairs which is the goal in question obtains,
independently of any decision as to whether the instructions have or have
not been carried out, then there is no theoretical impediment to one's
testing the instructions to see if they work. (Think of evaluating a set of
instructions for boiling an egg.) In such a situation one can recognize
whether the goal has been reached, and, independently of that, one can

recognize whether the directions have been followed; and so one can in principle ascertain the extent to which it was the following of those instructions that brought about that state of affairs. But if, on the other hand, the end state can only be recognized or adequately conceived by someone who has already carried out those instructions, then all normal forms of rational or objective evaluation fail to apply. And this difficulty is intensified when the end state in question is a state of mind. We have in such a case a structure of ideas present in many forms of traditional mysticism: there is a state of mind which cannot in any straightforward way be conceived by, or communicated to, one who does not already enjoy it; and there are procedures for realizing this state – procedures that must, however, appear arbitrary and unjustified in the absence of any conception of what that state itself is. This structure of ideas is present in Husserl's account of the phenomenological reduction. Indeed, the reduction itself is a procedure for inducing in us a particular state of mind of which no adequate conception can be formed by those who have not already successfully performed the reduction and thus achieved that state. In this connection Husserl himself was deeply concerned at what he saw as the problem of 'motivating' the reduction; for if it is only when one has performed it that one can know its value, then someone who has not performed it can have, and can be given, no cogent reason for doing so. [10]

In such a situation there seem to be only two options open to someone who wishes to evaluate a set of instructions. The first is, in effect, to try and implement them and see what happens. Well, I have tried to follow Husserl's instructions for the performance of the phenomenological reduction, and I have to report that nothing of any philosophical interest occurred – and certainly there was not opened up to me 'a new region of being never before delimited in its peculiarity'.

There is – to put it no stronger than this – something dismal and dogmatic about a philosophy whose utility, cogency, and plausibility depend essentially, not on objective arguments, rational analyses, or the critical consideration of evidence available to all, but rather on the individual philosopher's having undergone some esoteric experience the nature of which he is then in principle unable to communicate. In so far as one's ability to *do* Husserlian phenomenology (as distinct from one's being able to talk about doing it) depends upon one's having performed the phenomenological reduction, adoption of that phenomenology cannot be a matter for rational deliberation, but only for something suspiciously like conversion as a response to personal revelation. In his last work, the *Crisis*, Husserl himself came close to acknowledging this:

Perhaps it will even become manifest that the total phenomenological attitude and the epoché belonging to it are destined in essence to effect, at first, a complete personal transformation, comparable in the beginning to a religious conversion. (*Crisis* §35/p.137)

As if this were not bad enough, he then adds that, over and above this, such a transformation

> bears within itself the significance of the greatest existential transformation which is assigned as a task to mankind as such. (*ibid.*)

The second and only remaining option open to someone who wishes to evaluate a set of directions or instructions, in those cases where one has no independent access to the end state the directions are intended to bring about, is to transform them into the most nearly corresponding assertoric sentences, and then assess the latter for truth, consistency, ability to solve problems, and the like. The closest relevant assertoric sentences would seem to be those concerning the possibility of the states of affairs in question. In effect one transforms imperatives of the form 'Bring it about that such-and-such' or 'Refrain from doing such-and-such' into assertions of the form 'Such-and-such is possible' or 'It is possible to refrain from doing such-and-such'. This is a relevant procedure if only because the truth of such an assertion is a necessary condition for the cogency of the corresponding instruction. This is (though not always explicitly) the procedure I will adopt in what follows.

Talk of the transcendental or phenomenological reduction, in the singular, is slightly misleading; for Husserl quite often speaks as though there were more than one of them. In *Ideas*, for instance, he distinguishes between a 'philosophic' reduction (§18), a reduction with respect to the natural sciences (§30), one concerning the mental sciences, and especially psychology (§64), one concerning logic (§59), and another, the 'material eidetic' sciences such as geometry and kinematics (§60). But these can, and I think should, be seen as merely separate phases in, or aspects of, a single overriding procedure which incoporates them all. (Cf. *Crisis* §41/p.150.) In what follows I shall use the expressions *the reduction*, *the phenomenological reduction*, *the transcendental reduction*, and *the epoché* synonymously, to refer to this all-encompassing procedure. *This* reduction will always be sharply distinguished from other, quite different procedures that Husserl also calls 'reductions' – the eidetic reduction, for example, and the abstractive reduction.[11]

The transcendental reduction and subjectivity

Construed in one way,[12] the transcendental reduction is a procedure whose point of departure is something called the natural attitude, whose terminus is something called transcendental subjectivity, and whose central component is the 'neutralization' or 'suspension' of every commitment which, either tacitly or explicitly, appears within or in any way determines that natural attitude. And here the natural attitude, its characteristic commitments, their neutralization, and transcendental subjectivity are all to be construed as mental acts, or attitudes, or states. Roughly speaking, on this model the reduction takes us from one state of mind to another.

The natural attitude comprises the complex system of interlocking and mutually supporting beliefs, preferences, commitments, and habits of mind which permeate and regulate our everyday conduct and our everyday understanding of things. With respect to any given person, this system of commitments will doubtless include many that are very specific in content, and perhaps also some that are merely idiosyncratic or cranky. But at the most general and fundamental level, at least in the community of which I am a member, the following beliefs are so widely shared as to be virtually universal. There is, for example, the belief in the existence of an external, material reality that is extended in space, that persists through time, and that contains objects that interact causally with one another. Our shared system of commitments also includes the belief that the world contains conscious individuals who, by and large, enjoy sensations, perceptions, thoughts, and emotions similar to the ones we enjoy. It includes the belief that, on the whole, the world is very much as we perceive it and conceive it to be. It includes a belief in the applicability of logic, the reliability of mathematics, and the truth of the uncontentious parts of natural science. And so on. Commitments of the kind constitutive of the natural attitude not only underlie and make possible our everyday activities and thoughts, they also underlie and make possible the pursuit of objective truth by the natural and human sciences. And, for Husserl, the most significant characteristic of the natural attitude is its philosophical naivety; a naivety which it therefore transmits to the natural and human sciences; a naivety which simply consists in the uncritical and largely unconscious adoption of all of these philosophically problematic commitments.

More specifically, Husserl believes that the commitments which comprise the natural attitude, and which are ultimately responsible for its philosophical naivety, are all ontological commitments.[13] They are commitments, for example, to the existence of physical objects, the existence of properties, of facts, of the past, of other minds, of a causal nexus, of space, and so forth. In introducing the reduction, Husserl's guiding thought is a simple one: If ontological commitment is the source of philosophical naivety, then the way to remove that naivety would be to remove those commitments. And the transcendental reduction is just that: it is a procedure for reducing to zero the ontological commitments that comprise the natural attitude. 'Instead of remaining in this attitude,' Husserl writes, 'we propose to alter it radically' (*Ideas* §31/p.107). The alteration takes the form of a neutralization of each component ontological commitment, so that

> although it remains what it is in itself, we put it 'out of action', we 'exclude it', we 'bracket it'. It is still there, like the bracketed matter inside a pair of parentheses . . . but we make no use of it.
>
> We put out of action the entire ontological commitment (*Generalthesis*) that belongs to the essence of the natural attitude, we place in brackets whatever it includes with respect to being. (*Ideas* §32/p.111)

Not only all our consciously held beliefs but also all our tacitly assumed presuppositions concerning natural existence are to be put out of action in the transcendental reduction.

What exactly does this 'bracketing' or 'putting out of action' consist in? In his *Begriffsschrift* of 1879, in the section entitled 'Judgement', Gottlob Frege had written:

> A Judgement is always to be represented [in the concept-script] by means of the sign
>
> $$\vdash$$
>
> This stands to the left of the sign or complex of signs in which the content of the judgement is given. If we *omit* the little vertical stroke at the left end of the horizontal stroke, then the judgement is to be transformed into *a mere complex of ideas*; the author is not expressing his recognition or non-recognition of the truth of this. Thus let
>
> $$\vdash A$$
>
> mean the judgement: 'unlike magnetic poles attract one one another.' In that case
>
> $$\longrightarrow A$$
>
> will not express this judgement; it will be intended just to produce in the reader the idea of the mutual attraction of unlike magnetic poles . . . . In this case we *qualify* the expression with the words 'the cir-cumstance that' or 'the proposition that'. . . . Assertion, which is expressed by the vertical stroke at the left end of the horizontal one, relates to the whole thus formed. The horizontal stroke I wish to call the *content-stroke*, and the vertical the *judgement-stroke*.[14]

The transformations which Frege signals by the omission of the vertical assertion stroke from the expression of a judgement correspond closely to the transformations which, for Husserl, comprise the phenomenological reduction.[15] What are these transformations? The first is the cancellation of assertoric force, or of what in the *Logical Investigations* Husserl had called 'positing act-quality.' Crucially important here, for both Frege and

Husserl, is the difference between suspending a judgement, on the one hand, and denying or negating it on the other. In the move from |——— A to ——— A, the content remains constant: exactly the same thought (content, proposition, or sense) is now asserted, now merely entertained or grasped non-committally. Such is not the case, however, in the move from an assertion or judgement, |——— A, to its negation, |——— NOT-A. In the latter case the assertoric force remains and is not cancelled; and the content, sense, or judgement does not remain constant but is transformed into its contradictory. As Husserl repeatedly insists, it is these two factors which at the very outset distinguish the transcendental reduction from the Cartesian procedure based on methodical doubt. When I perform the reduction, according to Husserl, although I refrain from passing judgement on the world, 'I do not thereby *deny* this world, as though I were a sceptic. Rather, I perform the phenomenological epoché, [and this merely] bars me from *using* any judgement that concerns spatio-temporal existence' (*Ideas* §32/p.111).

The new attitude, achieved as a result of implementing the reduction, is not only to be distinguished from doubt and denial, it is also to be distinguished from assumption and supposition, from suspicion, aesthetic contemplation, and from imagination too. Doubting, denying, supposing, imagining, suspecting, and assuming are, like asserting or judging, specific qualities of acts – or 'doxic modalities' as Husserl now prefers to call them. His radical suggestion is not that we systematically replace certain such qualities by others, but that in performing the reduction we do away with all such qualities or modes of belief entirely. Neutralized, post-reduction consciousness consists in acts which, though they have of course content or sense, nevertheless lack all positing quality whatsoever. As Husserl was fully aware, however, ontological commitment is not only acquired as a result of the positing quality or assertoric force of acts, but also as a result of the *reference* which those acts seem to possess. So post-reduction consciousness must also be innocent of any reference to the world or to anything in it.

This brings us to the second transformation brought about as part of the transcendental reduction: the move from the natural to the neutralized attitude involves the substitution of a radically different subject matter for our conscious acts to be about. Clearly, after the reduction we can hardly go on talking and thinking about the same old world as if nothing had happened. Apart from anything else we are no longer allowed to pass judgement on it, to think about it, or to refer to it. So what *can* we talk about after the reduction? As Husserl remarks, 'it is necessary now to make really transparent the fact that we are not left with just a meaningless, habitual abstention' (*Crisis* §41/p.151).

The subject matter or content that remains after performance of the reduction is not something for which we need to cast about, something that we could, as it were, misidentify or even fail to find; for in bracketing everything that transcends consciousness, we are necessarily and immediately presented with what is immanent in consciousness. And so, although the transcendental reduction results in our adopting an attitude in which we eschew all reference to, or thought about, the natural world external to consciousness, we are nevertheless left with a 'phenomenological residuum': '*consciousness itself* has a being of its own which in its own absolute essence remains unaffected by the phenomenological reduction' (*Ideas* §33/p.113).

> This 'phenomenological epoché' or 'parenthesizing' of the objective world . . . does not leave us confronting nothing. On the contrary, we gain possession of something by it; and what we (or more accurately, what I, as the one who is meditating) acquire by it is my pure living, with all the pure subjective processes making this up, along with everything meant in them purely *as* meant in them; i.e., the world of *phenomena*. (*CM* §8/p.20)

We have to tread carefully here. Performance of the reduction requires me to abstain from reference to the world and everything in it. This means that I must bracket all judgements and beliefs about the physical world studied by the natural sciences. But it also means that equally, I must bracket all judgement about or reference to the items which comprise the subject matter of the human sciences, and especially such things as conscious beings, minds, mental events, conscious states, and the like, which belong within the subject matter of psychology. And here we come up against what Husserl calls 'the difficult, even paradoxical relation between psychology and transcendental phenomenology' (*Crisis* §58/p.203). The difficulty or 'paradox' is this: on the one hand, the existence of conscious states, mental acts, contents of consciousness and so forth must be subject to the phenomenological reduction. After the reduction we cannot appeal to such things, acknowledge their existence, or make any use of them. On the other hand, however, the reduction is claimed to present us with 'absolute or pure transcendental consciousness [which] is left over as a residuum' (*Ideas* §55/p.170). According to Husserl, after I have performed the epoché I come to realize that

> I, with my [mental] life, remain untouched in my existential status, regardless of whether or not the world exists . . . . This ego, with its ego-life . . . necessarily remains for me by virtue of such epoché. (CM §11/p.25)

So here at the very threshold of transcendental phenomenology there is an apparent contradiction: we are told that reference to our own mental acts is forbidden, but also that it is mandatory. If this apparent contradiction cannot be resolved, then 'transcendental phenomenology' as

Husserl conceived it is a nonsense. Resolution, for its part, requires that we find an acceptable sense in which it is true that

(1) Reference to myself, my mental acts and their contents is outlawed by the transcendental reduction,

while at the same time there is a sense in which it is true that

(2) Reference to myself, my mental acts and their contents is *all* that is allowed by the transcendental reduction.

The form which Husserl's attempted resolution of this difficulty takes is clear: he isolates an ambiguity or equivocation in such phrases as 'myself', 'my mind', 'mental acts', 'states of consciousness' and the like, which permits him to claim that there is a legitimate way of reading those phrases according to which (1) turns out to be true (and (2) false), while on another equally legitimate way of reading them, (2) turns out to be true (and (1) false). Understood in the former way, the phrases in question designate ordinary, everyday objects and events of the kind that occur in the natural world. Here we have 'data belonging to the world, which is presupposed as existing – that is to say, data taken as psychic components of a man' (*CM* §14/p.32). We may acknowledge the existence of these things before, but not after the reduction. On the second way of construing the terms in question they are understood to mean, not worldly or natural entities, but absolute or transcendental ones. And we can refer to these things after, but not before performance of the reduction: it is precisely the reduction which reveals their existence to us for the first time, Husserl claims.

Transcendental being

An attempt to resolve the problem along these lines will be workable only to the extent that a coherent account can be given of 'transcendental being', and of its relation to ordinary, natural existence. As only transcendental subjectivity has transcendental being, what we require minimally is an acceptable explanation of exactly what transcendental subjectivity is, and how it differs from ordinary subjectivity; of transcendental phenomenology, and how it differs (as it now does) from descriptive psychology; and of the transcendental ego, and how it differs from what we would normally call the mind. As his *Nachlass* reveals, over the next fifteen years Husserl devoted a considerable amount of effort and time to struggling with precisely this family of problems – in the end unsuccessfully. For if we construe Husserl's pronouncements about transcendental ontology literally – and clearly he intended that we should – then ultimately he fails to provide any clear account of what 'transcendental being' is, or any cogent reason for acknowledging or positing it.

Husserl intended there to be an irreducible distinction between two realms or regions of being, that is, between (i) the natural world, including my empirical self, my mind, and its acts and states; and (ii) the transcendental world which is coextensive with transcendental subjectivity and which includes my transcendental ego. These two ontological regions do not at any point overlap, and in particular the transcendental ego is no part of the natural world, and the empirical ego is no part of the transcendental world (cf. *Ideas* §33/p.112; *CM* §11/p.25). Transcendental being is autonomous, that is, it is 'absolutely independent' in the sense of that phrase elucidated earlier in connection with Husserl's theory of wholes, parts, and moments. The natural world, on the other hand, is ontologically dependent: it can only exist in relation to, or as a moment of, transcendental being. 'The realm of transcendental consciousness', Husserl writes, 'is in a quite definite sense a realm of "absolute" being. It is the original category of being as such . . . in which all other regions of being have their roots' (*Ideas* §76/p.212).

One bizarre consequence of Husserl's tendency to transpose his epistemological theories into an ontological mode is his doctrine concerning the 'splitting of the ego' that supposedly occurs during the reduction. The conscious acts of an ego or mind are normally 'turned towards the world', and are themselves events that occur within that world. With the phenomenological epoché, however, not only is thought directed towards the natural world no longer allowed, but equally thought *by* an ego that is part of the world must be bracketed as well. So the thoughts and other conscious acts that occur after the reduction cannot be performed by, or ascribed to, the natural, everyday ego. 'The phenomenological reduction thus tends to split the ego' (*PV* p.15/p.16). It brings with it 'a splitting of the ego, in that the phenomenological ego establishes himself as "disinterested onlooker" above the naively interested ego' (*CM* §15/p.35). And this phenomenological ego, in sharp contrast to the natural ego from which it has broken free, is nothing less that an 'absolute sphere of egological being' (*ibid.*). Now the natural ego is the object of study for the empirical science of psychology, whereas the transcendental or 'absolute' ego is the appropriate object of study for phenomenology. But, given that both egos are capable of thinking, perceiving, reasoning, and so forth, this leads, as Husserl acknowledges, to a massive and systematic reduplication; for there is no truth of psychology that does not have its exact phenomenological counterpart, and *vice versa*.[16] Husserl seems to have been struck by the peculiarity of the fact that we have here two exactly isomorphic theories for one and the same field, but he seems not to have had any adequate explanation of why we should need both of them.

The only motive that I have been able to find for Husserl's adoption of a 'transcendental ontology' is his belief that every science worthy of the name must have some specific and unique region of being assigned to it –

an assignment which, he believes, is just as necessary for the rigorous science of phenomenology as it is for the ordinary natural sciences. And if phenomenology is to be a transcendental discipline, then its ontological realm will presumably have to be a realm of 'transcendental being'. It is difficult to find anything that can be said in support of this line of thought, the most unacceptable aspects of which are that it is based on a simple-minded caricature of how science actually functions; it involves an unintelligible extension of the notion of something's being *transcendental*; it is ontologically reduplicative; and it is devoid of genuine explanatory power.

Fortunately it is possible to disentangle and discard Husserl's doctrine of the absolute being of transcendental consciousness. In order to do so, however, we need to reinterpret his ontological talk of 'absolute existence', 'transcendental being', and 'ontological regions' in a way which will enable it to contribute towards a solution of the *epistemological* problems that are in fact his ultimate goal. And this we do by taking his apparently ontological distinctions between regions of being to be distinctions between kinds of knowledge, or perhaps between ways of viewing the cognitive relations in which consciousness stands to reality. In which case 'the transcendental ego' is the name neither of some entity distinct from the empirical ego, nor of something that inhabits a region of absolute being. Instead we can say that the transcendental ego is merely the empirical ego, or mind, viewed transcendentally; pure or absolute consciousness is just common-or-garden consciousness in so far as it has a certain epistemological or transcendental role assigned to it. And *here* the notion of a transcendental role is the intelligible Kantian notion we examined earlier. An enquiry or theory is transcendental, we said, in virtue of its concerning the *a priori* and non-natural conditions of the possibility of objective knowledge in general. And although in this sense there can be such things as a transcendental theory, say, or a transcendental investigation, discipline, proof, or point of view, it is by no means clear what a 'transcendental region of being' could possibly be.

But even if we were to allow that the notions of 'transcendental being' and 'absolute consciousness' are intelligible, they would nevertheless remain objectionable; for in Husserl's hands they perform no work. This is because whenever the absolute being of consciousness is called upon to perform an explanatory task, it is always, so to speak, its epistemological and not its ontological independence that does the work. The situation arises in the following way. The phenomena studied by Husserlian phenomenology have one important property in common with the mental phenomena studied by Brentanian descriptive psychology: with respect to phenomena of both kinds there is in principle no possibility of distinguishing between what they are in and of themselves and how they seem to be to the person who is aware of them. 'The truly absolute *datum*

170

is the pure phenomenon' (*The Idea of Phenomenology*, p.5). Epistemically, phenomena are *given* absolutely, which is to say that they are
presented to consciousness in such a way that for them appearance and
reality coincide. The relations between how things seem and how they
actually are 'in the sphere of the psychical are totally different from those
in the physical sphere . . . . [Concerning] psychical being, being as
'phenomenon' . . . there is no distinction between appearance and being'
(*PRS* in *HSW* p.179). And it is this characteristic of absolute knowability,
so to speak, rather than their supposed absolute being, which allows
phenomena to discharge their transcendental function in explaining the
possibility of objective knowledge in general. If this is right, then we can
adopt Kant's deflationary approach and accept that the principles governing a transcendental investigation into the nature of human understanding
'are merely rules for the exposition of appearances [or phenomena]; and
the proud name of an Ontology . . . must therefore give place to the
modest title of a mere Analytic of pure understanding'.[17]

The doctrine of the absolute being of transcendental consciousness is
redundant in another, more specifically Husserlian respect. On the one
hand it is not a *consequence* of the transcendental reduction – Husserl
explicitly introduces and defends the doctrine 'without as yet having
carried out the phenomenological suspension of judgement', that is,
'without troubling with any phenomenological epoché . . . and without
forsaking the natural standpoint' (*Ideas* §§33,34/pp.113,114). But equally,
on the other hand, the doctrine is not a *requirement* of the phenomenological programme, which could hardly claim to be presuppositionless if
depended on the prior, massive, and indeed barely intelligible assumption
that the natural world is just a moment of absolute consciousness. In
short, Husserl is not entitled to, and does not in fact need this doctrine,
and I suggest we ignore it.

For these reasons, then, it seems desirable to construe the
phenomenological reduction, charitably, as enabling us to undergo a
change of attitude as a direct result of which we will be able to see
consciousness (ordinary consciousness) in a new light – as fulfilling a role
within a transcendental theory whose aim is to explain the nature of
objectivity and rationality – rather than as enabling us to enter some new
'region of being' that is separate from, but the foundation of, the spatio-
temporal universe. For the moment, however, I postpone detailed examination of the mechanisms by which the transcendental reduction brings
about these changes, and turn instead to the insights which, according to
Husserl, accrue to those who have successfully performed it. We shall,
that is, 'keep our eyes fixed on the region of consciousness, and study
what we find immanent in it' (*Ideas* §33/p.113). This rather roundabout
procedure is necessary because most of the information we possess
about the nature of the phenomenological reduction is in fact information

about what, in Husserl's opinion, performance of it enables us to see.

Structures of consciousness

Overview

Husserl's mature account of how consciousness functions, of how the mind works so as to yield meaningful experience, is thoroughly Kantian in structure.[18] It is articulated, like Kant's, in terms of a series of dichotomies, all of which in principle coincide, and each of which marks just one aspect of that basic dichotomy by appeal to which the possibility of objective experience is to be explained. In Husserlian terms, 'there emerges necessarily, as a radical difference, the difference between *hyletic data* and *intentional functionings*' (*FTL* §107(c)/p.286). Coextensive with this is a series of further distinctions, including those between the matter and the form of experience; between sensibility and understanding; sensations and concepts; passive receptivity and active synthesis (the 'given' and the 'made'); what is manifold and what is unitary (the 'many' and the 'one'); what is in a perpetual state of flux and what has stability and permanence; and finally, between what is intrinsically meaningless and what makes sense. 'The stream of phenomenological being,' Husserl says, 'has a twofold bed: a *material* one, and a *noetic* one' (*Ideas* §85/p.251). The former consists of sensuous *hyle* or *hyletic data*, the latter is an *intentional morphe*, or *noesis*.

The material components or hyletic data comprise sensations, feelings, sense data, and other non-intentional 'sensory stuffs', such as 'the data of colour, touch, sound, and the like', as well as 'sensory impressions of pleasure, pain, tickling, etc.,' and also the sensory or quasi-sensory moments, if any, that belong to emotional feelings, desires, acts of will, memory, imagination, and so forth. These are items which are simply given to consciousness, or which, conversely, consciousness passively receives (Cf. *Ideas* §85/pp.246–51; *FTL* §107(c)/pp.286–9).

By contrast, the second, 'noetic' aspects of consciousness have the task of making sense of, or bestowing meaning on, the first: 'Over those sensory phases lies, as it were, an "animating", *meaning-bestowing* stratum . . . a stratum through whose agency, out of the sensory element, which contains in itself nothing intentional, the concrete intentional experience takes form and shape' (*Ideas* §85/p.247). The function of the noetic aspect of consciousness is to create unity in diversity, identity in difference, form in what is intrinsically formless, and, ultimately, to deliver stable, coherent, and intelligible intentional experience on the basis of sensory data that are themselves non-intentional and without meaning. Following Kant, Husserl attempts to explain how all of these functions are discharged as a result of the mind's synthetic activity, an activity which brings it about that the concept of an object in general finds application within experience. Kant calls the bare concept of an object as such 'the transcendental object = X'; Husserl calls it 'the empty X' which is 'the object-core' of an intentional experience. And both philosophers maintain in effect that to make sense of experience, to create unity by combining different elements within the flux of sensory data, to organize hyletic data so that the concept of an undetermined X finds application to them, to enjoy intentional experience, and to refer to objects in the empirical world – all these are ultimately different aspects of one and the same process. The process is called *synthesis*, and for both Kant and Husserl the notion of the mind's synthetic activity stands at the very centre of an idealist theory intended to show how objective knowledge is possible, given only the subjective awareness we have of our immanent, sensory contents of consciousness. And this theory crucially involves an exploration of the explanatory relations in which the notions of *intentionality, synthesis, object, concept, identity, reference*, and *meaning* stand to one another.

Any parts or moments of a mental act in virtue of which that act is intentional, or in virtue of which it possesses a sense, Husserl calls 'its *noetic moments* or *noeses* for short' (*Ideas* §85/p.249); and the sense itself he calls the act's *noema* (*Ideas* §90/p.261).

Hyletic data

The exclusively sensory components, or hyletic data, that comprise the primitive raw materials of consciousness are distinct from all noetic or intentional aspects in virtue of possessing the following attributes. (i) They are merely undergone or registered: the mind, in other words, is purely passive in the reception of such material. The sensory material, for its part, is straightforwardly 'given'; it is, in the most literal sense, a *datum*. And so (ii) the sensations and feelings in question are typically neither referred to any object, nor are they themselves 'objectified' or referred to. Hyletic data, as such, are just *had*, and are neither intentional experiences nor the intentional objects of experiences. (iii) They are exclusively sensory, that is they are without intellectual or conceptual articulation of any sort. And for Husserl this means that they are intrinsically meaningless or senseless. (iv) They are such that, for them, *esse* is *percipi* – at least in the sense that a hyletic datum cannot coherently be supposed to survive a break in awareness of it. They are, in Hume's phrase, 'internal and perishing existences', which 'succeed each other with an inconceivable rapidity, and are in a perpetual flux and movement'.[19] And (v) they are what Husserl calls *really* immanent (as distinct from being merely intentionally immanent) contents of conscious experience: 'Such concrete data of experience are to be found *as component parts* in concrete experiences of a more inclusive . . . intentional kind' (*ibid.*).

Two objections of considerable weight have been levelled at theories of this kind from within the phenomenological tradition itself – and both have received their most forceful expression in the works of Merleau-Ponty. The first objection is that, as a matter of fact, experience simply does not contain anything corresponding to the notion of a pure hyletic datum: 'this notion corresponds to nothing in our experience, and the most rudimentary *factual perceptions* that we are acquainted with, in creatures such as the ape or the hen, have a bearing on relationships, and not on any absolute terms'.[20] If this is right, then so-called 'formless matter of experience' is a theoretical entity posited for its explanatory value, rather than something of which we have any immediate experience. But in that case no appeal to it ought to be made within a genuinely phenomenological theory, which requires 'the absolutely faithful description of that which really lies before one' and 'the keeping at a distance all interpretations that transcend the given' (*Ideas* §90/p.262). This objection does not, of course, imply that there are no such things as sensations, pains, feelings, visual impressions, and the like, but merely that such things are not the intrinsically independent, meaningless, formless, passively registered atoms of sensory experience that Husserl's theory requires; for, as Merleau-Ponty writes, 'if we try to seize "sensation" . . . we find not a psychic individual, a function of certain known variables, but a formation already bound up with a larger whole, already endowed with a meaning'.[21]

The second objection is not so much to the notion of a hyletic datum as such, as to any theory which, like Husserl's, depends upon there being a radical distinction between the meaningless raw material of sensory intuition, on the one hand, and the sense-bestowing activities of the understanding, on the other. The objection is that on any model of consciousness which has this structure the mind is assigned the task of 'interpreting' something that is intrinsically totally without meaning; and this is an impossible task.[22]

Noeses

The term 'noesis' is introduced by Husserl to designate a certain complex of dependent moments and independent parts present in each intentional act – namely those parts and aspects which are responsible for the act's being intentional or meaningful in the first place (*Ideas* §85/p.249). The noetic elements in an intentional act are whatever real, immanent elements 'animate' or 'bestow sense' on the inert hyletic data. (Husserl also at times uses the term 'noesis' to refer, not to a certain type of element present within a concrete act, but to a whole concrete act in its entirety; but I shall ignore this usage here.) The noetic components within an act contrast with the act's hyletic elements: indeed, a noesis is nothing more than a whole concrete intentional act minus whatever sensory data it may encompass.

But what are we left with, when we subtract its hyletic data from a given complex intentional act? Surely not any specific or well-defined kind of thing – something that we could then call a 'noesis'. On the contrary, we are left with a heterogeneous conglomeration which (depending on the nature of the particular act in question) might include independent component acts, emotional aspects, ontological commitments, synthetic moments, moments to do with attention, with intensity, with temporality, with degree of determinacy, with fulfilment, and so forth. The concept of a noesis is not a sortal concept; and in answer to the question 'What *is* a noesis?' we have to say: It's anything and everything that can possibly occur as a real part or moment of an intentional experience – with the exception of hyletic data. The term 'noesis', in other words, signifies merely a ragbag concept; it is not a name for some specific sort of thing or kind of activity.

When complex, noeses can be decomposed into their real constituent elements by a process of whole-part analysis. This 'real' or 'noetic' analysis yields items that actually occur *in* the analysandum; it contrasts, therefore, with intentional or noematic analysis which concerns items that, although immanent, do not occur as component parts within a concrete experience. To a first approximation we might say that real analysis is applied to concrete noeses, while intentional analysis concerns ideal or 'irreal' noemata. Husserl takes it as axiomatic that there is the strictest isomorphism between noesis and noema, or between what, in a given case, real noetic analysis and intentional noematic analysis will respectively reveal. Noesis and noema are, he says, 'strictly correlative' (*Ideas* §88/p.258).

At this point we can usefully examine a particular noesis and the analysis which it receives in Husserl's hands. Suppose, then, that I walk into my garden and take a look at the apple tree that stands there. As I do so I undergo a complex series of visual experiences, as I walk towards the tree, walk round it, examine its blossom, its bark, its leaves, its movement in the wind, and so on. If we now go over to the phenomenological point of view, we perform the reduction and reflect on the nature of this visual experience as it is exclusively in and of itself, regardless of any putative facts concerning the natural world. 'What do we really find *in* the perception as pure experience,' Husserl asks, 'included within it as its parts, pieces, and moments?' (*Ideas* §97/p.283). And he answers that on the one hand there are the brute sensations, the visual hyletic data that impinge on my consciousness, and on the other hand there are 'the noetic component parts' which transform the former into a coherent, significant perceptual experience.

At any given moment during this experience there will, for example, be a quite particular 'colour-sensation [or] hyletic moment of the concrete experience'. This hyletic datum is, however, a fleeting, perishing thing – and at another moment during the experience there will be some other colour-sensation numerically distinct from, and (we can suppose) qualitatively dissimilar to, the first. Both of these colour-sensations, in spite of their distinctness and dissimilarity, are somehow related to my experience of an intentional object whose colour remains constant: 'one and the same noematic colour, which I am aware of *as* one and the same throughout the . . . perceptual consciousness, . . . is adumbrated by a continuous multiplicity of colour-sensations' (*ibid.*). If we reflect on these colour-sensations and what they adumbrate, Husserl claims, 'we see immediately that the various adumbrative colours belonging to some fixed colour of a thing are related to that fixed colour as continuous "multiplicity" is related to "unity"' (*ibid.*).

Now, as Husserl analyses the situation, it is only the diverse elements comprising the 'multiplicity' that are actually *given*; their 'unity', by contrast, is not given and must therefore be created. A process taking a plurality of things and yielding a unity made out of them is, by definition, a process of synthesis – and synthesis is the most important function performed by the non-hyletic moments in an intentional act. In the case of the example at hand, a given multiplicity of different colour-sensations can be synthesized if they are taken to be sensations whose colour-content is the colour *of something* – of a tree, say, or a leaf, or an apple. It is worth noting, in passing, that the relation signified by the word 'of' in this context is not the intentional relation in which a conscious act stands to that *of* which it is conscious, but rather the possessive 'of' that indicates property ownership, and which is elucidated by appeal to the nature of predication. The sensed green that is my hyletic datum at a particular moment must be taken by me to be, say, the green *of* a leaf. Confusingly, this of course requires that I am *aware of* the leaf – and that relation is the intentional one. As we will see, the three relations of (i) a property to its bearer, (ii) an act of predication to its subject, and (iii) consciousness to its intentional object, are for Husserl intimately bound up with one another.

In the transition from a changing multiplicity of colour-sensations to an awareness of the stable, self-same colour of a given object a number of considerations have simultaneously become relevant. Amongst others, the notions of *synthesis, unity, identity, permanence,* and *intentionality*, as well as the distinction between an *object* and its *properties*, have all come into play at the same time. Roughly speaking, in the context of the example we have been examining, they are related to each other as follows: to synthesize a plurality of different colour-sensations is to unite them by predicating them, as properties, of one and the same intentional object which is taken to be capable of persisting through changes in those properties. So in *Ideas*, just as in the *Logical Investigations*, the taking of sensory properties to be co-instantiated lies at the very heart of primitive synthesis. And Husserl's introduction of 'the empty X' is precisely the introduction of a formal notion in terms of which to elucidate the phenomenon of co-instantiation. 'The X' which forms the innermost core of every noema is the materially undetermined subject of predication, the bearer of properties:

> The sensory content of that which is given in perception itself continues indeed to be reckoned as other than the true thing as it is in itself, but the *substratum*, the bearer (the empty X) of the perceived determinations still continues to count as that which is determined . . . by having predicates assigned to it. (*Ideas* §40/p.129)

Predicates, Husserl says, are always 'predicates of "something"'. And, he adds, 'this "something" belongs inseparably to the [noematic] nucleus: it is the central point of unification . . . . it is the nodal point of connection, or bearer of the predicates'; and he calls it 'the pure X in abstraction from all predicates'. (*ibid.*)

At the most elementary level, then, the noetic moments of an intentional experience are charged with the responsibility of making that experience intentional; and this they do by taking various hyletic elements to be co-instantiated properties. A necessary condition of the performance of this task is the organization of experience so that the purely formal notion of an object in general – of an X which is *that in which* the properties are instantiated – becomes applicable within that experience. Experience which possesses this form is, therewith, intentional. Synthesis and intentionality are so intimately related that, according to Husserl, 'only elucidation of the process we call synthesis makes fruitful the exhibition of the cogito (i.e., the intentional subjective process) as consciousness-*of*, that is to say, Franz Brentano's significant discovery that "intentionality" is the fundamental characteristic of "mental phenomena"' (*CM* §17/p.41). Husserl's theory thus involves the claim that 'the "object" of consciousness . . . is an "intentional effect", produced by the synthesis of consciousness' (*CM* §18/p.42).

When we earlier examined the account of unity, synthesis, and the relation between sensory and conceptual aspects of experience provided by Husserl in the *Logical Investigations*, we noted that there was some equivocation as to whether all complex unity in experience should be construed as synthetic unity, that is, as the result of synthetic activity, or whether straightforward sensory intuition might not possess a unity that is given, rather than synthesized. In *Ideas* and subsequent works this equivocation is resolved in favour of the Kantian doctrine that all complex unity whatsoever is the result of synthesis: 'even in the immanent "internality" of the ego, there are *no objects beforehand*, and no evidences that merely take in what already exists beforehand' (*FTL* 107(c)/p.286).

Nevertheless, Husserl's earlier equivocal distinction between sensory, non-synthetic unity, as against conceptual unity that must be constructed, does not merely disappear: it is transformed into the later distinction between 'passive' and 'active' synthesis. (Cf. *CM* §38; *PP* §12/pp.73ff; *Hus* XI, *passim*.) Passive synthesis is responsible for the 'ready-made' items of experience, for things which appear to be there 'beforehand', and, in particular, for the perceptible objects which together constitute the environment whose existence I take for granted in the natural attitude. 'Thanks to passive synthesis . . . the ego always has an environment of "objects"' (*CM* §38/p.79). Active synthesis, on the other hand, is reponsible for the constitution of objects which 'present themselves to consciousness *as products*':

> Thus in collecting the collection is constituted; in counting, the number; in predicating, the predicate and the predicational state of affairs; in inferring, the inference; and so forth. Original consciousness of universality is likewise an activity, one in which the universal becomes constituted as an object'. (*ibid.*)

As this list makes clear, while most elementary and primitive sensory unities result from passive synthesis, active synthesis is responsible for all 'higher', intellectual and rational complex wholes – though items of the latter kind always depend upon those of the former kind as their foundation.

Up to this point we have been talking about real or noetic analysis insofar as this is focused on the synthetic functions of consciousness, the all-important functions which account for the unity, stability, and significance of conscious experience. It is perhaps worth noting, however, if only briefly, that noeses also possess other aspects and attributes revealed by real analysis. There are, for example, those aspects of mental acts concerning what in the *Logical Investigations* Husserl called 'act-quality', and in terms of which positing acts are distinguished from non-positing ones. There are aspects which concern the degree of intensity, say, or the degree of determinacy that a particular noesis possesses, and others which concern fulfilment and adequacy. There are, moreover, complex structures of multiply-embedded noeses which require analysis – as for example when I formulate a value judgement that incorporates a factual judgement which in turn is founded on my memory of a perception. I will not discuss these matters here, however, as Husserl's account of them does not differ interestingly from that which he had earlier outlined in the *Logical Investigations*.

There is one family of noetic structures which, however, has not been mentioned yet, but which plays a crucial role within Husserl's mature philosophy, and which will have to be investigated in detail – namely those structures which determine the 'horizons' which are essentially possessed by all intentional objects. This topic is examined on pp. 188–97.

Noemata

In so far as our interest has until now been with the noetic aspects of consciousness, our primary concern has been with events, processes, and activities – with things that *happen*. And as we have seen, amongst the most important of the things that happen within consciousness are, on the one hand, the reception of sensory data, and on the other, the synthesizing, uniting, predicating, and referring activities that the mind performs in making sense of the former – though there are, in addition, 'higher' acts like attending, judging, valuing, and inferring which are founded on them. But in so far as we turn now to consider the noematic aspects of consciousness, our concern will predominantly be with object-like entities and their properties, rather than with events and processes. More specifically, our interest will centre on *that which* is united, identified, synthesized, and referred to in noetic activity.

This does not, however, mean that we are here changing the subject, so to speak. To tell a noematic story is not to tell a story different to the corresponding noetic one: ultimately we need to introduce neither new characters nor a new plot at this point. Instead, we tell exactly the same story again, but this time we use a language that is rather more substantive than gerundive. We talk, that is, of intentional objects rather than of intendings, of referents rather than of referrings, and of the things synthesized and identified rather than of synthesizings and identifications. 'There is no noetic moment without a noematic moment that belongs specifically to it' (*Ideas* §93/p.271). Noetic and noematic structures, according to Husserl, are entirely 'correlative'. To enjoy consciousness of an intentional object, for instance, just *is* to have performed certain acts of unification, identification and the like, no more and no less. 'Corresponding at every point to the manifold . . . of real, noetic elements there is a manifold of correlative noematic elements, a *noema* for short' (*Ideas* §88/p.258; cf. *CM* §17/p.40).

A very great deal has been written recently in an effort to establish exactly what a Husserlian noema is. And a wide variety of options have been canvassed; amongst them that noemata are intentional objects, linguistic meanings, essences, Fregean senses, and either the appearances, or the perspectival aspects, or even the parts, of physical objects.[23] But if we take seriously the claim that noemata are in every respect isomorphic with their correlative noeses, and if the concept of a noesis is merely a ragbag concept in whose extension belong all sorts of radically different kinds of things, then we should resist the temptation to think that a noema is some particular sort of object, or that the concept of a noema is a genuine sortal concept. On the contrary, noemata include any and every factor capable of determining an act's significance that is not a real (and hence noetic) part of that act. The concept of a noema is a ragbag concept too: it can, for example, apply to items belonging to the utterly heterogeneous categories that Frege distinguished under the titles of *force, sense, reference, indication, idea,* and *logical form.*

I think it likely that the temptation to construe noemata as objects of some particular category originates, at least partly, in the mistaken assimilation of indirect questions to singular terms. Constructions such as 'Henry asked what makes the sky look blue', or 'John wants to know what "zeolite" means' are reports whose bases are the direct questions 'What makes the sky look blue?' and 'What does "zeolite" mean?' – neither of which can appropriately be answered by specifying an object. Yet because of their grammatical form, expressions like 'what makes the sky look blue' and 'what "zeolite" means' are easily, though mistakenly, taken to be singular referring expressions, purporting to designate some particular object or other. The phrase 'what makes the sky look blue' is then tacitly construed as more or less equivalent to 'that which makes the sky look blue', and an indirect question has been allowed to generate a spurious singular term. But it is nonsense to ask which thing is what makes the sky look blue. Now Husserl, as we have seen, wants to know what makes an experience significant; but unfortunately he then introduces a singular term, 'the noema', whose function is in effect to stand for *what makes an experience significant.* But there is no such thing: the italicized phrase is a spurious singular term – though it is a perfectly good indirect question. In short, then, the only proper answer to the question 'What *is* a noema?' involves rejecting the question as grammatically malformed; for it is tantamount to asking 'What is what makes an experience significant?' which is nonsense. There remains, however, an acceptable use for the term 'noematic': something is noematic in so far as it is an immanent, but non-real contributory factor in the possession by an act of significance or meaning.

The device that Husserl most often employs to elucidate or specify what a noema is makes use of grammatical constructions that have the form: *the –ed as –ed,* or *the –ed as such,* or *the x as –ed.* Thus he talks about 'the intended as intended', 'the meant as meant', 'the perceived as such', as well as about 'the tree as perceived', 'the house as intended', and so on. (He also employs phrases even less perspicuous, but whose meaning seems to be similar, such as 'the appearing tree as appearing', 'the object in the How of its determinations', and even 'the noematic "object in the How"', (*der noematische 'Gegenstand im Wie'*).) We have met expressions of this general grammatical type before (see pp. 97–8), in connection with Husserl's formal ontology; and it was suggested there that they do not comprise genuine syntactic units – and hence, *a fortiori,* are not singular referring terms – but are complex sentential fragments whose apparent integrity breaks down under analysis. 'x *qua* φ', it was argued, should be taken to have the force of the fragment: 'x is φ, and it is in virtue of being φ that it . . .'. So when Husserl seems to refer to some object called 'the tree as perceived', say, or 'the house as intended', we should take him, rather, to be using an intelligible but highly misleading *façon de parler* in which no such reference is in fact involved. Not only are there no such things as 'noemata', there is also no category of things to which, say, 'trees-as-perceived', 'houses-as-intended', or 'the meant-as-meant' belong.

According to the theory outlined in *Ideas*, the most important noematic factors present in a given intentional experience are, in summary, as follows. First in order of importance are those which concern the intentional object of the experience, in other words, those factors in virtue of which the experience is indeed intentional in the first place. Such elements belong to what Husserl calls the noematic core or nucleus, and they are of three types. There is, (i), the 'empty X', the mere indeterminate 'something' which acts as the bearer of substantive content. There are (ii) the elements which comprise this substantive content or sense, namely the intentional attributes or properties which the intentional object is experienced as having. This sense, Husserl writes, 'cannot be lacking in any noema, nor can its necessary centre, the point of unification, the pure, determinable X. No "sense" apart from this empty "something" and, again, [no "something"] without "determining content"' (*Ideas* §131/p.367). And (iii) there are those factors which determine the degree of concreteness or fulness of the intentional object. Together these three elements comprise what Husserl calls 'the full nucleus' of the noema: 'We shall accordingly reckon the concrete fulness of the noematic constituent in question as the *full nucleus*, that is, *the sense, taking into account the way it is fulfilled* (*den Sinn im Modus seiner Fülle*)' (*Ideas* §132/p.369).

Secondly, and lying beyond the limits of the noematic core, so to speak, there are noematic factors of a different kind, the most important being those which in the *Logical Investigations* Husserl had called positing act-qualities, and which he now calls thetic moments (*thetische Momente*, sometimes translated as 'posited moments', or 'posita'). The thetic moments included in a noema are the noematic correlates of the noetic qualities that differentiate acts involving belief, certainty, suspicion, doubt, denial, and the like.

Husserl's fundamental intuition seems to have been the Kantian–Fregean one that while significance in general depends upon the applicability of the concept of an object, no object can be presented in experience, either perceptually or conceptually, without being presented *in some way*. An object cannot just be given, it must be given somehow – from a certain angle, within a certain perspective, as possessing certain properties, as having a certain appearance, or as related in some way to other objects. If one accepts this very plausible intuition then a number of distinctions become mandatory. One needs, for example, to distinguish between the object itself, which is *what* is intended (regardless of *how* it may be presented), the putative objective properties of the object which comprise its 'mode of givenness' on any particular occasion, and the subjective properties of the act in which the object is presented. To take a concrete example, when I see a tree I necessarily perceive it as possessing certain properties (of colour, size, shape, movement, and so forth), and my perceiving itself also has characteristics (perhaps of clarity, intensity, pleasurableness, stability, and the like). Now the last-mentioned 'subjective' aspects of the perception are not referred to the object as its properties, and so form no part of the noematic nucleus. The description of the intentional object, in other words, 'avoids all "subjective expressions"'.

> From the description of this meant objective as such, all expressions like 'perceptual', 'remembered', 'clearly intuited', 'conceptual', and 'given' are *excluded*. They belong to another order (or dimension) of description; not to *the objective we are aware of*, but rather to *the way in which we are aware of it*. (*Ideas* §130/p.364)

Concerning the intentional object, however, there remains the distinction between the object itself and its mode of presentation on any particular occasion. This distinction is identified by Husserl with that between a subject of predication and the predicates which are ascribed to it. Every experience has its intentional objective:

> [if we] carry out a noematic description of this objective, exactly as it is meant, . . . we acquire a certain set of predicates . . . and these predicates, in their modified meaning, determine the *content* of the object-nucleus of the noema in question. (*Ideas* §130/p.364)
>
> But the predicates are predicates *of something*, and this something also belongs, inseparably, to the nucleus in question. It is the nodal point of connection, the bearer of the predicates. [In] noematic description of what is meant, as such, and at the time, . . . the self-same intentional 'object' evidently separates itself from the shifting and changing 'predicates'. It becomes separated as the central noematic moment: the object, the objective, the self-same thing, the determinable subject of its possible predicates, the pure *X* in abstraction from all predicates . . . or rather, predicate-noemata. (*Ideas* §131/p.365–6; I have substantially simplified Husserl's punctuation.)

This leads Husserl to distinguish two notions of an intentional object: the one is a purely formal notion of a materially undetermined subject of predication, the 'empty X'; the other is that of the object along with whatever properties it is presented as having in a given experience. Thus, on the one hand, I can say that my perception is of an X, such that it is a tree, is blossoming, is in my garden, and so forth. Or, on the other hand, I can say my perception is of a blossoming tree in my garden. The two ways of talking, if they are both equally accurate descriptions of one and the same experience, must be equivalent.

Now 'the empty X' or 'intentional object *simpliciter*' is not in fact an intentional object at all: it is not something of which we can be directly aware, or which can be given in experience – for otherwise it would have to be possible for something to be presented in no way, presented without any properties or determinations whatsoever. Rather, it is 'a sort of abstract *form* inherent in the noema as a whole' (*Ideas* §132/p.368); it is, as the corresponding noetic analysis makes clear, a principle of organization, the final explanation of which is in terms of the co-instantiation of different properties, or the attribution to a single subject of different predicates.

This, then, is the very heart of Husserl's mature theory of intentionality, and it is a disappointment; for in the last analysis it merely substitutes one mystery for another. In answer to the question: How is it possible for a conscious act or state to be *of* an object distinct from it? We are told that this is possible to the extent that a number of different properties can be predicated *of* a subject distinct from them. As to how the latter is possible, however, we are not told. A great deal has been written recently about the Husserlian notion of 'noematic sense', in the apparent hope that it will shed some light on the nature of intentionality. But the noematic sense of an act is merely a set of predicates sharing the same subject, and in the absence of any account of predication, this gets us no further forward. Moreover this general strategy looks intrinsically unattractive as a whole; for in so far as it attempts to explain the nature of intentionality by appeal to the nature of predication it gives every appearance of circularity. To predicate something of a subject, to ascribe a property to a thing, to subsume an object under a concept, or to judge that something is thus-and-so; these are activities which are themselves already intentional.

Even more damaging for Husserl's overall strategy is the fact that these activities of predicating and judging are 'higher' intentional acts which, as such, ought to be founded on prior, primitive, and 'straightforward' acts of perception. (Cf. *CM* §38/p.79.) The incoherence at the heart of Husserl's philosophy of mind, then, is not merely that the notion of intentionality is used in the explanation of what intentionality is, but, more seriously, that the entire hierarchical structure – of primitive acts of perception underlying founded moments of intellectual or conceptual consciousness – simply collapses. The so-called 'founding stratum' of perceptual experience turns out in fact to depend for its existence on the existence of intellectual acts of judgement, predication, and subsumption from which it is ultimately inseparable. And this means that Husserl's talk of 'foundations', 'independence', and 'absolute grounding' is inapplicable in the present context.

We noted earlier that in *Psychology from an Empirical Standpoint* Brentano adopts a theory of mind according to which there is no fundamental difference between intellectual and sensory presentations, between concepts and percepts. We noted also that this was one of the very few distinctively Brentanian doctrines that Husserl rejected, from the very beginning, in its entirety. Husserl rejected the assimilation of the sensory and the intellectual, insisting, to the contrary, that contents of consciousness necessarily belong to two radically different sorts, and that those belonging to concrete, sensory, perceptual experience are prior to, and the foundation of, all those that are in any way abstract, conceptual, discursive, or categorial. What we have been examining here are symptoms of Husserl's failure to formulate a coherent alternative account of the mind's powers and properties with which to replace the Brentanian theory he had rejected. And in the last analysis this failure is a consequence of his having retained a commitment to another Brentanian doctrine, one which effectively rules out the possibility of an acceptable alternative account. The commitment is to a theoretical framework within which an essential role is assigned to pure sensory data that are simply *present* to consciousness, but which are without intrinsic meaning or significance. Within such a framework, as Merleau-Ponty has argued, it is almost inevitable that 'perception becomes "interpretation" of the signs that our senses provide, . . . a "hypothesis" that the mind evolves to "explain its impressions to itself"'. And as a consequence 'judgement is brought in to explain the excess of perception over retinal impressions'. In the end, however, such 'intellectualist analysis makes a nonsense of the perceptual phenomena which it was designed to elucidate'.[24] Husserl's acceptance of brute hyletic data is incompatible with his doctrine that all conceptual and intellectual acts 'trace back ultimately to sense perception, to a seeing and grasping of something itself' (*PP* §38/p.148), because all seeing and grasping of something, indeed all intentionality whatsoever, is from the very start *already* an intellectual, conceptually articulated affair. And for a theory of this kind the distinction between sensory perception and judgement disappears: 'This distinction disappears in intellectualism, because judgement is everywhere where pure sensation is not – that is, *absolutely everywhere*'.[25]

The transcendental reduction and meaning

On pp.163–8 we examined the phenomenological or transcendental reduction, construing it there as a procedure whose starting point is a mental state called the natural attitude, and whose performance supposedly makes accessible to each of us, individually, our own transcendental subjectivity or 'absolute consciousness'. There is, however, another way of viewing the reduction, another way of construing both the procedure itself and the nature of its results.

More often than not the phenomenological reduction is introduced via the metaphor of 'bracketing' or 'parenthesizing' the natural world and all that belongs within it – and in the present context a great deal hangs on just how we understand this metaphor. How we understand it will, in particular, determine what we take to be the 'phenomenological residuum' which is left over after performance of the reduction and which comprises the subject matter of Husserlian phenomenology. Now concerning precisely this problem Husserl wrote in the margin of one of his copies of *Ideas*: 'Is there any sense in asking for that which "remains"? As a matter of fact the expression is objectionable because . . . it carries with it the thought of doing away with one part of a whole, one part of a real context' (*Hus* III, p.70). Elsewhere he offers the following gloss on what 'bracketing' means: 'To put it metaphorically, the bracketed matter is not wiped from the phenomenological slate but only put into brackets, and thereby *provided with an index*. With this index, however, the bracketed matter remains a part of the main theme of the inquiry' (*Ideas* §76/p.212; my italics). It is the nature of this 'index' that I want to examine here.

There are two aspects to the phenomenological reduction which sit uneasily together. On the one hand performance of the reduction is clearly supposed to prevent us from referring to or making use of the denizens of the natural world: objects, events, properties, facts, and laws, whether physical or psychological, must all be bracketed. And yet on the other hand, and in spite of the very radical nature of that proposal, Husserl time and again claims that performance of the reduction 'neither cancels anything nor produces anything' (*Ideas* §109/p.306), that after it 'everything remains as before' (*Ideas* §88/p.260), and that, 'strictly speaking we have lost nothing' (*Ideas* §50/p.154). One problem we need to address, therefore, is how the reduction can at the same time be a radical transformation of our attitude to the world as a whole, and yet something that ultimately leaves everything as it is. What sort of 'index' or 'brackets' could have these consequences?

Husserl comes closest to providing the materials for a solution to this problem in a notorious passage in which he contrasts what, on the one hand, we would say in the natural attitude about an apple tree that we can see, and what, on the other hand, we should say about it phenomenologically, after performance of the reduction. In the natural attitude the tree is ascribed its familiar spatial, temporal, causal, botanical, aesthetic, and other sorts of property. Next, Husserl writes, let us pass over to the phenomenological standpoint. The transcendent world enters its 'brackets'; . . . we exercise the epoché . . . . And yet [we find] everything remains as before . . . . The tree has not forfeited the least nuance of all the moments, qualities, or characteristics with which it appeared in this perception. (*Ideas* §88/p.260)

So, even after the reduction, the tree is still described as 'this apple tree, in bloom, in the garden', and so forth. Yet,

it is clear that all these descriptive statements, though sounding very similar to statements concerning reality, have undergone a *radical* modification of sense; just as the thing described, though it is given as 'precisely the same', is still something radically different, in virtue, so to speak, of a change in signifying orientation. In the reduced perception . . . we find, as belonging indissolubly to its essence [what we express as] 'material thing', 'plant', 'tree', 'blossoming', and so forth. The *inverted commas* are clearly significant; they express that change in signification, the corresponding radical change in the meaning of the words. (*Ideas* §89/p.260)

And, elsewhere, he writes that

there belongs to [a] noema 'something objective' – in inverted commas – with a certain noematic constitution explicated in a definitely limited description . . . [in which] are employed formal ontological terms, such as 'object', 'property', and 'state of affairs'; material ontological terms, such as 'thing', 'figure', and 'cause'; and material determinations like 'rough', 'hard', and 'coloured' – all having their inverted commas and, thus, a noematically modified sense. (*Ideas* §130/p.364)

This use of inverted commas may well sound utterly mysterious; but to those familiar with Frege's writings the claim that there is a functor which cancels assertoric force, which effects a systematic modification of sense, which 'neutralizes' reference to objects and properties in the external world, but which nevertheless results in an expression having both a determinate sense and a reference (as long as the expression to which it is applied has a determinate sense) – the claim that there is such an operator should come as no surprise. Any expression creating an 'indirect' or oblique context does just that. And if this is right, it provides us not only with the beginnings of a semantics for post-reduction language, but also with an explanation of how the transcendental reduction works.

On the Fregean model, a free-standing, well-formed indicative sentence, like

(1) The tree is in blossom

serves, in normal contexts of use, to make an assertion or to express a judgement, and in virtue of this it is capable of possessing a truth-value. The assertion here has the form of a claim, concerning a certain object, that it possesses a certain property (or that it falls under a certain concept). In order to do this, the sentence must contain elements that refer to that object and to that property. These elements, a singular term and a predicate, respectively, successfully refer to the entities in question in virtue of their having a sense which comprises identity conditions of those entities: the reference is simply that thing, if there is one, which satisfies those identity conditions. The sentence as a whole has a sense and expresses a thought – indeed, for Frege, they are one and the same: a thought is the sense expressed by an indicative sentence. In these ways Frege relates the notions of *assertion, truth-value, reference, sense, identity, judgement,* and *thought*, with respect to a sentence like (1).

If we now embed sentence (1) in an intensional context, say,

(2) John thinks that the tree is in blossom

we find, according to Frege, that its semantic properties have altered quite radically. As it occurs in (2), sentence (1) no longer possesses assertoric force, and so no longer serves to express a judgement. If we ask what function it does now serve, the most plausible answer is that its role in (2) is to identify or refer to *what John thinks*, i.e., a thought. As it occurs in (2), then, sentence (1) no longer expresses a judgement or possesses assertoric force; and it no longer refers to any object or property in the natural world. Rather, it refers to a thought, that is, a *sense*: its reference is now the sense it expressed before it was embedded. In short, the expression 'John thinks that. . .' functions in many ways like Husserl's inverted commas. It is not, however, the 'index' we require in the present context, first because it can only be prefixed to indicative sentences, not to non-indicative sentences or to non-sentential expressions; and second because prefixing it to a sentence results in a sentence which, like (2), is itself assertoric and referential in the normal way.

We can overcome these deficiencies by introducing a sign, say 'Σ:', which will have the following properties. It may prefix meaningful expressions belonging to any syntactic category; it will not alter the syntactic category of any expression to which it is prefixed; it will act as a functor mapping all expressions within its scope onto their normal sense; and it will cancel the assertoric force, if any, of expressions to which it is applied. It is similar, therefore, to the English phrase *'the sense of'*, with the major difference that it does not convert sentences into singular terms, but leaves expressions syntactically unaltered. And so, while sentence (1) is assertoric and brings with it ontological commitment to items in the natural world,

(3) Σ: *the tree is in blossom*

does neither. It does indeed express a thought, a sense, which is identical with the thought or sense it refers to, but it expresses no judgement and concerns no items in the natural world. In particular, for instance, it involves no reference to a tree, but only to something called 'Σ: *the tree*'; but this is merely the sense that the expression 'the tree' possesses in normal contexts.

On this Fregean model, senses are not inhabitants of the natural world at all, but are rather abstract, atemporal, non-causal entities whose existence is independent of natural phenomena. And this corresponds closely to Husserl's doctrine concerning the nature of the noematic contents to which the reduction takes us:

> The tree plain and simple, the thing in nature, is as different as can be from this *perceived tree as such*, which, as perceptual sense, belongs inseparably to the perception. The tree plain and simple can burn away, decompose into its chemical elements, and so on. But the sense – the sense of this perception . . . – cannot burn away; it has no chemical elements, no forces, no real properties. (*Ideas* §89/p.260)

If this Fregean model is appropriate, then the phenomenological reduction is not in any straightforward way restrictive or limiting. It involves, for example, no retreat from the world as a whole to some part or region of it, and in particular it involves no renunciation of objectivity in favour of a restricted focus on subjective psychological states. It is, rather, a philosophical device, the purpose of which is to enable us to chart the bounds of sense by allowing us to refer directly to the sense or content of our thoughts, perceptions, and concepts. And, as Husserl puts it, 'If transcendental subjectivity is the universe of possible sense, then an outside is precisely – nonsense' (*CM* §41/p.84).

This last quotation raises a problem: What precisely is the relation between the transcendental reduction viewed as on pp. 163–8 as a renunciation of the natural world with the consequent immersion in transcendental subjectivity, and on the other hand, the reduction taken (as here) to be an operation that substitutes abstract senses for our normal objects of reference? Husserl's answer, I suppose, would be that the two conceptions are strictly speaking correlative: according to the former the reduction is stated in predominantly noetic terms, while the latter states the same thing in noematic terms. And the two are mutually dependent in that noetic activity always concerns sense-bestowal, while noematic analysis concerns precisely the senses thus bestowed.

Horizons and essences

An important corollary of the doctrine that our experience of objects is always aspectival, in other words, that objects are always presented in some way or other, is the thesis that our experience of objects is intrinsically partial: the object 'is always more than we actually perceive of it' (*PP* §6/p.45; cf. *CM* §20/p.48). For example 'the actual house stands there in bodily actuality and yet at the same time in such a way that it, this house, enters into particular perceptions only according to a part of its determinations' (*ibid.*). I can see, or remember, or imagine it from the front, or from the rear, from inside or from above. I can have a presentation of a whole side or, moving closer, of the kitchen window, or of one pane of glass in that window, or of a small fault in that glass, and so forth; but there is no possibility of a presentation which, as it were, embraces the house in its entirety and contains an element representing every single part and property of the house. Husserl calls the various partial, perspectival aspects under which a given object can be presented its 'adumbrations' (*Abschattungen*).

If we examine the nature of these adumbrations phenomenologically, they are found to possess a complex internal structure which has a surprising property: it enables them to stand in internal relations to other adumbrations that are not present. Now the phrase 'not present' here is ambiguous, having both a temporal and, so to speak, a modal sense. To say that an adumbration is not present can mean either (temporally) that it is not at present an item of awareness, or (modally and timelessly) that it is a merely possible but non-actual item of awareness. As we shall see, the temporal notion is emphasized in the account Husserl gives of the nature of sense perception, while the modal notion is dominant in his theory of essences, eidetic intuition, and the eidetic reduction.

When we think about some particular concrete perceptual experience – say, the visual experience which I have at a given moment while looking at the front of my house – there is perhaps a temptation to think naively that what I am actually presented with, the literal content of my experience, is something more or less static, inert, and self-contained. It is, we might say, something that could in essence be captured in a photograph, something of which we could conceivably make a self-contained picture or copy. Husserl attacked this atomistic way of thinking in virtually every work he produced, from the *Logical Investigations* to the *Cartesian Meditations*. His attack is conducted on two fronts, one descriptive, the other a part of his 'transcendental analytic'.

The descriptive objection is simple in form, but none the less compelling: actual perceptual experience, he argues, is simply not like that. Perceptions are not self-contained units of experience, one replacing or succeeding another without any intrinsic or internal relation between them, as if they were photographs appearing one after another in an album. On the contrary, any given perception contains within it, as an essential part of its sense, tacit allusions both to past experiences and to possible future ones. When I see the front of my house, what I see is, precisely, *the front* of *my house*, and my experience, if it is to be characterized accurately, would have to be described in terms such as these. In other words my intentional object is a three-dimensional physical object that possesses a back and sides, an inside, a location, a function, a history. And although I doubtless have none of these things explicitly in mind as I stand in the garden looking at it, my perceptual experience would nevertheless be radically different were my tacit awareness of these factors simply absent. Moreover, as I look at the house and my gaze shifts from one part of it to another,

> not only does what has become invisible *remain* in [my] grasp and continue to determine the [object], but at every place the appearing of the object *anticipates in advance*; the object is, so to speak, an object determined in advance, before it has been actually determined by a specific perception. It has an empty horizon of yet unknown features . . . to which the progressing perception brings the fullness that fits into it. (*PP* §35/p.139)

In the *Logical Investigations* Husserl provided a nice example of this anticipation inherent in perception: 'If I see an incomplete pattern, e.g., in this carpet partially covered over by furniture, the piece I see seems clothed with intentions pointing to further completions – we feel as if the lines and coloured shapes go on "in the sense" of what we see' (*LU* VI, §10/p.700). Every adumbration, in other words, contains within it a structure of 'retentions' and 'protentions' that are a function of memory, imagination, expectation, and habit. An adumbration stands internally related, in virtue of its sense, to other past or merely possible adumbrations. And this provides, as it were, a system of cross-referencing between experiences which is an intrinsic part of their nature: 'an intentional *horizon of reference* to potentialities of consciousness that belongs to the process itself' (*CM* §19/p.44).

> The features which enter into perception always point to completing features, which themselves might appear in other possible percepts, either definitely or more or less indefinitely, according to the degree of our 'empirical acquaintance' with the object. (*LU* VI, §10/p.700)

To say that an intentional object appears under some aspect, but that that appearance contains within it tacit allusions to other possible ways in which it might also appear is, in Husserlian terms, to say that every adumbration is surrounded by *a horizon* of other, possible adumbrations. Within the structure of the intentional object of a given experience, that is, we can distinguish between those aspects of the object that are explicitly present, as actual, and those that are present, but only tacitly, as possible. Every intentional object is surrounded by 'an empty horizon of possibilities' which, despite being only 'dimly apprehended' (*Ideas* §27/p.103), are nevertheless present in the experience of that object and contribute to determining its nature. (Cf. *CM* §20/p.46).

The second front along which Husserl attacks the atomistic conception of perceptual experience is not so much descriptive as analytic. In effect he argues, not that an accurate description of actual experience will falsify that conception, but rather that the conception itself is incoherent: if percepts were self-contained units of experience, then perceptual experience would be impossible. The system of cross-referencing must obtain, 'otherwise we would have to say that in every phase a different object were perceived' (*PP* §35/p.138). And if this were the case, consciousness would fail to be intentional. As Husserl wrote in the *Logical Investigations* : 'All perceiving and imagining is, on our view, a web of partial intentions, fused together in the unity of a single, total intention . . . . Only in this way can we understand how consciousness reaches out beyond what it actually experiences. It can, so to say, mean beyond itself and its meaning can be fulfilled' (*LU* VI, §10/p.701). If adumbrations had no intrinsic relation to one another – so that, for instance, no one of them could fulfil, or confirm, or make more determinate, or resolve an ambiguity in any other – then coherent experience of a single world would be impossible.

There are perhaps two points here. One is a conceptual one. There are certain clear cases in which an intentional act is internally related to one or more other intentional acts: 'we have only to think of the [relation] between wishful intention and wish fulfilment, between voluntary intention and execution, or the fulfilment of hopes and fears, the resolution of doubts, the confirmation of surmises, and so on' (*LU* VI §10/p.699). Now, mainly as a result of Wittgenstein's influence,[26] it has become widely accepted that, for example, an expectation, or a wish, is internally related to that which fulfils or satisfies it. Though Husserl would doubtless also accept this, his point is a rather different one. An expectation is intrinsically related not only to the expected event, but also to possible *experiences of* that event – and analogously in the cases of desiring, hoping, intending, fearing, predicting, guessing, and the like. This seems quite right, as far as it goes. But Husserl also wants to make the much stronger claim that precisely this sort of internal relation holds analytically between any given perception and an indefinite number of other possible perceptions of the same object. As against this it can be objected, however, that *those* relations are not analytically ascertainable: they may be empirically discoverable (as was suggested above), it may even be the case that their obtaining can be asserted *a priori* and synthetically (see below), but no amount of conceptual analysis can show that two different percepts are internally related. *Percepts*, unlike hopes, intentions, expectations, predictions and the like, do not have the conceptual, even propositional articulation necessary in order for that sort of conceptual analysis to be applicable to them.

The second point is a Kantian one. Roughly speaking the argument runs as follows. If the stream of consciousness is to make sense, then the primitive elements that compose it must undergo synthesis. For intentionality to be possible those elements must be capable of being combined to form representations of objects not present within that stream itself. The elements must, however, *be capable* of being combined. Otherwise, as Kant argued, 'it would be entirely accidental that appearances should fit into a connected whole of human knowledge. For even though we should have the power of associating perceptions, it would remain entirely undetermined and accidental whether they would themselves be associable'.[27] Kant is therefore led to ask, 'how are we to make comprehensible to ourselves this thoroughgoing affinity of appearances'?[28] Now, according to Husserl, a necessary condition of our being able to synthesize a number of different experiences, by taking them to be partial or aspectual experiences of one and the same object, is that those experiences should be, however indeterminately, *already* intrinsically related to one another. Even though the experiences in question may be utterly different from one another in specific content – as different, say, as my visual perception of the front of my house in bright sunlight is from my tactile experience of groping my way round it during a power failure – they must nevertheless in some sense 'agree', or 'be in harmony', or 'support each other'. If they did not, they would be incapable of being combined, as parts, into one overall representation of a single object, and 'we would have to say that in every phase a different object [was] presented' (*PP* §35/p.138). In the *Cartesian Meditations* Husserl echoes closely the view which he had first expressed some twenty-eight years earlier in the *Logical Investigations*, that only by appeal to the horizon structure of consciousness, with its system of inherent, tacit, non-conceptual cross-referencing, can one account for the intentionality of consciousness, for how coherent consciousness is possible in the first place:

> intentional analysis . . . as intentional, reaches out beyond the isolated subjective processes . . . . By explicating their correlative *horizons* it brings the highly diverse anonymous processes into the field comprising those that function 'constitutively' in relation to the objective sense of the cogitatum in question – that is to say: not only the actual but also the *potential* subjective processes, which, as such, are 'implicit' and 'predelineated' in the sense-producing intentionality of the actual ones and which, when discovered, have the evident character of processes that explicate the implicit sense. Thus alone can the phenomenologist make understandable to himself how, within the immanency of conscious life . . . anything like fixed and abiding objective entities can become intended. *The horizon structure* belonging to every intentionality thus prescribes for phenomenological analysis and

description methods of a totally new kind which come into action whenever consciousness and object, or intending and sense, . . . or experience, judgement, evidence and so forth present themselves as names for transcendental problems. (*CM* §20/p.48; my italics)

In previous chapters of this book we examined Husserl's struggles in the *Philosophy of Arithmetic* and the *Logical Investigations* to come to terms with what is universal, purely conceptual, and 'ideal' in experience, as distinct from those aspects of experience that are individual, sensory, contingent, and 'real'. The earlier work contained a naive and incomplete account of how concepts are abstracted from sensory experience. In the *Logical Investigations* this was modified and amplified to become in effect a theory of how we synthesize the ideal or categorial entities called 'species' and 'universals'. This theory in turn gives way to a third, concerning ideation, eidetic seeing, or the intuition of essences, outlined for example in *Ideas*, and, more fully, in *Phenomenological Psychology*.

Husserl's three attempts to address this matter have much in common. All, for instance, take it as axiomatic that what is concrete and real is prior to, and forms the foundation of, whatever is abstract and ideal. This is the case ontologically: 'In respect of its being, reality has precedence to every irreality whatsoever, since all irrealities relate back essentially to an actual or possible reality' (*FTL* §64/p.168). And it is the case epistemologically: 'experience traces back ultimately to perception, to a seeing and grasping of something itself; and all other intuition, as it founds the procuring of eidetic insights, is merely a modal variation of perception' (*PP* §38/ p.148). All three attempts aim to show that we can have a direct quasi-perceptual awareness of (respectively) concepts, or species, or essences. All are then presented with the central problem of how this possibility is to be explained: How, on the basis only of our purely sensory (including imaginative) experience of concrete, individual, contingent particulars, can we come to enjoy an awareness of things that are not real but ideal (or 'irreal'), that are not individual but universal, and that are not in any way contingent but are, precisely, the medium of necessity, universality, and all that is essential? And all three theories offer solutions of the same structural kind: 'Empirical or individual intuition *can be transformed* into essential intuition . . . which gives the essence' (*Ideas* §3/p.54; my italics). The major element in Husserl's repeated attempts to explain this aspect of human conscious life, in other words, is always the description of some process or procedure, something we *do*, as a result of which concrete intuition is transformed into an awareness whose object is universal and ideal. This is especially true of the process of ideation and its formalization in the eidetic reduction.

Ideation is a procedure which takes the awareness we have of an individual object ('object' in Husserl's broad sense, which encompasses objects, properties, states of affairs, and events – actual and imaginary), and transforms that awareness into an awareness of a universal or essence (*Wesen, Eidos, Essenz*). The relation between this procedure and the doctrine of horizons that we examined earlier is this: by implementing that procedure we as it were plot the limits to a given horizon, we plot the limits within which something can be imagined to vary, without its ceasing to be that thing. And to plot such limits is, according to Husserl, to establish its essence, that is, its 'horizons of potentiality' (*CM* §34/p.71). If an object (in the broad sense) can be imagined to be other than it is with respect to one of its parts or properties, *F*, without ceasing thereby to be that object, then possession of *F* cannot be essential to the object. But on the other hand, if to imagine a given object changed in some respect, *G*, is *ipso facto* to imagine a numerically distinct object, then we are presented with something that belongs to its essence: the object is essentially *G*.

The method for performing this procedure of ideation is as follows. We take either a perception or an imaginative presentation of one instance of the universal we wish to see, and we vary that instance in imagination. We vary it quite freely – though always making sure that it remains, precisely, an instance of the universal in question. If we do this, then – lo and behold – we will *see* an essence. This may sound fatuous and utterly naive, but Husserl's own descriptions of the process are no better. This, for instance, is how Husserl believes we should go about acquiring a grasp of what the essence of *perception* is:

> Starting from this table-perception as an example, we vary the perceptual object, table, with a completely free optialness, yet in such a manner that we keep perception fixed as perception of something, no matter what. Perhaps we begin by fictively changing the shape or the colour of the object quite arbitrarily, keeping identical only its perceptual appearing. In other words: Abstaining from acceptance of its being, we change the fact of this perception into a pure possibility, one among other quite 'optional' pure possibilities – but possibilities that are possible perceptions . . . . Accordingly from the very start we might have taken as our initial example a phantasying ourselves into a perceiving, with no relation to the rest of our *de facto* life. Perception, the universal type thus acquired, floats in the air, so to speak – in the atmosphere of pure phantasiableness. (*CM* §34/p.70)

The suggestion that in order to gain an understanding of what perception is, we ought to start by looking at a table and imagining it to have a different colour or shape, is surely not one that can be taken seriously. And, when we penetrate through the verbiage in passages like the one above, the specification of the procedure itself amounts to little more than the simple and, I take it, empirically false claim that if we imagine different perceptions we will grasp the essence of perception. Moreover, as an account of how we come to possess a grasp of that essence, it is straightforwardly circular; for implementation of the procedure clearly depends upon our already having a very firm grasp of what is and what is not essential to perception.

It is natural to take Husserl's theory of ideation – as, indeed, I have taken it so far – to be a description or explanation of how *in general* anyone progresses from experience of what is contingent and particular, to an awareness of what is universal and essential. This, for example, is how the theory is presented in Husserl's lectures on phenomenological psychology (cf. *PP* §8/pp.51–65); and it is plausible to see the mature theory of 'ideation' as addressing the same set of problems as his earlier theory of 'abstractive ideation' in the *Logical Investigations* . If the theory was intended in this way, it is an unmitigated failure. It is possible, however, that Husserl did not intend it to fulfil this role at all; for the very same procedure of 'ideation' outlined above also appears in Husserl's writings under the guise of something called 'the eidetic reduction'. And in *that* guise it seems intended, not as a description of how we are able in principle to transcend the particularity of our basic experience, but rather as a specifically *philosophical* technique, aimed at making clearer or more distinct the universal 'ideas' which we already possess and use in everyday life, albeit in a more or less indistinct and unclear way.[29] Construed as a philosophical device the eidetic reduction takes elements of that tacit everyday understanding and transforms them into something more explicit, clear, and complete. It takes, for example, our normal vague and unsystematic grasp of what perception is, and transforms it into a philosophically more adequate grasp. In analogy with Quine's recommendation that in philosophy we practise 'semantic ascent', the eidetic reduction can be seen as Husserl's requirement that we perform 'eidetic ascent', so to speak, and instead of merely making use of ideas, we turn our attention to them and study them in their own right. And if this is the case, then clearly the objection that the procedure is circular is misplaced: on the contrary, the procedure *requires* that there already be a tacit, pre-theoretical grasp of universal ideas which can subsequently be brought to explicit clarity by means of it.

There are, however, a number of things amiss with the eidetic reduction viewed in this way. In the first place, it is inadequate. Even if we grant that possessing and exercising imaginative ability is a necessary condition for achieving a full understanding of a given concept, it is hardly a sufficient condition: the imagination must be exercised to some degree systematically, if only to avoid what Wittgenstein diagnosed as a 'main cause of philosophical disease – a one-sided diet: one nourishes one's thinking with only one kind of example'.[30] Husserl notes this fact, and warns against incorporating 'secret' and 'unnoticed' restrictions on the imaginative variations we contemplate (*PP* §8(a)/p.55). But he has no suggestion as to how such bias might be removed.

Second, the eidetic reduction is objectionable because it aims at the wrong *result*. According to Husserl the end product is a direct acquaintance with an object:

> The essence (*Eidos*) is a new sort of object. Just as the datum of individual or empirical intuition is an individual object, so the datum of essential intuition is a pure essence.
>
> Here we have not a mere superficial analogy, but a radical community of nature. Essential insight is still an intuition, just as the eidetic object is still an object . . . . Essential intuition is the consciousness of something, of an 'object', a something towards which its glance is directed. (*Ideas* §3/p.55)

But the achievement of understanding, especially the achievement of a philosophical or scientific understanding, cannot be captured in terms of this simple-minded and inappropriate model. Such understanding does not consist in, and is not brought about by, simply *looking at an object* – regardless of how idiosyncratic we make the looking, or the object looked at, or both. Intellectual understanding is not a species of acquaintance. It is, minimally, a complex state involving abilities, dispositions, and a capacity to apply explanatory theory to problematic phenomena. Genuinely to know *what perception is*, for instance, would involve mastery of a considerable amount of theory, possession of solutions to a large number of problems, the ability to evaluate evidence, and much else besides. And this is neither something one acquires by simply gazing at something, nor is it something that consists in having some *object* in mind. To repeat: performance of the eidetic reduction can at best yield, as a result, acquaintance with an object; what we *need* at this point, however, is an account of the complex system of abilities and techniques that together comprise a theoretical understanding of something. Husserl seems to believe, mistakenly, that the former is an acceptable substitute for the latter.

Husserl's doctrine of essential intuition is objectionable, finally, because of its methodological consequences; for it forms an essential ingredient in Husserl's view of phenomenology as a discipline that proceeds exclusively by a method of 'pure description'. 'Phenomenology is, in fact, a *purely descriptive* discipline which explores the field of transcendentally pure consciousness in the light of *pure intuition*' (*Ideas* §59/p.176). Husserl is guided in this respect by what he dignifies with the title 'The Principle of All Principles', namely,

> that every intuition which gives its object originally (*jede originär gebende Anschauung*) is a source of justification for knowledge, that

whatever presents itself in the 'intuition' originally . . . is simply to be accepted as it presents itself. (*Ideas* §24/p.92)

Husserl takes this to imply that, for phenomenology, 'the decisive factor lies, above all, in the absolutely faithful description of what is actually present in phenomenological purity, and in keeping at a distance all interpretations that transcend the given' (*Ideas* §90/p.262).

What contemporary philosophers of science have dubbed 'the myth of the given' achieves its apotheosis in Husserl's rigorous science of philosophy. It is not so much that he allows that there are 'pure data' which present themselves to us exactly as they are; nor that he believes we can provide the one, unique 'absolutely faithful' description of such data; nor that he believes that this description will itself subsequently determine rigorous scientific theory. What is ultimately unacceptable in this respect is that, within so-called rigorous science, *there is no subsequent theory.* To offer an absolutely faithful description of what is given, without explanation, interpretation, extrapolation, hypotheses, or models of any sort, is the final and only goal of pure phenomenology. Not only must phenomenology begin with the description of what is immediately given, it must end with it as well: the first sin in phenomenology is to 'transcend the given'.

As a result, Husserlian phenomenology is intrinsically not only one of the most timidly conservative, but also one of the most dogmatic of all philosophical standpoints. Having absolved himself in principle from any obligation to provide arguments, proofs, or justifications for his conclusions – indeed, having absolved himself from any obligation to provide *conclusions* at all – the Husserlian phenomenologist is free of all the normal accoutrements of objective, rational, philosophical enquiry. In the last analysis, all that a rigorous scientist may do is describe his own intuitions; and the dogmatism and subjectivity inherent in this proposal is not in the least mitigated by the fact that those intuitions are supposed to strike him as self-evident intuitions of essence.

Wittgenstein once called intuition 'an unnecessary shuffle',[31] and at least this much seems true: given a pure intuition of the kind Husserl believes himself to have isolated, all one *could* do with it would be to describe it. But there seems to be no philosophical problem to which such a description could be the solution, no philosophical use to which it could be put.

The Individual
and the *Lebenswelt*

Introduction

The overall framework of ideas that we examined in the last chapter is one
of transcendental solipsistic idealism. It concerns, that is, the *a priori*
conditions of the possibility of objective experience in general; and, it
turns out, the conditions on which that possibility depends make no
essential or ineliminable reference either to the independent existence of
an extra-mental world, or to the existence of a plurality of conscious
beings. 'The existence of a world is the correlate of certain complexes of
experience' (*Ideas* §49/p.150). 'The term "object" is for us always a name
for essential connections of consciousness' (*Ideas* §53/p.164). And these
complexes of experience and connections of consciousness are such that
they can obtain within, and determine an objective world for, an individual ego considered in isolation. In *Ideas* Husserl maintains that transcendental *subjectivity* is 'the absolute, within which everything transcendent, and thus the entire physical and psychological world, is constituted'
(*ibid.*). And yet some sixteen years later, in *Cartesian Meditations*, he was
to write: 'The intrinsically first being, the being that precedes and bears
every worldly objectivity is transcendental *intersubjectivity*' (*CM* §64/
p.156). The present chapter concerns the nature of this move from solipsism to intersubjectivity, from the transcendental 'I' to the transcendental
'we' (*CM* §49/p.107), and in particular it concerns the consequences this
shift of perspective has for Husserl's solutions to problems concerning
the nature of objectivity – to problems concerning such notions as
rationality, evidence, knowledge, truth, existence, transcendence, and
reality.

Harmony and the exploding noema

In the final chapter of *Ideas*, entitled 'Reason and Reality' (*Vernunft und*

Wirklichkeit), Husserl offers a solipsistic solution to the problem of how we are, individually, to escape the very subjectivity to which each of us is apparently confined as a result of the phenomenological reduction. In outline, that solution has two phases.

First phase

In its primitive form, the form on which all 'cognitions of a higher level' are founded, conscious experience requires the bestowal of an 'objective' sense on brute hyletic data; and here we encounter the first, minimal, purely formal ingredient in what will eventually be a full-blooded conception of objectivity. *'Gegenständlichkeit'* ('objectivity' in inverted commas) as we noted earlier is merely the property of being directed towards an (intentional) object, the property, that is, of being organized around an empty X. To say that an experience has *Gegenständlichkeit* is to claim no more than that the experience has the formal property of manifesting unity in diversity, or identity in difference. To synthesize, to unify what is diverse and manifold in experience, to direct different moments in an act to a single object, to introduce the formal notion of identity, to endow an act with intentionality, and to bestow an 'objective' sense on the data of experience – these are all ultimately one and the same synthetic function. The resulting 'objectivity' can of course be something which, in a different sense, is entirely subjective: in reflection, for example, I can have my own psychological states or my subjective sensations and feelings as the intentional objects of my acts. Likewise, for something to be *gegenständlich* does not imply that it actually exists or is real. Imaginary and fictional entities, for instance, are 'objective' without being real.

Although *Gegenständlichkeit* is by no means the same as objectivity (i.e. non-subjectivity), it is nevertheless the essential first step towards it. There could be no such thing as objective knowledge were we not capable, at a primitive level, of discerning unity in the diverse elements of sensory experience, that is, of uniting such elements in a way which allows the formal, materially undetermined concept of an object in general to be applied to them.

Second phase

Transition to the second stage in the analysis of objectivity is signalled by Husserl's introduction of a number of important questions:

> The X [at the centre of] different acts and act-noemata, and with its different 'determining contents', is necessarily experienced as the same. But *is it really the same*? And *is the object itself 'real'*? . . . . What does it *mean* to say that an object given to consciousness is 'real'? (*Ideas* §135/p.376).

199

The problem is clear: given that an object can have *Gegenständlichkeit* and yet be something subjective like a sensation, or something merely imaginary like a gryphon, in virtue of what does an object count as fully and objectively real, as actually existing in the external world?

What distinguishes something psychologically subjective from something that exists objectively and actually is the fact that the latter is *transcendent*: it does not exist immanently within consciousness, but, on the contrary, leads a life of its own in the external world. Husserl sees his task, therefore, as providing a phenomenological analysis of what transcendence consists in, and of how such transcendence can be explained exclusively by reference to what *is* immanent in transcendental subjectivity. This analysis takes place in two steps. The first of these makes use of the doctrine of horizons, and the second concerns something Husserl calls 'harmony'.

As we have seen, intentional objects that appear as physical objects can only appear in adumbrations: 'In principle a real thing, [i.e.] a being which has that sense, can appear only *'inadequately'* in a finite appearance' (*Ideas* §138/p.384). And this, in and of itself, is sufficient to distinguish putative physical objects from purely subjective, immanent, mental entities. An objectively real thing, Husserl writes,

> is transcendent to the perception of it, and, moreover, to every consciousness whatsoever of it, not merely in the sense that the thing is not
> . . . a real constituent part of consciousness, but also . . . that, in
> absolutely unconditioned generality and necessity, a thing cannot be
> given as really immanent in *any* possible perception or any possible
> consciousness. Thus a basic and essential difference arises between
> *being as experience* and *being as a thing*. [The former] is perceivable in
> immanent perception, but it is of the essence of a spatial thing that this
> is not possible . . . . Thus the thing itself, *simpliciter*, we call transcendent. (*Ideas* §42/p.133)

For something to be transcendent, then, is for it to be such that it always and necessarily exceeds the grasp consciousness has of it; it essentially surpasses the mind's ability to be aware of it in its entirety. And that an object *does* have this property is something we can know on the basis of our own, subjective experience. We have here an analysis of 'transcendence' that can be couched solely in phenomenological terms; for our awareness of transcendence is a function of our awareness of the potentially infinite horizons of possibility that are a part of the presentation we have of any such object.

To talk about an objectively real object, or an actually existing thing is to talk about something that contrasts not only with psychologically subjective things like sensations and mental images, but also with purely imaginary things like mermaids and gryphons. The first step in the analysis of objectivity bears on the former contrast; in the second step Husserl turns to that element in the concept of transcendence which concerns the *existence* of those objects we take to be objectively real. The question, now, is: What phenomenological explanation can we give of the difference between an intentional object which, like a gryphon, doesn't actually exist, and one like a lion, which clearly does? (Cf. *Ideas* §138; *CM* §§25f.)

This question brings us face-to-face with an issue whose treatment in Husserl's middle period works we have not yet considered. The issue concerns the *rationality* of our intentional acts. In so far as I merely undergo experiences, have sensations or perceptions, entertain thoughts, and perform acts of imagination, I do nothing that can be assessed as rational or irrational. Merely to imagine an animal with an eagle's head and wings and a lion's body, say, or idly to entertain the thought that my typewriter is made of butter, is, as yet, to do nothing which is intrinsically irrational. The possibility of such a condemnation does arise, however, as soon as I in any way commit myself to the existence of gryphons, or come to believe that my typewriter really is made of butter. In Husserlian terms, the possibility of rationality, or irrationality, is a function of the thetic characteristics, the ontological *positings*, present in some of my acts: 'the specific character of rationality belongs to the positing moment (*Setzungscharakter*) intrinsically and as a distinguishing mark' (*Ideas* §136/p.380). It is only in so far as my mental acts involve some form of commitment – be it a tacit ontological commitment, or an explicit judgement that some state of affairs obtains – that they can be evaluated as correct, accurate, relevant, true, proper, justified, or not. To say that such a commitment is rational is, trivially, to say that it is justified; and this is to say that there exists, and that I am aware of, sufficient evidence in its favour. Rationality, for Husserl, is a function of the availability of *Evidenz*. We might call this his verificationist theory of rationality. (Cf. *Ideas* §136; *CM* §26.)

Evidence has always the same form for Husserl. According to the theory which he inherited from Brentano and never abandoned, genuine evidence is taken to consist in *self*-evidence, in other words, in the presence to consciousness of the thing itself, in person. (See, e.g., *HSW* p.114; *LU* Prol. §51/p.195; *Ideas* §136/p.379; *CM* §5/p.13; *FTL* §58/p.155; *Crisis* §34(d)/p.127; *EU* §4/p.20, etc.) There are, for example, cases in which the datum is an essence, and is given in an act of intellectual intuition. In such a case it is possible, Husserl maintains, not only that the object is given 'in person', but also that it is given 'adequately' – not aspectively, but transparently and without remainder. On the other hand, in sensory intuition an object can itself be presented *in propria persona*, but only 'inadequately', with its indeterminate horizons and opaque aspects.

> The act which posits a thing on the basis of its appearance 'in person' is
> clearly a rational act, even though the appearance is never more than a
> one-sided and 'imperfect' appearance. (*Ideas* §138/p.384)

But what is it that makes it rational to ascribe actuality or real existence
to a thing? In what circumstances is a positing act justified? Husserl's
answer is that *any* fulfilled act, no matter how partial or fleeting the
fulfilment may be, constitutes in itself rational justification for an
ontological commitment, but that this commitment is intrinsically and for
ever provisional. At the most basic level, I am justified in my commitment
to the existence of an object (or property, event, state of affairs, etc.)
in so far as I *seem* to have a direct experience of that object and, importantly, in so far as that experience is not contradicted or subverted by any
other experience. And it is the inexhaustibility of an object's horizons of
possibility, combined with the reference to presently unknown future
actualizations of those horizons, which together make all rationality
inescapably provisional.[1] In a train of thought to which Quine, for
example, also subscribes, Husserl sees his verificationism as entailing a
theory which is also holistic, radically fallibilistic, and which places a
crucial emphasis on the notion of coherence.[2] Experience can provide us
with warranted certainty: we can be sure of something in a way which is
entirely rational, and yet in a way which at the same time is, by its very
nature, entirely defeasible. Warranted certainty is by no means the same
as 'absolute' certainty.

> What about . . . experience of what is in the world, experience of what
> I am immediately certain of as existing spatio-temporally? It *is* certain;
> but this certainty can modalize itself, it can become doubt, it can
> dissolve in the course of experience into illusion: no immediate expe-
> riential assertion gives me an entity as what it is in itself, but only
> something meant with a certainty that must verify itself in the course
> of my experiencing life. But the verification which lies merely in the
> harmonious character of actual experience does not prevent the pos-
> sibility of illusion. (*Crisis* §73/Appendix IV, p.335)

In Husserl's metaphorical terms, as long as a fulfilled noema remains
harmonious it constitutes rational justification for an assertion of actual
existence, even if that fulfilling is partial, perhaps even slight. But noemata
can explode:

> the thetic components and the sense of the earlier course of perception
> [can] suffer cancellation; . . . under certain circumstances the percep-
> tion [can] explode, so to speak, and break up into 'conflicting thing-
> apprehensions', into *suppositions* concerning things; . . . and the posit-
> ings in these suppositions [can] annul one another. (*Ideas* §138/p.384)

Gareth Evans has argued persuasively that we need to 'take the notion of *being in an informational state with such and such a content* as a primitive notion for philosophy'; and he identifies 'the most general term for the deliverances of the informational system' as 'the way things *seem* to the subject'.[3] This seems right. And Husserl would add that any harmonious seeming is *eo ipso* rational grounds for some commitment – for a judgement, a belief, an inference,[4] or just the tacit taking of something to exist that is part and parcel of normal perceptual experience – until such time, that is, as it is overturned by further, refractory seemings out of harmony with it. Ultimately only experience can substantiate or undermine experience; and in the coherent, harmonious, fulfilling course that our normal experience takes, as a whole, we have all the justification we will ever get – and all we will ever need – of the rationality of our commitments to 'actually existing' objects in the external world.

Disembodied egos

According to the doctrines we have examined so far, it is within individual, disembodied consciousness that are located all the resources we need to account for meaning, knowledge, objectivity, rationality and the like. And in this respect those doctrines belong squarely within the mainstream of the Cartesian tradition in philosophy. It is ironical, therefore, that it should have been in a series of lectures delivered in the Amphithéâtre Descartes of the Sorbonne, and later published under the title *Cartesian Meditations*, that Husserl began to explore a line of thought that is profoundly anti-Cartesian in its implications.[5] Ultimately these considerations lead us away from solitary, immaterial, self-subsistent consciousness, as the focal point of philosophy, and indicate instead the importance of the body, of the existence of a plurality of conscious beings, and of the life-world or *Lebenswelt* which they share. These new thoughts receive a final – though hardly a definitive – expression in Husserl's last, unfinished work, *The Crisis of European Sciences and Transcendental Phenomenology* (1936).

A solipsistic phenomenology like Husserl's can come to seem inadequate in a number of different respects. For instance, in so far as it concerns itself exclusively with contents of consciousness as they immediately present themselves, that phenomenology is badly placed to say anything interesting either about *the body* and its role in determining human nature and human experience, or about the *dispositional* properties of the mind – as against straightforwardly occasional or episodic phenomena.

Moreover, the solipsistic point of view can come to seem inadequate, not only with respect to one's knowledge and understanding of oneself, but also, and perhaps especially, with respect to one's knowledge and understanding of *others*. This latter worry has, for Husserl, two points of focus. One concerns the nature of our awareness of other conscious individuals, the phenomenology of our experience of other minds; the other has to do with the epistemic roles performed by such things as inherited tradition, common practices and institutions, and the existence of a shared culture and history. These roles, Husserl came to believe, are fundamental in determining and constituting not only one's subjective point of view, but also the nature and possibility of objectivity. I will deal with the problems concerning one's own ego, body, and dispositions in the present section, and with those concerning the egos, bodies, and practices of others in the next.

The notion of the ego (or the mind, the self, the 'I', the subject of mental acts and states, that which has thoughts and perceptions, etc.) had a chequered history in the development of Husserl's thought. In the original edition of the *Logical Investigations* (1901) Husserl denied the existence of any such thing: 'I must frankly confess', he wrote, 'that I am quite unable to find this ego, this primitive necessary centre of relations' (*LU* V, §8/p.549). By the time of the second edition of that work in 1913 he had changed his mind, and in a footnote added to the last quoted sentence he announced: 'I have since managed to find it'. In the first book of *Ideas*, also published in 1913, there is, however, hardly more than a passing mention of the ego.[6] The concern in *Ideas* is with a bipartite, 'correlative' structure involving noeses and noemata, intentional acts and their intentional objects, the *cogito* and its *cogitata*. And that work gives every impression that mental states and acts can be studied phenomenologically without reference to anything that has or performs them. But this overall structure is, it seems, replaced in subsequent works by a tripartite one involving *ego, cogito*, and *cogitatum*: the agent, the act, and its object (cf. *Crisis* §50/p.171). And with this there is introduced – again apparently – a new discipline to which Husserl gives the appalling name '*Egology*'. Indeed phenomenology itself 'begins . . . as a pure egology and as a science that apparently condemns us to a solipsism, albeit a transcendental solipsism' (*CM* §13/p.30).

> It thus becomes a transcendental-solipsistic science. It is therefore not the *ego cogito*, but a science about the ego – a pure egology – which becomes the ultimate foundation of philosophy . . . [But only the foundation], not the fully developed phenomenology, because to the latter, of course, belongs the further development from transcendental solipsism to transcendental intersubjectivity. (*PV* p.12/pp.11–12)

In actual practice, however, this change turns out to be largely nominal rather than substantial; for Husserl does *not* posit the existence of any substance or individual that is distinct from, but the owner or subject of, mental acts. On the contrary, the transcendental ego is indistinguishable from 'the processes making up his life' (*CM* §30/p.65). So, in practice, 'egological analysis' is very largely noetico-noematic analysis of the familiar kind, and not the analysis of some newly discovered entity. Strawson has coined the phrase 'no-ownership' or 'no-subject' doctrines of the self for those, like Hume's, say, or Wittgenstein's in the *Tractatus*, which deny that there is a subject or bearer or owner of mental acts distinguishable from those acts themselves.[7] And Husserl's, too, is a no-ownership theory of the self.

The matter, however, is complex and elusive; and unfortunately becomes more so in the case of a philosopher whose texts are replete with apparent references to a thing, or things, called 'the transcendental ego', 'the monadically concrete ego', 'the active subject of consciousness', 'the substrate of habitualities', 'the empty pole of identity', 'the monad', 'the empirical psyche', and even 'the empirically factual transcendental ego', and who, moreover, seems to be exercised by the baffling problem of how, 'by his own active generating, the ego *constitutes himself*' (*CM* §32/p.67; my italics).

We can begin by directly confronting this last problem, the problem of the ego's 'self-constitution'. As we already know, Husserl believed that wherever a multiplicity of subjective acts are united in such a way as to constitute different presentations of one and the same object, this is a function of synthetic activity, an activity which thus 'constitutes' the object in question. Constitution is not, however, a matter of creation *ex nihilo* but, more modestly, of unifying various data so that they come to possess a certain sense. And this is as true of the object I call 'my mind' as it is of any other intentional unity. Now the ego's constitution of itself can easily be made to seem as great a mystery as, say, divine self-causation: How can God be *causa sui*, the cause of His own existence? Surely He must already exist before He can be the cause of anything. In which case we seem forced to choose between two equally unacceptable alternatives: either something can exist before it exists, or something non-existent can have causal powers. Likewise, talk of the constitution by the ego of itself is sometimes construed as though it involved a mysterious process whereby the ego somehow creates itself out of nothing. What Husserl has in mind, however, is a procedure considerably more mundane and intelligible than this. In the first place, there are *data*, things that are *given*, and it is on the basis of these that the synthesis proceeds. Second, that synthesis proceeds as normal, in the way that we have already examined with respect to intentional objects in general: there is an 'empty *X*', to which data are ascribed as its properties, both actual and 'horizonal':

> But it is to be noted that this centering ego is not merely an empty pole of identity, any more than any object is such. Rather, according to a law of 'transcendental generation', with every act emanating from him

205

and having a new objective sense, he *acquires a new and abiding property.* (*CM* §32/p.66; my italics)

What is interesting about Husserl's treatment of these issues in his last works, and what marks a break with his earlier treatments of them, is the emphasis he now places on dispositional characteristics ('habitualities'), and the role they play in explaining the nature of the self. When I make a decision, say, or undergo some experience, I 'acquire a new property' in the trivial sense that it becomes true of me for all time that *at such-and-such a time I performed such-and-such an intentional act.* But it is not with this trivial claim that Husserl is concerned; neither is he concerned especially with the fact that it is possible that on subsequent occasions I may undergo further episodic experiences directly and explicitly related to the earlier one. I may, for example, remember the earlier decision, or, thinking about it, come to change my mind and make another decision cancelling it, and so forth. Rather, Husserl wishes to emphasize that 'I acquire a new *and abiding* property' in so far as I acquire dispositions, habits, propensities, inclinations – in short, 'an abiding style . . . a personality' (*CM* §32/p.67).

> For example: If in an act of judgement I decide for the first time [that such-and-such is the case], the fleeting act passes; but from now on *I am abidingly the ego who is thus and so decided* . . . . That, however, does not signify merely that I remember the act, [or even that] I *can* remember it later. I could do this even if I had given up my conviction. . . . As long as it is accepted by me, I can . . . repeatedly find it as mine, *habitually* my own opinion, or correlatively, find myself as the ego who is convinced, who, as the persisting ego, *is determined by this abiding habitus or state.* (*ibid*; my italics)

And the contrast between these dispositional states and any conscious episodes is explicitly stressed by Husserl:

> The persisting, the temporal enduring, of such determining properties of the ego . . . manifestly is not a continuous filling of immanent time with subjective processes – just as the abiding ego . . . is not a process or a continuity of processes. (*ibid*; cf. *Crisis* §40/p.149.)

But, we still need to ask, what exactly is this 'abiding ego'? Taken all-in-all, taken, as Husserl says, 'in its full concreteness', the ego is a complex whole that comprises the individual events, both hyletic and intentional, which make up the stream of consciousness, along with the dispositional characteristics which supervene on them, and the horizons of potentiality that are instrinsic to them. 'The monadically concrete ego includes the whole of actual and potential conscious life' (*CM* §33/p.68). (Husserl borrows Leibniz's term for the unitary ego in its entirety, calling it 'the monad'.) The self-constitution of the ego, it turns out, is merely the synthesis which unites these disparate elements into that complex *whole*. There is, in other words, no such thing as The Ego – if by that we mean something distinct from 'the flowing multiformity of intentional life'. There is, for Husserl, no owner of experiences separate from those experiences themselves. On the other hand, however, it would be wrong to construe Husserl's theory as, like Hume's, a 'bundle' theory of the self. The ego is not a weak whole, or mere agglomeration. On the contrary it is a *synthetic* whole, a genuine unity – but a unity which encompasses all the diverse elements of consciousness, and does not stand over against them as their bearer, or owner, or subject. In this way Husserl manages to steer between, on the one side, the metaphysical excesses involved in positing a substantial transcendental ego, and, on the other side, the difficulties which defeated Hume in his attempts to develop an atomistic account of the self. And the result is a theory in which – despite the strong impression to the contrary created by Husserl's unfortunate way of expressing the matter – the transcendental ego is nothing but the ordinary, common-or-garden *mind*, albeit viewed from within a philosophical or transcendental perspective. 'As transcendental ego, after all, I am the same ego that in the worldly sphere is a human ego. What was concealed from me in the human sphere I reveal through transcendental enquiry' (*Crisis* §72/p.264). And this 'human ego' or mind is nothing but a massively complex, interrelated system of conscious acts and states, possessing dispositions and, ultimately, a style and personality of its own.

In articulating this theory, Husserl's appeal to 'habitualities' plays a crucial role. We will need to return to this notion in subsequent sections; for it has another, a vital part to play, in Husserl's final assault on problems concerning objectivity, rationality, and reality.

Conscious bodies

For over forty years, in the works he published, Husserl subscribed unquestioningly to the Brentanian doctrine that mental *acts* are the elements which make up one's conscious life, and which are, therefore, the proper objects of study both for descriptive psychology, and for its successor, transcendental phenomenology.[8] At an early stage, it is true, he recognized the inappropriateness of the term 'act', warning that 'in talking about "acts" . . . we must steer clear of the word's original meaning: all thought of activity must be rigorously excluded'. And, he added, 'we define "acts" as intentional experiences, not as mental activities' (*LU* V, §13/p.563). It nevertheless remains the case that with few exceptions the intentional experiences which comprise the subject matter of Husserl's published philosophy, from the time of the *Philosophy of Arithmetic* until he came to write the *Cartesian*

Meditations, belong to the category of *events* – dateable occurrences within a stream of consciousness which is made up of such events. But this commitment began to crumble, under the pressure exerted on it by a number of other doctrines which came increasingly to seem incompatible with it.

We have already mentioned two of those doctrines. One concerns the horizon-structure of intentional experience, the other concerns Husserl's growing emphasis on 'habitualities'.[9] Neither 'tacit infinite potentialities' on the one hand, nor 'dispositional characteristics' on the other can be easily assimilated into a theory that implicitly restricts its domain to episodes of conscious awareness. This is because neither is an episodic phenomenon and, moreover, both can exist even though there is no explicit, conscious awareness of them. In short, neither is, strictly speaking, a *phenomenon*. In addition to the foregoing, however, there is a third issue whose emergence in Husserl's later writings places the earlier doctrine of disembodied mental acts under considerable strain – not surprisingly; for the issue concerns the human body, and in particular, one's own body.

In one sense my own body is a physical object, a material, spatio-temporal object like any other: it has a weight, a size, a chemical composition, a history, and so forth. Husserl's term for the human body viewed merely as a physical object is *der Körper*. Quite clearly, however, there is also a sense in which my own body is not given to *me* in that way: it is experienced and known by me in ways quite different from those in which I experience or know other physical objects. I do not, as it were, stumble across my body in the course of experience in anything like the way in which I can come across a building, say, or another person. It is not simply that my own body is very familiar to me, nor even that it is 'always there', like some substantial shadow from which I can never escape.[10] It is rather that, at a certain level, my 'relation' to my own body is not strictly speaking a relation at all: it is not, at least, a relation between *me* and *some other object*. Although my body is certainly a physical object, and is, moreover, the intentional object of many of my acts of perception, conception, and memory, there is also a sense in which my own body is a *subject*. And in this sense my body is unique amongst intentional physical objects in that it belongs, also, on the subjective side of the intentional relation. My body can feel tired, my legs can feel stiff, my hands can feel the warmth of the fire, and so forth. My own body is (in terms unfortunately more often associated with Merleau-Ponty than with Husserl) an object-subject, or a body-subject. Husserl calls the human body viewed in this way *der Leib*, a term which I shall translate as 'the living body'.

In spite of their being in fact one and the same object, from a phenomenological point of view 'the physical body and the living body are essentially different' (*Crisis* §28/p.107). Husserl identifies four phenomenological characteristics which together serve to define the notion of the living body, and to distinguish it from all other intentional objects. First, my living body is immediately expressive: when I am tired, or amused, or in pain, it is *that* object which yawns, smiles, or cries out. Like Wittgenstein, Husserl emphasizes the spontaneity and immediacy of expressive behaviour:

> A human being is not a mere combination or aggregation of one thing, called a body, and another called a mind. The human body is through and through a conscious body: every movement of the body is 'full of mind' – coming, going, standing still, laughing, dancing, speaking, etc.[11]

And, as we will see, for both Husserl and Wittgenstein it is the spontaneity of 'the primitive, the natural, expression of sensation' which makes it possible for us to understand the mental life of someone else.

Second, and obviously, the living body is sensitive: I do not pull my hand out of the fire as I would my glove, because otherwise it will get damaged. I pull it out because it hurts. Here one should resist the temptation to ascribe the pain to something incorporeal, to something other than the body (perhaps on the confused grounds that a 'material' object cannot have something 'mental' like a sensation); for when the experience is described accurately, the description will make essential reference to the bodily location and nature of the pain. When I put my hand too close to the fire, it is, when all is said and done, *my hand* that hurts.

Third, the living body has motility ('kinaesthesia' as Husserl mistakenly calls it), that is, it has the power to act. My living body is 'the organ of my will, and the medium (*Träger*) of free movement'.[12] It is 'the only object which is immediately and spontaneously moveable' by my pure will. In this respect it is important to note that it is not *the experience* of moving and acting that is at issue here, but *the fact* that I can and do act. Indeed, as Wittgenstein observed:

> *Doing* itself seems not to have any volume of experience. It seems like an extensionless point, the point of a needle. The point seems to be the real agent. And the phenomenal happenings only to be consequences of this acting. 'I *do* . . .' seems to have a definite sense, separate from all experience.[13]

In Husserl's last works there is a marked tendency to emphasize physical behaviour, the '*I do* . . .', and the '*I can* . . .', so to speak, at the expense of the earlier, Cartesian focus on mental acts and the disembodied '*I think* . . .'. What becomes increasingly important is the fact that I am intentionally related to things 'through the living body', and this means that I am related to them neither as a pure ego, nor as one physical object is related to another; rather, the expression 'being related via the living body'

> refers to the kinaesthetic, to functioning as an ego in this peculiar way
> – primarily through seeing, hearing, etc; and of course other modes of
> the ego belonging to this (for example, lifting, carrying, pushing, and
> the like). (*Crisis* §28/p.108)

These are some of the activities possible for a bodily ego or body-subject
(*leibliche Ichlichkeit*); and clearly we have here, in all but name, the
notion which Merleau-Ponty called *motor intentionality*, and which he
explored at length in *The Phenomenology of Perception*.

Husserl's fourth, and final, characterization is of '*der Leib als
Orientierungszentrum*' (*Ideas* II, §41 in *Hus* IV, p.158). The living body,
that is, functions as the absolute point about which all spatial relations are
experienced as orientated. Phenomenologically, the space I inhabit and
move about in, the space which characterizes my perceptions and experiences, does not present itself to me as unorientated, uncentred,
abstract Euclidian space; rather, spatiality is experienced in ways which
call for description in egocentric terms: things are near me or far away,
above me or below, facing me or facing away, to the right or to the left,
moving with respect to me, receding perspectivally towards the horizon,
and so forth. But regardless of how much objects may change their spatial
positions, and regardless, too, of how much I might change mine, 'a firm
zero of orientation persists, so to speak, as an absolute *Here*'.[14] The living
body is always 'the middle point of a surrounding world',[15] it is
necessarily the geometrical centre, the *Nullpunkt* of orientated,
egocentric space.

We have already examined the notion of self-constitution as it applies
to the pure or transcendental ego; and we found that in Husserl's view the
unity of the human mind, viewed as a whole, is a function of straightforward synthesis applied to a plurality of items of awareness, the items
being themselves experiences of which we are aware in reflection. Now
the human body is also a complex whole, and so its unity, too, must be a
function of synthetic activity that forms a plurality of component parts
and aspects into a single whole. In so far as my body is an intentional
object for me, the synthesis proceeds as it does for any intentional object:
I refer certain of my visual, tactile, and other sensations to my body as the
object which has the properties corresponding to them. I can see my own
body, touch it, hear it, observe its behaviour, and so on, in just the way in
which I can see, hear, touch, or observe someone else's body, or some
inanimate physical object. According to Husserl the way I synthesize the
intentional object which is my physical body is not fundamentally different from the way I synthesize any intentional object whatsoever.

But clearly this explanation is inapplicable to the body as *subject*,
which is, precisely, not an intentional *object* for me, but the point from

which intentionality radiates, my point of view on the world. 'My living body is not constituted in the same way as external objects' (*Hus* XV, text No.37, p.648). Husserl's thinking is this. Given that, by definition, the living body is not an intentional object – when it is, it becomes 'the physical body' – it cannot be the case that the living body is synthesized *as* an intentional object. But given, on the other hand, that the living body is undoubtedly a complex unity, and so must be constituted synthetically, the problem that faces us is to explain the nature of this synthesis. This is a pressing problem, because the only model of synthetic activity we possess at this point is the mental synthesis of intentional objects: and the living body is not an intentional object but rather a *subject*, and it is not a mental phenomenon but, precisely, a *bodily* one.

This makes a great deal of sense, even when, perhaps especially when, we abstract from the rather artificial constraints imposed by Husserl's architectonic. The knowledge and understanding that I have of my own body, and likewise the control which I have over it, are of two categorially distinguishable sorts. On the one hand, a great deal of that knowledge is little different in kind from the knowledge I have of any arbitrary physical object with which I am acquainted: both of them have the same source, the same forms of justification, and the same formal properties. I know that my body has a certain colour, or weight, or smell in the way that I know that any other object of acquaintance has such properties. My knowledge is based on observation, and is justified if the observations were made responsibly and in appropriate conditions. The resulting knowledge is contingent, empirical, and conceptually articulated: on the basis of observation I judge that such-and-such is the case. Likewise, with a bit of ingenuity, I can move parts of my body around in just this way. I can reach out, grasp an object with my hand, pick it up, and put it down in another place; and this is as true of my own hand as it is of my ashtray. But there are other forms of bodily knowledge and control which stand in sharp contrast to these. I normally know where my hand is, say, or the direction in which my eyes are pointing without, as it were, first having to find out. I do not need first to *locate* my hand, to ascertain its position in objective space on the basis of observation, in order to go about moving it or using it to perform some task. And, most obviously of all, when I move my hand I typically do not move it *with* anything.

It makes sense, I am suggesting, to say that in normal circumstances I spontaneously *know* where my hand is, that its position is *given* to me – as long as we do not assimilate this sort of knowledge to the conceptually articulated, empirical knowledge mentioned before. When I move my hand normally, I do not first judge or acquire a belief that a certain state of affairs obtains, namely, that my hand occupies such-and-such a position in space. In the case of normal and spontaneous movement, I do not make a judgement at all; and my knowledge is not *based on* anything, neither experience, nor observation, nor inference, nor kinaesthetic sensation.[16] Of course, as Wittgenstein reminds us, 'A sensation *can* advise us of the movement or position of a limb. (For example, if you do not know, as a normal person does, whether your arm is stretched out, you might find out by a piercing pain in your elbow.)' But although such cases as this are possible, as too are those in which I learn of the position or movement of a limb by observation, they are the exceptions that prove the rule.

The upshot of these considerations is that it is not in terms of any appeal to mental activities of perception, conceptualization, synthesis, judgement, or inference, that we are to analyse the living body and its knowledge of itself. On the contrary, the analysis reveals the existence of a complex whole whose unity is of a new kind – it is ultimately an *organic* whole, and its unity is a function of *movement*, not thought. In a chapter entitled 'The Synthesis of One's Own Body', Merleau-Ponty reaches a conclusion that is entirely Husserlian:

> Thus the connecting link between the parts of our body, and that between our visual and tactile experience, are not forged gradually and cumulatively. I do not translate the 'data of touch into the language of seeing' or *vice versa* – I do not bring together one by one the parts of my body . . . . We do not merely behold as spectators the relations between the parts of our body, and the correlations between the visual and tactile body: we are ourselves the unifier of these arms and legs, the person who both sees and touches them. The body is, to use Leibniz's term, the 'effective law' of its changes.[17]

Moreover this organic or bodily whole possesses, and manifests in action, a species of knowledge: the knowledge which a living body has of itself, unmediated by intellectual understanding or even empirical observation. And this, I think, is what Husserl too means when he writes that 'the living body is constituted via kinaesthetic functions' (*Hus* XV, *Beilage* xviii, p.295), that it constitutes itself 'in *practice* in relation to itself' (*ibid*. p.300). In the *Crisis* Husserl repeats the familiar claim that all perception is aspectival, and that an 'exhibiting of' an object is necessarily one-sided. He then adds:

> We soon note that these systems of 'exhibiting of' are related back to correlative multiplicities of kinaesthetic processes having the peculiar character of 'I do', 'I move' (to which even 'I hold still' must be added). The kinaestheses are different from those movements of the living body which exhibit themselves merely as those of a physical body, yet are somehow one with them. (*Crisis* §47/p.161)

And elsewhere he amplifies this thought as follows:

All kinaestheses, each being an 'I move', 'I do', are bound together in a comprehensive unity . . . . Clearly the aspect-exhibitions of whatever physical object is appearing in perception, and the kinaestheses are not processes [simply running] alongside each other; rather, they work together in such a way that the aspects have the ontic meaning of, or the validity of, aspects of the object only through the fact that they are those aspects continually required by the kinaesthesis. (*Crisis* §28/p.106)

This passage, if I understand it correctly, implies that rationality is only possible given the powers of movement possessed by the living body. The validity of one's ontological commitments, the very possibility of objectivity, depend essentially upon one's physical motility. Now this is certainly a far cry from the Cartesian rationalism which characterized *Ideas*, and according to which the constitution or synthesis of objects is to be assigned to pure, transcendental consciousness. Husserl comes very close indeed to an explicit rejection of *that* model of rational consciousness in the following passage:

Sensibility, the ego's active functioning of the living body or the bodily organs, belongs in a fundamental, essential way to all experience of objects. It proceeds in consciousness, *not* as a mere series of object-appearances, as if these in themselves, through themselves alone and their coalescences, were appearances of objects; rather, they are such in consciousness *only* in combination with the kinaesthetically functioning living body, the ego functioning here in a peculiar sort of activity and habituality. (*ibid*, p.107)

Husserl's ground for making this claim about the essentially physical or bodily foundation of all intentional experience is, in part, that otherwise we cannot account for the stability and integrity of that experience. Take a trivial, concrete example: I open my eyes and am presented with a momentary visual field articulated in a certain way and containing various items. If I close my eyes, turn my head through 90 degrees, and open them again, I will be presented with an entirely different momentary visual field, one which, let us say, contains not a single item that was present in the first. The integration of these two utterly different visual fields, fields which *ex hypothesi* have no element in common, depends upon its being the case that I have turned my head. Their being brought into significant relation with each other, so that they come to comprise merely two 'views' of one and the same environment, depends upon its being the case that, without changing my location, I was initially facing in one direction, then in another. The synthesis of these two experiences, we might say, essentially goes *via* the body: they can only be integrated into a coherent whole, as two visual experiences of one and the same room, say, on the assumption that they are two perceptions *had by a body that changed its orientation without changing its location*. And here reference to the body occurs in *oratio recta*. It is not 'my body as I experience it' or 'my body as an intentional object' that is in question here, but my living body as it actually exists in and moves about the real world.

It might be thought that the integration of various discrete and dissimilar perceptions into an intrinsically connected experience of a single environment is a problem that has already been dealt with, under the heads of 'adumbrations' and the 'horizonal structure of intentionality'. In a sense this is true; but what Husserl came eventually to realize is that the system of cross-references intrinsic to a given perception, and in virtue of which it is internally related to other actual and possible perceptions, itself goes *via* the living body. Such an internally interrelated system of actual and possible perceptions Husserl calls a *perceptual field*, and he argues that the possibility of one's having a perceptual field at all depends upon the existence and the motility of one's own body:

the familiar, total system of kinaestheses . . . is perpetually bound to a [general] situation in which physical objects appear, i.e., that of the field of perception. To the variety of appearances through which an object is perceivable as this one-and-the-same object correspond, in their own way, the kinaestheses which belong to this object. As these kinaestheses are allowed to run their course, the corresponding required appearances must show up in order to be appearances of this object at all. (*Crisis* §28/p.107)

And this means, I take it, that the content of a given perceptual horizon includes such implicit components as 'what the object would look like from over there', 'what it would feel like if I were to reach out and touch it', 'what I would see if I were to turn it round', 'what it will look like tomorrow', and so forth. And if I *do* look at it from over there, touch it, turn it round, come back again the next day, and the like, then indeed 'the corresponding required experiences must show up in order to be appearances of this object at all'. If they do not show up, then we have a case of an exploding noema; and I have to conclude that I suffered an illusion, made a mistake, had an hallucination, or the like. Note, however, that in the description of this situation, essential reference is made to my living body, that is, to a real item in the world that is sentient, capable of spontaneous movement, and which comprises the only absolute point of orientation, my point of view on the world.

Subjectivity, intersubjectivity, and the world

Introduction

The considerations examined in the last section have taken us a long way from the philosophical vision which predominates in *Ideas* and Husserl's other middle-period works. The pure ego has been transformed into a physical, sentient organism, a human being; the cogito has been replaced by something capable of 'kinaesthesis'; the single perceptible object has made way for an integrated perceptual field, or environment; and the original phenomenological method has been broadened to become something Husserl at one point calls 'the phenomenological-*kinetic* method' (*Ideas* III; *Hus* V, p.1; my italics). But these changes did not emerge suddenly, and never emerged clearly in Husserl's thought. Moreover, they developed alongside other, older, more traditional doctrines with which they co-exist in uneasy tension. An example of this uneasy amalgam of the old and the new is provided by Husserl's approach to the issue of formulating a phenomenological analysis of the experience one conscious being has of another.

In one respect his treatment of this problem marks another decisive step in his move away from the earlier philosophical standpoint, dominated as it was by Descartes and Brentano. And in particular it marks Husserl's attempt to transcend the solipsistic bias inherent in that standpoint. And yet, in another respect, Husserl is never more totally committed to that earlier solipsistic perspective than when (for example in the fifth of the *Cartesian Meditations*) he explicitly addresses the problems concerning the subjectivity, the privacy, and the solipsism to which that perspective apparently restricts him. For, in effect, what Husserl there tries to organize is a solipsistic escape from solipsism.

According to Husserl himself, the most pressing problem he faces in this respect is this: 'When I, the meditating I, reduce myself to my absolute transcendental ego by phenomenological epoché, do I not become *solus ipse*; and do I not remain that, as long as I carry on a consistent self-explication under the name of phenomenology?' (*CM* §42/p.89). And if the answer is affirmative, then how can phenomenology reasonably hope to 'solve the transcendental problems pertaining to the objective world'? (*ibid.*). Now it is worth emphasizing that, as set up in this way, the problem is not a general or genuine philosophical problem at all. It is, quite simply, a difficulty for phenomenology, one of its own making, one *created* by the adoption of a certain restrictive phenomenological method. Husserl sees his task, in other words, as reconciling on the one hand his commitment to the method of the phenomenological reduction, with the egocentric perspective which this inevitably imposes, and on the other hand his commitment to the goal of

215

explaining the nature of 'the objective world' and our knowledge of it. As a result his contribution to our understanding of what *is* a genuine philosophical problem – the analysis of the nature of our experience of other conscious beings – is too often submerged and distorted by the defence which he mounts of the very method that creates his problem in the first place. Time and again his remarks have merely the force: 'This is what we must say if we are to protect phenomenology', and not: 'This is what we must say if we are to solve a real problem of philosophy'.

This criticism applies especially to the use he makes of a new methodological procedure that he introduces at this point and which he calls 'the abstractive epoché'. This epoché is examined in the following section, which is largely negative and aims merely to clear the ground so that Husserl's genuine philosophical insights can be discerned more clearly.

Another reduction

The materials which Husserl is prepared to allow himself in his escape from 'the solipsistic predicament' are severely restricted; and in order to set limits to them he introduces another reduction: 'the abstractive reduction' or 'the reduction of transcendental experience to the sphere of ownness' (*CM* §44/p.92).

> As regards method, a prime requirement for proceeding correctly here is that first of all we carry out, inside the universal transcendental sphere, a peculiar kind of epoché with respect to our theme. For the present we exclude from the thematic field everything now in question: we *disregard all constitutional effects of intentionality relating immediately or mediately to other subjectivity*, and delimit first of all the total nexus of that actual and potential intentionality in which the ego constitutes within himself a peculiar ownness. (*ibid.*)

As this passage indicates, Husserl's motive for insisting on the performance of another reduction is to prevent the subsequent analysis from being vitiated by the presence within it of question-begging assumptions and presuppositions. If one's aim is to show that other minds and other human beings are constituted entirely from within one's own transcendental subjectivity, then one must take care not to assume in advance that such things exist beyond or independently of that subjectivity. This seems right (though it leaves open the question of why one should have that aim in the first place). It is far from clear, however, that the abstractive epoché is an appropriate means to the securing of that result.

In his first published work of philosophy, 'On the Concept of Number' (1887), Husserl had subscribed to a naive theory of abstraction according to which 'to "abstract" from something merely means to pay no special attention to it' (*HSW* p.116). In subsequent works this theory was first modified, and later rejected in favour of a theory of synthesis. But in the abstractive reduction, it seems, the act of 'paying no special attention' to something is once again to be given an important philosophical role to perform. Now my conscious life, even the life of consciousness that remains after performance of the transcendental reduction, contains within it experiences that, as an intrinsic part of their sense, make tacit or explicit reference to other egos or subjects of consciousness: not only my experiences of other people and animals, of course, but also my experiences of artifacts (works of art, buildings, tools, machines, etc.), of cultural or social institutions (universities, political parties, voting procedures and the like), of a shared objective world (even an unpopulated landscape has the sense 'there for everyone'), and, indeed, of any physical object whatsoever. 'Within myself, within the limits of my transcendentally reduced pure conscious life, I *experience* the world (including others) – and, according to its experiential sense, *not* as (so to speak) my *private* synthetic function, but as other than mine alone, as an *intersubjective* world, actually there for everyone' (*CM* §43/p.91). The function of the abstractive reduction is, precisely, to 'abstract' from the intersubjective sense that normally characterizes elements present in transcendental subjectivity, thereby revealing (we are told) the existence of a prior, primordial, 'transcendental sphere of peculiar ownness'. This revelation is to be achieved as a result of my ignoring everything in transcendental subjectivity that is tainted by reference to what is 'alien', 'other', 'belonging to the surrounding world', 'not-mine', and so on.

Husserl's motive for introducing the abstractive reduction may be sound, but the procedure itself is vacuous at best, and at worst it is incoherent. As a practical device for ensuring that we do not surreptitiously import commitments which will make the subsequent analysis circular, it amounts to no more than the injunction: if you do not wish to beg the question, ignore everything that would beg the question. The entire machinery of 'reduction' to the primordial 'full concretion of ownness' has no more substance than that, and is therefore a sham.

Not only is the reduction useless as a practical procedure, it also brings with it theoretical commitments that are untenable; for it makes no sense to 'abstract from' the very factors that are *constitutive* of a given experience. One is not then left with a sphere of primordial experience, one is left with nothing. Let us suppose that there do exist circumstances in which I can, either spontaneously or intentionally, experience a certain thing 'in abstraction' from all the other things with which it in fact appears and is bound up. It may be, for example, that I am able to focus my attention on just one object in my environment, or on just one aspect of that object (its colour, say), in such a way that conscious awareness of all other objects and aspects ceases. With sufficient skill perhaps I can then describe that experience, the 'reduced' experience of something in abstraction from its normal surroundings and properties. This seems, at least, to be the situation that Husserl has in mind and which he uses as a model in terms of which to explain the abstractive reduction (cf. *CM* §44/pp.93–6). There are, however, two considerations which show this to be an inapplicable model.

In the first place, it makes no sense to claim that one can abstract from that which is constitutive of something, while still being left with a part or aspect of that thing. One cannot, for instance, abstract from an object's identity, but still claim that what is left is somehow connected to *that* object. Or again, one cannot think about the sense of the word 'red', in abstraction from everything to do with red's being a colour. That red is a colour is constitutive of what we mean by 'red' – and one cannot 'ignore' this, in the hope that one can then concentrate, as it were, on 'the sense of the word "red" in so far as it is independent of any connection with colour'. This makes no sense. And neither, for the same reason, does talk of 'my experience, independently of the sense which it has'. The abstractive reduction requires me to consider my experience, in abstraction from the sense that it in fact makes, that is, independently of the essentially *intersubjective* sense with which all my primitive perceptual experience is through and through permeated. But the sense it makes is constitutive of an experience: its identity, its existence, and its essence are functions of this sense. And so, when one abstracts from this sense, one is not left with something, like a colour-moment, on which one can concentrate to the exclusion of other factually present phenomena; one is simply left with nothing that makes sense.

The second objection can be stated simply. The fact that in a given case one *can* indeed make some object, or some part or moment of an object, the exclusive focus of one's attention, has no tendency whatsoever to show that what one focuses on is in any way independent of, or more fundamental than, the whole from which it is abstracted. On the contrary, when one becomes aware of an abstract moment via abstraction, the intentional object of one's attention is essentially *dependent*, being incapable of existence or presentation without the whole to which it belongs.[18] So even if the abstractive epoché were possible, this would in no way show, as Husserl claims, that performance of it reveals 'an essentially founding stratum' of experience that can exist independently of, but is yet the necessary condition for, all other types of experience whatsoever (*CM* §44/p.96).

The constitution of intersubjectivity

But regardless of what we make of the abstractive epoché – and henceforth I shall ignore it – there remain two problems concerning one's experience of other people with which we must now deal. One is a local, but none the less a substantial problem, and concerns the adequacy of the analysis of intentionality as we have it at this point. The other is a fundamental philosophical problem in its own right, concerning the relation between my awareness of another's body and behaviour and my awareness of his or her psychological states.

Let us assume that we are already in possession of an acceptable Husserlian theory of intentionality which explains how it is possible for a mental act to be directed towards an object that is not itself mental and is not a proper part or immanent content of that act. The theory is egocentric in that its primitive terms refer only to one's sensory data, synthetic activity, dispositions, and perhaps also to the motility of one's own living body. And it provides an analysis and justification of the claim that in straightforward sense perception I have an experience of a physical object which is directly presented to me – even though it is only ever presented partially or aspectivally. But however persuasive that analysis might be, and however strong that justification, there nevertheless remains a large and crucially important class of experiences to which the theory necessarily fails to apply. The members of that class are those experiences of mine which are not of a *physical* object, and are not of an object that is ever *directly presented* to me, either perspectivally or in any other way. They are, that is, intentional experiences directed towards a mind, or ego, or consciousness other than my own; and these experiences possess structural properties which the theory of intentionality as it has been developed up to this point lacks the resources to explain.

In straightforward perception of an inanimate object like a tree, the object is presented 'originally' and 'in person'; what I experience is not an image, a sign, or a representation of the tree, neither is it something from which I deduce or infer the existence and nature of the tree. My intentional object is *a tree*. I do not perceive it in its entirety, of course, but only one-sidedly. Even so, my experience is such that the adumbrations that *are* present act as the bearers of a sense which refers to other possible adumbrations and perspectives which could be, but are not at the moment, given to me originally. My experience of other people is not, however, analysable in these terms, as Husserl makes very clear:

> Experience is original consciousness; and in fact we generally say, in the case of experiencing a man: the other is himself there before us 'in person'. On the other hand, this being there in person does not keep us from admitting forthwith that, *properly speaking*, neither the other ego himself, nor his subjective processes, nor his [experiences] themselves . . . becomes given in our experience originally. (*CM* §50/p.109)

Husserl intends his point to belong to common sense: the psychological and subjective states of another person are not *directly* accessible to me. I never perceive or experience another's consciousness in the way that I can, say, directly experience or perceive a tree.

219

Husserl's response to this state of affairs is sophisticated. He does not, for example, even for a moment yield to the temptation to think that because another's mind is not directly accessible to me, it is therefore not accessible to me at all, or is something whose knowability or existence is in any way dubious. He does not, moreover, see *his* task as either the refutation of scepticism about the existence or the knowability of other minds, or the justification of the knowledge claims we normally make about them. His goal is, rather, to understand the nature of the experience one person manifestly *can* have of another. And Husserl is undoubtedly right that essential to such experience is my awareness not only that other people are conscious, but also that their consciousness is not directly accessible to me. This latter fact is not, however, cause for regret; for it constitutes neither a theoretical problem, nor a practical obstacle in the way of intersubjective understanding. On the contrary, as Husserl deftly points out, that fact is nothing more than a necessary condition of there being *other* conscious beings at all. For if it were not the case that another's subjective states were in some sense inaccessible to me, that is,

> if what belongs to the other's own essence were *directly* accessible, it would merely be a moment of my own essence, and ultimately he himself and I myself would be the same person. (*CM* §50/p.109)

In other words, the fact that your conscious states and processes are not given 'originally' to me is not an impediment to my coming to know and understand you as another person; it is simply what makes you *another* person in the first place. If 'your mind' were directly given to me as my experience, if I were to have your thoughts, sensations, feelings and the like, then there wouldn't *be* two minds, but only one: mine.

These considerations provide a strong and sophisticated framework within which to address the problems that concern us; but those problems still need to be addressed. In particular, we have to ask, what analysis are we to provide of intentionality in those cases where the intentional object is something of which I can, in principle, have no direct experience?

The key to solving this problem lies in acknowledging that under normal circumstances I do not have to come to terms with another 'ego' or another 'consciousness', as such, but with another person. Wittgenstein writes:

> 'I noticed he was out of humour.' Is this a report about his behaviour or about his state of mind? ('The sky looks threatening': is this about the present or the future?) Both: not side-by-side, however, but about one *via* the other.[19]

The other person's state of mind is not, and cannot be presented to me as an item of immediate awareness – otherwise it would be my state of mind: the identity conditions of an arbitrary conscious mental state, *S*, are such that if a person, *x*, is immediately and directly aware of *S*, then *x* is the owner or bearer of *S*. By contrast, however, what can be, and is, directly presented to me is the other person's body and behaviour. The question is now: How must the physical behaviour and the mental states of another person be internally related one to another, if it is to be possible for me to experience and understand the one *via* the other? Husserl introduces a technical term in order to refer to precisely this relation: he calls it '*appresentation*'.

> There must be *a certain mediacy of intentionality* here, . . . making present to consciousness something that is 'there too', but which nevertheless is not itself there and can never become an 'itself-there'. We have here, accordingly, a kind of making co-present, [not a direct presentation but] a kind of 'appresentation'. (*CM* §50/p.109)

I can have a direct presentation of another person's body and behaviour, and this is 'the perception proper that functions as the underlying basis' for an appresentation of that person's states of mind. I perceive those states of mind – not directly, however, but 'along with' or 'through' my perceptions of the body.

What is interesting here is Husserl's insistence that appresentation is an essentially perceptual matter: 'Quite rightly we speak of *perceiving* someone else'; for 'what I actually see is not a sign and not a mere analogue; . . . on the contrary, it is someone else' (*CM* §55/p.124). As a consequence Husserl is adamant in his rejection of any theory according to which the relation between perceived behaviour and recognized mental state is one of inference, whether deductive, inductive, or merely analogical. (Cf. *Crisis* §67/p.231.) It involves, he says, 'no inference from analogy' and is, indeed, not an inference of any sort; for it is 'not an act of thinking' (*CM* §50/p.111). I *see* another person, I see that they are conscious, that they are in pain, and so forth. These are typically not hypotheses that I form, or conclusions at which I arrive on the basis of a consideration of the evidence – a point which Wittgenstein also makes: 'My attitude towards him', he writes, 'is an attitude towards a soul. I am not of the *opinion* that he has a soul'.[20]

If this is right, then a correct phenomenological description of one's experience of another conscious being will involve the claim that 'the other's living body and his governing ego are given in the manner that characterizes a *unitary transcending experience*' (*CM* §51/p.114). The intentional object of this unitary experience is a psychophysical entity, a living body, or a human being. To this single entity both physical and mental predicates can be assigned, the latter in and through the former.

Moreover, as a transcendent object another person is necessarily perceived aspectivally, as possessing horizons of possible but non-actual
adumbrations that may be revealed in the course of future experience. All
knowledge and understanding that we have of another person is therefore
intrinsically provisional and defeasible:

> The experienced living body of another continues to prove itself as an
> actual living body, solely in its changing but incessantly harmonious
> 'behaviour'. Such harmonious behaviour (as having a physical side that
> indicates something psychic appresentatively) must present itself fulfil-
> lingly in original experience. (*CM* §52/p.114)

So far we have been examining the appropriate form in which our
experience of other conscious beings should be described. There remains,
however, the rather different question of how that experience should be
analysed and explained. What, for instance, are the mechanisms which
explain how experience, described in this way, comes about? If my
perception of another person is a 'presentation-appresentation', then what
is the intentional structure, and what are the synthetic or other activities,
in virtue of which a straightforward presentation comes to possess an
indirect or appresentational sense?

It may well be a fact that I can see another person, see that they are
happy or in pain: 'If we stick to our *de facto* experience of someone else as
it comes to pass at any time, we find that actually *the sensuously seen body*
is experienced, forthwith, as *the body of someone else*, and not merely as
an indication of someone else'. But, Husserl immediately asks, 'is this fact
not an enigma?' (*CM* §55/p.121). Another person is an intentional object
for me, and as such must possess a unity that is the product of synthetic
activity – Husserl never relinquishes this claim. He is committed, therefore, to the conclusion that 'only a precise explication of the intentionality actually observable in [my] experience of someone else, and a
discovery of the motivations essentially implicit in that intentionality, can
unlock the enigma' (*ibid.*). In unlocking this enigma Husserl develops his
theories of 'empathy' and 'analogical apperception', according to which
the possibility of my perceiving another's physical body *as* the living
body of a conscious being is a function of my ability to transfer or project
onto it an understanding that I originally acquire only from my own case.

Now my own living body is the sole absolute point of reference, the
unique 'geometrical centre', of egocentric or orientated space. And the
most basic phase in the complex process of constituting another person as
an intentional object is, so to speak, the decentralization of this space.

My own body constitutes, in Husserl's terms, an absolute 'Here', in
relation to which all other physical objects are situated 'There'. But in
virtue of the living body's motility it is in principle possible for me to
reverse these egocentrically identified locations, making what was

'There', 'Here', and *vice versa*. 'By free modification of my kinaestheses, particularly those of locomotion, I can change my position in such a manner that I convert any There into a Here' (*CM* §53/p.116). This is, moreover, not merely a contingent fact concerning the motility of my body, it is something which intrinsically and essentially characterizes the very sense of my perceptual experience: my perception of an arbitrary physical object involves a horizonal structure in which there is implicit reference to 'what the object would look like from over there, from the rear, from nearer to it', and so forth. And one element in this horizonal structure is the possibility of spatial reversal, with its corresponding perceptual reversal, whereby what was Here becomes There, and *vice versa*. 'This implies that, perceiving from There, I shold see the same physical things, only in correspondingly different modes of appearance' (*ibid.*). Now the physical body of another person is presented to me, in egocentric space, as 'There'. But intrinsic to the sense of such a presentation, as part of its horizons, is, crudely speaking, 'what things would look like *from* over there, looking back in this direction'. But one of the things that one would see from over there, looking back here, is of course *me*. This is the crucial move in the decentralization of egocentric space. I am now envisaging a situation in which my own body is no longer the central '*Here*' around which the whole of phenomenal space is orientated, but rather one in which my own body has become just another object, occupying a location which is '*There*' from a different point of view. To put it metaphorically, space no longer radiates out from a single centre, which is my living body; now space *has* no single centre, and my living body is something that can be Here from one point of view, but equally There from another.[21]

What I have called the decentralization of egocentric space is one crucial phase required in the appresentation of another conscious being. Another such phase is what Husserl calls the living body's reflexive relation to itself:

> Touching kinaesthetically, I perceive with my hands, I also perceive with my eyes, and so forth . . . . As perceptively active I experience (or can experience) all of nature, *including my own living body*, which is thus reflexively related to itself. That becomes possible because I can perceive one hand 'by means of' the other, an eye by means of a hand, and so forth – a procedure in which the functioning organ must become an object, and the object a functioning organ. (*CM* §44/p.97)

This possibility allows Husserl to claim that not only do I know what it *is like* to pick up an object, say, or scratch an itch, yawn with boredom, or smile with amusement, I also know what it *looks like* for me to do these things. Not only is my living body capable of action, it is also capable of perceiving the actions which it itself performs. This is important, for this reflexive perceptual awareness provides an essential ingredient in the sense that I transfer, in the appresentation of another conscious being, from my own living body to the physical body of the other. We need now to bring together the two aspects we have so far identified – the de-centralization of space, and the living body's reflexive awareness of itself. If, in my own case, a certain type of perception becomes associated with a certain type of physical movement, and if, again in my own case, movements of that type have a certain *sense*, then that association should continue to hold whenever I perceive movements of that type – even when it is not *my* body that is performing them. That is to say, because of the decentralization of space and the possibility which that brings with it of my awareness of 'myself as I would look from over there', or of 'myself as I appear to be, not just to myself, but quite generally', the associative mechanism which links together (i) the appearance of a physical movement and (ii) the sense or meaning of that movement, can itself find application quite generally, and not merely in my own case. So when I directly perceive another physical body yawning, smiling, scratching itself and so forth, that perception itself is imbued, via association, with an intrinsic sense that encompasses not just physical movement but also its expressive significance, in connection with 'boredom', 'amusement', 'itching', and the like. I spontaneously see another's behaviour as expressive; and what enables me to do this is, first, the fact that my own body is expressive, and, second, the fact that I can have an imaginative awareness of my own body and its appearance *in general* and not merely from my own, restricted, egocentric point of view. The association between a particular kind of expressive meaning and a particular kind of physical or behavioural appearance is one that is capable of having the physical and behavioural appearances of others as its instances. This is, I think, what Husserl has in mind when he writes:

> The natural body . . . appresents the other ego by virtue of a pairing association with my living body. (*CM* §55/p.123)
>
> In this appresentation . . . the body in the mode *There*, which presents itself in *my* monadic sphere, is apperceived as another's living body . . . . That body indicates 'the same' body in the mode *Here* as the body experienced by the other ego in *his* monadic sphere. Moreover it indicates the 'same' body concretely, with all the constitutive intentionality pertaining to this mode of givenness in the other's experience. (*CM* §53/p.117)
>
> Thus the assimilative apperception becomes possible and established, by which the external body over there receives analogically from mine the sense *living body*. (*CM* §54/p.118)

One of the most remarkable and ingenious aspects of this analysis is the role it assigns to the 'objectification of oneself', as a necessary condition of the discernment of subjectivity in others. As long as I remain in an exclusively egocentric perspective, genuine reciprocity is impossible: there can only be one space, one ego, one living body, and one intentional world: *mine*. It is only in so far as I can remove myself, in imagination from the geometrical centre of that perspective that there is created so much as the possibility of another ego, say, or of an objective space which contains me and other things on an equal footing. And I accomplish this abdication through imaginative projection in which I imagine, for example, what I would perceive if I were not Here, but over There, looking in this direction instead. Imaginative projection is important in that it brings an awareness that I am potentially just one more perceptible object, existing in a space which does not have me at the centre. Imaginative projection is also important, however, in the process of 'empathy'; for 'what I would see from there, looking over here' is precisely what I attribute to the person who *is* over there, looking at me.

In this way genuine reciprocity becomes intelligible: as I look at you I perceive a body, and apperceive a person who is looking at me – and the content that I ascribe to your perception is structurally the same as that which characterizes my own. You are perceiving a body, and apperceiving a person who is looking at you . . . and so on. Neither experience has priority over the other, neither person can be construed as The Centre, in such a way as to reduce the other to a mere item within an egocentric perspective. On the contrary, the experience of both is permeated through and through by horizons in which *the other's experience* is an inerradicable element. And this is what Husserl means by 'intersubjectivity'. It is not merely the weak, we might say arithmetical, notion of a plurality of egos; it is the richer, Leibnizian notion of a harmonious community of conscious beings, the members of which stand in reciprocal relations whereby the internal states of any one can be mirrored and registered by those of any other. The earlier talk of 'monads' turns into a genuine monadology:

> What remains, now, is not a multiplicity of separated souls, each reduced to its pure interiority, but rather: just as there is a sole universal nature as a self-enclosed framework of unity, so there is a sole psychic framework, a total framework of all souls, which are united, not externally, but through the intentional interpenetration which is the communalization of their lives . . . . This means that within the vitally flowing intentionality in which the life of an ego-subject consists, every other ego is already intentionally implied in advance by way of empathy and the empathy-horizon. (*Crisis* §71/ p.255; cf. *CM* §60/p.139f)

This is a remarkable vision. Every individual consciousness, *from out of its own resources*, as it were, is intrinsically and essentially determined by its relations to other such centres of consciousness. Even at the most rudimentary level of intentional experience, at the level, say, of a straightforward sensory perception of an inanimate object, my experience possesses a sense that is partly comprised by horizons in which reference is made to possible perceptions of *others*. And not the least remarkable aspect of this vision is the attempt it makes to reconcile, on the one hand, what is compelling in the Cartesian appeal to subjectivity and egocentricity with, on the other hand, the urgent need to escape the solipsistic consequences of that appeal. In his last works Husserl increasingly came to see intersubjectivity, not as a problem confronting the solitary, solipsistic ego, but rather as a dimension or structure that characterizes our intentional life at its very core.

The *Lebenswelt*

Husserl is right to maintain (e.g. *CM* 55/p.123) that as a consequence of his analysis of intersubjectivity, there remains no phenomenological problem about the existence of a shared, communal *world*: the analysis of the one is at the same time an analysis of the other. This is not because we can, after the event, as it were, bring in the world and identify it with what a community of monads have in common – though they do indeed have this in common. It is rather that the notion of a shared environment has from the beginning played a crucial role in the analysis of intersubjectivity; and that analysis can itself now be transformed into an account of objectivity, rationality, and 'external existence'. The two are strictly 'correlative.'

In order to see this we need to reflect that, typically, my ascription of even the most rudimentary intentional states to another being presupposes that I share with it a common environment. To say of some being that it is trying to avoid an obstacle, say, that it is moving towards food, or that it can see a light source makes sense only if the obstacle, the food, and the light source are themselves taken to be intentional objects of which there is an awareness by more than one consciousness. It is, according to Husserl, part of the very sense of my perception of another's living body that that body inhabits the same environment as me. This is the case, not merely in the weak sense that the other body is *in* the same environment as me, but in the stronger sense that it is *aware of* the same things as me:

> The following should be noted in this connection. It is implicit in the sense of my successful apperception of others that their world, the world belonging to their appearance-systems, must be experienced *forthwith* as the same as the world belonging to my appearance-systems; and this involves an identity of our appearance-systems. (*CM* §55/p.125)

And conversely, in those cases where there exist intentional objects that are present to one being but not to others, we do not talk about physical objects or the real world at all, but about dreams, after-images, hallucinations, visions, fantasies, delusions, and the like. Husserl takes this to imply that 'the objective world has existence by virtue of a harmonious confirmation of the apperceptive constitution . . . a confirmation thereof by the continuance of experiencing life with a consistent harmoniousness' (*ibid.*). The *Lebenswelt* or 'life-world' is the noematic correlate of this harmonious, intentional, intersubjective experience. That world, however, is the world *we inhabit*; and as such it is a complex whole that possesses physical, mythical, social, political, aesthetic, mathematical, sexual, historical, and ethical properties and dimensions. If it is to avoid distortion and over-simplification, a phenomenological description of this life-world must, therefore, capture all of these aspects, along with the complex relations in which they stand to one another.

On pp. 198–203 we examined the theory of objectivity and rationality that Husserl provides in *Ideas*. We found that theory to be solipsistic in form: it is couched exclusively in terms of the sensory data, the synthetic activities, the horizons, and the harmony which together characterize the continuing experience of a single ego. Virtually all of these explanatory structures are retained in Husserl's last works, but they are there transposed into the plural. The world is no longer *my* world: 'the world is our world' (*Crisis* §28/p.108). The solitary transcendental ego is replaced by 'the transcendental *we*', capable of 'we-synthesis' (*Crisis* §50/p.172); and 'fully developed phenomenology' moves from 'transcendental solipsism to transcendental intersubjectivity' (*PV* p.12/p.12). In spite of this transposition from the singular to the plural, however, many elements in Husserl's last works mirror faithfully those to be found, for instance, in *Ideas*. Objectivity and rationality are still explained as properties of experience which it possesses defeasibly in virtue of its internal structure, its ontological commitments, its habitualities, and the harmony and coherence of its horizons as they are fulfilled by the subsequent course of experience. The signal difference is that it is now *our* experience, the shared experience of a community of conscious beings, to which appeal is made. But this intersubjective experience, in so far as it is objective and rational, still has its functional structure, its ontological commitments, horizons, habitualities, fulfilments, and the like.

This way of viewing the development that Husserl's philosophy underwent in its last phase is, however, potentially misleading; for it masks the revolutionary and fundamental nature of the modifications, both methodological and doctrinal, which that development brought in its wake. The last phase of Husserl's philosophy is marked by much more than a substitution of the transcendental 'we' for the transcendental 'I'.

Although Husserl at no point subscribed to an extreme form of atomism, his early works nevertheless manifest a number of recognizably atomistic tendencies. One is his willingness to countenance isolated, disembodied, self-contained centres of consciousness. Another is the methodological approach adopted in the *Logical Investigations* and *Ideas*, which can be roughly characterized in terms of its conformity to the maxim: Begin by isolating what is most simple and, therefore, most fundamental, and proceed to explain what is complex and inessential on that basis. Thus, for example, we learn first about hyletic data, as the most primitive elements given to consciousness, then about simple syntheses of identification which combine such data into complex wholes; and only eventually (if at all) do we work up to a full description of intentional life in its rich variety, which includes aesthetic experiences, value judgements, emotions, and the experiences of other people. Perhaps the most radical change Husserl's thought finally undergoes is the rejection, in its entirety, of this approach. In its place he adopts – as did Wittgenstein at almost exactly the same time – a profoundly holistic point of view. What is *given*, the datum with which one must needs begin, is not any atom of experience, or anything either ontologically or epistemically simple. And in particular 'one must not go straight back to the supposedly immediately given "sense data", as if *they* were immediately characteristic of the purely intuitive data of the life-world' (*Crisis* §34(a)/p.125). Rather, it is the *Lebenswelt* as a whole that is the sole datum with which phenomenological analysis must begin.[22]

> We, in living together, have a world pre-given . . . as existing for us and to which we together belong, the world as world for all, pre-given with this ontic meaning. (*Crisis* §28/p.109)
>
> Each thing that we experience, that we have to do with in any way whatever – and this includes ourselves when we reflect upon ourselves – gives itself, whether we notice it or not, *as* a thing in the world. (*Crisis* §71/p.251)
>
> Straightforward experience, in which *the life-world is given*, is the ultimate foundation of all objective knowledge. (*Crisis* §66/p.226)

According to this vision, the *Lebenswelt* comprises the sole absolute foundation of all our moral, scientific, philosophical, and everyday practices. And here, as always for Husserl, the notion of an *absolute foundation* is that of an ontologically autonomous whole whose parts and moments not only depend for their existence on their participation in that whole, but, moreover, are knowable only to the extent that we have the capacity, via a process of abstraction, to distinguish them as partial aspects within that whole. Individual physical objects, persons, properties, facts, values, numbers, hyletic data, and so forth, are merely dependent moments abstracted from the prior *Lebenswelt* in its entirety. It follows, therefore, that the physical universe – the inanimate, material world studied by the physical sciences – is merely one partial and dependent aspect of the life-world; an aspect that is revealed as a consequence of our having abstracted from all the social, psychological, aesthetic, moral, and cultural aspects with which that life-world is also permeated. 'Science is a human spiritual accomplishment which presupposes as its point of departure . . . the intuitive surrounding world of life, pregiven as existing for all in common' (*Crisis* §33/p.121).

In placing the intersubjective community of conscious beings at the very centre of his philosophical concerns, and in then applying to that community concepts such as 'horizon', 'habituality', and 'praxis' which he had earlier applied to the isolated ego, Husserl came to recognize the constitutive role played by such factors as culture, tradition, common practise and, especially, history in determining the everyday life of that community, and hence in directly determining its life-world. The life-world shared by the members of a given society, the environment which they take themselves to be inhabiting, is essentially a reflection of the culture they have in common. But this culture or civilization is manifest primarily in the *dispositions* of the individuals and institutions that belong within it, and is, moreover, a phenomenon whose determinants are largely *historical*.

We examined earlier the account which Husserl provides in *Ideas* and elsewhere of the 'habitualities' in terms of which the unity of the isolated ego is explained and upon which the possibility of the ego's 'self-constitution' depends. As Husserl's focus of attention shifts, in the late works, from the individual ego to the intersubjective unity of the community, the notion of a habituality itself undergoes reinterpretation and redeployment in a communal, intersubjective context. In the *Crisis*, for example, an important explanatory purpose is served by the notion of *Selbstverständlichkeiten* – the things that the members of a given community are disposed to take, usually unthinkingly, as entirely natural, obvious, and unproblematic. The identity and the integrity of a society or culture, according to Husserl, are functions of the possession by its members of a body of beliefs and practices 'taken for granted' and 'made use of as unquestioned and available' (*Crisis* §29/p.112). And when we become aware of the existence of such a body of inherited commitments:

> there opens up to us, to our growing astonishment, an infinity of ever new phenomena belonging to a new dimension, coming to light only through consistent penetration into the meaning- and validity-implications of what was thus taken for granted. (*ibid.*)

On this point Husserl's thought is very close to Wittgenstein's. In *On Certainty*, for example, Wittgenstein argues that one's convictions depend upon, and make sense only within, a largely tacit picture of the world that one inherits unavoidably as a member of a given community.

'But I did not get my picture of the world by satisfying myself of its correctness,' he writes, 'nor do I have it because I am satisfied of its correctness. No: it is the inherited background against which I distinguish between true and false'.[23] Moreover, both Husserl and Wittgenstein stress the importance of practical action and training, rather than of theoretical thought, in the process of assimilating the *Selbstverständlichkeiten* that define a given culture. According to Wittgenstein: 'Sure evidence is what we *accept* as sure, it is evidence we go by in *acting* surely, acting without any doubt.'[24] And Husserl concludes similarly that 'that which is *taken for granted* and which is presupposed by all thinking' is 'everyday praxis'. This praxis, and the life-world it determines, 'constantly functions as a subsoil':

> The world is pregiven to us, the waking, always somehow practically interested subjects, not occasionally but always and necessarily as the universal field of all actual and possible praxis, as a horizon. To live is always to live-in-certainty-of-the-world. (*Crisis* §37/p.142).

And the world in which we live, the world as it is for us, 'becomes understandable as a structure of meaning formed out of elementary intentionalities' (*Crisis* §49/p.168). The most elementary of these intentionalities, Husserl suggests, are those involved in the activities of the living body, in so far as these activities are shaped and given significance only within the context of an inherited, intersubjective system of practices and values. The task of phenomenology, as Husserl now sees it, is 'to go back to the intentional *origins* . . . of the formation of meaning' (*ibid.*; my italics) – a task which, he thinks, requires a phenomenological investigation of the factors that have, over the ages, determined our culture and, hence, our life-world.

In his attempt to understand the intersubjective constitution of the life-world, and the role played in it by inherited tradition and received practice, Husserl perhaps inevitably came to emphasize the importance of historical considerations and historical methods of enquiry. 'A historical, backward reflection', he writes, 'is actually the deepest kind of self-reflection aimed at self-understanding in terms of what we are truly seeking as the historical beings we are' (*Crisis* §15/p.72). 'We have become what we are thoroughly and exclusively in a historical–spiritual manner', and accordingly we can only understand ourselves and our life-world 'through a critical understanding of the total unity of history – *our* history' (*ibid.*). The inevitability of a historicism of this sort is not, however, purely philosophical; for one can, like Wittgenstein, adopt a holistic point of view in which a constitutive function is assigned to such factors as culture, tradition, convention, and community, without therewith accepting that a philosophical understanding of that function must needs be couched in historical or genetic terms. In Husserl's case the impetus towards a radical historicism is in large part psychological. Every phase in the development of his thought, from the *Philosophy of Arithmetic* onwards, is marked by a strong tendency towards a genetic style of explanation and analysis. Time and again Husserl's first impulse is to examine 'the origin and nature' of whatever puzzling phenomena he might be concerned with. And throughout his life he proceeded on the assumption that an investigation of the origin of a phenomenon would be sufficient, or anyway necessary, for an understanding of its nature. The historicism that emerges in the late works results from the application of this prejudice in favour of genetic modes of thought to the problem of accounting for the essentially intersubjective and communal sense that our experience possesses. To understand the nature of the constraints that our communal inheritance imposes on us, he seems to feel, requires that we examine the origin and the development of those constraints – that we turn, in other words, to history.

In Husserl's last works, and especially in the *Crisis*, (intersubjective) history comes to perform the same role with respect to transcendental philosophy that (individual) psychology had performed in his earlier works. And in both cases the underlying problem is the same: How can contingent facts – whether they concern the subjective life of an isolated ego, or the history of an entire civilization – act as the foundation of a transcendental philosophy whose results are supposed to be essential, *a priori* insights into the very nature of things? Husserl, unfortunately, offers us no solution to this problem; for, as Derrida rightly observes: 'Though it is constantly *practiced* in the *Crisis* . . . this new access to history is never *made a problem* there'.[25]

But even if one does not subscribe to a historicism quite as extreme as Husserl's, it is nevertheless the case that with the emergence of factors like culture, tradition, and convention as determining the life-world of a given community, one's phenomenological descriptions and analyses will possess a validity that is restricted, precisely, to a given community:

> in the social group united with us in the community of life, we arrive at 'secure' facts . . . . But when we are thrown into an alien social sphere, that of the Negroes of the Congo, Chinese peasants, etc., we discover that their truths, the facts that for them are fixed, generally verified or verifiable, are by no means the same as ours. (*Crisis* §36/p.139; cf. *CM* §57/p.133)

Finally, therefore, with the growing realization that phenomenology had not only become inescapably holistic, but had also transformed itself into a discipline whose results could never be more than historically and culturally parochial, Husserl abandoned the conception of phenomenology that had informed his thought for nearly thirty years. The ideal of philosophy as the only 'absolutely rigorous science', aiming at an 'absolutely faithful description' of the essence of 'things themselves' came, rightly, to seem incompatible with a view according to which the sole datum is an entire life-world, and according to which, moreover, philosophical understanding will require an understanding of the historical forces shaping a whole civilization. The earlier demands for universality, apodicticity, and exactness, along with the various philosophical methods designed to secure them, are rendered irrelevant by a vision of reality that is holistic, culture-relative, and indeterminate. Three years before his death Husserl wrote:

> Philosophy as science, as serious, rigorous, indeed apodictically rigorous science – *the dream is over*.[26]

Husserl's dream of philosophy as a rigorous science was always insubstantial and naive. The tragedy is that he did not live to develop further the insights that are adumbrated in his last works – insights that emerged out of, and owe their existence to, the gradual but ultimately total disintegration of that very dream.

Notes

Prolegomenon: Brentano's Legacy

1 On the other hand, for what little evidence there is, see, e.g., manuscripts Q7, 8, and 9 in the Husserl Archives, Louvain; especially *Aus der Metaphysik von Franz Brentano* of 1882.

2 From a sketch by Frau Malvine Husserl, quoted in Schuhmann, K. (1977) *Husserl-Chronik. Denk- und Lebensweg Edmund Husserls*, The Hague: Nijhoff, p. 11. See also *Hus XXI*, p. lxix.

3 For further details of Husserl's relationship with Brentano see Husserl's 'Recollections of Franz Brentano', translated by R. Hudson and P. McCormick, in *HSW*, pp. 342–8.

4 See, e.g., Peters, R.S. (ed.) (1953) *Brett's History of Psychology*, London: Allen & Unwin, pp. 554ff.

5 Wundt, W. (1874) *Die Grundzüge der physiologischen Psychologie*, Leipzig: W. Engelmann; translated by E.B. Titchener (from the 5th edition, 1902), and published as *The Principles of Physiological Psychology*, London: Swan Sonnenschein, 1904.

6 Boring, E.G. (1957) *A History of Experimental Psychology*, New York: Appleton-Century-Crofts, (2nd edition), p. 316; cf. Klein, B.B. (1970) *A History of Scientific Psychology*, London: Routledge & Kegan Paul, pp. 824ff.

7 Wundt, W. (1874) (Titchener translation), p. 5.

8 Brentano, F. (1874) *Psychologie vom empirischen Standpunkt*, Leipzig: Duncker und Humblot; *Psychology from an Empirical Standpoint*, ed. L.L. McAlister, translated by A.C. Rancurello *et al.*, London: Routledge & Kegan Paul, 1973. For the rest of this chapter, unqualified page numbers in the text refer to the English edition of this work.

9 Stumpf, C. (1976) 'Reminiscences of Franz Brentano', translated by L.L. McAlister and M. Schättle, in L.L. McAlister (ed.) *The Philosophy of Brentano*, London: Duckworth, p. 16.

10 *ibid.*

11 See, e.g., Spiegelberg, H. (1982) *The Phenomenological Movement* (3rd edition), The Hague: Nijhoff, pp. 26–7; Chisholm, R.M. (1976) 'Brentano's Descriptive Psychology' in L.L. McAlister (ed.), *op. cit.* pp. 91–3; and

Chisholm, R.M. (1967) 'Brentano on Descriptive Psychology and the Intentional' in E.N. Lee and M. Mandelbaum (eds), *Phenomenology and Existentialism*, Baltimore: Johns Hopkins, pp. 1–6.

12 The use here of the term 'phenomenology' in connection with Brentano's philosophy should be understood, for the moment, as leaving entirely open the question whether Brentano and Husserl had any conception of phenomenology in common, and if so, what.

13 Brentano, F. (1969) *The Origin of Our Knowledge of Right and Wrong*, p. xv; quoted by O. Kraus in his 'Introduction' to *Psychology from an Empirical Standpoint*, 1924 edition; see *PES* p. 370.

14 I should perhaps reiterate at this point that I am concerned with Brentano's philosophy only to the extent that it helps shed light on Husserl's texts. As the influence which he had on Husserl does not seem to change significantly after about 1890, I shall simply ignore the many developments which Brentano's thought underwent after this date.

15 Kant, I. (1933) *Critique of Pure Reason*, translated by N. Kemp Smith, London: Macmillan, p. 148 (*A*. 127).

16 Unfortunately, the use which Brentano and, following him, Husserl make of the expression 'mental act' means that any psychological verb in the gerund form ('seeing', 'dreaming', 'hearing', 'thinking', 'wanting', 'imagining', etc.) will stand for such an act. This is unfortunate because of course hearing, dreaming, and wanting, for instance, are not *acts* at all: they are not things we perform. This usage can be accepted, however, (with some linguistic discomfort) because in the hands of Brentano and Husserl it is not in fact philosophically pernicious. The expression 'mental act' should, then, be construed widely, to encompass also those mental activities and states which are not properly speaking acts at all. As Husserl says: 'In talking of "acts" . . . we must steer clear of the word's original meaning: *all thought of activity must be rigidly excluded*' (*LU* V, §13/p. 563).

17 Brentano, it seems, came to recognize this more fully after the publication of *PES*. In his lectures more than a decade later, for example, he stressed that 'to be a phenomenon something must be in one. All phenomena should be called "inner"'. See Brentano, F. (1982) *Deskriptive Psychologie*, R.M. Chisholm and W. Baumgartner (eds), Hamburg: Meiner, p. 129.

18 One possible source of misunderstanding should perhaps be mentioned here. It concerns the term 'in-existence', which does not mean 'non-existence' – it derives, rather, from the notion of one thing's existing *in* another. In other words, in-existence is a form of existence (the form of existence enjoyed by the immanent content of a mental act) and is by no means a form of actual or possible non-existence. (The possibility of confusion comes about as follows: it was not until well after the publication of *Psychology from an Empirical Standpoint* that Brentano introduced an entirely new doctrine of intentionality, a part of which consisted in provision of a criterion of intentionality according to which a relation is intentional if that relation can hold even though one of its terms does not exist (see Appendix to *PES*, pp. 271–307, written in 1911). Thus, for example, one can think of, imagine, want, or expect a unicorn. The possibility, in terms of the later theory, of the *non-existence* of a term in an intentional relation is easily confused with what

234

the earlier doctrine calls the *in-existence* of a mental content.) See also McAlister L.L. (1976) 'Chisholm and Brentano on Intentionality', in L.L. McAlister (ed.) *op. cit*, pp. 151–9.

19 And so Husserl's objection (*LU* VI, Appendix §6/p. 864) – that Brentano is confused in allowing that 'an external object (a house)' and 'a content . . . present as a real part of a perception' are both 'physical phenomena' – is based on a misreading of Brentano. See also Kraus's remarks, in *PES* pp. 80n and 393.

20 Ryle, G. (1949) *The Concept of Mind*, London: Penguin Books, p. 178.

21 Brentano sometimes implies that secondary consciousness is necessarily present whenever there is primary consciousness (e.g., *PES* p. 121), and sometimes that they are only contingently (though invariably) related (*PES* p. 218).

22 Cf also Brentano, F. (1966) *The True and the Evident*, ed. by O. Kraus; translated by R.M. Chisholm *et al.*, London: Routledge & Kegan Paul, p. 33.

23 Brentano sometimes asserts, and sometimes denies, that a *mere* presentation, i.e. a presentation with no evaluative or emotional aspects whatsoever, is possible. Perhaps his considered opinion is that expressed at *PES* p. 265, where he writes that the 'phenomena of the three fundamental classes are most intimately intertwined . . . there is no mental act in which all three are not present'.

24 Russell, B. (1917) 'Knowledge by acquaintance and knowledge by description', in *Mysticism and Logic*, London: Allen & Unwin, (1963 edition), p. 108.

25 That Russell believes knowledge by description to be essentially sentential or propositional does not emerge clearly in his essay 'Knowledge by acquaintance and knowledge by description', where he actually defines it in terms of the essential occurrence in its expression of at least one definite description. It follows, however, from his theory of definite descriptions as incomplete symbols that they *can* only occur in complete sentences.

26 For further details of Brentano's non-propositional theory of judgement, see e.g. Chisholm, R.M. (1982) 'Brentano's Theory of Judgement', in his *Brentano and Meinong Studies*, Amsterdam: Rodopi, pp. 17–36; and also his (1978) 'Brentano's Conception of Substance and Accident', in *Die Philosophie Franz Brentanos*, R.M. Chisholm and R. Haller (eds), Amsterdam: Rodopi, pp. 197–210. And for details of Brentano's reconstruction of syllogistic logic, see e.g. *PES* pp. 201–34 and 295–306; and Körner, S. (1978) '*Über Brentanos Reismus und die Extensionale Logik*' in R.M. Chisholm and R. Haller (eds) *op. cit.*, pp. 29-43.

27 The first of these issues is dealt with on pp. 14–17 below, the second is the topic of the following section 'The Analysis of Phenomena'.

28 Frege, G. (1979) 'A Brief Survey of my Logical Doctrines', in *Posthumous Writings*, ed. by H. Hermes *et al.*, translated by P. Long *et al.*, Oxford: Blackwell, p. 198.

29 F. Brentano, *The True and the Evident*, p. 39.

30 *ibid.*

31 For justification of this claim as it relates to Kant, see Bennett, J. (1974) *Kant's Dialectic*, Cambridge: Cambridge University Press, pp. 9-20; and as it relates to Frege see Bell, D. (1979) *Frege's Theory of Judgement*, Oxford: Clarendon

Press, *passim*; and Bell, D. (1987) 'Thoughts', *Notre Dame Journal of Formal Logic*, 28, pp. 36–50.

32 For a quite different reading of Brentano on this matter, cf. Stegmüller, W. (1969) *Main Currents in Contemporary German, British and American Philosophy*, Dordrecht: Reidel, pp. 54–5.

33 Dummett, M.A.E. (1981) *The Interpretation of Frege's Philosophy*, London: Duckworth, p. 39.

34 Cf. Chisholm, R.M. (1978) 'Brentano's Conception of Substance and Accident', especially pp. 11–16.

35 Within the analytic tradition this issue would most suitably be dealt with in terms of the difference between singular and plural reference; see pp. 63–8 below.

36 See Brentano, F. (1981) *The Theory of Categories*, translated by R.M. Chisholm and N. Guterman, The Hague: Nijhoff, pp. 111–15, 191f. (The theory of wholes and parts defended in that work, however, differs significantly from that contained in *PES*.)

37 For an examination of Brentano's account of how we can have knowledge of such matters, see pp. 23–8 below.

38 Cf. J.N. Findlay's verdict on the doctrine of secondary consciousness, and on its Aristotelian ancestor: 'There can be no doubt that the theory of Aristotle and Brentano is the purest nonsense imaginable.' (1963) *Meinong's Theory of Objects and Values*, Oxford: Oxford University Press, p. 232.

39 Though my beliefs would necessarily be true, they would not, of course therewith be necessary truths. In the situation envisaged, it would necessarily be the case that if I believe p then p is true: $\Box$ (Bel$(p) \supset p$). But here p itself could very well be contingently true. In fact Brentano's doctrine of inner perception is, I think, guilty of the slide from (i) $\Box$ (Bel$(p) \supset p$), to (ii) Bel(p) $\supset \Box$ p; which is why he believes that inner perception yields *a priori* knowledge. This is not, however, a matter that needs to be pursued here.

40 See Brentano, F. *Deskriptive Psychologie*, p. 85; cf. Mulligan, K. and Smith, B. (1985) 'Franz Brentano on the Ontology of Mind', *Philosophy and Phenomenological Research*, 45, pp. 633–4.

Chapter I   The Philosophy of Arithmetic

1 *Über den Begriff der Zahl. Psychologische Analysen*, Heynemann'sche Buchdruckerei (F. Beyer), Halle a.d.S., 1887. Reprinted in *Hus* XII, pp. 289-338; translated as 'On the concept of Number' by D. Willard, in *HSW* pp. 92–119.

2 *Philosophie der Arithmetik. Psychologische und logische Untersuchungen*, C.E.M. Pfeffer (R. Stricker), Halle a.d.S., 1891. Reprinted in *Hus* XII, pp. 1–283.

3 For the remainder of this chapter unqualified page numbers will refer, as here, to the Husserliana edition of *Philosophie der Arithmetik* (i.e. *Hus* XII).

4 The influence that Frege's works exercised on Husserl during the period 1886–1900 was, I believe, vast – though its nature and extent are matters I shall not pursue here. It is however worth noting briefly that, contrary to wide-spread opinion, Frege's influence did not begin (or, for that matter, end) with his devastating review of the *Philosophy of Arithmetic* which appeared in 1894.

As an antidote to such a view it should be remembered, first, that in the *Philosophy of Arithmetic* itself Husserl refers more often to Frege, and devotes more space to the discussion of his ideas, than he does to any other mathematician or philosopher. And, second, that in 1891 Husserl wrote to Frege: 'allow me to acknowledge the large amount of stimulation and encouragement I derived from your *Foundations of Arithmetic*. Of all the many writings that I had before me when I worked on my book, I could not name another which I studied with as much enjoyment as yours.' (Frege, G. (1980) *Philosophical and Mathematical Correspondence*, ed. by G. Gabriel *et al.*, translated by H. Kaal, Oxford: Blackwell, pp. 64–5).

5 Frege, G. (1884) *Die Grundlagen der Arithmetik*, W. Koebner: Breslau, §62; translated by J.L. Austin, as *The Foundations of Arithmetic*, Oxford: Blackwell, 1964, p. 73.

6 For a detailed and scholarly examination of the relation between Brentano's and Husserl's 'psychology', see de Boer, T. (1978) *The Development of Husserl's Thought*, translated by T. Plantinga, The Hague: Nijhoff, chs 2,3, and 5.

7 There are many possibilities here for confusing the various senses of the words 'object', 'thing', and 'content' and, sadly, virtually all of them are present in Husserl's text. In what follows I shall try to resolve this confusion by adopting what seems to be the most defensible set of conventions governing their use – conventions to which, indeed, Husserl himself sometimes conforms. (1) By 'thing' I shall mean a content of consciousness which is a strong whole, i.e., a content which is neither an aggregate nor a moment. (2) By 'object' – and especially by '*physical* object' – I shall mean a non-phenomenal, extra-mental denizen of the external world. As we shall see, the nature and the existence of such objects is no concern of descriptive psychology. (3) I shall try to avoid the use of 'object' in the sense of 'intended object' (e.g. in phrases like 'the object of his mental act'), preferring to use the term 'content' instead. The early Husserl followed the early Brentano in construing the intentional object of a mental act as an immanent content of that act. In short, then, descriptive psychology dispenses with physical objects, restricting its universe of discourse to mental acts or states and their immanent contents (which can be in-existing *things, aggregates* or *moments*).

8 For more detailed elaboration of the distinction between the 'analytic' and the 'genetic' tasks of descriptive psychology, see, e.g., Husserl's writings on the foundations of geometry, in *Hus XXI*, pp. 262–3, 302–3, 404–5. Cf. also Stumpf, C. (1873) *Über den psychologischen Ursprung der Raumvorstellung*, Leipzig, pp. 3–4.

9 I am here of course distinguishing sharply between *numbers* and *numerals*. Token numerals, or numerical signs, like '2', 'ii', 'two', '1+1' and the like, are perceptible objects which signify numbers. The previous four numerical signs, for example, all signify one and the same number; and it is the perceptibility of this *number* that is, to say the least, problematic. (The relation between our sensory awareness of numerals and other signs, and our non-sensory grasp of (large) numbers is precisely the topic of the *Philosophy of Arithmetic*, Part II.)

10 Husserl's semi-technical terms '*Vielheit*' and '*Einheit*' are poorly translated by the English terms 'multiplicity' and 'unity', in the first place because the

English terms are by no means as contrastive, almost contradictory, as are the German; in the second place because the word 'multiplicity' carries with it the unwanted suggestion that a not inconsiderable number of items are at issue; and third because the word 'unity' suggests the integrity of a whole, rather than, with the German, its singularity. Something of the precise meaning Husserl attaches to the terms might be indicated by rendering them, respectively, as 'more-than-one-ness' and 'exactly-one-ness'.

11 For a more detailed account of Husserl's theory of abstraction, and of its deviations from the traditional theory, see pp. 41–6 below.

12 I shall be concerned here almost exclusively with mental powers and capabilities that Husserl took, at this time, to be of central *cognitive* relevance; so I shall largely ignore, e.g., emotion, imagination, volition, feeling, and the like.

13 Stumpf, C. (1873) *Über den psychologischen Ursprung der Raumvorstellung*, Leipzig, p. 109.

14 *ibid*, p.113.

15 It is revealing that the examples of 'concrete things' which Husserl provides are almost always such *phenomena* as sounds, colours, mental acts and the like (e.g. pp. 19, 80, 136–7 etc.), rather than such objects as tables, chairs, and houses. And even when he comes closest to talking about the denizens of the external world, he is usually careful to distinguish the material object (to which no reference can properly be made in descriptive psychology), from its *appearance*, which is of course a genuine phenomenon. (See, e.g., the discussion of the 'genuine presentation of the outer appearance of a house', pp. 193–4. The reference on pp. 16–17 to such material objects as trees, apples, the sun, the moon, and Mars is an apparent exception to this rule. The context, however, makes it clear that Husserl is talking not about *Objekte* as such, but about *Vorstellungsobjekte*, i.e. about *Vorstellungen*, *Inhalte*, and *Phänomene*.)

16 From Husserl's *Tagebuch*; quoted in the Editor's Introduction to *Hus* XII, pp. xxvi-xxvii.

17 Wittgenstein, L. (1975) *The Blue and Brown Books*, Oxford: Blackwell, p. 55.

18 If this account of the origin of concepts is to be coherent, then 'similarity' between moments must be taken to be a qualitative likeness between different individuals, not the numerical identity of a single, shareable attribute. Moreover, if the account is to avoid circularity, then it must be possible to *see* similarities, i.e. to perceive them, independently of, and prior to, any conceptualization of them. For a powerful investigation into the possibility of seeing similarities, aspects, and other 'abstract moments', see Wittgenstein, L. *Philosophical Investigations*, Part II, section xi, pp. 193–229. Cf. Bell, D. (1979) 'Epistemology and Abstract Objects', *Proceedings of the Aristotelian Society*, suppl. vol.53, pp. 135–52.

19 The relation between the accounts provided by Husserl and Frege of the abstractive process are interestingly explored in Simons, P.M. (1981) 'Abstraction and Abstract Objects', in E. Morscher *et al* (eds), *Essays in Scientific Philosophy*, Bad Reichenhall: Comes Verlag, pp. 355–70.

20 Frege, G. *The Foundations of Arithmetic*, pp. 74–5.

21 It might seem here that the objective attributes or properties that belong to a

thing are being confused with the subjective percepts and concepts which a person might have of that thing. But because our investigation is *ab initio* restricted to phenomena, i.e. to mental acts and their contents as they appear to consciousness, there *is* no distinction that can be drawn between a thing which is presented and the content of a presentation, or, likewise, between a shareable property and a general concept. The impossibility of distinguishing the way they appear to be from the way they really are is, as we noted earlier, precisely one of the hallmarks of phenomena.

22 See, e.g., Kneale, W. and M. (1962) *The Development of Logic*, Oxford: Oxford University Press, pp. 318f; and Russell, B. (1903) *The Principles of Mathematics*, London: Allen & Unwin, 2nd edition 1937, pp. 66–8.

23 The definition is of course an oversimplification: it ignores a number of irrelevant complexities in ecclesiastical doctrine and history.

24 Husserl would have rejected them if only because he believed that zero was not in fact a number of any sort.

25 For details see Mill, J.S. (1961) *A System of Logic*, London: Longmans, pp. 164–84; cf. also Skorupski, J.M. (1989) *Mill*, London: Routledge, ch.5.

26 Frege, G. *The Foundations of Arithmetic*, p. 11 (my italics).

27 See Russell, B. (1937) *The Principles of Mathematics*, second edition, pp. 76, 103–6; cf. Husserl's remark: 'There is an essential difference between multiplicity as such, i.e. multiplicity thought of as multiplicity, and multiplicity thought of as unity' (p. 156).

28 Some of the considerations alluded to here run closely parallel to those which exercised Wittgenstein in the *Tractatus*. Cf. Wittgenstein, L. (1961) *Tractatus Logico-Philosophicus*, translated by D.F. Pears and B. McGuinness, London: Routledge & Kegan Paul, 3.141–3.143, 4.122, etc.

29 See, e.g., Kant's remarks to the effect that 'the combination of a manifold can never come to us through the senses . . . for it is an act of spontaneity . . . . Of all representations, *combination* is the only one which cannot be given through objects. Being an act of the self-activity of the subject, it cannot be executed save by the subject itself.' (Kant, I. (1933) *Critique of Pure Reason*, translated by N. Kemp Smith, London: Macmillan, p. 151 (*B* 130).)

30 Part I of *Philosophy of Arithmetic* is addressed to epistemological problems concerning aggregates (*Inbegriffe*); but in Part II Husserl begins to talk instead of groups (*Menge*). As far as I can see the difference is this: an aggregate is a (small) multiplicity of things united authentically by collective combination, whereas a group is a (larger) multiplicity of things united inauthentically or symbolically. Both are, however, aggregates in the formal sense already defined.

31 The examples here are, merely for brevity's sake, physical objects rather than genuine 'phenomena'. Instead one could talk of, say, 'an intuition whose immanent content was one describable as of *a stand* (of trees)' – but in the present context the complication is unnecessary.

32 Frege, G. (1984) 'Review of E.G. Husserl, *Philosophie der Arithmetik I*', in *Collected Papers* ed. by B. McGuinness, translated by M. Black *et al.*, Oxford: Blackwell, p. 201.

33 Cf. Wittgenstein, L. *Philosophical Investigations*, §381.

34 Benacerraf, P. (1965) 'What Numbers Could Not Be', reprinted in

P. Benacerraf and H. Putnam (eds), *Philosophy of Mathematics. Selected Readings*, Cambridge: Cambridge University Press, (2nd edition), pp. 272–95. All further quotations in the present paragraph are from pp. 290–3 of this work.

35 Cf. Husserl's almost identical conclusion: 'Arithmetic is usually defined as "the science of numbers", but the definition is insufficiently clear. Considered in isolation, the individual numbers themselves give rise to no organized body of knowledge; [the latter can only concern] characteristics which belong to a given number *in virtue of the specific relations that link it to other individual numbers*, or whole classes of numbers. It is only in the relations in which numbers stand to one another that there originate propositions for logical treatment. It would be better, therefore, to define arithmetic as *the science of numerical relations*' (p. 256; my italics).

36 Cf. Husserl's criticism of formalistic or 'nominalistic' theories of number, pp. 170–8. Benacerraf, incidentally, makes the same claim for his account of number: because of the rules governing the use of the sequence of numerals in counting, 'one can . . . be this sort of formalist without denying that there is such a thing as arithmetical truth other than derivability within some given system'.

37 Although lack of space precludes explicit discussion of them, and although my understanding of Husserl's treatment of these topics is often in disagreement with them, I have nevertheless profited from the following works: Farber, M. (1943) *The Foundation of Phenomenology*, Cambridge (Mass.): Harvard University Press, especially ch.2; Miller, J.P. (1982) *Numbers in Presence and Absence. A Study of Husserl's Philosophy of Mathematics*, The Hague: Nijhoff; Simons, P.M. (1982) 'Number and Manifolds', in B. Smith (ed.), *Parts and Moments. Studies in Logic and Formal Ontology*, Munich: Philosophia Verlag, pp. 160–98; Sokolowski, R. (1964) *The Formation of Husserl's Concept of Constitution*, The Hague: Nijhoff, especially ch.1; Sukale, M. (1970) *Comparative Studies in Phenomenology*, The Hague: Nijhoff, especially chs.2–3; Willard, D. (1984) *Logic and the Objectivity of Knowledge. A Study of Husserl's Early Philosophy*, Athens (Ohio): Ohio University Press.

38 The labels are rather general and, in the present context at least, uninformative. Their generality is, however, a strength; for, shortly after completing the first volume of the *Philosophy of Arithmetic*, Husserl began to see the reconciliation of the conflicting claims of 'subjectivity' and 'objectivity', not merely within the foundations of arithmetic but quite generally, as the first and most fundamental task of philosophy: 'I became more and more disquieted by doubts of principle, as to how to reconcile the objectivity of mathematics and of all science in general, with a psychological foundation for logic . . . . I felt myself more and more pushed towards general critical reflections on the essence of logic, and on the relationship, in particular, between the subjectivity of knowing and the objectivity of the content known.' (*LU* Foreword (1st ed.)/ p. 42).

39 Some of the material intended for the second volume is contained in *Hus* XII, pp. 341ff.

40 Frege, G. *Collected Papers*, p. 198.

41 *ibid*, p. 207 (my italics).

42 Fodor, J.A. (1980) 'Methodological Solipsism Considered as a Research

Strategy in Cognitive Psychology', in *The Behavioural and Brain Sciences*, 3, p. 67. See also Putnam, H. (1975) 'The Meaning of "Meaning"', in *Mind, Language and Reality*, Cambridge: Cambridge University Press, p. 220.

43 They are, I shall argue later, germane not merely to an understanding of the descriptive psychology of the *Philosophy of Arithmetic*, but also to under standing the motive for and the status of the phenomenological reduction and the restriction to transcendental subjectivity that it entails. See pp. 163–8 below.

44 Frege, G. *Collected Papers* p. 209 (my italics).

45 Although, I believe, it is perfectly clear that Husserl did *not* confuse objective, external objects and properties with the subjective presentations that we have of them, it is equally clear that in 1890 he had no explanation whatsoever to offer of the relation in which the two stand to one another. And so in the last analysis it remains unclear *how* the epistemological and the ontological parts of Husserl's early theory are related. As we will see, this very issue became increasingly problematic for Husserl, and its resolution required extensive modification to the theory of intentionality which he had inherited from Brentano.

46 Cf. Frege, G. *The Foundations of Arithmetic*, pp. 68ff.

47 Admittedly, this characterization ignores the nature and indeed the importance of general assertions in arithmetic (e.g. 'every number has exactly one successor', 'There is only one even prime', and the like); but in the natural order of things one wants to know what numbers are, before one begins to quantify over them.

48 '*Zur Logik der Zeichen (Semiotik)*', and '*Zur Lehre vom Inbegriff*', in *Hus* XII, pp. 341–73, and 385–407.

49 Simons, P.M. 'Number and Manifolds', p. 165 (my italics). An exception to these generalizations can be found in Bertrand Russell's early writings, e.g. *The Principles of Mathematics*, ch. VI; and also *Introduction to Mathematical Philosophy*, pp. 167ff, and Ch. XVII.

50 Ironically, this tendency is particularly clearly expressed in Tyler Burge's treatment of *aggregates*, in which aggregates of individual things are themselves taken to be singular, individual things. Burge writes that aggregates could also be handled if we were to 'change the logic underlying our semantic theory so as to admit plural subjects . . . . But although this alternative is doubtless worth exploring . . . the most natural tack is to treat [a subject term like "the people presently in this room"] as a singular term'. Burge, T. (1977a) 'A theory of Aggregates', *Nous*, 11, p. 98.

51 In *Word and Object*, for example, Quine mentions the possibility of plural reference just once – and then only in order to dismiss it. See Quine, W.V.O. (1960) *Word and Object*, Cambridge (Mass.): MIT Press, p. 118.

52 Personally I do not know what the term 'the Beatles' designates – an individual, an aggregate, a mereological sum, an abstract object, a legal entity (like a limited company), or what have you. The answer will depend, for example, on whether we take the Beatles to be capable of surviving changes in its membership; on whether the Beatles can have properties independently of those possessed by the individuals concerned, and so forth. I rather suspect that 'the Beatles' designates different things, perhaps radically different kinds

of things, in different contexts and at different times. Here and now, however, I shall simply stipulate that 'the Beatles' is to designate just: John, Paul, Ringo, and George.

53 A caveat is in order here: the remarks that follow go beyond anything to be found explicitly in Husserl's text, though they are, I hope, entirely Husserlian in spirit.

54 As we will see, (H4) and (H5) create certain difficulties when Husserl comes to account for the numbers one and zero.

55 For details, see Bell, D. *Frege's Theory of Judgement*, pp. 143–8.

56 I deal with zero and one below, pp. 69–71.

57 We should beware the temptation to think that (5) must be construed in terms of classical (Fregean) quantification theory; for in the present context this would beg the very question at issue. Quantification theory, that is, is itself yet another device for de-pluralization, for eliminating plurally referring terms: variables of quantification are *individual* variables, and predicate-letters are all *singular*. Thus '$(\exists x)(F(x))$' is read (roughly) as 'There is at least one thing such that it is F'.

58 The strong notion of a *collective* property should be distinguished from the weaker notion of a merely *non-distributive* property. ϕ will be non-distributive if $\phi[x: F(x)] \supset \sim (x)(F(x) \supset \phi(x))$.

59 Black, M. (1971) 'The Elusiveness of Sets', *Review of Metaphysics*, 24, p. 631.

60 For the sake of simplicity I have here taken (5) to mean that there are three coins (at least) in the fountain, rather than that there are three coins (exactly) in the fountain.

61 Frege, G. *Collected Papers*, p. 206.

62 Frege, G. *The Foundations of Arithmetic*, p. 65.

63 Peter Simons, to whom I am indebted, brings this out clearly in 'Numbers and Manifolds', p. 187.

64 Cf. Quine, W.V.O. *Set Theory and its Logic, passim*; and Burge, T. 'A Theory of Aggregates', p. 101.

65 On the nature and importance of one-to-one mappings of a sequence into itself, in relation to numbers and counting, see also Brouwer, L.E.J. *Collected Works*, vol.1, pp. 15ff.

66 Frege, G. *The Foundations of Arithmetic*, p. 28.

67 Aggregates can also be specified by *listing* their members. But this too can, trivially, be construed as involving a concept. The aggregate specified as '[a, b, c]' can be taken to involve tacit contraction from '[x: x=a v x=b v x=c]', i.e. as involving the concept: *being identical with either a, b, or c*.

68 Cf. the fragment 'Arithmetic as an *a priori* science', in *Hus* XII, pp. 380–4.

69 See, e.g., Frege, G. *The Foundations of Arithmetic*, pp. 29-36; *Collected Papers*, pp. 195–209; *The Basic Laws of Arithmetic*, Introduction, pp. 10–25.

70 Frege is quite clearly guilty of such a misreading; but so too are some more recent (and more sympathetic) commentators on the *Philosophy of Arithmetic*, many of whom have tried in vain to show that Husserl's talk about concepts and presentations of numbers and aggregates was really, and in spite of appearances, intended to be a contribution to our understanding of the nature of numbers and aggregates as they are *an sich*. See, e.g., Willard, D. (1974)

'Concerning Husserl's View of Number', *Southwestern Journal of Philosophy*, 5, pp. 97–109; Sukale, M. (1970) *Comparative Studies in Phenomenology*, Ch.4; Smith D.W. and McIntyre, R. (1982) *Husserl and Intentionality*, Dordrecht: Reidel, p. 171; Bachelard, S. (1968) *A Study of Husserl's Formal and Transcendental Logic*, Evanston: Northwestern University Press, p. xix.

71 See Husserl's letter to Meinong of 20 November 1894, in *Husserl-Chronik*, p. 43.

72 This aspect of Husserl's development has been explored in Willard, D. (1980) 'Husserl on a Logic that Failed', *Philosophical Review* 89, pp. 46–64.

73 The words are Weierstrass's, as quoted by Husserl in *PdA* p. 12n. Cf. also *PdA* pp. 294ff.

74 Letter from Husserl to Stumpf, 1891; quoted in Willard, D. 'Husserl on a Logic that Failed', p. 63.

75 Kant, I. *Critique of Pure Reason*, p. 283 (*A* 271 = *B* 327).

76 From Husserl's diary; quoted in de Boer, T. (1978) *The Development of Husserl's Thought*, The Hague: Nijhoff, p. 267n (my italics).

77 Cracks had begun to appear in the Husserlian edifice as early as 1894, the year in which 'Psychological Studies on Elementary Logic' appeared. The distinction between the transcendent *object* as against the immanent *content* of a mental act developed in this article would certainly have required the re-working of parts of the *Philosophy of Arithmetic*.

78 Strictly speaking, Husserl's naturalism reached its apogee in the first edition of the *Logical Investigations* (i.e. the edition of 1900–1). This was subsequently revised, though not completely rewritten, for the second edition, some of it in 1913, the rest in 1920, i.e. long after Husserl had abandoned naturalism and had taken his transcendental turn. Unfortunately matters are complicated for the English reader by the fact that J.N. Findlay's English version of the *Logical Investigations* is a translation of the second edition, and as a result the text at times contains an uneasy and confusing mixture of both naturalistic and transcendental points of view.

Chapter II   *Logical Investigations*

1 Cf. Husserl's complaints at having been misunderstood, made, e.g., in *LU* VI, Foreword/p. 662; 'A Draft "Preface" to the *Logical Investigations*', pp. 18ff, 52ff; 'Philosophy as a Rigorous Science' in *HSW*, pp. 183f; and *Ideas*, Introduction/p. 42.

2 See pp. 4–7.

3 Although my aim in the present chapter is a critical reading of Husserl's naturalistic investigations into logical theory, the *locus classicus* of which is the first edition of the *Logical Investigations* (1901), there are a number of other texts on which, either tacitly or explicitly, I have drawn. They include, from Husserl's naturalistic period, such articles as 'The Deductive Calculus and Intensional Logic' (1891); 'Review of Schröder's *Vorlesungen über die Algebra der Logik*' (1891); 'Psychological Studies on Elementary Logic' (1894); and 'A Reply to a Critic of my Refutation of Logical Psychologism' (1903), as well as Husserl's lectures 'Introduction to Logic and Theory of

Knowledge' (delivered 1906–7, published 1984). But, in addition, considerable light is shed on Husserl's early naturalistic philosophy by works written after he had abandoned that position. They include not only the second edition of the *Logical Investigations* (1913, 1921), but also 'A Draft of a "Preface" to the *Logical Investigations*' (written 1913, published 1939); *Formal and Transcendental Logic* (1929); and *Experience and Judgement: Investigations in a Genealogy of Logic* (written c.1929, published 1939).

4 There is, however, an exception to this generalization: Investigation III is alone in belonging within formal logic, rather than phenomenological philosophy. See pp. 93–5.

5 Cf. Natorp, P. (1901) for some perceptive (and influential) comments, '*Zur Frage der logischen Methode*', *Kant Studien*, 6, pp. 270ff; and Husserl's response in 'A Draft of a "Preface" to the *Logical Investigations*', pp. 20ff.

6 The distinction, though not the terminology, is Husserl's. Cf. *FTL* §12/p. 48; *LU Prol.*, §71/p. 244.

7 Cf. Bachelard, S. *A Study of Husserl's Formal and Transcendental Logic*, pp. 6–10. Bachelard is surely right to claim that the examples of formal absurdity (*Widersinn*) provided by Husserl in the *Logical Investigations* are inadequate and misleading. She writes: 'Formal countersense [i.e. absurdity] is a purely formal incompatibility, abstraction being made from all material cognition. [Yet] by and large the examples given in the *Logical Investigations* are material examples'. (*ibid*, p. 7; cf. *LU* IV, §12/p. 517).

8 See, e.g., *LU Prol.* §§62–71/pp. 225–46. Also *Hus.* XXIV, pp. 5–6; *FTL* §28/pp. 91f; and 'A Draft of a "Preface" to the *Logical Investigations*', pp. 28ff.

9 See Hylton, P. (1989) 'Logic in Russell's Logicism', in D. Bell and N. Cooper (eds), *The Analytic Tradition: Meaning, Thought and Knowledge*, Oxford: Blackwell.

10 This and the immediately succeeding quotations are from *EU* §3/p. 17.

11 See pp. 23–6.

12 The issues here, concerning fallibilism, holism, verificationism, and the relations between (say) truth, rationality, knowledge, evidence, self-evidence, and the like go far deeper than the present naive and merely impressionistic remarks might suggest. These very issues, however, became increasingly central in the development of Husserl's thought – and they are taken up again below, pp. 198–203.

13 Quine, W.V.O. and Ullian, J.S. (1970) *The Web of Belief*, New York: Random House, p. 26.

14 Eugen Fink's editorial comments, in 'A Draft of a "Preface" to the *Logical Investigations*', p. 15.

15 The expression 'formal ontology' does not occur in the first edition of the *Logical Investigations*, but was inserted at a number of points in the second edition (e.g. at *LU* III, Introduction/p. 435). Nevertheless, the *discipline* of formal ontology was certainly present, in all but name, from the very start. See next footnote; cf. Husserl's own remarks in *FTL* §27/p. 86.

16 The notion first appeared in Husserl's earliest work, 'On the Concept of Number', and in *PdA* where it played a crucial role (see pp. 51–3 below). Cf. *LU Prol.*, §62/p. 226; and *FTL* §42(b)/pp. 113ff.

17 See, e.g., Smith, B. and Mulligan, K. (1983) 'A Framework for Formal Ontology', *Topoi*, 3, pp. 73–85.

18 And this fact renders insecure any interpretation of the *Logical Investigations* that takes Husserl's point of view in the third Investigation to be characteristic of that work as a whole. In sharp contrast to the 'Prolegomena' and the other five Investigations, Investigation III is in fact written from a non-phenomenological, indeed naively realist standpoint; which may explain why so many naive realists are attracted to it. In fact, however, its non-phenomenological, philosophically naive standpoint is merely a reflection of the fact that its subject matter belongs not to philosophy but to formal logic. (See also *FTL* §37/pp. 105ff; and *LU* III, Introd./p. 435.)

19 Developments in whole-part theory since Husserl are usefully summarized in Smith, B. and Mulligan, K. 'Pieces of a theory', in B. Smith (ed.) *Parts and Moments*, pp. 45–109.

20 Husserl was later to adopt a more Fregean or 'analytic' point of view. See, e.g., *FTL* §54/pp. 143–48, where formal ontology and logical syntax are said to be 'correlative'.

21 See pp. 17–23 and 38–9.

22 Husserl's theory is intended to be entirely formal, that is, to abstract from all material or contingent constraints. It is important, therefore, that such material constraints are not tacitly imported at this point. So, for example, the notion of 'co-existence' should not be interpreted as a temporal notion; there is no suggestion of simultaneity here. Likewise the notion of a kind or species should not be restricted to that of a natural kind.

23 To be genuinely formal, however, both the objects and the species must remain unspecified. (So the concrete examples of the preceeding paragraph clearly do not belong within formal ontology.) Husserl writes: 'The pure forms of *wholes and parts* are determined by the *pure forms of law*. Only what is *formally* universal in the foundational relation . . . is then relevant . . . . In formalization we replace the names standing for the sort of content in question by indefinite expressions [i.e. variables]'. (*LU* III, §24/p. 482).

24 As I shall use them, no systematic or significant difference is intended between expressions of the following forms: 'a φ as such'; 'an object in so far as it is a φ'; or 'an object *qua* φ'. The variety is merely stylistic.

25 This point is convincingly argued by Peter Simons, whom I follow here: see 'The Formalization of Husserl's Theory of Wholes and Parts', in Smith, B. (ed.) *Parts and Moments*, pp. 131–33.

26 *LU* III, §14/p. 463. All six theorems are quoted from this section. I have changed the style of variable: Husserl uses lower-case Greek letters.

27 In fact, Husserlian abstracta correspond more closely to Fregean functions than they do to Fregean abstract objects – at least in so far as both abstracta and functions are said to be 'incomplete', 'unsaturated', 'non-selfsubsistent' and 'in need of supplementation'. The Fregean distinction between concrete and abstract objects corresponds more closely to Husserl's distinction between real and ideal objects.

28 This is, of course, a contentious statement, and will be judged so especially by those who like to see in the *Logical Investigations* a reflection of their own 'realist' prejudices. My own, 'non-realist' reading will be defended explicitly

below; for the moment that reading is merely assumed.

29 Wittgenstein, L. (1958a) *Philosophical Investigations*, translated by G.E.M. Anscombe, Oxford: Blackwell, p. 193. Throughout the remainder of the present section unqualified page references are to this work.

30 See pp. 41–6. Cf. *LU* I, §§30–35; II, Introd. and §§1, 4, 21, 40–42; VI, §§40–58. The transition from *PdA* to *LU* is most clearly seen in Husserl's article 'Psychological Studies on Elementary Logic', §§2–3, in *HSW* pp. 128–30. See also in this connection Husserl's disavowal at *LU* VI, §8/p. 694n.

31 Kant, I. *Critique of pure Reason*, translated by N. Kemp Smith, p. 151 (*B* 129).

32 Husserl himself is quite clear as to the difference between these two notions of identity: see *LU* VI, §8/pp. 696–7.

33 See, e.g., *LU* V, §38/p. 639 for Husserl's views on the possibility of a many-rayed act whose unity is not a product of synthesis. See also *Ideas* §133/p. 369.

34 On this point Kant, Wittgenstein, and Husserl are broadly speaking in agreement. In Wittgenstein's phrase we have here 'the echo of a thought in sight'; Kant assigns all synthetic activity to the understanding; and according to Husserl, when we move from primary to categorial perception 'this means that the sphere of "sensibility" has been left, and that of "understanding" entered'. (*LU* VI, §47/p. 792).

35 Smith, D.W. and McIntyre, R. (1982) *Husserl and Intentionality. A Study of Mind, Meaning and Language*, Dordrecht: Reidel, p. 87.

36 This misunderstanding is further encouraged by the misidentification of 'physical' objects in Husserl's sense (i.e non-mental *phenomena*) with physical objects in the usual sense (i.e. material objects existing independently of us in the natural world).

37 This distinction, although of relatively minor importance in the *Logical Investigations*, was subsequently to assume a central role in accounting for the possibility of the phenomenological reduction. See pp. 164 ff.

38 Cf. Kant's distinction between apprehensions and representations in the 'Second Analogy', i.e., *Critique of Pure Reason*, translated. by N. Kemp Smith, p. 219 (*A* 190 = *B* 235).

39 Kant, I. (1952) *The Critique of Aesthetic Judgement*, translated by J.C. Meredith, Oxford: Oxford University Press, p. 45.

40 This doctrine is later transformed, terminologically, into the claim that the real hyletic moments of a noesis are informed by a noematic sense to yield an experience of an object. (Cf. *Ideas*, §§128f.).

41 Wittgenstein, L. *Philosophical Investigations*, §432.

42 Cf. Bell, D. *Frege's Theory of Judgement*, pp. 13–24.

43 Wittgenstein, L. *Philosophical Investigations*, p. 178. There are many suggestive and subtle relations between Husserl's account of how linguistic behaviour can serve as a sign of 'inner experience' and Wittgenstein's investigations of the same topic – particularly in connection with Wittgenstein's use of notions like 'criterion', 'symptom', 'seeing . . . as . . .', 'expressive behaviour', and above all in connection with his examination of the relation between an 'inner process' and the 'outward criteria' that it stands in need of. These topics are taken up again (pp. 218–26) in connection with Husserl's analysis of intersubjectivity and the life-world.

44 Mohanty, J.N. (1982) *Husserl and Frege*, Indiana University Press, p. 43.

45 For further details, see Bell, D. (1984) 'Sense and Reference: An Epitome', *Philosophical Quarterly*, 34, pp. 369-72; and (1987) 'Thoughts', *Notre Dame Journal of Formal Logic*, 28, pp. 36–50.

46 Frege, G. (1980) *Philosophical and Mathematical Correspondence*, G. Gabriel *et al.* (eds), translated by H. Kaal, Oxford: Blackwell, pp. 63–4.

47 Clearly in the present context I am using the terms 'real', 'actual' and the like in their normal, and not in their Husserlian senses. So here real or actual objects are items that exist, independently of our cognitive or other acts, in the external world. Amongst those who interpret Husserl's theory as assigning such objects to acts as their 'objective correlates' or 'intentional objects' are Dummett, M. (1989) in 'Thought and Perception: the Views of Husserl and Frege' in D. Bell and N. Cooper (eds), *The Analytic Tradition: Meaning, Thought and Knowledge*; Mohanty, J. N. (1972) *The Concept of Intentionality*, St Louis: Green, p. 68; Olafson, F. (1975) 'Husserl's Theory of Intentionality in Contemporary Perspective', *Nous* , 9, pp. 74–5; Smith, D.W. and McIntyre, R. (1982) *Husserl and Intentionality. A Study of Mind, Meaning and Language*, p. 87; Welton, D. (1983) *The Origins of Meaning*, The Hague: Nijhoff, p. 98; and Findlay, J.N. 'Translator's Introduction' to English version of *LU*, p. 27.

48 There is, in fact, one way in which a relational theory of intentionality can be reconciled with a univocal account of singular thought: following Meinong, one can maintain in effect that there *is* always an object to which an intentional act is genuinely related – it's just that in some cases the object exists, and in some cases it doesn't. I shall ignore this theory, however, because, on the one hand, it is not clear that it has anything to recommend it, and on the other it is clear that Husserl did not subscribe to it.

49 This dilemma forms a focus of one of the liveliest debates in contemporary philosophy: the debate concerning the nature of *de re* thoughts and whether their existence is compatible with the programme of methodological solipsism. See, e.g., Bach, K. (1982) '*De re* Belief and Methodological Solipsism', in A. Woodfield (ed.), *Thought and Object*, Oxford: Oxford University Press; Burge, T. (1977) 'Belief *De Re*', *Journal of Philosophy*, 74; Dennett, D. (1982) 'Beyond Belief', in A. Woodfield (ed.) *op. cit.*; Fodor, J.A. (1980) 'Methodological Solipsism Considered as a Research Strategy in Cognitive Psychology', *The Behavioural and Brain Sciences*, 3; McDowell, J. (1984) '*De re* Senses', in C. Wright (ed.) *Frege: Tradition and Influence*, Oxford: Blackwell; Noonan, H. (1986) 'Russellian Thoughts and Methodological Solipsism', in J. Butterfield (ed.) *Language, Mind and Logic*, Cambridge: Cambridge University Press; Putnam, H. (1975) 'The Meaning of "Meaning"', in *Mind, Language and Reality*, Cambridge: Cambridge University Press.

50 These remarks are clearly not true of the use that Husserl makes of the terms 'actual', 'real', 'external' and the like at *LU* V, Appendix to §§11 and 20/p. 595. This passage is explicitly examined, below pp. 138–40.

51 Husserl's use of this notion of *Gegenständlichkeit* is not restricted to *LU*: it appears in a number of other works (see, e.g., *Ideas* §§ 90, 119, 128, 130 etc.; cf. also *CM* §20/p. 47).

52 *LU* V, §11/p. 559. The greater part of §11 is devoted by Husserl to recording

the extent both of his agreement and of his disagreement with Brentano's account of '*immanente Gegenständlichkeit*'.

53 On Husserl's understanding and use of the notion of *Widersinn*, see above, pp. 88–90.

54 This is not, of course, a reductivist programme: the sense of 'foundation' relevant here is that introduced and explored in Investigation III (see above, pp. 97 ff.).

55 For a non-phenomenological examination of this problem – the problem of the putative identity of non-existent or merely intentional objects – see Geach, P.T. (1972) 'Intentional Identity' in *Logic Matters*, Oxford: Blackwell, pp. 146–153; and 'The Perils of Pauline', *ibid*, pp. 153–66.

56 Husserl's discussion occurs at *LU* VI, §§6 and 8. My own discussion concentrates exclusively on what Husserl calls the case of 'dynamic union' in which intellectual and sensory acts occur at different times, rather than on 'static union' where the different elements are somewhat harder to distinguish from each other.

57 Here the term 'object' is intended to range over nominal, propositional, real, and ideal entities; and correspondingly 'perception' must be taken to include categorial intuition of ideal objects like species.

58 Patzig, G. (1977) 'Husserl on Truth and Evidence', in J.N. Mohanty (ed.), *Readings on E. Husserl's "Logical Investigations"*, The Hague: Nijhoff, p. 194.

Chapter III   Solipsistic Idealism

1 *Ideen zu einer reinen Phänomenologie und phänomenologischen Philosophie. Erstes Buch: Allgemeine Einführung in die reine Phänomenologie*, published in *Jahrbuch für Philosophie und phänomenologische Forschung*, vol.1 (1913); reprinted in *Hus* III. Translated as *Ideas. General Introduction to Pure Phenomenology* by W.R. Boyce Gibson, London: Allen & Unwin, 1931. (This translation includes the 'Author's Preface to the English Edition'.) Also translated (1982) as *Ideas Pertaining to a Pure Phenomenology and to a Phenomenological Philosophy* by F. Kersten, The Hague: Nijhoff. (This translation omits the 'Author's Preface to the English Edition'.)

2 These lectures have been published as *Die Idee der Phänomenologie. Fünf Vorlesungen* in *Hus* II. Translated as *The Idea of Phenomenology* by W.P. Alston and G. Nakhnikian, The Hague: Nijhoff, 1966.

3 Quine, W.V.O. (1969) 'Ontological Relativity', in *Ontological Relativity and Other Essays*, New York: Columbia University Press, p. 26.

4 Quine, W.V.O. (1981) 'Five Milestones of Empiricism', in *Theories and Things*, Cambridge (Mass.): Harvard University Press, p. 72.

5 Spiegelberg, H. 'Glossary', in *HSW* p. 370.

6 Putnam, H. (1975) 'The Meaning of "Meaning"', in *Mind, Language and Reality*, Cambridge: Cambridge University Press, p. 220.

7 Cf. Williams, B. (1972/3) 'Wittgenstein and Idealism', in G. Vesey (ed.) *Understanding Wittgenstein. Royal Institute of Philosophy Lectures*, 7, pp. 76–95; and Kripke, S. (1981) 'Wittgenstein on Rules and Private Language' in I. Block (ed.) *Perspectives on the Philosophy of Wittgenstein*, Oxford: Blackwell, pp. 238–312. See also *Crisis* §15/p. 71 and §34(e)/p. 130.

8 Kant, I. *Critique of Pure Reason*, p. 59 (*A* 12 = *B* 25).

9 See, e.g., *The Idea of Phenomenology*, p. 13, where Husserl distinguishes between 'science of the natural sort' and 'philosophic science': 'the former originates from the natural, the latter from the philosophical attitude of mind.'

10 Cf. Fink, E. (1970) 'The Phenomenological Philosophy of Edmund Husserl and Contemporary Criticism', in R.O. Elveton (ed.) *The Phenomenology of Husserl: Selected Readings*, Chicago: Quadrangle.

11 The eidetic reduction is examined on pp. 194–7; the abstractive reduction on pp. 216–18.

12 This is not, however, the only way in which the reduction can be viewed; cf. pp. 184–8.

13 The influence on Husserl's thought of Brentano's theory that all judgement is existential judgement is still detectable here: Husserl comes very close to affirming this when he says (*Ideas* §31/p. 108) that whoever attempts to doubt anything is attempting to doubt 'being' of some form or other, and that judgement, as such, is essentially a matter of ontological commitment (i.e. thetic or positing quality).

14 Frege, G. *Begriffsschrift* §2; translated (1952) by P.T. Geach and M. Black, in *Translations from the Philosophical Writings of Gottlob Frege*, Oxford: Blackwell, pp. 1–2.

15 This correspondence is closer and more suggestive than the present brief remarks indicate; cf. pp. 185–7.

16 See, e.g., *Ideas* §76/p. 213; *PP* §3/p. 32.

17 Kant, I. *Critique of Pure Reason*, p. 264 (A 247 = B 303).

18 The story is essentially that told by Kant in the so-called 'subjective deduction' of the first edition of the *Critique of Pure Reason*, A 95 – A 130.

19 Hume, D. (1978) *A Treatise of Human Nature*, Oxford: Oxford University Press, pp. 194, 252.

20 Merleau-Ponty, M. (1962) *The Phenomenology of Perception*, translated by C. Smith, London: Routledge & Kegan Paul, p. 3.

21 *ibid*, p. 9.

22 Cf. *ibid*, pp. 27–34.

23 Options such as these have been canvassed, for example, by Dreyfus, H.L. (1970) '*Sinn* and Intentional Object', in R.C. Solomon (ed.) *Phenomenology and Existentialism*, New York: Harper & Row; Gurwitsch, A. (1967) 'Husserl's Theory of the Intentionality of Consciousness in Historical Perspective', in E.N. Lee and M. Mandelbaum (eds) *Phenomenology and Existentialism*, Baltimore: Johns Hopkins; Küng, G. (1972) 'The World as Noema and as Referent', *Journal of the British Society for Phenomenology*, 3, pp. 15–26; McIntyre, R. and Smith, D.W. (1975) 'Husserl's Identification of Meaning and Noema', *The Monist*, 59, pp. 115–32; Olafson, F.A. (1977) 'Husserl's Theory of Intentionality in Contemporary Perspective', in F.A. Elliston and P. McCormick (eds), *Husserl: Expositions and Appraisals*, Notre Dame: University of Notre Dame Press; and Solomon, R.C. (1970) 'Sense and Essence: Frege and Husserl', *International Philosophical Quartely*, 10, pp. 378–401.

24 Merleau-Ponty, M. *The Phenomenology of Perception*, p. 33.

25 *ibid* p. 34; my italics.

26 See, e.g., Wittgenstein, L. *Philosophical Investigations*, §437–452.

27 Kant, I. *Critique of Pure Reason*, p. 145 (A 122).

28 *ibid*, p. 139 (*A* 113).

29 Here I follow Husserl in using the terms 'idea', 'essence', 'concept', and 'universal' interchangeably.

30 Wittgenstein, L. *op. cit.*, §593.

31 *ibid*, §213.

Chapter IV   The Individual and the Lebenswelt

1 I ignore here those vanishingly rare cases in which one is supposed to enjoy an 'adequate' intellectual perception of an essence in its entirety.

2 See, e.g., Quine, W.V.O. 'Two Dogmas of Empiricism', in *From a Logical Point of View*, pp.20–46; and 'Five Milestones of Empiricism', in *Theories and Things*, pp.67–72.

3 Evans, G. (1982) *The Varieties of Reference*, ed. by McDowell, J., Oxford: Oxford University Press, the quotations are from pp.123 and 154 respectively.

4 Although I will not pursue the matter here, it is interesting to note in passing that Husserl also believes in the radical defeasibility of logical laws: 'Even an ostensibly apodictic evidence can become disclosed as deception and, in that event, presupposes a similar evidence by which it is "shattered"' (*FTL* §58/ p.156; cf. *Crisis* §73/Appendix IV, p.336). Dagfinn Føllesdal makes this point in an unpublished paper, 'Husserl on Evidence and Justification'.

5 The lectures themselves were entitled 'Introduction to Transcendental Phenomenology', and they have since been published in *Hus* I (as *Pariser Vorträge*), and in English translation (1985), by P. Koestenbaum, as *The Paris Lectures*, The Hague: Nijhoff. The lectures were expanded and rewritten to become the *Cartesian Meditations*, first published, in French translation, in 1931. The German edition is in *Hus* I; and the English translation (1973) is by D. Cairns, The Hague: Nijhoff.

6 See, e.g., *Ideas* §57/p.173, where the topic is postponed for later treatment in *Ideas* II.

7 Strawson, P.F. (1958) 'Persons' , in H. Feigl, M. Scriven and G. Maxwell (eds), *Minnesota Studies in the Philosophy of Science*, 2, University of Minnesota Press; also (1959) *Individuals*, London: Methuen, chapter 3.

8 This, at least, is the case with respect to the works which Husserl published himself. The *Nachlass* reveals, however, that many of the doctrines and theories that we are about to examine, and which were first published in *CM* and *Crisis*, had in fact been formulated by Husserl as early as 1910 – in his private papers, in the manuscripts of works which remained unpublished, and in his university lectures. See, e.g., *Hus* XIII, *Zur Phänomenologie der Inter- subjektivität. Texte aus dem Nachlass. Erster Teil. 1905–1920*; and *Ideas* II, published as *Hus* IV.

9 Cf. Husserl's lecture 'Phenomenology and Anthropology' (delivered in 1931): 'The ego, which makes its appearance at first as a centre without content, brings with it problems of its own, namely, the problems of dispositional qualities' (*HSW* p.321).

10 Husserl sometimes emphasizes the fact that my body always seems to be '*mit dabei*' (see e.g. *Ideas* II, §36, in *Hus* IV, p.144). But perhaps the most sane response to this line of thought, and certainly one of the most delightful, is

Wittgenstein's. 'I am tempted to say: "It seems at least a fact of experience that at the source of *the visual field* there is mostly a small man with grey flannel trousers, in fact L.W." – Someone might answer to this: It is true that you almost always wear grey flannel trousers and often look at them.' (Wittgenstein, L. 'Notes for Lectures on "Private Experience" and "Sense Data"', reprinted in O.R. Jones (ed.) (1971) *The Private Language Argument*, London: Macmillan, p.255.)

11 Section entitled 'Body and Expression', in *Hus* XIII, Beilage XV, p.69. Cf. Wittgenstein's remarks in *Philosophical Investigations*, §§244, 249, 257 etc.

12 This quotation and the next are from *Ideas* II §38, in *Hus* IV, pp.151, 152. Cf. also *Ideas* III §2(b), in *Hus* V, p.7.

13 Wittgenstein, L. *Philosophical Investigations*, §620.

14 Husserl, E. (1946) '*Die Welt der lebendigen Gegenwart und die Konstitution der ausserleiblichen Umwelt*', edited by A. Schütz, in *Philosophy and Phenomenological Research*, 6, p.342. Translated as 'The World of the Living Present and the Constitution of the Surrounding World External to the Organism', in *HSW*, p.250.

15 *Ideas* II §50, in *Hus* IV, p.185; cf. *ibid* §41, in *Hus* IV, p.158.

16 On the irrelevance of kinaesthetic sensations to one's knowledge of one's own movements and the disposition of one's limbs, see Wittgenstein, L. *Philosophical Investigations*, Part II, vii, p.185. The next quotation in the text is from this passage.

17 Merleau-Ponty, M. *The Phenomenology of Perception*, p.150.

18 Cf. Husserl's discussion of the abstraction of moments in *LU* III, *passim*, and VI §52/p.800.

19 Wittgenstein, L. *Philosophical Investigations*, II, v, p.179.

20 Wittgenstein, L. *ibid*, II, iv, p.178.

21 Cf. Ricoeur, P. (1976) *Husserl: An Analysis of his Phenomenology*, translated by E.G. Ballard and L.E. Embree, Evanston: Northwestern University Press, pp.145–51.

22 This thought also receives expression in Wittgenstein's assertion that 'What has to be accepted, the given, is – so one could say – *forms of life.*' (*Philosophical Investigations*, II, xi, p.226).

23 Wittgenstein, L. (1969) *On Certainty*, ed. by G.E.M. Anscombe and G.H. von Wright, translated by D. Paul and G.E.M. Anscombe, Oxford: Blackwell, §94, p.15.

24 Wittgenstein, L. *On Certainty*, §196, p.27.

25 J. Derrida, 'Translator's Introduction' to Husserl, E. (1962) *L'Origine de la géométrie*, translated by J. Derrida, Paris: Presses Universitaires de France, p.8; cf. also Ricoeur, P. *Husserl: An Analysis of his Phenomenology*, pp.143–74.

26 *Crisis*, Appendix IX/p.389; *Hus* VI, Beilage XXVIII, p.508.

Bibliography

In spite of its length, this bibliography is by no means intended to be exhaustive. With the exception of the second section, it contains only works by or about Husserl that I have cited in the text, along with works which bear directly on the philosophical problems that Husserl addresses and which I have found particularly useful or interesting.

Works published by Husserl

Über den Begriff der Zahl. Psychologische Analysen (Habilitationsschrift), Halle: Heynemann'sche Buchdruckerei (F. Beyer), 1887. (Reprinted in *Hus* XII.)

Philosophie der Arithmetik. Psychologische und logische Untersuchungen, vol.1, Halle: C.E.M. Pfeffer (R. Stricker), 1891. (Reprinted in *Hus* XII.)

'Der Folgerungscalcul und die Inhaltslogik', *Vierteljahrschrift für wissenschaftliche Philosophie* 15, pp. 168–89.

'E. Schröder: *Vorlesungen über die Algebra der Logik*', *Göttingen gelehrte Anzeigen*, 1891, pp. 243–78.

'Psychologische Studien zur elementaren Logik', *Philosophische Monatshefte*, 30, 1894, pp. 159-91.

Logische Untersuchungen. Erste Teil: Prolegomena zur reinen Logik, Halle: Niemeyer, 1900. (Reprinted in *Hus* XVIII.)

Logische Untersuchungen. Zweite Teil: Untersuchungen zur Phänomenologie und Theorie der Erkenntnis, Halle: Niemeyer, 1901. (Reprinted in *Hus* XIX, vols 1 and 2.)

'Philosophie als strenge Wissenschaft', *Logos*, 1, 1910–11, pp. 289-341.

Logische Untersuchungen, vol.1 and part one of vol.2 (second edition), Halle: Niemeyer, 1913. (Reprinted, Tübingen: Niemeyer, 1980; also reprinted in *Hus* XVIII and XIX/1.)

Ideen zu einer reinen Phänomenologie und phänomenologischen Philosophie. Erstes Buch: Allgemeine Einführung in die reine Phänomenologie, in *Jahrbuch für Philosophie und phänomenologische Forschung*, 1, 1913, pp. 1–323. (Reprinted, Tübingen: Niemeyer, 1980; also reprinted in *Hus* III.)

'Erinnerungen an Franz Brentano', in O. Kraus, *Franz Brentano. Zur Kenntnis seines Lebens und seiner Lehre*, Munich: Beck, 1919, pp. 153–67.

Logische Untersuchungen, vol.2, part two (second edition), Halle: Niemeyer, 1921. (Reprinted, Tübingen: Niemeyer, 1980; also reprinted in *Hus* XIX/2.)

'Vorlesungen zur Phänomenologie des inneren Zeitbewusstseins', M. Heidegger (ed.), *Jahrbuch für Philosophie und phänomenologische Forschung*, 9, 1928, pp. 367–498. (Reprinted in *Hus* X.)

'Formale und transzendentale Logik. Versuch einer Kritik der logischen Vernunft', in *Jahrbuch für Philosophie und phänomenologische Forschung*, 10, 1929, pp. 1–298. (Reprinted in *Hus* XVII.)

'Phenomenology', in *Encyclopaedia Britannica*, 14th edition, London, 1929, pp. 699-702. (Reprinted in *Hus* IX.)

Méditations cartésiennes, translated into French by G. Peiffer and E. Levinas, Paris: Colin, 1931. (German version, *Cartesianische Meditationen*, in *Hus* I.)

'Die Krisis der europäischen Wissenschaften und die transzendentale Phänomenologie: Eine Einleitung in die phänomenologische Philosophie', *Philosophia*, 1, 1936, pp. 77–176. (Reprinted in *Hus* VI.)

The Husserliana edition of Husserl's Collected Works

Husserliana - Edmund Husserl, Gesammelte Werke, The Hague: Nijhoff, 1950ff. Consists of the following volumes:

I   *Cartesianische Meditationen und Pariser Vorträge*, S. Strasser (ed.), 1950.

II   *Die Idee der Phänomenologie: Fünf Vorlesungen*, W. Biemel (ed.), 1950.

III   *Ideen zu einer reinen Phänomenologie und phänomenologischen Philosophie. Erstes Buch: Allgemeine Einführung in die reine Phänomenologie*, W. Biemel (ed.), 1950.

IV   *Ideen zu einer reinen Phänomenologie und phänomenologischen Philosophie. Zweites Buch: Phänomenologische Untersuchungen zur Konstitution*, M. Biemel (ed.), 1952.

V   *Ideen zu einer reinen Phänomenologie und phänomenologischen Philosophie. Drittes Buch: Die Phänomenologie und die Fundamente der Wissenschaften*, M. Biemel (ed.), 1952.

VI   *Die Krisis der europäischen Wissenschaften und die transzendentale Phänomenologie. Eine Einleitung in die phänomenologische Philosophie*, W. Biemel (ed.), 1954.

VII   *Erste Philosophie (1923–1924). Erste Teil: Kritische Ideengeschichte*, R. Boehm (ed.), 1956.

VIII   *Erste Philosophie (1923–1924). Zweiter Teil: Theorie der phänomenologischen Reduktion*, R. Boehm (ed.), 1959.

IX   *Phänomenologische Psychologie. Vorlesungen Sommersemester 1925*, W. Biemel (ed.), 1962.

X   *Zur Phänomenologie des inneren Zeitbewusstseins*, R. Boehm (ed.), 1966.

XI   *Analysen zur passiven Synthesis (1918–1926)*, M. Fleischer (ed.), 1966.

XII   *Philosophie der Arithmetik. Mit egänzenden Texten (1890–1901)*, L. Eley (ed.), 1970.

XIII–XV   *Zur Phänomenologie der Intersubjektivität. Texte aus dem Nachlass*, three vols, I. Kern (ed.), 1973.

XVI   *Ding und Raum. Vorlesungen 1907*, U. Claesges (ed.), 1973.

XVII   *Formale und transzendentale Logik. Versuch einer Kritik der logischen Vernunft*, P. Janssen (ed.), 1974.

XVIII   *Logische Untersuchungen. Erster Band: Prolegomena zur reinen Logik*, E. Holenstein (ed.), 1975.

XIX/1   *Logische Untersuchungen. Zweiter Band: Untersuchungen zur Phänomenologie und Theorie der Erkenntnis. Erster Teil*, U. Panzer (ed.), 1984.

XIX/2   *Logische Untersuchungen. Zweiter Band: Untersuchungen zur Phänomenologie und Theorie der Erkenntnis. Zweiter Teil*, U. Panzer (ed.), 1984.

XX   [In preparation]

XXI   *Studien zur Arithmetik und Geometrie. Texte aus dem Nachlass (1886–1901)*, I. Strohmeyer (ed.), 1983.

XXII   *Aufsätze und Rezensionen (1890–1910)*, B. Rang (ed.), 1979.

XXIII   *Phantasie, Bildbewusstsein, Erinnerung. Zur Phänomenologie der anschaulichen Vergegenwärtigungen. Texte aus dem Nachlass (1898–1925)*, E. Marbach (ed.), 1980.

XXIV   *Einleitung in die Logik und Erkenntnistheorie. Vorlesungen 1906–1907*, U. Melle (ed.), 1984.

XXV   *Aufsätze und Vorträge (1911–1921)*, T. Nenon and H.R. Sepp (eds), 1987.

XXVI   *Vorlesungen über Bedeutungslehre. Sommersemester 1908*, U. Panzer (ed.), 1987.

XXVII   *Aufsätze und Vorträge (1922–1937)*, T. Nenon and H.R. Sepp (eds), 1988.

English translations of Husserl's works

Ideas. A General Introduction to Pure Phenomenology, translated by W.R. Boyce Gibson, London: Allen & Unwin, 1931. [*Ideen zu einer reinen Phänomenologie und phänomenologischen Philosophie. Erstes Buch*].

Cartesian Meditations, translated by D. Cairns, The Hague: Nijhoff, 1973. [*Cartesianische Meditationen*].

'Phenomenology and Anthropology', translated by R.G. Schmitt, in R.M. Chisholm (1960) (ed.), *Realism and the Background to Phenomenology*, Glencoe: The Free Press, pp. 129–42. Reprinted in *HSW* pp. 315–23. ['Phänomenologie und Anthropologie'].

The Phenomenology of Internal Time-Consciousness, translated by J.S. Churchill, Bloomington: Indiana University Press, 1964. [*Vorlesungen zur Phänomenologie des inneren Zeitbewusstseins*].

The Idea of Phenomenology, translated by W.P. Alston and G. Nakhnikian, The Hague: Nijhoff, 1964. [*Die Idee der Phänomenologie: Fünf Vorlesungen*].

The Paris Lectures, translated by P. Koestenbaum, The Hague: Nijhoff, 1985. ['Pariser Vorträge'].

'Philosophy as Rigorous Science', translated by Q. Lauer in *Phenomenology and the Crisis of Philosophy*, New York: Harper & Row, 1965, pp. 71–147. Reprinted in *HSW* pp. 166–97. ['Philosophie als strenge Wissenschaft'].

Formal and Transcendental Logic, translated by D. Cairns, The Hague: Nijhoff, 1969. ['Formale und transzendentale Logik'].

Logical Investigations, translated by J.N. Findlay, London, Routledge & Kegan Paul, 1970. [*Logische Untersuchungen* (2nd edition)].

The Crisis of European Sciences and Transcendental Philosophy, translated by D. Carr, Evanston: Northwestern University Press, 1970. ['Die Krisis der europäischen Wissenschaften und die transzendentale Phänomenologie'].

Experience and Judgement. Investigations in a Genealogy of Logic, L. Landgrebe (ed.), translated by J.S. Churchill and K. Ameriks, London: Routledge & Kegan Paul, 1973. [*Erfahrung und Urteil. Untersuchungen zur Genealogie der Logik*].

'A Draft of a "Preface" to the *Logical Investigations* ', translated by P.J. Bossert and C.H. Peters, in Husserl, E. (1975) *Introduction to the Logical Investigations*, The Hague: Nijhoff. ['Entwurf einer "Vorrede" zu den *Logischen Untersuchungen*'].

Phenomenology and the Foundations of the Sciences, translated by T.E. Klein Jr and W.E. Pohl, The Hague: Nijhoff, 1980. [*Ideen zu einer reinen Phänomenologie und phänomenologischen Philosophie. Drittes Buch*].

Ideas Pertaining to a Pure Phenomenology and to a Phenomenological Philosophy, translated by F. Kersten, The Hague: Nijhoff, 1982. [*Ideen zu einer reinen Phänomenologie und phänomenologischen Philosophie. Erstes Buch*].

Works by other authors

Adorno, T.W. (1940) 'Husserl and the Problem of Idealism', *Journal of Philosophy*, 35, pp. 5–18.

Ameriks, K. (1977) 'Husserl's Realism', *Philosophical Review*, 86, pp. 498–519.

Anscombe, G.E.M. (1968) 'The Intensionality of Sensation' in R.J. Butler (ed.) *Analytic Philosophy*, second series, Oxford: Blackwell, pp. 158–80.

— (1975) 'The First Person', in S. Guttenplan (ed.) *Mind and Language*, Oxford: Oxford University Press, pp. 45–65.

Aquila, R. (1982) 'On Intensionalizing Husserl's Intentions', *Nous*, 16, pp. 209-26.

Bach, K. (1982) '*De Re* Belief and Methodological Solipsism', in A. Woodfield (ed.) *Thought and Object*, Oxford: Oxford University Press, pp. 121–51.

Bachelard, S. (1968) *A Study of Husserl's Formal and Transcendental Logic*, translated by L.E. Embree, Evanston: Northwestern University Press.

Baldwin, T. (1988) 'Phenomenology, Solipsism and Egocentric Thought', *Proceedings of the Aristotelian Society*, suppl. vol. 62, pp. 27–44.

Bar-Hillel, Y. (1956) 'Husserl's Conception of a Purely Logical Grammar', *Philosophy and Phenomenological Research*, 17, pp. 362–69.

Bell, D. (1979a) *Frege's Theory of Judgement*, Oxford: Oxford University Press.

— (1979b) 'Epistemology and Abstract Objects', *Proceedings of the Aristotelian Society*, suppl. vol. 53, pp. 135–52.

— (1984) 'Sense and Reference: An Epitome', *Philosophical Quarterly*, 34, pp.

369-72; also in C. Wright (ed.) (1984) *Frege: Tradition and Influence*, Oxford: Blackwell, pp. 184–88.

(1987) 'Thoughts', *Notre Dame Journal of Formal Logic*, 28, pp. 36–50.

(1988) 'Phenomenology, Solipsism and Egocentric Thought', *Proceedings of the Aristotelian Society*, suppl. vol. 62, pp. 46–60.

Bell, D. and Cooper, N. (1989) (eds) *The Analytic Tradition: Meaning, Thought and Knowledge*, Oxford: Blackwell.

Bennett, J. (1966) *Kant's Analytic*, Cambridge: Cambridge University Press.

(1974) *Kant's Dialectic*, Cambridge: Cambridge University Press.

Benacerraf, P. (1965) 'What Numbers Could Not Be', *Philosophical Review*, 75, pp. 47–73; also in P. Benacerraf and H. Putnam (eds) (1983) *Philosophy of Mathematics: Selected Readings*, second edition, Cambridge: Cambridge University Press, pp. 272–95.

Black, M. (1971) 'The Elusiveness of Sets', *Review of Metaphysics*, 24, pp. 614–36.

Boring, E.G. (1957) *A History of Experimental Psychology*, second edition, New York: Appleton-Century-Crofts.

Brentano, F. (1973) *Psychology from an Empirical Standpoint*, ed. by L.L. McAlister, translated by A.C. Rancurello, D.B. Terrell, and L.L. McAlister, London: Routledge & Kegan Paul.

(1966) *The True and the Evident*, ed. by O. Kraus, translated by R.M. Chisholm, I. Politzer, and K.R. Fischer, London: Routledge & Kegan Paul.

(1981) *The Theory of Categories*, translated by R.M. Chisholm and N. Guterman, The Hague: Nijhoff.

(1982) *Deskriptive Psychologie*, R.M. Chisholm and W. Baumgartner (eds), Hamburg: Meiner.

Brouwer, L.E.J. (1975) *Collected Works*, ed. by A. Heyting, vol. 1, Amsterdam: North Holland.

Burge, T. (1977a) 'A Theory of Aggregates', *Nous*, 11, pp. 97–117.

(1977b) 'Belief *De Re*', *The Journal of Philosophy*, 74, pp. 338–62.

(1986) 'Cartesian Error and the Objectivity of Perception', in P. Pettit and J. McDowell (eds) *Subject, Thought and Context*, Oxford: Oxford University Press.

Carr, D. (1975) 'Intentionality', in E. Pivčević (ed.) *Phenomenology and Philosophical Understanding*, London: Hutchinson, pp. 17–36.

(1973) 'The Fifth Meditation and Husserl's Cartesianism', *Philosophy and Phenomenological Research*, 34, pp. 14–34.

(1977) 'Husserl's Problematic Concept of the Life-World', in F.A. Elliston and P. McCormick (eds) *Husserl: Expositions and Appraisals*, Indiana: University of Notre Dame Press, pp. 202–12.

Chisholm, R.M. (1960) (ed.) *Realism and the Background to Phenomenology*, Glencoe: The Free Press.

(1967) 'Brentano on Descriptive Psychology and the Intentional', in L. Lee and M. Mandelbaum (eds) *Phenomenology and Existentialism*, Baltimore: Johns Hopkins University Press pp. 1–23.

(1976) 'Brentano's Descriptive Psychology', in L.L. McAlister (ed.) *The Philosophy of Brentano*, London: Duckworth, pp. 91–100.

(1978) 'Brentano's Conception of Substance and Accident' in R.M. Chisholm and R. Haller (eds) *Die Philosophie Franz Brentanos*, Amsterdam:

Rodopi, pp. 197–210.

(1982) *Brentano and Meinong Studies*, Amsterdam: Rodopi.

Chisholm, R.M. and Haller, R. (1978) (eds) *Die Philosophie Franz Brentanos*, Amsterdam: Rodopi.

Cooper, N. (1989) *see* Bell, D. and Cooper, N.

De Boer, T. (1978) *The Development of Husserl's Thought*, translated by T. Plantinga, The Hague: Nijhoff.

Dennett, D. (1982) 'Beyond Belief', in A. Woodfield (ed.) *Thought and Object*, Oxford: Oxford University Press.

Derrida, J. (1973) *Speech and Phenomena*, translated by D.B. Allison, Evanston: Northwestern University Press.

(1978) *Edmund Husserl's Origin of Geometry: An Introduction*, translated by J.P. Leavy Jr, New York: Nicholas Hays.

Dreyfus, H.L. (1972a) '*Sinn* and Intentional Object', in R.C. Solomon (ed.) *Phenomenology and Existentialism*, New York: Harper & Row, pp. 196–210.

(1972b) 'The Perceptual Noema: Gurwitsch's Crucial Contribution', in L.E. Embree (ed.) *Life-World and Consciousness: Essays for Aron Gurwitsch*, Evanston: Northwestern University Press, pp. 135–70.

(1982) (ed.) *Husserl, Intentionality and Cognitive Science*, Cambridge (Mass.): MIT Press.

Dufrenne, M. (1966) 'Wittgenstein and Husserl', in *Jalons*, The Hague: Nijhoff, pp. 188–207.

Dummett, M.A.E. (1973) *Frege: Philosophy of Language*, London: Duckworth, (second edition, 1981).

(1978) *Truth and Other Enigmas*, London: Duckworth.

(1981) *The Interpretation of Frege's Philosophy*, London: Duckworth.

(1989) 'Thought and Perception: The Views of Husserl and Frege', in D. Bell and N. Cooper (eds) *The Analytic Tradition: Meaning, Thought, and Knowledge*. Oxford: Blackwell.

Elliston, F.A. and McCormick, P. (1977) (eds) *Husserl: Expositions and Appraisals*, Indiana: University of Notre Dame Press.

Elveton, R.O. (1970) (ed.) *The Phenomenology of Husserl: Selected Critical Readings*, Chicago: Quadrangle Books.

Embree, L.E. (1972) (ed.) *Life-World and Consciousness: Essays for Aron Gurwitsch*, Evanston: Northwestern University Press.

Evans, G. (1982) *The Varieties of Reference*, edited by J. McDowell, Oxford: Oxford University Press.

Farber, M. (1943) *The Foundations of Phenomenology*, Cambridge (Mass.): Harvard University Press.

Findlay, J.N. (1963) *Meinong's Theory of Objects and Values*, second edition, Oxford: Oxford Univeristy Press.

(1970) 'Translator's Introduction', in E. Husserl, *Logical Investigations*, translated by J.N. Findlay, London: Routledge & Kegan Paul, pp. 1–40.

Fink, E. (1970) 'The Phenomenological Philosophy of Edmund Husserl and Contemporary Criticism', in R.O. Elveton (ed.) *The Phenomenology of Husserl: Selected Critical Readings*, Chicago: Quadrangle Books, pp. 73–147.

Fodor, J.A. (1980) 'Methodological Solipsism Considered as a Research Strategy in Cognitive Psychology', *Behavioural and Brain Sciences*, 3; also in H. L.

Dreyfus (ed.) *Husserl, Intentionality and Cognitive Science*, Cambridge (Mass.): MIT Press, pp. 277–303.

Føllesdal, D. (1958) *Husserl und Frege*, Oslo: Aschehoug.

(1969) 'Husserl's Notion of Noema', *Journal of Philosophy*, 66, pp. 680–7.

(1978) 'Brentano and Husserl on Intentional Objects of Perception', *Grazer Philosophische Studien*, 5, pp. 83–94.

(Unpub.) 'Husserl on Evidence and Justification'.

Frege, G. (1953) *The Foundations of Arithmetic*, translated by J.L. Austin, Oxford: Blackwell.

(1964) *The Basic Laws of Arithmetic*, ed. and translated by M. Furth, Berkeley and Los Angeles: University of California Press.

(1979) *Posthumous Writings*, ed. by H. Hermes, F. Kambartel, *et al.*, translated by P. Long and R. White, Oxford: Blackwell.

(1980) *Philosophical and Mathematical Correspondence*, ed. by G. Gabriel *et al.*, translated by H. Kaal, Oxford: Blackwell.

(1984) *Collected Papers*, ed. by B. McGuinness, translated by M. Black, *et al.*, Oxford: Blackwell.

Gadamer, H.G. (1972) 'The Science of the Life-World', *Analecta Husserliana*, vol.2, pp. 173–85.

Geach, P.T. (1972) *Logic Matters*, Oxford: Blackwell.

Gurwitsch, A. (1964) *The Field of Consciousness*, Pittsburg: Duquesne University Press.

(1967a) 'On the Intentionality of Consciousness', in J.J. Kockelmans (ed.) *Phenomenology: The Philosophy of Edmund Husserl and Its Interpretation*, New York: Doubleday, pp. 118–36.

(1967b) 'Husserl's Theory of the Intentionality of Consciousness in Historical Perspective', in E. Lee and M. Mandelbaum (eds) *Phenomenology and Existentialism*, Baltimore: Johns Hopkins, pp. 25–58.

(1970a) 'Towards a Theory of Intentionality', *Philosophy and Phenomenological Research*, 30, pp. 354–67.

(1970b) 'Problems of the Life-World', in M. Natanson (ed.) *Phenomenology and Social Reality: Essays in Memory of Alfred Schütz*, The Hague: Nijhoff, pp. 35–61.

Haller, R. *see* Chisholm, R.M. and Haller, R.

Harney, M.J. (1984) *Intentionality, Sense and the Mind*, The Hague: Nijhoff.

Hintikka, J. (1975) *The Intentions of Intentionality and Other New Models for Modalities*, Dordrecht: Reidel.

Howarth, J.M. (1980) 'Franz Brentano and Object-Directedness', *Journal of the British Society for Phenomenology*, 11, pp. 239–54.

Hume, D. (1978) *A Treatise of Human Nature*, L.A. Selby-Bigge (ed.), Oxford: Oxford University Press (second edition).

Hylton, P. (1989) 'Logic in Russell's Logicism', in D. Bell and N. Cooper (eds) *The Analytic Tradition: Meaning, Thought and Knowledge*, Oxford: Blackwell.

Ingarden, R. (1972) 'What is New in Husserl's *Crisis*?', translated by R. George, *Analecta Husserliana*, 2, pp. 23–47.

(1975) *On the Motives which Led Husserl to Transcendental Idealism*, translated by A. Hannibalsson, The Hague: Nijhoff.

(1976) 'Letter to Husserl about the *VI Investigation* and "Idealism"', translated by H. Girndt, *Analecta Husserliana*, 4, pp. 418–38.

Kant, I. (1933) *The Critique of Pure Reason*, translated by N. Kemp Smith, London: Macmillan.

(1952) *The Critique of Judgement*, translated by J.C. Meredith, Oxford: Oxford University Press.

Kern, I. (1964) *Husserl und Kant: Eine Untersuchung über Husserls Verhältnis zu Kant und zum Neukantianismus*, The Hague: Nijhoff.

Klein, B.B.(1970) *A History of Scientific Psychology*, London: Routledge & Kegan Paul.

Kneale, W. (1968) 'Intentionality and Intensionality', *Proceedings of the Aristotelian Society*, suppl. vol. 42, pp. 73–90.

Kneale, W. and M. (1962) *The Development of Logic*, Oxford: Oxford University Press.

Kockelmans, J.J. (1967) (ed.) *Phenomenology: The Philosophy of Edmund Husserl and Its Interpretation*, New York: Doubleday.

Körner, S. (1978) 'Über Brentanos Reismus und die extensionale Logik', in R.M. Chisholm and R. Haller (eds), *Die Philosophie Franz Brentanos*, Amsterdam: Rodopi, pp. 29–43.

Kripke, S. (1981) 'Wittgenstein on Rules and Private Language' in I. Block (ed.) *Perspectives on the Philosophy of Wittgenstein*, Oxford: Blackwell, pp. 238–312.

Küng, G. (1969) 'The Role of Language in Phenomenological Analysis', *American Philosophical Quarterly*, 6, pp. 330–4.

(1972) 'The World as Noema and as Referent', *Journal of the British Society for Phenomenology*, 3, pp. 15–26.

(1975) 'The Phenomenological Reduction as *Epoché* and as Explication', *Monist*, 59, pp. 63–80; also in F.A. Elliston and P. McCormick (eds) *Husserl: Expositions and Appraisals*, pp. 338–49.

Kwant, R.C. (1967) 'Merleau-Ponty's Criticism of Husserl's Eidetic Reduction', in J.J. Kockelmans (ed.) *Phenomenology: The Philosophy of Edmund Husserl and Its Interpretation*, New York: Doubleday, pp. 393–412.

Landgrebe, L. (1973) 'The Phenomenological Concept of Experience', *Philosophy and Phenomenological Research*, 34, pp. 1–13.

(1978) 'The Problem of Passive Constitution', translated by D. Wellan, *Analecta Husserliana*, 7, pp. 23–36.

(1981) 'Regions of Being and Regional Ontologies in Husserl's Phenomenology', in W. McKenna *et al.* (eds) *Apriori and World: European Contributions to Husserlian Phenomenology*, The Hague: Nijhoff, pp. 132–51.

Lee, E. and Mandelbaum, M. (1967) (eds) *Phenomenology and Existentialism*, Baltimore: Johns Hopkins University Press.

Levin, D. (1970) *Reason and Evidence in Husserl's Phenomenology*, Evanston: Northwestern University Press.

McAlister, L.L. (1976a) 'Chisholm and Brentano on Intentionality', in L.L. McAlister (ed.) *The Philosophy of Brentano*, London: Duckworth, pp. 151–9.

(1976b) (ed.) *The Philosophy of Brentano*, London: Duckworth.

Mackie, J.L. (1975) 'Problems of Intentionality', in E. Pivčević (ed.) *Phenomenology and Philosophical Understanding*, Cambridge: Cambridge University Press, pp. 37–52.

McCormick, P. *see* Elliston, F.A. and McCormick, P.

McDowell, J. (1984) *'De Re* Senses', in C. Wright (ed.), *Frege: Tradition and Influence*, Oxford: Blackwell, pp. 98–109.

McIntyre, R. and Smith, D.W. (1975) 'Husserl's Identification of Meaning and Noema', *Monist*, 59, pp. 115–32.

    see also Smith, D.W., and McIntyre, R.

Merleau-Ponty, M. (1962) *The Phenomenology of Perception*, translated by C. Smith, London: Routledge & Kegan Paul.

Mill, J.S. (1961) *A System of Logic*, London: Longmans.

Miller, J.P. (1982) *Numbers in Presence and Absence: A Study of Husserl's Philosophy of Mathematics*, The Hague: Nijhoff.

Mohanty, J. N. (1964) *Edmund Husserl's Theory of Meaning*, The Hague: Nijhoff.

    (1972) *The Concept of Intentionality*, St Louis: Green.

    (1977) (ed.) *Readings on E. Husserl's 'Logical Investigations'*, The Hague: Nijhoff.

    (1982) *Husserl and Frege*, Bloomington: Indiana University Press.

Mulligan, K. and Smith, B. (1982) 'Pieces of a Theory', in B. Smith (ed.) *Parts and Moments*, Munich: Philosophia, pp. 15–109.

    (1983) 'A Framework for Formal Ontology', *Topoi*, 3, pp. 73–85.

    (1985) 'Franz Brentano on the Ontology of Mind', *Philosophy and Phenomenological Research*, 45, pp. 627–44.

Natanson, M. (1966) (ed.) *Essays in Phenomenology*, The Hague: Nijhoff.

    (1970) (ed.) *Phenomenology and Social Reality: Essays in Memory of Alfred Schütz*, The Hague: Nijhoff.

    (1973) *Edmund Husserl: Philosopher of Infinite Tasks*, Evanston: Northwestern University Press.

Natorp, P. (1901) 'Zur Frage der logischen Methode mit Beziehung auf Edmund Husserls Prolegomena zur reinen Logik', *Kantstudien*, 6, pp. 270–83.

Noonan, H. (1986) 'Russellian Thoughts and Methodological Solipsism' in J. Butterfield (ed.) *Language, Mind and Logic*, Cambridge: Cambridge University Press.

Olafson, F.A. (1977) 'Husserl's Theory of Intentionality in Contemporary Perspective', in F.A. Elliston and P. McCormick (eds) *Husserl: Expositions and Appraisals*, Indiana: University of Notre Dame Press, pp. 160–7.

Patzig, G. (1977) 'Husserl on Truth and Evidence' in J. Mohanty (ed.) *Readings on E. Husserl's "Logical Investigations"* , The Hague: Nijhoff, pp. 179-96.

Peters, R.S. (1953) (ed.) *Brett's History of Psychology*, London: Allen & Unwin.

Pivčević, E.(1970) *Husserl and Phenomenology*, London: Hutchinson.

    (1975) (ed.) *Phenomenology and Philosophical Understanding*, Cambridge: Cambridge University Press.

Prior, A.N. (1968) 'Intentionality and Intensionality', *Proceedings of the Aristotelian Society*, suppl. vol. 42, pp. 91–106.

Putnam, H. (1975) 'The Meaning of "Meaning"', in *Language, Mind and Reality*, Cambridge: Cambridge University Press, pp. 215–71.

Quine, W.V.O. (1960) *Word and Object*, Cambridge (Mass.): MIT Press.

(1961) *From a Logical Point of View*, second edition, New York: Harper & Row.

(1963) *Set Theory and Its Logic*, Cambridge (Mass.): Harvard University Press.

(1969) *Ontological Relativity, and Other Essays*, New York: Columbia University Press.

(1976) *Ways of Paradox and Other Essays*, revised edition, Cambridge (Mass.): Harvard University Press.

(1981) *Theories and Things*, Cambridge (Mass.): Harvard University Press.

Quine, W.V.O. and Ullian, J.S. (1970) *The Web of Belief*, New York: Random House.

Rancurello, A.C. (1968) *A Study of Franz Brentano*, London and New York: Academic Press.

Ricoeur, P. (1966a) 'Kant and Husserl', *Philosophy Today*, 10, pp. 145–68.

(1967) *Husserl: An Analysis of his Philosophy*, translated by E.G. Ballard and L.E. Embree, Evanston: Northwestern University Press.

(1967b) 'Husserl and Wittgenstein on Language', in E. Lee and M. Mandelbaum (eds) *Phenomenology and Existentialism*, Baltimore: Johns Hopkins University Press, pp. 207–18.

Russell, B. (1917) 'Knowledge by Acquaintance and Knowledge by Description', in *Mysticism and Logic*, London: Allen & Unwin, pp. 152–67.

(1919) *Introduction to Mathematical Philosophy*, London: Allen & Unwin.

(1937) *The Principles of Mathematics*, second edition, London: Allen & Unwin.

(1956) *Logic and Knowledge*, ed. by R.C. Marsh, London: Allen & Unwin.

Russell, B., and Whitehead, A.N. (1913) *Principia Mathematica*, Cambridge: Cambridge University Press.

Ryle, G. (1949) *The Concept of Mind*, London: Penguin Books.

Sartre, J.P. (1970) 'Intentionality: A Fundamental Idea of Husserl's Phenomenology', translated by J.P. Fell, *Journal of the British Society for Phenomenology*, 1, pp. 4–5.

Schumann, K. (1977) *Husserl–Chronik. Denk-und Lebensweg Edmund Husserls*, The Hague: Nijhoff.

Searle, J. (1983) *Intentionality*, Cambridge: Cambridge University Press.

Simons, P.M. (1981) 'Abstraction and Abstract Objects', in E. Morscher *et al.* (eds) *Essays in Scientific Philosophy*, Bad Reichenhall: Comes, pp. 355–70.

(1982a) 'The Formalization of Husserl's Theory of Wholes and Parts', in B. Smith (ed.) *Parts and Moments*, Munich: Philosophia, pp. 113–59.

(1982b) 'Numbers and Manifolds', in B. Smith (ed.) *Parts and Moments*, Munich: Philosophia, pp. 160–98.

(1982c) 'Plural Reference and Set Theory', in B. Smith (ed.) *Parts and Moments*, Munich: Philosophia, pp. 199-260.

Skorupski, J.M. (1989) *Mill*, London: Routledge.

Smith, B. (ed.) (1982) *Parts and Moments*, Munich: Philosophia.

see Mulligan, K. and Smith, B.

Smith, D.W. and McIntyre, R. (1982) *Husserl and Intentionality. A Study of Mind, Meaning and Language*, Dordrecht: Reidel.

Sokolowski, R. (1964) *The Formation of Husserl's Concept of Constitution*, The

Hague: Nijhoff.

(1968) 'The Logic of Parts and Wholes in Husserl's *Investigations*', *Philosophy and Phenomenological Research*, 28, pp. 537–53; also in J. Mohanty (ed.) *Readings on E. Husserl's 'Logical Investigations'*, pp. 94–111.

(1974) *Husserlian Meditations*, Evanston: Northwestern University Press.

Solomon, R.C. (1970) 'Sense and Essence: Frege and Husserl', *International Philosophical Quarterly*, 10, pp. 378–401.

(1972) (ed.) *Phenomenology and Existentialism*, New York: Harper & Row.

(1977) 'Husserl's Concept of the Noema', in F.A. Elliston and P. McCormick (eds) *Husserl: Expositions and Appraisals*, Indiana: University of Notre Dame Press, pp. 168–81.

Spiegelberg, H. (1960) *The Phenomenological Movement: A Historical Introduction*, vols I and II, The Hague: Nijhoff.

(1973) 'Is the Reduction Necessary for Phenomenology? Husserl's and Pfänder's Replies', *Journal of the British Society for Phenomenology*, 4, pp. 3–15.

(1976) '"Intention" and "Intentionality" in the Scholastics, Brentano and Husserl', translated by L.L. McAlister and M. Schättle, in L.L. McAlister (ed.) *The Philosophy of Brentano*, London: Duckworth, pp. 108–27.

Stegmüller, W. (1969) *Main Currents in Contemporary German, British, and American Philosophy*, Dordrecht: Reidel.

Strawson, P.F. (1958) 'Persons', *Minnesota Studies in the Philosophy of Science*, 2.

(1959) *Individuals. An Essay in Descriptive Metaphysics*, London: Methuen.

Stumpf, C. (1873) *Über den psychologischen Ursprung der Raumvorstellung*, Leipzig: Hirzel.

(1976) 'Reminiscences of Franz Brentano', translated by L.L. McAlister and M. Schättle, in L.L. McAlister (ed.) *The Philosophy of Brentano*, London: Duckworth, pp. 47–56.

Sukale, M. (1970) *Comparative Studies in Phenomenology*, The Hague: Nijhoff.

Taylor, C. (1959) 'Phenomenology and Linguistic Analysis', *Proceedings of the Aristotelian Society*, suppl. vol. 33, pp. 93–110.

Tragesser, R. (1984) *Husserl and Realism in Logic and Mathematics*, Cambridge: Cambridge University Press.

Tugendhat, E. (1970) *Der Wahrheitsbegriff bei Husserl und Heidegger*, second edition, Berlin: De Gruyter.

(1977) 'Phenomenology and Linguistic Analysis', in F.A. Elliston and P. McCormick (eds) *Husserl: Expositions and Appraisals*, Indiana: University of Notre Dame Press, pp. 325–37.

Van De Pitte, M.M.,

Van De Pitte, M.M. (1977) 'Husserl's Solipsism', *Journal of the British Society for Phenomenology*, 8, pp. 123–5.

Welton, D. (1973) 'Intentionality and Language in Husserl's Phenomenology', *Review of Metaphysics*, 27, pp. 260–98.

(1983) *The Origins of Meaning*, The Hague: Nijhoff.

Whitehead, A.N. *see* Russell, B. and Whitehead, A.N.

Willard, D.A. (1972) 'The Paradox of Husserl's Psychologism: Husserl's Way Out', *American Philosophical Quarterly*, 9, pp. 94–100; also in

J. Mohanty (ed.) *Readings on E. Husserl's 'Logical Investigations'*, pp. 43–54.

    (1974) 'Concerning Husserl's View of Number', *Southwestern Journal of Philosophy*, 5, pp. 97–109.

    (1980) 'Husserl on a Logic that Failed', *Philosophical Review*, 89, pp. 46–64.

    (1984) *Logic and the Objectivity of Knowledge. A Study of Husserl's Early Philosophy*, Athens (Ohio): Ohio University Press.

Williams, B. (1974) 'Wittgenstein and Idealism', in J. Vesey (ed.) *Understanding Wittgenstein. Royal Institute of Philosophy Lectures*, 7 (1972/73), London: Macmillan pp. 76–95.

Wittgenstein, L. (1958a) *Philosophical Investigations*, translated by G.E.M. Anscombe, Oxford: Blackwell, second edition.

    (1958b) *The Blue and Brown Books*, Oxford: Blackwell.

    (1961) *Tractatus Logico-Philosophicus*, translated by D.F. Pears and B. McGuinness, London: Routledge & Kegan Paul.

    (1969) *On Certainty*, ed. by G.E.M. Anscombe and G.H. von Wright, translated by D. Paul and G.E.M. Anscombe, Oxford: Blackwell.

    (1971) 'Notes for lectures on "Private Experience" and "Sense Data",' in O.R. Jones (ed.) *The Private Language Argument*, London: Macmillan, pp. 232–75.

Wright, C. (1983) *Frege's Conception of Numbers as Objects*, Aberdeen: Aberdeen University Press.

Wundt, W. (1904) *The Principles of Physiological Psychology*, translated by E.B. Titchener, London: Swan Sonnenschein, fifth edition.

Zaner, R.M. (1975) 'On the Sense of Method in Phenomenology', in E. Pivčević (ed.) *Phenomenology and Philosophical Understanding*, Cambridge: Cambridge University Press, pp. 125–42.

Index

265